CHALLENGING THE POTENTIAL

**Related Research and Policy Publications
From the High/Scope Press**

*Changed Lives: The Effects of the Perry Preschool Program
on Youths Through Age 19*

*Young Children Grow Up: The Effects of the Perry Preschool Program
on Youths Through Age 15*

*Consequences of Three Preschool Curriculum Models
Through Age 15*

*The High/Scope Perry Preschool Program and Its Long-Term Effects:
A Benefit-Cost Analysis*

Available from

High/Scope® Press
*A division of the
High/Scope Educational Research Foundation
600 N. River Street, Ypsilanti, MI 48198-2898
(313) 485-2000   FAX (313) 485-0704*

Sherri Oden

Mario A. Kelly

Zhenkui Ma

David P. Weikart

CHALLENGING THE POTENTIAL

*Programs for Talented
Disadvantaged Youth*

High/Scope® Press
Ypsilanti, Michigan

**A division of the High/Scope
Educational Research Foundation**

Marge Senninger, High/Scope Press Editor

Linda Eckel, Cover and Text Design
Margaret FitzGerald, Typesetting and Keylining

Library of Congress Cataloging-in-Publication Data

Challenging the potential: programs for talented disadvantaged youth/by Sherri Oden . . . [et al.].
   p. cm.
   Includes bibliographical references.
   ISBN 0-929816-35-8
   1. Gifted children—Education—United States. 2. Minority students—United States. 3. Socially handicapped children—Education—United States. I. Oden, Sherri.
LC3993.9.C48   1992
371.95—dc20   92-35023
                                             CIP

International Standard Book Number: 0-929816-35-8

Printed in the United States of America

High/Scope Educational Research Foundation
600 North River Street
Ypsilanti, Michigan 48198-2898
(313)485-2000

The High/Scope Educational Research Foundation is an independent nonprofit organization formally established in 1970 by Dr. David P. Weikart. High/Scope is internationally known as a center for research, curriculum development, professional training, and public policy work. High/Scope's work centers on the learning and development of children from infancy through adolescence, with a special emphasis on the early childhood years.

A Word About Reading This Book

Challenging the Potential: Programs for Talented Disadvantaged Youth was written and designed to be read according to different levels of interest. For those who are interested in the larger issues related to a topic, text in the margins (in green) capsulates the key points discussed in more detail in the nearby main text. For those interested in the detailed treatment of a given topic, the margin text can serve as a guide for locating more detail. For an initial reading or a review of specific topics or chapters, the words IN SUMMARY or SUMMARIZING THIS CHAPTER earmark paragraphs that sum up the pre-

ceding section or chapter. For similar quick-reference, major parts of the book are printed on green pages. On such pages, readers can find summaries of the programs studied and of the High/Scope longitudinal study.

All readers should read Part 3, An Overview: Future Directions for Policy and Development. This part contains summaries of the book's major research findings and proposes recommendations for educators, program developers, and policymakers seeking to advance the achievement of talented disadvantaged youth.

Contents

Tables and Figures

Tables

Figures

Acknowledgments

Many individuals and organizations made important contributions to this book. The research reported in the book was made possible by funding from The Skillman Foundation, The Ford Foundation, and the Detroit Edison Foundation. Barbara Scott Nelson, from The Ford Foundation, was helpful in facilitating contacts with the programs described in Part 1 of the book. We are grateful to the students, directors, teachers, and staff of these programs for their cooperation in this project and their time and receptivity during site visits.

The research presented in Part 2 of the book was conducted with the cooperation of the Detroit Public Schools and the Crawford, Ogemaw, Oscoda, and Roscommon (COOR) Intermediate School District of Michigan. We especially want to express appreciation to George Johnson, the COOR District's Director of Planning and Finance, for his facilitation of the research. Roberta Volker-Foreman, Executive Director of Region 7B's Employment and Training Consortium in Michigan, and her staff also provided much-appreciated cooperation and assistance.

We want to acknowledge the work of many people who made significant contributions to the longitudinal research: Charles Hohmann gave considerable input to the project's early development; Ann Epstein and Larry Schweinhart gave input to the interview instrument; Sam Hannibal and Ann Rogers assisted in obtaining student location information from the schools; Karl Wheatley assisted interviewers in locating study subjects; Sherrie Hittler and Linda Hulton did most of the location work and interviewing; and Mary Achatz, Elizabeth Cole, and Christine Young also did some location work and interviewing. We also want to acknowledge the important contributions to the 1990 study made by Kimberly Browning, who collected and compiled data and wrote the case study profiles, and by Vincent Harris, who provided input to the High/Scope program summary. Many others assisted us with both the longitudinal and 1990 research: Mei-yu Yu helped with data analysis; Shirley Barnes did the word processing of the interview instruments and also provided secretarial assistance; Helena Hoas coordinated the development of the computer data coding system; and Kay Long conducted the data coding and entry, with help from Nancy Burandt, Heidi Keifer, Karen Parsell, and Brenlee Robinson.

We are especially grateful to Marge Senninger, who served as the

High/Scope Press editor. Her astute, thorough editing and stimulating critique made very significant contributions to the book. Steve McHugh and Karen Jones also provided much-appreciated editorial assistance. Finally, we want to thank Diana Knepp for her diligence and patience in doing the word processing of the manuscript, and Linda Eckel and Margaret FitzGerald for their creative and skillful design work.

CHALLENGING THE POTENTIAL

Chapter ONE

Introduction

THE POTENTIAL of our nation's talented disadvantaged and minority youth too often goes unrealized. The United States, though enriched by the diversity in religion, race, national origin, and cultural background among its people, has always faced a challenge in providing each citizen with adequate opportunity in education and employment. Today the challenge presented by diversity remains undiminished. And today, because of the vast changes that have occurred in the American workplace and family over the past 20 years, we face a new kind of challenge. Perhaps more than ever before, it is imperative that we develop innovative ways to encourage and develop the talents and skills of *all* our young people.

Tragically, the potential of talented children and teenagers can easily go unnoticed or unrecognized in contexts of impoverished conditions—in homes and communities where people struggle to secure the basic requirements for living. Surprisingly many American children—20% of them—are growing up in impoverished conditions. Breaking this down by major cultural groups, we find 44% of African American children, 36% of Hispanic American children, and 11% of non-Hispanic white children growing up in families with incomes below the poverty threshold (U.S. Bureau of the Census, 1990a). While some of the poverty can be attrib-

1

The talents of many of our young people are an untapped national resource.

▾

Amid social and economic obstacles—ranging from poverty and discrimination to changes in the workplace and family—even talented teenagers may not find the paths leading to achievement.

▾

uted to discriminatory practices and the increase in single-parent, female-headed households (where the poverty rate is 43%), another contributing factor is the change in the nature of the American workplace.

With the domestic decline in manufacturing jobs, today's workers with only a high school diploma or less find that getting or maintaining a job to support a family is increasingly difficult. The "working poor"—families where a sole parent or two parents are employed at jobs that pay low wages—are on the increase. Addressing this situation, a recent report from the Carnegie Council on Adolescent Development (1989) pointed out that in addition to its moral responsibility to further the higher education of disadvantaged and minority students, the United States faces an "economic imperative" to do so. Among minority students, in particular, too few go on to higher education; still fewer become leaders in science, mathematics, business, and other highly skilled professions. The need is increasing for *all* young people in America, including those from minority and disadvantaged backgrounds, to achieve higher education levels.

The essence of the problem is well articulated in the June 1990 report of the National Center on Education and the Economy. Warning that America faces a choice of either low skills and low wages, or high skills and high wages, the report concludes that "gradually, silently, we are choosing low wages." According to the report's statistics, the real earnings of young adults 24 to 34 years of age who do not have any postsecondary education have decreased by approximately 10% over the last decade. While the incomes of the highest-paid 30% of the population have increased since 1969, the other 70% of the population, faced by downward-spiraling incomes, are struggling to simply maintain their standard of living. The average weekly earnings (in 1989 dollars) of American workers have been steadily declining since 1969 and have now fallen to the level of earnings in 1959. Consequently, in most families, two wage earners have become a necessity.

Today great numbers of Americans are settling for

Both ethical and economic forces compel our nation to challenge the potential of all its young people.

▼

To retain international leadership and fortify our economic well-being, American workplaces of the future will demand higher skills.

▼

jobs that not only do not pay well but also do not challenge them to think critically or solve problems, to be innovative or take initiative. However, if we are to maintain our world leadership and avert economic decline, tomorrow's jobs must be ones that demand these higher-level skills. This means that in the future, the majority of all new jobs for men and women will require some postsecondary education. In somewhat the way that adolescents face turning points in their development, our nation is facing a turning point—technological changes in computers, travel, and international communication systems, and the growing sophistication of the international marketplace, challenge us to turn away from limited educational approaches and outmoded work-organization systems.

For individuals as well as for the nation as a whole, education is the key to gaining economic stability and prosperity. As stated in the recent report by the William T. Grant Foundation Commission on Work, Family, and Citizenship (1988), "Regardless of race or ethnic origin, the more years a person spends in formal education, the greater that person's annual earnings." However, though there is some evidence of economic progress among Americans from minority cultural backgrounds, they continue to face prejudice and discrimination. As summarized in the Winter/Spring 1990 *Carnegie Quarterly*, "Prejudice, discrimination, and social inequality continue to haunt the lives of poor and even middle-class minority youths" (Carnegie Corporation of New York, 1990). Though white males born in the United States represent nearly one half of today's work force, by the year 2000 they will represent less than one third of new entrants to the labor market (Hudson Institute, 1987). It is clear that greater numbers of young people from all cultural backgrounds must be more highly educated and skilled if the nation is to achieve economic vitality.

For disadvantaged and minority students who are talented, educational achievement beyond high school is critical for many reasons. Those who earn college or other postsecondary degrees go down a different life-

We must discover ways to captivate and direct the talents of disadvantaged students to prepare them to excel in workplaces of the future.

Minorities in America are becoming an increasingly large share of the work force.

track than did their families before them. They are in a better position to financially support their own families and to serve as role models for fostering their children's higher education. Instead of being unable to capitalize on their talents, or instead of squandering them, they can use their abilities to make contributions to their jobs and communities and thus contribute to the economic vitality of the nation. Increasing the higher education of talented minority and disadvantaged students means increasing the leadership of the future.

In this book, we discuss 13 nationally known model programs designed to enhance the educational futures of talented students from disadvantaged or minority backgrounds. The objectives of our discussion are (1) to focus on the achievement obstacles faced by these students and to propose interventions to deal with the obstacles, (2) to develop a model of ideal-program components, (3) to propose a research model and ways to use a data base for evaluating intervention programs, and (4) to offer recommendations aimed at policymakers as well as program evaluators, developers, and funders concerned with minority and disadvantaged youth.

In Part 1 of the book, Mario Kelly presents a review of the theoretical and empirical research on the achievement of disadvantaged and minority students. Kelly then uses this information to formulate the key components, or features, of an ideal intervention program. Part 1 concludes with Kelly's application of his ideal-program features in a report on his site visits to 12 nationally known intervention programs in mathematics and science.

Part 2 focuses on one other nationally known program, High/Scope's program for talented disadvantaged teenagers. In this part of the book, Sherri Oden, Zhenkui Ma, and David Weikart first analyze High/Scope's intervention program in light of the ideal intervention program's key components enumerated in Part 1. Subsequent chapters present the method and results of a 5-year follow-up study of students from the High/Scope 1982 and 1983 programs, as well as the

---

Existing model programs designed to propel disadvantaged and minority students into mathematics and science careers can provide insights and direction for program developers.

▾

From research and practice we can identify ideal-program features and set a course for research and policy initiatives.

results of a more recent study of the 1990 program. This research, both the longitudinal study and the 1990 evaluation, is presented as an illustration of what can be learned from systematic evaluation of a model program. The longitudinal study, in particular, demonstrates that such programs can increase the number of minority and disadvantaged students going on to higher education.

In Part 3, Sherri Oden and David Weikart summarize and examine the implications of the findings of Parts 1 and 2. They conclude with a list of recommendations for practitioners, funders, and policymakers regarding future program development and evaluation.

Part **ONE**

Improving Minority
Students' Achievement:
A Model for Academic Intervention

MARIO A. KELLY

Chapter TWO

Introduction to Part One

ACCORDING TO A REPORT from the National Commission on Excellence in Education (1983), American public education is in a state of crisis that places the nation at risk. Nowhere is the crisis graver or the nation placed at greater risk for economic, social, and moral failure than in the inadequate education of its high-potential minority[1] youth.

Telltale signs of the public education crisis, as it affects minorities, are everywhere. Census data summarized by the American Council on Education (1988) and the U.S. Department of Education (1988) reveal that large proportions of minority students, ranging from 17% of black to 31% of Latino 18- and 19-year-olds, are dropping out of high school. Many of those who do stay in school read substantially below grade level and graduate functionally illiterate, lacking the minimal skills for adequately completing a job application. Each year, decreasing numbers of those who complete high school are able or motivated to go on to college. And what is perhaps most threatening to the nation's well-being, gifted and talented minority children are often not identified and assisted to fulfill their potential, as Baldwin (1987) argued. The result is a tremendous waste of human potential.

Potential not used to benefit society does not just vanish; it is often misdirected to the peer culture of

2

The crisis in American public education is especially critical in its failure to identify and educate talented minority students. Too many of them lack the skills or motivation to go on to college.

We are all diminished—morally, personally, and economically—by our acceptance of this waste of human potential.

▾

urban streets, to creative ways of obtaining and pushing drugs, to innovative ways of committing crime (often with impunity), to creative means of extorting money from the welfare system, and to other antisocial uses. In the end, not only does the society fail to benefit but it actually loses. We all lose from the terrible waste of minds. Each of us is diminished physically and emotionally by the real or imagined threat of crime and violence perpetrated by many of those left on the fringes of society. Each of us is diminished economically by the abuses of the welfare system and the costs of the overburdened judicial system. Each of us is diminished morally and socially by the failure of others to achieve some substantive measure of their potential. A further and direct result of this waste of minds is a society divided along racial and economic lines, as is increasingly evident in large urban areas. Such a society is indeed at risk of decay from within.

The continuing loss of minority talent could not be occurring at a worse time. Scientific and technological advances of the last 20 years, and those envisioned for the next 20 years, are increasing exponentially the nation's need for research scientists, engineers, mathematicians, and highly skilled workers in technical fields. It is not surprising that one of the national goals for public education developed by President Bush and the nation's governors is for U.S. students to be first in the world in mathematics and science achievement by the year 2000 (U.S. Department of Education, 1991).

Large shortages of workers skilled in mathematics and science threaten our nation's next century.

▾

Unless this goal is met, the United States will face a shortage of over a half-million technically trained workers by the start of the twenty-first century, according to a report of the Task Force on Women, Minorities, and the Handicapped in Science and Technology (1989). The report also stated that since minorities are the fastest-growing sector of the population, the nation will have to depend heavily on them to meet its need for technically skilled persons. It is estimated that in the year 2010, minorities will account for over one third of all college-aged persons in the United States.

One place to turn in seeking intervention strategies that may improve the mathematics and science achievement of minority students is to a group of 12 well-known extracurricular precollege programs that have been in existence for the last 10 to 15 years. The ultimate goal of these model programs is to increase the number of minority professionals in mathematics- and science-based fields, such as engineering, computer science, and medicine. The programs intervene during middle (or junior high) school and high school to assist minority students in gaining admittance to and performing successfully in mathematics and science academic tracks. If these programs are successful in their strategies, students and educators throughout the country stand to benefit from the use of similar strategies. Unfortunately, at present, little empirical evidence of program success is available. Part 1 of this book, which reports on and analyzes the 12 model extracurricular precollege programs, is a first step in looking at the issue of program effectiveness.

To gain directives to assist talented disadvantaged youth, Part One examines 12 established extracurricular precollege programs designed to promote minority students' achievement—primarily in mathematics and science.

Overview

Part 1 analyzes 12 model intervention programs and their strategies in the light of available theoretical and empirical research on the psychological development and education of minority students. (While ethnic/racial minorities are the focus of the analysis, much of our discussion can also apply to nonminority students from economically disadvantaged backgrounds.) In our analysis, we enumerate and discuss components that appear to be essential for effective intervention programs and provide examples from the 12 model programs. Although mathematics and science programs are the main focus of Part 1, the discussion of components of effective programs for minorities is pertinent to education in other content areas as well.

The 12 model programs are briefly described in this chapter. The theoretical analysis is then developed in

The theory and empirical research pertinent to the development of minority academic achievement are also reviewed.

We first discuss key student characteristics that must be fostered— motivation, knowledge in subject areas, problem-solving strategies, and communication skills.

▼

We then propose a model that incorporates "ideal-program" components for fostering the key characteristics in minority students.

▼

Many of the ideal-program components are exemplified in the 12 model programs described in Part One.

▼

Chapters 3 and 4, with Chapter 3 describing and examining the national crisis in the academic achievement of minority students.

Chapter 4 looks in detail at the characteristics that are not being sufficiently fostered in minority students—characteristics that *must* be fostered if those students are to fill the roles the nation needs. The chapter consists of a critical review of the literature on the cognitive, psychological, and social development of minority students, including a discussion of the implications of current theory and research for the improvement of educational practice. The *enhancement of motivation* in minority students, their *acquisition of knowledge* about specific subjects, and their *development of problem-solving strategies* and *effective communication skills* are of particular focus in this chapter.

In Chapter 5, the implications of the issues discussed in earlier chapters are integrated into a model of "ideal-program" components for fostering minority academic achievement, and features of individual programs that exemplify the components of the model are cited. Chapter 5 includes a summary description of each program. Chapter 6 discusses the relative strengths and weaknesses of the programs in the national context.

Brief profiles of the experiences of students and staff in the programs are interspersed throughout Part 1. Each profile is the result of an in-depth interview with an individual or, in the case of the first profile, with a small group. The personal experiences related in the profiles are representative of the experiences of persons in similar roles in other programs.

In recent years, several descriptive studies of programs designed to improve the achievement of minority youths in mathematics and science have been conducted. Perhaps most notable among these is the descriptive analysis of a sample of 50 engineering education programs that was conducted by Gordon et al. (1987) for the National Action Council for Minorities in Engineering, Inc. (NACME). In its introduction to the published report, NACME described it as "the most significant assessment of the minorities-in-engineering effort ever prepared." The Gordon et al. report, and other reports, have provided significant assessments of various programs and, based on their findings, have provided important recommendations for improving the programs.

The present report is similar in many respects to previous ones. However, it differs from them in important ways. First, whereas other reports were based on mail-in surveys of programs, this study is based on site visits and in-person interviews with program directors, other program staff, teachers, and students. Less limited than mail-in surveys, personal interviews and site visits can convey more qualitatively how programs operate day-to-day and, in particular, how program components are perceived not only by the staff who implement them but also by the students who are affected by them. A second difference between this and previous reports is that the present one includes an extensive review of recent research on the psychological development and education of minority students. Then, based on this review, we propose ideal strategies for improving minority students' achievement. Individual components of actual programs are then described in terms of the degree to which they employ the ideal strategies.

> Our study of these programs was largely based on qualitative methods—review of written materials, interviews, site visits.
> ▾

The Study of Model Programs

Selection of Programs

In terms of geographic location and in terms of the specific racial/ethnic groups served, the 12 programs selected for this report provide a representative sample of model programs across the nation. At least one program from each region of the country—the Northeast, the Southeast, the Northwest, the Southwest, and the Midwest—was chosen. The selected programs include at least one serving a large number of Native Americans, at least one serving a large number of African Ameri-

> The 12 model programs represent a wide range of U.S. regions and serve talented students who are African, Hispanic, and Native Americans.
> ▾

AISES (Boulder, CO)

AIUD (Boulder, CO)

CAHMCP (Chicago, IL)

CMEA (Denver, CO)

DAPCEP (Detroit, MI)

MASSPEP (Boston, MA)

MESA, CA (Berkeley)

MESA, WA (Seattle)

PRIME (Philadelphia, PA)

PREP (Pittsburgh, PA)

PRIS²M (Rochester, NY)

SECME (Atlanta, GA)

Most of the model
programs are funded by
private foundations and
take place in settings away
from students' schools.

cans, and at least one serving a large number of Hispanic Americans. Other racial/ethnic groups were not a focus in selecting programs.[2] A list of the programs follows:

- *American Indian Science and Engineering Society (AISES)*—Boulder, Colorado
- *American Indian Upward Bound Science and Self-Determination Program (AIUB)*—Boulder, Colorado
- *Chicago Area Health and Medical Careers Program (CAHMCP)*—Chicago, Illinois
- *Colorado Minority Engineering Association, Inc. (CMEA)*—Denver, Colorado
- *Detroit Area Pre-College Engineering Program (DAPCEP)*—Detroit, Michigan
- *Massachusetts Pre-Engineering Program for Minority Students, Inc. (MASSPEP)*— Boston, Massachusetts
- *Mathematics, Engineering, and Science Achievement Program (MESA, CA)*— Berkeley, California
- *Mathematics, Engineering, and Science Achievement Program (MESA, WA)*— Seattle, Washington
- *Philadelphia Regional Introduction for Minorities to Engineering, Inc. (PRIME)*—Philadelphia, Pennsylvania
- *Pittsburgh Regional Engineering Program (PREP)*—Pittsburgh, Pennsylvania
- *Program for Rochester to Interest Students in Science and Math (PRIS²M)*— Rochester, New York
- *Southeastern Consortium for Minorities in Engineering (SECME)*—Atlanta, Georgia

General characteristics of the 12 programs, such as the race/ethnicity and grade level of the students served, are presented in Table 2.1. The programs serve students from a range of economic backgrounds, with some programs serving both low- and middle-income students. Most students served are in middle (or junior high) school and high school. The current and prior levels of academic achievement of students vary widely, as do the criteria for entry into and continued participation in the programs.

Most of the programs are extracurricular. With rare exceptions, they are funded by private corporations and foundations and are staffed by nonteaching personnel not subordinated to the school district whose students they assist. The programs usually are housed not in offices of the school district but rather in those of a local

Table 2.1

General Characteristics of Precollege Programs

Program	Race/Ethnicity of Students	Grades Served	Criteria for Admission & Continued Participation
AISES	American Indians	Junior & senior high school	Being in top ½ of class, 2.5 GPA, & teacher recommendation
AIUB	American Indians	High school	Combination of grades (no cutoff), recommendations, "potential for college"
CAHMCP	Primarily African Americans	Grades 7–12	Combinations of grades, scores on standardized tests, teacher/counselor recommendations
CMEA	Hispanic, African, & Native Americans; large number of rural Hispanic Americans	Grades 7–12	3.0 GPA
DAPCEP	African, Hispanic, & Native Americans	Junior & senior high school	Combination of grades (2.0 GPA), teacher recommendation, and personal information (e.g., attendance record)
MASSPEP	African, Hispanic, & Native Americans; primarily African Americans	Middle & high school	High interest & ability
MESA, CA	African & Hispanic (primarily Mexican) Americans; recent outreach to Native Americans	Grades 4–12	Interest and aptitude (measured by grades, standardized tests)

Table 2.1 (continued)

General Characteristics of Precollege Programs

Program	Race/Ethnicity of Students	Grades Served	Criteria for Admission & Continued Participation
MESA, WA	African, Hispanic, & Native Americans	Middle & high school	Interest & aptitude, but some students with low GPA
PREP	Primarily African Americans	Middle & high school	Teacher recommendation, math course each year in high school, no grade requirement for entrance
PRIME	African, Hispanic, & Native Americans	Middle & high school	Overall B average with at least B average in both math & science; teacher recommendation
PRIS^{2}M	Primarily African Americans	Grades 7–12	50th percentile or better on CAT, teacher recommendation, request from parent or student, 2.5 GPA, math/science course each semester
SECME	African, Hispanic, and Native Americans	Grades 4–12	Combination of GPA, test scores, teacher recommendation, enrollment in math & science courses; varying by state

Most of the programs have their own staff and occur during nonschool hours or days, or in the summer.

▾

university or a local business. Moreover, the program activities for the minority youths who are enrolled usually occur during nonschool hours, such as on Saturday mornings or in the summer.

Procedures for Acquiring Program Information

The basic research approach was qualitative. Each program was treated as a case study. The director of each program was telephoned and told about the study and about the nature of his or her participation in it, should he or she agree to participate. Originally, 13 of 14 program directors agreed to participate. However, the information provided by one of the 13 programs was insufficient for its inclusion in the report.

Descriptions of the 12 participating programs were derived from (1) written material in the form of pamphlets, handouts, or magazines provided by directors and staff, and (2) individual face-to-face interviews with program directors, staff, and students. In addition to staff from the programs, various teachers and, sometimes, principals from schools participating in the programs were also interviewed. The information and insights gathered from these face-to-face interviews were particularly important for purposes of describing what typically occurs in programs.

Students Served by the Programs

Two types of minority students are served by the participating programs: high-achievers and underachievers (that is, low-achievers who are perceived as having the potential to improve considerably with some guidance, instruction, and enhancement of motivation). Of course, some of the "high-achievers" may also be underachieving if they are failing to fully exploit their potential. The high-achievers are probably best represented by the group of magnet-school students described in Profile 1 on the next page. The underachievers are more like Jerome, the struggling 10th-grade student described in Profile 5 on page 65.

Much of the literature reviewed in Part 1 of this book is about underachieving minority students, like Jerome, whose academic performance is less than it could be and who are from low-income families. There has been insufficient research comparing underachieving talented minority students (like Jerome) and their high-achieving counterparts, although the need for such research clearly exists. The position taken here is that the best of the strategies used by the programs are effective with both groups.

> **The programs serve both high-achieving and "underachieving" students.**

> **Most of the research that is reviewed here focuses on the "underachieving" students.**

Profile 1

Students at a Math/Science Magnet School

The high school is located in a poor inner-city neighborhood of a large city. It is a magnet school with a mathematics and science theme. We (myself and a staff member from the extracurricular precollege math/science program) drive to the school from the "nice" side of town. The closer we get to the school, the more desolate the neighborhood appears. Surprisingly, human figures appear in the portals of buildings whose largely boarded-up windows suggest abandonment. We park in the school parking lot, and the staff member removes a metal contraption from the trunk of his car and uses it to physically lock the steering wheel and column. "I hope it [the car] is here when we get back," he says. "You're kidding," I say. "I'm not," he replies.

The facade of the school is not much better than those of surrounding buildings. However, we enter and are suddenly in a different world. While the building, its fixtures, and furnishings are obviously old, it is brightly painted and vibrant. I meet with about 10 students around a large table. I say "about 10" because several wandered in and out during the course of the meeting, as the program advisor was able to locate them and as their schedules permitted.

They are a bright, articulate, self-confident, highly motivated group. They talk about their experiences in the program, the hands-on science activities, the visits to local industry, their special mathematics class. Most of all, they talk about their past summer experiences—what it was like living on campus, interacting with university faculty and graduate students. There is a certain genuineness in their voices and in their eyes that leads me to believe that despite some small amount of exaggeration, they are not just providing the usual *pro forma* laudatory comments. They really enjoy and feel they have benefited from the program.

Compared with many students I have talked with in extracurricular precollege programs, this group almost seems not to need such a program. Despite the poverty of the surrounding neighborhood, their school—a magnet school—has a very good reputation, and the students I am speaking with were attracted by its math/science theme. Largely from middle-class families, they have parents who hold college degrees, including a couple of doctorates. Asked to imagine themselves in 10 years, these students see engineers, actuarial scientists, and the like. They give the distinct impression that they will reach these goals. In most ways, they are the cream of the crop. They have been academically successful in the past, and they would most likely continue to be, even without the benefit of a special program.

It is not that they receive no benefit from the program. On the contrary, the program has acquainted them with an expanded range of options. For example, I learned only recently what an actuarial scientist does; these students already have an intimate knowledge of the field and its requirements. However, they would probably have made something of themselves in any event. They have the ability, and perhaps more important—being middle-class in speech, appearance, and values—they come from the "right" background. They are perceived as talented, both by themselves and by their teachers. In this magnet-school setting, they experience peer pressure to be, rather than not to be, academically successful.

The chapter that follows paints a picture of how serious the problem of minority low achievement is. It also introduces the four characteristics that academic intervention programs must nurture in minority students in order to change this picture.

ENDNOTES

1. The term *minority*, because of its prevalence in the literature, is used in this report to refer to African, Hispanic, and Native Americans. However, two common misconceptions about the term should be avoided. First is the assumption that the term is demographically accurate. In fact, the term *minority* may be inappropriately applied in many regions of the country where "minorities" are rapidly becoming majorities. This is the case in 23 of the 25 largest cities in the U.S. and will be the case in many other cities by the turn of the century (Quality Education for Minorities Project, 1990).

The second and graver misconception is the assumption that except for superficial differences in language, food, and clothing, all minorities are alike. Educators and program staff unfamiliar with the breadth and depth of cultural differences, as these were recently described by Kinsler, Romero, Kelly, Graves, and Mercado (1991), must guard against unduly minimizing intergroup differences. Similarly, cultural differences within each group should not be minimized. For example, Cubans, Puerto Ricans, Mexicans, and Central Americans, although collectively referred to as Hispanic, differ from one another in substantive ways, despite certain common historical and linguistic traditions (Marsella, 1990).

Consistent with their use in the literature, in referring to the specific minority groups, we use the terms *African American* and *black* interchangeably, and we use the terms *Hispanic American* and *Latino*(a) interchangeably. Consistent with their use in the literature, and with the recommendations of staff of the programs visited, we also use the terms *American Indian* and *Native American* interchangeably.

2. African Americans, Hispanic Americans, and Native Americans are all underrepresented in mathematics- and science-based fields and are therefore the minorities discussed in Part 1. Consistent with the amount of information about each group in the theoretical and research literature, African Americans are discussed in the greatest depth. However, the general principles illustrated by specific studies, as well as the recommendations derived from research and theory, are in most instances applicable to all three groups.

Chapter THREE

Academic Achievement of Minorities

THE OUTLOOK for minorities at all levels of education is a complex and generally dismal one. On the one hand, the number of minority high school graduates who enroll in college has increased in recent years. On the other hand, too few of these students persist in college to receive a 4-year degree. Moreover, in comparison with whites, the number of minority students who enroll in college as well as the number who receive 4-year degrees is disproportionately low. A major contributing factor to these relatively low college-enrollment and college-completion rates is the students' less-than-adequate preparation, in high school, for achievement in college. Large numbers of minority students leave high school without the basic academic skills they need to succeed in college. Moreover, inner-city high schools as well as those in other poor school districts often do not offer the advanced mathematics and science courses that are required for acceptance to math- and science-oriented degree programs in college (Task Force on Women, Minorities, and the Handicapped in Science and Technology, 1989).

Two major indexes of the educational outlook for minorities are presented in this chapter. First, the college achievement of minority students, as measured by the number of degrees conferred in recent years, is

Minority students have relatively low college-enrollment and college-completion rates; too many are insufficiently prepared for college course work.

compared with that of nonminority students; recent facts about college enrollment of minorities are also discussed. Second, the high school achievement of minority students in the basic skills of mathematics, writing, and reading, as measured by standardized tests, is compared with that of nonminority students. Basic skills, of course, are prerequisites for achievement in mathematics and science in high school and beyond. Statistics presented throughout this chapter are taken primarily from recent reports by the American Council on Education (1991) and by the U.S. Department of Education (1988), which were based on census data.

Achievement in Higher Education

Hispanic Americans

While there has been some increase in the number of Hispanic Americans going on to college, they still are disproportionately represented in higher education.

▼

Between 1981 and 1989, the number of bachelor's degrees awarded to Hispanics increased by 36%; the number of master's degrees, by 12%; and the number of doctoral degrees, by 23%. An overly optimistic interpretation of these increases must be tempered by two realizations: First, the small *number* of degrees awarded each year makes almost any percentage increase seem dramatic. For example, the 570 doctoral degrees received by Hispanics in 1989 were only 106 more than the 464 received by them in 1981 (American Council on Education, 1991, pp. 31–34). Second, despite these gains, Hispanics continue to earn disproportionately fewer degrees than nonminorities do. While Hispanics composed 8% of the U.S. population, they accounted for only 2.9% of bachelor's, 2.4% of master's, and 1.6% of doctoral degrees conferred in 1989 (American Council on Education, 1991; Task Force on Women, Minorities, and the Handicapped in Science and Technology, 1989). These statistics are particularly alarming in light of the youthfulness of the Hispanic population relative to the non-Hispanic population (37% of Hispanics are between the ages of 5 and 24, whereas only 28% of non-

Hispanics, the fastest-growing minority group, accounted for only about 3% of bachelor's degrees and 2% of master's and doctoral degrees in 1989.

▼

Hispanics are in this age group) and in light of the growth rate of the Hispanic population relative to that of the non-Hispanic population (the Hispanic population grew by 39% between 1980 and 1989, whereas the non-Hispanic population grew by only 7.5%; American Council on Education, 1991).

The problems just described will likely worsen, given recent declines in the college enrollment of the 18- to 24-year-old Hispanic high school graduates, the age group that usually constitutes the core of college enrollment. College enrollment among this group declined from a high of 35.8% in 1976 to a low of 26.9% in 1985, and it has fluctuated between 28% and 31% since then. Nor does it bode well that the high school completion rate for Hispanics, after peaking at 62.9% in 1985, declined to 55.9% in 1989. This recent rate was much lower than the 1989 high school completion rates of both whites (82.1%) and blacks (76.1%) (American Council on Education, 1991).

Native Americans

Between 1981 and 1989, the number of bachelor's degrees awarded to Native Americans increased by 12.6%; the number of master's degrees, by 9.5%; and the number of doctoral degrees, by 9.5%. As stated earlier, an overly optimistic interpretation of these percentage increases must be tempered by the realization that small numbers are behind the percentages, and Native Americans continue to earn disproportionately fewer degrees than nonminorities do. While Native Americans made up 0.6% of the U.S. population, they received only 0.4% of bachelor's and master's degrees and 0.3% of doctoral degrees awarded in 1989 (American Council on Education, 1991; Task Force on Women, Minorities, and the Handicapped in Science and Technology, 1989). It is unlikely that these statistics will improve significantly as long as Native American students, compared with students from other racial/ethnic groups, take longer, on the average, to complete high school and also com-

College enrollment among Hispanic Americans declined from approximately 36% in 1976 to 27% in 1985.

▾

Hispanics' high school completion also has declined—from about 63% in 1985 to 56% in 1989. This latter rate compares with 82% for whites and 76% for blacks.

▾

Also making progress in higher education are Native Americans, but they are not yet proportionately represented.

▾

plete high school at one of the lowest rates. For example, only 67% of Native American high school students who were sophomores in 1980 graduated on schedule, in 1982. In comparison, 72% of Hispanic, 78% of black, 86% of white, and 93% of Asian American 1980 sophomores graduated on schedule (American Council on Education, 1991).

African Americans

Of all minority groups, the educational picture is most dismal for African Americans. Between 1981 and 1989, bachelor's degrees awarded to African Americans *decreased* by 4.3%, master's degrees *decreased* by 17.8%, and doctoral degrees *decreased* by 19.9% (American Council on Education, 1991).

African Americans have the most dismal higher education picture: They decreased by about 4% in bachelor's degrees, about 18% in master's degrees, and 20% in doctoral degrees from 1981–1989.

▼

The 1981–89 decrease in the number of conferred degrees was particularly salient among black *males*: 8.7% fewer bachelor's degrees, 15.5% fewer master's degrees, and 35.2% fewer doctoral degrees were awarded to black males. During the same period, the number of bachelor's and doctoral degrees received by black *females* also declined, but only by 1.4% and 5.0%, respectively. However, the number of master's degrees received by black females fell considerably, by 19.1% (American Council on Education, 1991).

Black males, in particular, have been declining in all levels of college and university degrees.

▼

The percentage of 18- to 24-year-old blacks graduating from high school increased from 70.9% in 1981 to 76.1% in 1989. The percentage of those students going on to college fluctuated between 28% and 31% during the same period.

There were some slight gains during the 1980s in African Americans completing high school and getting started in college.

▼

In recent years an increased number of college degrees have been awarded to African Americans in technical fields such as engineering. However, in relation to whites, blacks continue to earn disproportionately fewer college degrees, in general, and fewer math- and science-based degrees, in particular. For example, while blacks made up 12% of the U.S. population, they earned only 5.7% of all bachelor's, 4.6% of all master's, and 2.3% of all doctoral degrees awarded in 1989 (American

Council on Education, 1991). Moreover, blacks generally do even less well in math- and science-based fields: They receive only 5% of the bachelor's and 1% of the doctoral degrees in science and engineering, and they make up only 2% of all employed scientists and engineers (Task Force on Women, Minorities, and the Handicapped in Science and Technology, 1989). There have been increases in the number of blacks earning college degrees in math- and science-based fields in recent years. However, these increases may have been at the expense of the field of education, the traditional higher-education field for blacks. For example, between the 1975–76 and the 1984–85 academic years, the number of engineering bachelor's degrees awarded to African Americans increased by almost 50%. During that same period the number of education bachelor's degrees awarded to black Americans decreased by over 60% (American Council on Education, 1988). As a consequence, an already-existing shortage of black educators is further exacerbated.

College Enrollment Patterns of Minorities and Whites

Minority students are more likely than white students to take nontraditional routes to acquiring a college degree. They are more likely to attend college on a part-time basis, to attend college intermittently over many years, and to enroll initially at 2-year rather than 4-year institutions. In 1988, for example, 46% of minority students enrolled in 2-year, as opposed to 4-year, institutions. In contrast, only 36% of white students enrolled in 2-year institutions (American Council on Education, 1991). There are many reasons for taking nontraditional routes to a college degree, including poverty and, as will be discussed next, inadequate high school preparation. However, regardless of the reasons for taking them, nontraditional routes may, at best, considerably extend the time taken to earn a degree (as we discuss in Part 2 of this book) or, at worst, decrease the likelihood

Blacks earn only 5% of bachelor's degrees and 1% of doctoral degrees in science and engineering and make up only 2% of employed scientists and engineers.

While more African Americans have been choosing science and mathematics careers of late, this has coincided with their decline in other fields where they are needed, such as teaching.

Minorities are more likely than whites to attend college part-time, spread college out over more years, and begin college at 2-year rather than 4-year institutions.

of receiving a degree (Richardson & Bender, 1985).

The relatively small number of higher-education degrees awarded to minorities is not surprising if achievement in college is considered to be partly a function of achievement in high school. In general, minority high school students graduate less-prepared for college and with lower levels of basic academic skills than do their nonminority counterparts, as revealed by statistics presented next.

Achievement in High School

Upon high school graduation, minority students lag behind whites in major areas of academic achievement—mathematics, writing, and reading.

About the time of their graduation from high school at age 17 or 18, minority students score consistently below whites in *mathematics*, *writing*, and *reading*, as the following achievement test results substantiate:

Statistics from the Education Commission of the States (cited in U.S. Department of Education, 1988) revealed that in recent years the average 17-year-old white student correctly answered about 63% of the *mathematics* items on the National Assessment of Educational Progress (NAEP) test. In contrast, the average Hispanic student answered about 49% correctly, and the average black student answered about 45% correctly.

The Office of Research and Improvement of the U.S. Department of Education (cited in U.S. Department of Education, 1988) reported that while the average *writing* performance on the NAEP test was about 224 for 11th-grade white students, it was only about 200 for black and Hispanic students.

According to the National Institute of Education (cited in U.S. Department of Education, 1988), during the 1983–84 academic year, only 69% of Hispanic and 66% of black 17-year-olds tested on the NAEP test as *reading* at an "intermediate" level or higher. ("Intermediate" reading is defined as being able to search for specific information, interrelate ideas, and make generalizations about literature, science, and social studies materials.) In contrast, 89% of white students could read at or above this level. An even greater contrast is seen at the next-higher level of reading proficiency, "adept." ("Adept" reading is defined as being able to find, understand, summarize, and explain relatively complicated literary and informational material.) Almost half of all 17-year-old white students (45%) were adept readers, in contrast with only about one fifth (20%) of Hispanic and about one sixth (16%) of black students.

Overall, the educational state of minority students is particularly alarming when compared with the template of persons needed for tomorrow's technologically oriented world. Too many minority students graduate from high school lacking the basic skills necessary to succeed in college or at competitive jobs. A review of research on achievement and psychological development indicates that to achieve in mathematics and science, as well as in other fields, students need to have (1) *knowledge of one or more specific fields*, (2) *effective problem-solving strategies*, (3) *motivation*, and (4) *effective communication skills*. Although there may be other factors associated with achievement, these four characteristics are clearly essential and form the basis of the model to be proposed (in Chapter 5) for improving the achievement of minority students. A closer look at these characteristics follows.

The Characteristics Essential for Academic Achievement

Knowledge of One or More Specific Fields

Success in mathematics- or science-based fields requires a working knowledge of current theory, facts, and methods of inquiry. Bloom's taxonomy of educational objectives for the cognitive domain (Bloom, Englehart, Furst, Hill, & Krathwohl, 1956) is one particularly useful tool for conceptualizing not only the type of knowledge that students need to acquire but also possible

Of 17-year-old white students, 45% were "adept" readers on the NAEP tests. This compared with only 20% of Hispanic and 16% of African American students.

Success in math- or science-based fields requires specific knowledge and the ability to analyze, synthesize, and evaluate during learning and experimentation.

ways of evaluating their acquisition of that knowledge. In general, success in mathematics- or science-based fields requires an ability to function at the analysis, synthesis, and evaluation levels of Bloom's taxonomy. This is in part because wider application of existing technology, as well as discovery of new technology, is usually built on existing bodies of knowledge. Random, accidental discoveries are the exception rather than the rule. Moreover, motivation to succeed in any field of endeavor partially depends on the perception that one has the necessary tools for finding answers.

Effective Problem-Solving Strategies

Problem-solving ability is commonly described as "intelligence," which is a theoretically and empirically confusing concept, given the lack of agreement among social scientists on the definition and measurement of intelligence. Most likely, as proposed by Gardner (1983), Hale-Benson (1986), Hilliard (1976), and others, there are multiple intelligences and multiple ways of processing information for problem-solving purposes. A person's intellectual ability, however it is manifested, has to be acknowledged and accommodated in educational settings, especially if the potential to become a scientist is to be realized. To employ a cliché, instruction must be tailored to the needs of the individual learner. However, in practice the reverse is often true.

Motivation

Success in technological fields depends heavily on a student's internal motivation and not merely on the promise of some external reward. Typically, a student's internal motivation is reflected in a thirst for knowledge, a confidence in his or her ability to solve problems, a persistence in the face of failure, and a willingness to take risks. The sources of student motivation are many, but they probably include the student's perception that an endeavor is (1) interesting and relevant to real life; (2) challenging but within his or her abilities; and thus (3) in some sense, fun.

Current theorists, such as Gardner, propose that there are multiple intelligences and ways of processing information for problem solving.

Students must have strong internal motivation to achieve in technologically oriented fields.

Effective Communication Skills

To succeed academically, as well as to succeed in the sciences, students must be skilled receptors of the oral, written, and graphic communication of others. These skills are vital to keeping current with the ever-increasing volume of scientific information generated in our technologically oriented society. The successful student must also be an effective communicator of ideas in oral, written, and graphic form. In the United States today, effective communication skills require, at a minimum, fluency in standard English.

A number of factors may hinder disadvantaged and minority teenagers' development of effective communication skills and of the other essential characteristics we have been discussing. Because precollege intervention programs need to take these factors into account, the following chapter discusses the hindering factors in detail.

Effective communication skills are essential to students' academic success.

Chapter FOUR

Minority Students' Development and Academic Achievement

As BRONFENBRENNER (1979) pointed out, children live and interact in at least three environments—the family, the school, and the immediate community. Each environment has a unique impact on children's cognitive, affective, and social development. It is important for optimum development and academic achievement that children's experiences at home, at school, and in the community be complementary. However, they are not complementary for many low-income and minority children (Slaughter & Epps, 1987), as is made obvious throughout this chapter. It is in this context that development of the four key characteristics for academic achievement is discussed. Each characteristic is first considered in light of theoretical and empirical research. Then we discuss the problems and obstacles that minority students face in the acquisition of each characteristic.

Knowledge of One or More Specific Fields

Students should possess a working knowledge of current theory, facts, and methods of inquiry that allows them to function at the analysis, synthesis, and evalua-

4

Complementarity and consistency between home, school, and community foster children's development and achievement.

▾

By their middle school years, children should begin to actively engage in analyzing, synthesizing, and evaluating knowledge in at least one area of study.

▼

Minority students in inner-city schools often have no access to sufficiently advanced courses, equipment, and teaching.

▼

tion levels of Bloom's taxonomy of educational objectives (Bloom et al., 1956). Acquisition of such knowledge depends on several factors. Students must attend classes regularly, and they must be actively engaged in the business of constructing knowledge; they must spend adequate time on task, complete projects and assignments, and so on. Entry into math- and science-based professions requires an early interest in the field, so students may benefit by entering the right academic track in junior high school (or perhaps even in middle school).

However, according to staff and students at many of the programs visited, minority students in mathematics and science tracks in large, inner-city public high schools are often at a disadvantage compared with their private and suburban public school counterparts. Upper-level mathematics and science courses were reported to be missing from the curriculum of many inner-city public schools. Frequently, the classes offered were described as being taught by persons with limited expertise and as being inadequately supported with equipment and other resources. Because of these reported problems, several program directors complained that a grade of A in an upper-level mathematics or science course from an inner-city school is equivalent to a grade of B or C from a private school or a suburban public school with better-equipped labs, better-trained teachers, and so on.

Examples of how students perceive this difference in academic preparation and of how the design of the extracurricular mathematics and science programs helps students narrow the difference are presented in Profile 2.

Rosalind, described in Profile 2, is fortunate not only because she benefits from the extracurricular precollege program but also because she is in a math-and-science track in high school. For many reasons, most minority students do not enter a math-and-science track in high school. The reasons include factors endemic to a student's family setting (how the student is able or encouraged to use nonschool time, whether the student lives in poverty, whether the student comes from a single-parent household), as well as factors endemic to the educational setting. As already mentioned, for students to achieve academically, their experiences at home, at school, and in the community must be complementary. Thus we now look at factors in at least two of those settings—the home and the school—that have an impact on students' knowledge acquisition.

Profile 2

ROSALIND—A Student

Rosalind is the daughter of West Indian immigrants. She lives with her mother in a "not-too-nice area" of a large city. She has just completed the requirements for a bachelor of science degree and is hoping to go on to medical school. She attributes part of her academic success to the extracurricular mathematics and science program she has participated in since her sophomore year in high school. (As a college student, she has continued to take program courses and serves as a role model for high school students.) Most of her participation in program activities has been during summers. Each summer since high school, she has taken enrichment mathematics and science courses offered by the program. She has also been placed in different work environments (such as hospitals) related to the profession she aspires to.

According to Rosalind, the program helps because "it keeps me focused on what I want to do." The enrichment courses are also "a big plus." These are courses that really challenge high school students by giving them work equivalent to introductory work required of college students. Most disadvantaged or minority students, including those with high academic potential, are never challenged in this way. Instead, public school faculty and administration often assume that disadvantaged or minority students are not capable of meeting the requirements of even their regular classes. The program makes sure the course work will be challenging, but not be *too* challenging, for Rosalind and her peers by pretesting them to determine what they can handle.

Regarding the courses and their role in her academic success, Rosalind says: "All [of them] help you get ahead. They give you a head start to compete with prep-school students. *I would never have passed organic chemistry without the program.*"

Two other reasons the program helps, in Rosalind's opinion, are these: First, it provides information on what different professions involve. The program helps her clear up doubts about "Do I really want to do this?" Second, and perhaps equally important in her case, it helps develop a positive self-concept. Precisely what aspects of the program do that? "Talking to other students who have made it and been through difficult times," receiving academic help from those students, networking with others.

She also cites the fact that the program is "very personal," adding, "You can call the director up at any time." Perhaps that is why Rosalind is now giving back to the program by helping high school students, as she was helped.

Family Background Factors That May Hinder Knowledge Acquisition

Students' use of nonschool time. Many minority students spend too much time watching television to the detriment of homework. Although watching too much television might be said to be a condition of American children generally, statistics compiled by the National Assessment of Educational Progress (cited in U.S. Department of Education, 1988) reveal that black children, especially those of elementary school age, watch more television than their white peers do.

Assuming that the content of programs presented by the media is educational and that the language of presentation is grammatical, a positive impact on minority children is a logical expectation. Indeed, empirical evidence (Ball & Bogatz, 1972) indicates that for children of preschool or early elementary school age, viewing *educational* television programs (such as *Sesame Street*) may even enhance standardized test scores, preparedness for school, and interest in school. However, it seems reasonable to assume that large doses of *commercial* video and audio entertainment may simply reduce the time available for children and adolescents to study and do their homework. The result may be decreased academic performance, as measured by standardized achievement tests (Keith, Reimers, Fehrmann, Pottsbaum, & Aubey, 1986). Research reveals that children's writing performance decreases as frequency of television viewing increases (U.S. Department of Education, 1988), which may in part explain the previously discussed low writing-test scores obtained by black teenagers.

Another major concern is the minority students' use of their summers strictly for employment or leisure activities. The economic needs of low-income families make summer employment important for many minority students and their families. However, most students who obtain summer jobs—as well as many of those who do not—fail to participate in summer classes

How students are able to use nonschool time can impact their academic achievement.

Watching too much television is one use of nonschool time that can be detrimental to academic achievement. This is especially the case among minority students.

or other educational activities that could prevent the decline of knowledge and of academic work habits that often occurs over a summer. Summer educational activities that include attendance at local colleges or universities can give students a taste of university life and may thereby attract them to higher education. Activities that include a college or university residential component may also make the thought of attending college less threatening, a potentially important benefit for students who are the first in the family to attend college. Additionally, as discussed later in this chapter, the camplike atmosphere of residential summer classes may nurture positive feelings about self, leadership skills, and motivation in students from backgrounds not particularly rewarding of academic prowess.

Single-parent households. Census data reveal that the percentage of children living in single-parent families increased steadily between 1970 and 1989 (U.S. Bureau of the Census, 1990a): During the same period, however, higher percentages of black and Hispanic children than of white children lived in single-parent households. In 1989 approximately 57% of black children, 29% of Hispanic children, and 19% of white children lived in single-parent households. Of these households, about 87% were single-female-parent households.

Census data further reveal that single-female head-of-household status and poverty tend to go hand in hand. While approximately 44% of all black and 36% of all Hispanic children under the age of 18 lived in poverty in 1989, 63% of all black and 65% of all Hispanic children under age 18 in single-female head-of-household families lived in poverty. Furthermore 79% of all low-income black families and about 50% of all low-income Hispanic families were headed by single females (U.S. Bureau of the Census, 1990a).

Much has been said about the ability or inability of single-female parents to positively affect the academic performance of their children. The argument presented here is that being from a single-female-parent household does not always result in a child's poor academic

For many economically disadvantaged teens, use of nonschool time strictly for employment or leisure activities precludes participation in academic enrichment programs.

▾

In those single-parent households where poverty and its accompanying stresses prevail, children's learning can suffer.

▾

achievement. However, when poverty and stress accompany single parenthood, as they often do, these factors may have a negative impact on the child's academic achievement.

Specifically referring to divorced women, Hetherington, Cox, and Cox (1982) described single-female parents as suffering from feelings of unhappiness and frustration, along with task overload (having to deal alone with such tasks as child-discipline, which in a two-parent family would be shared by both adults). Not surprisingly, Hetherington, Camara, and Featherman (1983) found children of single mothers to be having difficulty with self-control and, perhaps as a consequence, to be performing poorly on standardized tests of intelligence and achievement.

These are not inevitable consequences of the phenomenon of single-female-headed households. Clark (1983) found that some low-income families headed by single mothers foster academic success in their children as effectively as do two-parent middle-income families. The determining factors seem to be parental outlook on life, interest in the children's education, and degree of parental control over children, particularly regarding educational matters. Poor black children who succeed academically tend to have parents who value education, exercise control over educational activities, and model and reinforce the belief that high achievement is possible; whether the family is intact (a two-parent family) or not seems to be less critical than these other family characteristics. Single-parent families, as well as intact families, who do not exhibit these characteristics tend to foster low academic achievement.

Parents' own upbringing. Parental engagement in promoting children's achievement may be affected negatively by parents' own upbringing. Some low-income minority mothers, despite the best intentions for their children's education, are simply unable, without external guidance, to engage in the behaviors that, according to Clark (1983), foster academic performance. The reason, it seems, is that as children, they themselves

However, whether in single-parent or two-parent low-income households, children can prosper when parents stress the value of education and reinforce educational activities.

were not exposed to such practices and hence do not have them in their repertoire of childrearing behaviors.

Parental poverty. Unfortunately, dealing with poverty has become an all-consuming enterprise for many families—especially for those headed by single, minority mothers. As a result of cutbacks in federal funding in the last decade, families frequently find themselves without the safety net of economic and other resources previously provided by federal programs. As a result of cultural and demographic changes, including the weakening of extended-family ties, parents (in particular, single mothers) may also lack traditional support from other adult family members. Consequently, the struggle against poverty may leave them with little energy to engage in the kind of academic-achievement-promoting behaviors described by Clark (1983).

Parental poverty affects children in other ways, too. As mentioned earlier, because they need to find jobs (or other means of earning money) to help support the family and acquire material goods, poor teenagers often show little interest in or have little time for academic achievement. Researchers at the Institute for Social Research at the University of Michigan reported that 8% of employed African American high school seniors contributed all or almost all their income to family expenses. Almost 64% contributed at least some of their income. The comparable figures for employed white high school seniors were 2% and 39%, respectively (Bachman, Johnston, & O'Malley, 1991).

A critical problem connected with family poverty is that some minority youths earn needed income not from jobs but from illegal activities such as selling drugs. In light of minorities' economic needs, the phenomenon of children helping to support their families with profits from the sale of drugs will grow if local, state, and federal policies affecting poor children are not changed significantly.

The economic needs of minority students were brought home to us during site visits to extracurricular mathematics and science programs. Staff of several

> Without guidance and resources for their own development, many parents cannot support their children's educational endeavors.

> Many teenagers from economically disadvantaged families need to hold jobs to help with family expenses.

programs revealed that teachers receiving small stipends for advising and tutoring the students often use some of their stipend money for the poorest students, to help them purchase clothing or materials or pay for field trips.

Educational Setting Factors That May Hinder Knowledge Acquisition

Abstract curriculum content and teaching methods. In high school as well as in college, students from all walks of life complain about the abstract nature of curriculum content and instruction and the perceived irrelevance of the knowledge they acquire. Students often ignore adult admonitions that the information will be useful, if not absolutely necessary, in subsequent years. In part, the students' attitude grows naturally out of their stage of cognitive development. Teenagers, as described by Elkind (1974), tend to feel invincible and to have little concern for the future. However, this "natural" tendency is probably exacerbated by the abstract nature of much school instruction.

The reliance on formal presentations of an abstract nature, which is typical of instruction in academic settings, may have a particularly negative effect on black students, if White's (1984) description of their cultural tradition has validity. According to White, African American tradition places a high value on direct experience. Consequently, not only may many minority students be *un*motivated by abstract knowledge and instructional methods, they may even be *negatively* motivated.

Curriculum omission of minority contributions. For many minority students, relating current education to the future is only one problem. They also experience difficulty because of an underreported past. As Alter, McDonald, Murr, and Padgett pointed out in their 1989 article, almost everyone has heard about George Washington Carver and Martin Luther King, Jr. However, the few blacks whose accomplishments are well known are

Certain factors in educational settings can discourage adolescents' academic achievement.

Teachers' formal instructional methods can result in students' being unmotivated or negative towards learning.

usually discussed only in connection with a unit of study during black history month. The important historical figures of other minority groups are treated similarly. Countless other contributions by minorities are not recognized and, more important, are not integrated into the retelling of Western history. The omissions may tell many minority students something about the status or worth of their ethnic group in the society, thereby decreasing the motivation of some students.

Inadequate counseling. Minority students are frequently encouraged to follow nonacademic tracks by well-meaning high school counselors who believe the students lack ability. Moreover, many counselors cannot adequately assist students in making career decisions because they (the counselors) are unfamiliar with the nature or expectations of many jobs that have a mathematics or science base.

Counselors have been known to encourage minority students to start their higher education by attending a community college, in order to "get their feet wet." However, some empirical evidence (Richardson & Bender, 1985) indicates that the chances of completing a baccalaureate degree may be lower for students who initially attend 2-year institutions than for those who start at 4-year institutions.

An African American colleague who now holds a doctorate degree is a good example of a talented student who received well-intentioned yet poor counseling. Upon graduation from high school, she was offered a scholarship to the local junior college. She decided to reject it in favor of an almost certain scholarship to a 4-year institution. Her counselor tried to convince her and her parents that attending the junior college was in her best interest. In the colleague's opinion, the counselor felt that she lacked intellectual ability. Fortunately, she ignored the counselor's advice.

IN SUMMARY   Minority students face many obstacles to acquiring knowledge about specific fields. Some obstacles—such as lack of parental control over how

The self-image of minority students suffers when the contributions of persons from ethnic minority groups are underreported or not well integrated in school curricula.

Counselors may underestimate minority students' potential for advanced achievement in math and science or other areas of study.

much nonschool time students spend in educational activities—originate in the home. Poverty and stress, which especially affect single-female-headed households, may play a significant role in limiting this parental control in many minority homes. School factors that may be obstacles to the acquisition of knowledge by minority students include pedagogy that relies too heavily on formal presentations of abstract content, inadequate recognition of minorities in the curriculum, and inappropriate counseling.

In addition to family background and the school-related factors discussed thus far, the acquisition of knowledge is also highly dependent on the interactions between the information-processing/problem-solving strategies of the learner and the methods of instruction. We turn to this topic next.

Intelligence and Effective Problem-Solving Strategies

Intellectual ability is necessary for problem solving in mathematics- and science-based fields, as it is in any field. However, experts disagree about what constitutes intellectual ability and about how it should be measured. *Intelligence* has been variously viewed as the operative structure of thinking that develops in adaptation to the environment (Piaget, 1983), as creativity (Torrance, 1965), as memory and problem-solving ability, and as that which intelligence tests measure (an example of this is defining intelligence as an IQ score). Educators and others often give too much credence to intelligence test scores, even though they are limited indicators of intelligence.

There are many views of intelligence, but too many educators view intelligence as restricted to what is measurable.

Educational Setting Factors That May Hinder Development of Problem-Solving Strategies

As measured throughout the school years by traditional intelligence tests, the intellectual performance of black children is about 15–20 points lower than that of whites, and in the general child population, the performance of low-income children is 10–15 points below that of middle-income children (Broman, Nichols, & Kennedy, 1975; Hall & Kaye, 1980; Kennedy, 1969). Many explanations of these discrepancies have been advanced.[1] A thorough discussion of them is beyond the scope of this report. However, this report will discuss the following practices that may hinder adequate assessement and development of children's intellectual abilities:

Use of standardized tests for early tracking. Of great concern for purposes of the present discussion is the practice of sorting students into high and low academic tracks on the basis of performance on standardized tests of intelligence and achievement. Minority students, because of their generally lower scores, are more likely to be assigned to low academic tracks early in their school experience. Once assigned to low tracks, they are likely to remain there. This is not necessarily problematic—if students in low tracks acquire the same content and skills as students in high tracks but do so at a different pace. However, low- and high-track classes are sometimes quite dissimilar in both content and method of instruction.

Eder (1986) found that minority students are very likely to be placed in low reading groups in their early school years, and they are very likely to remain there. Moreover, research by Collins (1986) suggests that whereas instruction in the high reading group tends to center on semantics (study of the meaning of words and sentences), instruction in the low reading group tends to center on phonology, particularly the proper pronunciation of words. As a result, in the different groups, children are likely to form different perceptions of the reading task.

According to Collins (1986) and Cook-Gumperz (1986), the interaction between the different teaching strategies and students' subconscious methods of processing information may result in strong unintended

On intelligence tests traditionally used by schools, blacks and some other minorities score lower than whites.

▼

Based on their lower standardized test scores, minority students are often tracked or grouped at an early age into less-challenging instructional groups.

▼

and undesirable effects in the low reading groups. These may be too complex to be remedied by a simple shift in teaching strategy, and the effect on subsequent learning may be deadly. It is logical to assume that what occurs in reading may occur in other subject areas as well.

Why are students who are placed in a low academic track likely to remain there? This is in part because the standardized tests used for placing students have very limited potential for diagnosing learning problems and prescribing remediation. They are, by nature, *product*-oriented, that is, designed to provide a score that describes how many correct answers each student can produce in relation to how many correct answers every other student can produce. They provide little or no information about the cognitive *processes* of students, about how they arrive at answers. Yet, children's cognitive processes (problem-solving strategies, learning styles) are frequently at the root of academic success or failure. To convert academic failure to achievement, the variations in children's strategies and styles must be identified and then accommodated or adjusted.

Lack of active-learning experiences. Not only should the evaluation of learning center on cognitive processes, but so should the instruction. In an age of exponentially increasing scientific knowledge, providing students with scientific content is only one, and not necessarily the most important, function of schools. Learning how to learn and how to adjust to new knowledge may be far more important. Thus, the development of critical thinking and effective problem-solving strategies should be a major goal of education. Methods of instruction that promote hands-on, *active learning* may be particularly useful for this purpose.

Research summarized by Bredderman (1983) indicates that economically disadvantaged elementary science students can derive considerable benefits from the hands-on, or active-learning, approach. The increased learning that resulted from activity-based instruction was found whether children were tested with standardized tests biased in favor of activity-based programs or

Assessments of intelligence and achievement should inform educators about students' cognitive strategies, or learning styles.

▾

Both instruction and assessment should center on active learning—nurturing and observing cognitive processes such as problem solving and critical thinking.

▾

with traditional types of standardized tests. While the scores were lower on tests of the latter type, they remained positive. In part, this dispels the popular misconception that activity-based learning fosters only a concrete level of understanding.

Lack of recognition of differences in learning styles. Individual people learn, process information, and solve problems in various ways. Many investigators (e.g., Hale-Benson, 1986) believe that variations in learning styles also exist among different ethnic groups. Specifically, Hale-Benson and others believe that the learning style of most whites is *analytic*, while the learning style of most blacks is *relational*. Analytic reasoners, according to Hale-Benson, process information by following a linear, or sequential, pattern of inductive or deductive reasoning. Relational reasoners, however, process information by considering multiple elements simultaneously rather than sequentially.

According to Hale-Benson (1986) and other proponents of ethnic differences in learning styles, schools are primarily analytic in their approach to teaching, and they expect students to mainly use analytic thinking in their work, thereby placing many black students at a disadvantage. One implication of this hypothesis is that deliberate efforts should be made to help teachers and all students understand and use *both* analytic and relational reasoning. This implication is an important and practical one, even if, as Shipman and Shipman (1985) concluded from their review of research, learning styles may vary as much *within* as *among* ethnic, racial, socioeconomic, and linguistic groups.

IN SUMMARY Perhaps the most important of the school obstacles discussed so far is the practice of using standardized tests to evaluate students' acquisition of knowledge and to place students in high and low academic tracks. Using instructional methods that involve hands-on learning and using assessment methods derived from information-processing techniques are recommended ways of fostering and assessing the de-

Students from different cultural backgrounds may vary in their styles of reasoning and acquiring knowledge.

velopment of critical thinking and problem-solving skills. Next we consider the important role motivation plays in improving minority academic performance.

Motivation

In Chapter 3, student motivation was described behaviorally as including thirst for knowledge, confidence in one's own problem-solving ability, persistence in the face of failure, and willingness to take risks. How do students come to be interested in mathematics and science and become motivated to succeed in these fields? They do so in the same manner that they become interested and motivated in any other field. They are invited, directly or indirectly, by adults or peers or both and are rewarded, directly or vicariously, for their interest and involvement. Examples of indirect invitation, by role modeling, exist in all strata of society. For example, Clift (1989) reported that three of President Bush's four sons have political aspirations. Similarly, the offspring of coal miners often become coal miners.

The role model that influences a child's interests need not be a parent, as in the preceding examples. However, from the perspective of social learning theory (Bandura, 1986), a role model is most often a person who is perceived by the child as powerful, warm, and similar to the child. For many minority children, the home and community do not provide models for academic achievement. One result is minority students' low motivation, which is discussed next. Normative developmental characteristics of children and classroom environments affecting motivation are also discussed.

Home and Community Factors That May Lower Motivation

Scarcity of positive role models. Low-income minority children, unlike their middle-income counterparts, have virtually no educated role models who might

Role models influence children's and adolescents' interests and motivation to achieve.

▾

inspire an interest in mathematics and science. There was a time, however, when low-income minority children had a wider spectrum of occupational role models than they have today. This was prior to the mid-1970s, when middle- and low-income minorities lived in the same, segregated neighborhoods.

In the early 1970s the success of the civil rights movement, along with other factors, began to have an effect on minority housing patterns. Middle-income minorities, taking advantage of opportunities for better jobs and housing, largely abandoned low-income minorities in the inner cities (Ellis, 1988; Wilson, 1987). As a result, in the early 1990s, inner-city minority neighborhoods are populated almost exclusively by the most economically disadvantaged segments of the minority community. Wilson refers to this group as the *underclass*, rather than the *lower class*, to emphasize the terrible state of these communities where middle-income, educated role models scarcely exist.

It is worth noting that parental achievement of middle-income status does not per se solve the problem of children lacking role models for higher educational achievement. Minority parents who are the first generation to acquire middle-income status may still maintain many features of their lower-income status, such as satisfaction with low educational attainment, which can relate to their children's poor academic performance.

The situation for the black middle class in the upstate New York city of Rochester offers an excellent example of this phenomenon. Because Rochester has a large and solid base of industrial firms, such as Eastman Kodak, Xerox, and Delco Products (a division of General Motors), in the 1970s previously unheard-of job opportunities became available to Rochester's blacks. Many worked on production lines, for high enough pay to essentially make them middle class. Others even obtained managerial positions for the first time. However, at least one major characteristic seemed to distinguish this new black middle class from the existing middle classes, both black and white. The new middle-class

Low-income minority students often lack educated role models to inspire and support achievement—especially in math and science.

▾

Many inner-city youngsters have few community role models who are adequately employed or educated.

▾

Other, middle-class, minority youths—like their white counterparts—see their parents experiencing employment problems brought on by increasing automation in the workplace.

▾

Young people can find many negative influences and role models in inner-city neighborhoods, where basic survival is the goal.

▾

workers, believing that high-paying production jobs would also be available for their children, did little to encourage or foster their children's educational ambitions and were not themselves role models for advanced educational achievement. As a result, the growing automation of industry is now returning to lower-class status their children who settled for a high school education or less.

Availability of negative role models. Many inner-city minority adolescents, faced with the departure of middle- and working-class role models from their communities, fill the resultant gap with role models who are antithetical to academic success. One cogent theory about how these negative role models develop, as well as a fairly comprehensive catalog of them, was offered by Ogbu (1978, 1985, 1986). Ogbu referred to the role models as constituting a *survival strategy*. This term describes his belief that the roles evolve in response to and are functional within the unique cultural ecology of the inner city, and they are a very logical way to survive socially and economically in spite of the overt and tacit restrictions placed on minorities by the larger society. According to Ogbu, survival strategies, once established, can be transmitted to succeeding generations through the process of socialization. Parents, relatives, guardians, peers, the larger society, and the media play a part in that transmission.

Ogbu's (1985) catalog of the negative role models available to inner-city black adolescents includes the following:

The *street gang*, teens who belong to the powerful peer group that has its "home" on the streets. They tend not to abide by the conventions of society's dominant group or even by the conventions of the minority group to which they belong.

The *cool cats*, who elevate to artistic levels the ability to project an unperturbed exterior while functioning under stress. Requisites for projecting a "cool" image include a neat appearance, superb verbal manipulative skill, and a catlike ability to walk the social fence without falling into serious trouble.

The *jesters*, who handle stress or pressure by behaving essentially like clowns, engaging in pranks and other mischievous acts. Consequently, these teens are often in trouble with the authorities.

The *antagonists*, who are the typical bullies of their peer groups. Their social status depends on their ability to harass, intimidate, and outperform others with their physical prowess.

An obvious omission from Ogbu's list is the following type of role model:

The *athletes*, who believe the principal or only path to success is to excel at sports. They tend to be interested in academic performance only to the extent needed to maintain their eligibility to participate in sports.

Academic performance of inner-city black youths is affected—directly and indirectly—by the negative role models. For example, many students who believe that to succeed at sports is the road to the ultimate goal of social and economic success regard academic success as unimportant. Their poor academic performance, even after major intervention, should surprise no one. The controversy over Proposition 42—the 1989 National Collegiate Athletic Association ruling regarding academic standards for athletes—may reflect the degree to which this antithesis has become tacitly institutionalized.

Peer pressure. Peer pressure to *not* succeed academically may be particularly relevant to the academic performance of many inner-city black youths. Black adolescents often view roles they associate with the dominant group (whites) as something to be avoided. This is how they view participation in curricular or extracurricular activities aimed at improving academic performance. The tendency to view roles in this way has been labeled *cultural inversion* by Holt (1972) and *secondary cultural difference* by Ogbu (1985).

In Profile 3, Zelma, a high school senior, describes the social costs of participating in an extracurricular mathematics and science program. To combat the kind

Although athletics has been embraced as a minority route to education, it is too limited a route for most students.

Profile 3

ZELMA—A Student

Zelma is a high school senior in a medium-sized city. The small school she attends is located in a mainly black suburb. Having been involved in an extracurricular mathematics and science program since the 10th grade, she remains with the program because, she says, "It's fun—it is educational, but also fun." She describes the fun and the educational aspects of the program as "knowing about the different fields of engineering and the way math and science apply to everyday experience."

The participants in the mathematics and science program at her school meet every other week. Usually only about half of the approximately 75 members of the group make it to each meeting. Zelma is vice president of the group and feels that in that capacity, she has developed some leadership skills. Particularly, she has had to "learn to keep order." She does this in part by "emphasizing control, respect for others talking, and so on." Her leadership skills have also been fostered by tutoring younger students (which is an optional component of the program) as well as

by participating in leadership workshops that are periodically offered as part of the program.

Comparing herself and her program-mates to other students in the school, ones who do not belong to the program, Zelma describes the program group as "more academically talented" (even though only a C average is required to remain a member). They also "behave differently"—they "act mature, [they do not get] involved in fighting or being disruptive in school."

The preceding year, such distinct behavior earned them the label of "college groupies." The term was not meant as an encomium. Zelma says she does not mind the label, "because I know what I want to be." Moreover, she says it felt good to be part of a group of academically successful students.

Zelma's parents belong to the Parent Group, which assists the program with various activities. The previous week, for example, the Parent Group had worked on an awards dinner. In this sense Zelma may be very fortunate. Direct parent involvement in these precollege intervention programs seems to be the

exception rather than the rule.

In addition to relying on her parents for their supportive involvement, Zelma relies for counseling on the teacher who runs the program at her school, as well as on the assistant director of the program. In fact, the assistant director seems to know her quite well, even though he is not on the school's staff. Happily, this is not an unfamiliar occurrence in these programs.

Zelma feels that she is intelligent and would probably be academically successful without participation in the program. However, she also feels that without the program, she would "probably not [be] in the same place." Now she knows more about "different professions and how to get in." Now she likes school more, because it "feels good to be part of a group."

of peer pressure Zelma and others experience—pressure *against* academic success—students in many precollege extracurricular programs have established peer support-groups. Based on years of experience, the staff of most programs expect and even foster the formation of such support groups.

One particularly fertile ground for fostering peer support appears to be the summer camp or summer classes for students, which most programs include. Staff report that they see program participants coalescing as a result of their joint summer experience, with individual participants appearing more motivated to learn and more confident of their own ability. Perhaps most important, program staff believe that the changes in motivation and confidence are sustained when students return from a summer program to their communities and schools, where academic success is often not rewarded. (It would be interesting to determine to what degree summer components of precollege programs are, in and of themselves, able to effect the type of behavioral changes described.)

Unfortunately, for many minority students, the effects of negative role models are not outweighed by the benefits of a peer support-group, and the negative-role-model effects may even be further exacerbated by the students' stage of ethnic identity and by the type of egocentrism generally found in adolescents.

Students' stage of ethnic identity. Synthesizing the conceptual models of ethnic identity development previously presented by Thomas (1971), Cross (1978), and Banks (1981), Gay (1985) proposed that ethnic identity in blacks develops in three stages: the *pre-encounter* stage, the *encounter* stage, and the *post-encounter* stage.

Blacks at the *pre-encounter* stage embrace the behaviors of the mainstream white culture, using these as yardsticks for their own behavior; they may even denigrate the values of their own ethnic group. Blacks at the *post-encounter* stage embrace values of their own, as well as those of other ethnic groups.

Many black high school students and young adults

Peer pressure for minority students is often "anti-achievement," with school success being viewed as something nonminority students value.

In extracurricular camps or classes for talented minority students, young participants can become a source of peer support, motivating one another to achieve.

Ethnic identity development moves in stages, from *pre-encounter*, to *encounter*, and finally to *post-encounter*.

are at the second of Gay's stages, the *encounter* stage. This means they have high levels of egocentric and ethnocentric ethnic affiliation, ideology, and associational preferences. They attempt to be attitudinally "blacker" than other blacks, and they may feel hostility and anger towards members of other ethnic groups, particularly towards whites.

Gay (1985) argued that the students' level of ethnic identity development influences their sense of reality and their psychological dispositions and thereby affects their responses to school environments and instructional processes. If Gay is right, then students at the encounter stage of ethnic identity may be particularly at risk for failure in academic settings they perceive as "Anglo." The traditional school curriculum, which most often ignores the contributions of minorities, may do little to circumvent the perceptions and related responses of students at the encounter stage.

Adolescent egocentrism. The academic performance of minority youths may be complicated further by the normative developmental characteristic of adolescence that Elkind (1974) referred to as *adolescent egocentrism*. Falsely secure in the belief that they are immune to the laws of morbidity, mortality, and probability, adolescents take all kinds of risks (Berger, 1986). One possible effect of adolescent egocentrism is that many inner-city minority youths simply fail to perceive the long-term consequences of imitating negative role models, such as the drug pusher or consumer. Those youths who observe in others the ugly consequences of engagement in illegal activities may believe that they themselves are different and will somehow escape those same consequences.

Specific minority-group membership. Motivation for academic success may differ among students as a function of their specific minority-group membership. Generally, Asian students are academically as successful, and often more so, than white students. The same is true of many first- and second-generation immigrant blacks and Hispanics. Ogbu (1978) distinguished among

In the *encounter* stage, minorities tend to reject achievement, seeing it as adopting white culture and abandoning the ethnic culture.

▼

The egocentrism of adolescents can increase the allure of following negative role models and rejecting the paths that lead to achievement.

▼

three types of minorities: *autonomous, immigrant*, and *castelike* minorities. These types, according to him, differ in ideological beliefs and expectations, and as a result, they may have different levels of motivation for academic success.

Autonomous minorities, according to Ogbu, are minorities not in the sense of status, but in a statistical sense. They may be identifiable in terms of distinctive religious, ethnic, linguistic, and cultural characteristics and may be victims of prejudice. However, as a group, they are not politically or economically subjugated by the majority group and do not play denigrated roles. On the contrary, they are often quite successful economically, and because their sociocultural frame of reference encourages achievement, they tend to perform well in school. Ogbu pointed to the Amish, the Jews, and the Mormons as examples of autonomous minorities in the United States.

Immigrant minorities, according to Ogbu, usually enter a country voluntarily, to improve their economic, social, and political status. They often play denigrated roles—by holding menial jobs, for example. Some were abjectly poor in their country of origin and, based on this reference point, perceive themselves as being much better-off than members of the dominant group in the United States perceive them to be. Many Haitian and Vietnamese boat people are examples.

Other immigrant minorities were of middle- or upper-class status in their countries of origin and perceive menial jobs in the United States as only a temporary setback, to be overcome eventually. Examples are Cuban immigrants to the United States following Fidel Castro's rise to power. Because they see America as the land of individual opportunity, and school achievement as a means (perhaps the only means) of succeeding in the new country, first- and second-generation immigrant minorities tend to do well in school.

Castelike minorities, unlike the previous two types, enter a country more or less involuntarily (by birth or by being brought in against their will). The birthright of

How ethnic groups originally entered the United States and how, historically, they have been received also affect their beliefs and expectations about achievement.

▾

castelike minorities is usually permanently low economic, social, and political status, brought about by
the dominant group subjugating them through the use
of social conventions (legal and nonlegal, spoken and
unspoken). As a group, castelike minorities accurately
perceive themselves as being at the bottom of the economic, social, and political ladders, which they believe
is the result of institutional racism on the part of the
dominant group. Group struggle, rather than individual
effort at educational achievement, is usually seen as the
best way to overcome racism and discrimination. Ogbu
sees blacks, Native Americans, and Mexican Americans
as examples of castelike minorities in the United States.

In recent years, the low motivation for academic
success in castelike minorities may be exacerbated by
the failure of parents to buttress their children emotionally against racism and by the high cost and perceived
unaffordability of higher education.

Lack of fortification against racism. In public
schools as well as on college and university campuses,
prejudice often takes the form of general doubt about
the academic ability of minority students. Minority
students who perceive such doubt on the part of faculty
see this as more prominent in the hard sciences than in
the social sciences and humanities (Harvard Committee
on Race Relations, 1980; Kelly, 1983).

To weather the motivational storms occasioned by
perceived racism on the part of some faculty and fellow
students, minority youth must be fortified emotionally
by their parents or other adults to maintain a positive
sense of self and race. In the past, minority parents
fortified their children emotionally to face discrimination. However, parents today, perhaps having been
lulled into a sense of security by the gains of the civil
rights movement, seem to spend less time informing
their children about racism and prejudice and buttress-
ing them emotionally against these experiences. They
may feel that it is no longer necessary or that schools
should take on the responsibility.

In light of the recent increase in incidents of racial

Ironically, because of
gains brought about by
the civil rights movement,
minority young people
today are perhaps less
equipped to cope with
prejudicial rejection than
were the generations
before them.

▾

tension in major cities and on college campuses across the country, it may be argued that minority children still do need preparation to deal effectively with racism and that schools are not providing such help in any significant or systematic way. Minority students ill-prepared to expect and deal with racism may be easily discouraged and hence suffer academically when they encounter it on campus (Bowman & Howard, 1985). As a black high school junior explained during an interview, "The first time somebody called me 'nigger,' I was really hurt, because I had always thought that my generation didn't have those problems, that we were all equal."

Perceptions of higher-education costs. The perception that college is unaffordable probably factors strongly into the low motivation of many minority students, who often come from poverty-stricken communities. Most parents and students in families earning 12 thousand dollars or less annually find prohibitive the average cost of several thousand dollars for tuition, room, and board at a public college or university. The even-higher cost for attendance at a private educational institution must seem even more so, especially to parents with less than a high school education and little knowledge of the financial aid system. Knowledge about financial aid, other than sports scholarships, is hard for minority families to come by. Even when families know about available aid, the process for obtaining it may appear daunting because most aid involves a combination of loans, scholarships, and employment. First-generation middle-class families—many of whom are only a few paychecks away from lower-class status—may perceive the financing of postsecondary education in the same way that lower-class families do.

Faced with tremendous economic difficulties, low-income parents may simply look forward to a time when their children can support themselves or perhaps even contribute financially to the family, and thus they may think of college as a costly delay. Many parents need help to take a longer-term view. They need to understand and successfully handle the difficult process of

College costs and how to obtain financial aid can seem overwhelming or mysterious to minority and disadvantaged students and their families.

obtaining funding for higher education. For example, in one program, a staff member meets at least once with each 11th-grade student in the program and with his or her parents to discuss the college admissions process and, in particular, the process for obtaining funding.

Educational Setting Factors That May Lower Motivation

It is easy to blame the victim—the student, the student's immediate family, and the student's community—for low academic motivation. However, a number of classroom factors also play a large role.

Low teacher-expectations. Do teacher expectations affect learning? Studies conducted over the last 20 years have yielded conflicting findings about the existence and effects of teacher expectations (Brophy & Good, 1974; Raudenbush, 1984). However, Good and Brophy (1987) recently presented an insightful analysis of the controversy. They argued that the conflicting results were primarily from studies like Rosenthal and Jacobson's (1968), which involved the experimental manipulation of teacher knowledge about students. Studies that involved observations of teacher behavior in the classroom (with no experimental manipulation of teacher perceptions) have rather consistently found major differences in teachers' expectations of and behavior towards students of different status (different gender, ethnic background, income level).

> Research shows that teachers often have low expectations for minority students to achieve in academic subjects.

The potentially powerful effect of teacher expectations on student academic performance may apply particularly to minority children, who are often treated differently from other students by public school teachers (Brophy & Good, 1974) as well as by college professors (Trujillo, 1986). Among other treatment differences, teachers and professors have been found to take less time in answering the questions of minority students, to ask simpler questions of them, and to respond less frequently to eye contact initiated by them (Good & Brophy, 1987). For example, in a study of a racially integrated first-grade classroom, Cadmus (1974) found that poor black children received approximately 75% of the teacher's negative comments, whereas affluent white students received approximately 75% of the teacher's positive comments.

There are many likely sources of low teacher-expectations. One worthy of discussion is teachers' lack of familiarity with minority cultures. This frequently results in their misinterpretations of student behavior and ensuing assumptions that minority students are incapable of learning or unwilling to learn. An example of this is found in an early study by Gottlieb (1966), who compared white middle-class teachers with black teachers who had lower-class origins, in terms of their perceptions of a group of lower-class students. The same students described by white teachers as "talk-ative," "lazy," "fun-loving," and "rebellious" were de-scribed by black teachers as "happy," "cooperative," "energetic," and "ambitious."

In addition to producing low academic expecta-tions, unfamiliarity with minority cultures may result in too much hesitation on the part of nonminority teachers in setting and enforcing standards of behavior. Teachers often accept as *cultural*, behaviors they need not and should not accept. Sometimes the fears teachers have about enforcing standards are justified, as in some large inner-city schools, where student possession of handguns is not anomalous. However, in many situa-tions that are not similarly threatening, some students avoid academic work by behaving in ways they know teachers will accept as cultural.

One teacher who is culturally aware enough to know how and when to confront students is Ms. Jones, who is described in Profile 4. She provides the kind of external motivation—in the form of realistic expecta-tions—that teachers might and should provide. Ms. Jones's being black, like many of her students, may simplify her task. However, the argument being made here is that *all* teachers have to become culturally aware enough to have realistic expectations of their minority

When they are unsure or ignorant of minority cul-tural norms, nonminority teachers hesitate to enforce high standards of behavior and to expect high levels of academic performance.

▾

and disadvantaged students. At present, far too few have reached this level of awareness. Staff of many of the extracurricular precollege programs examined in this study *are* culturally aware and thereby serve the educational, social, and psychological needs of many students. In fact, students in one program that appeared to

---

Profile 4

**MS. JONES—
A Science Teacher and
Program Advisor**

Ms. Jones is a young black science teacher in her late 30s or early 40s. She also serves as advisor to an extracurricular mathematics and science program in the small suburban school where she teaches. As a science teacher who is neither male nor white, she is an exception to the rule. She is a little over 5 feet tall, with medium build, and has a deep, somewhat raspy voice. Despite her relatively diminutive stature, she has what in theatrical circles is referred to as size, or presence. Her personality is strong but not overpowering, and there is a certain self-assurance in her manner.

Ms. Jones's students give the following reasons for her being a good advisor: "First of all, she believes in us and will never let us get down on ourselves." "She cares, she tells it like it is, no matter what." "She pushes us, not in a forceful way." In

response to my question, "Can we train someone to be like her?" their response is, "No, it comes from the heart. She is very dedicated."

Talking about herself, Ms. Jones says she took on the job because she thought the kids needed it. Perhaps she would have gone further in *her* career had she received the kind of encouragement she is providing for her students. She is partial to students who are having some difficulty, because "everybody caters to the upper, elite students."

She strongly believes that the high school science modules being used in her school district are too show-and-tell-like, and "need to be refined and made more challenging for the high school level." Moreover, she feels that knowing and being able to teach her subject matter is only half the battle. The other half is "personality, knowing when to stand firm and when to give." She has obviously won both halves of the battle, as have so

many of her colleagues from coast to coast. In fact, a white science teacher in another extracurricular program, whose students were principally Hispanic, was in many respects similar to Ms. Jones.

Echoing the remarks of two of her students (from a separate, previous interview with students), Ms. Jones says "I never say what a student cannot do. They [speaking about the two students] were too scared to fill out applications to go to college [and in particular, to take the SAT]." She encouraged and perhaps even pushed them to do it. She also put the students in touch with professors at local universities. One student has already been accepted to a good engineering program. The other is still waiting to hear.

Ms. Jones takes her job very seriously because she believes that "America cannot continue to leave out bright minority minds. They [America] need to bring them in; otherwise they will not be able to compete with Japan."

lack such staff expressed concern over this matter.

The many potential consequences of low teacher-expectations of minority students include the likelihood that students will conform to low expectations. Common sense and research evidence (e.g., Soar & Soar, 1979) suggest that poor students learn less in classrooms where they receive a high frequency of negative messages from teachers who expect little of them. Therefore, differential expectations and treatment of minority students may result in a vicious circle in which teachers react negatively to behaviors they do not understand and do not like, and students in turn find it increasingly difficult to learn or excel (Soar & Soar, 1979; Hetherington & Parke, 1986).

A study by Wells (1986) provides an example of how this circular reaction can be set in motion. Wells found children from working-class families to be very skilled communicators at home, despite the fact that they were perceived as less responsive than middle-class children to questions posed by their teachers at school. Wells suggested that the children's poor school performance, rather than being the result of limited competence, may be a context-bound response to an environment that is discontinuous with home in terms of adult expectations and behavior. Of course, the cumulative result of similar experiences over time may well *be* limited competence. According to Dweck (1986) such experiences may eventually result in a maladaptive motivational pattern of learned helpless behavior towards one or more academic subjects. This helpless behavior is characterized by a tendency to avoid challenge and by low persistence in response to failure. Considering this, it is not surprising that as Kunjufu (1985) suggested, many low-income African American and Hispanic American children who start school roughly on an academic par with whites achieve considerably less by the fourth grade. Moreover, eventually their desire to learn may be rechanneled to acquiring "street smarts," if the peer group is more rewarding.

Teacher gender and ethnicity. Kunjufu (1985)

> Students' learned helplessness—having low motivation, avoiding challenges, and not persisting—is a likely result of an accumulation of negative experiences related to low teacher-expectations.

argued insightfully that the problem of low teacher-expectations is particularly salient for low-income black males. The problem is also salient for Latino males. During the last two decades, the percentages of black and Latino females completing high school have increased more than the percentages of black and Latino males have (American Council on Education, 1991). The academic attrition of black and of Latino males is so great that several directors of extracurricular precollege mathematics and science programs interviewed made such comments as, "We have a large number of girls in the program, because by high school most of the boys are lost."

The plight of elementary school black and Latino males may be due in large measure to demographic characteristics of schools (gender and ethnicity of staff), as Hare and Castenell (1985) and Kunjufu (1985) pointed out. They suggested that middle-income white females, who make up the teaching staff of most elementary and middle schools, tend to perceive as threatening, behaviors that are appropriate for low-income black males within their subcultures. Before long the boys find the peer culture—with its opportunities for demonstrating competence, its rewards, and its allowance for the maintenance of self-esteem—far more attractive than school. Street knowledge becomes the knowledge for which the boys thirst; the "street gang," the "antagonists," and the "cool cats" become the role models they want to imitate.

IN SUMMARY   Several factors in the home, community, and school environments combine to lower the achievement motivation of many minority students. Major factors are the scarcity of positive role models and preponderance of negative role models in inner-city neighborhoods, the lack of complementarity between the students' level of ethnic identity and the traditional curriculum (which takes little note of the contributions of minorities), and the inadequate preparation of students at home for effectively dealing with racism at school. Another important factor involves the demo-

> **Black and Latino *males* in particular seem to be failing to reach upper levels of academic achievement.**

graphic characteristics of schools—-namely, the combined effects of income differences, ethnic differences, and, sometimes, gender differences on student and teacher perceptions of each other and on their behaviors towards each other.

The demographic characteristics of schools—middle-income white teachers instructing low-income minority students—may also have an impact on the effectiveness of student-teacher communication, one of the most important aspects of the educational process. To this issue we turn next.

Effective Communication Skills

In middle-class American society, facility in the oral and written reception and production of standard English is a necessary but not sufficient feature of "effective" communication skills. Another requirement is what Hirsch (1988) called *cultural literacy*, the possession of basic information about various domains of human activity that is common knowledge to the middle classes. Perhaps even more important than this is another skill, described by Campbell (1986), the ability to demonstrate knowledge in socially prescribed ways.

Educational Setting Factors That May Hinder Acquisition of Communication Skills

Acquisition of the aforementioned aspects of effective communication skills depends on at least three factors: the possession of *cognitive ability*, the possession of *linguistic ability*, and *a supportive social-psychological environment*. The first two interact in the production and comprehension of texts, according to researchers such as Bernstein (1972) and Vygotsky (1962). According to Cook-Gumperz (1986), the social-psychological environment is crucial because literacy is also the product of social interactions between teacher and student, who jointly construct much of what is to be acquired.

Effective communication skills involve more than facility with standard English.

There are many barriers to minority students' mastery and use of standard English.

▾

Most minority teenagers, like their white counterparts, do have the requisite cognitive and linguistic abilities. These abilities are amply demonstrated by the fact that most minority teens are skilled, if not excellent, communicators within their own subculture. Inner-city blacks, for example, who are illiterate in terms of middle-class culture and the use of standard English, are quite literate in terms of their knowledge of inner-city culture and black English. The latter language, contrary to popular misconception, has a grammar of its own, one distinct from that of standard English, as Labov (1972) pointed out.

Given their demonstrated cognitive and linguistic abilities, the deficits many minority students exhibit in middle-class literacy skills are then probably due to numerous problems in the social-psychological domain. Several of these factors were discussed previously in this chapter. For example, it was indicated that minority students may, in general, spend disproportionately large amounts of time in activities that entertain rather than educate, and that those students who would probably benefit the most from summer academic experiences often do not have them. A major problem affecting the acquisition of standard English literacy skills that has not yet been discussed is the volatile political issue of minorities wanting to maintain the integrity of their cultures (including their distinct languages) in the face of what is perceived, by many, as the majority culture's desire to stamp out cultural differences.

Attempts to eliminate nonstandard English. As previously stated, for many minority persons, standard English is a second language. Intricately intertwined with the first language acquired from early childhood experiences is what, for lack of a better term, we may refer to as a *cultural self*—valued memories and emotions about one's family, culture, childhood joys, significant others, and, perhaps most important, the self at the center of all these memories and emotions. Language is not just a tool for communication. It is one of the most tangible representations of that cultural self.

Few would disagree that effective use of standard English is a requirement for all but the most menial jobs in American society. Few would disagree with the proposition that minority students should acquire standard English communication skills because of the importance of such skills to employment. However, these propositions are often translated into public and educational policy in ways that, at worst, do violence to the cultural self of many minorities and, at best, are politically unpalatable to many minorities. Such is the case when teachers attempt to completely eliminate students' home language and replace it with standard English. Students may be made to feel ashamed of their way of talking at home. Students may also misunderstand the intentions of educators. In both instances the end result may be the same: Students perceive school policy as a repudiation of all that their home language represents.

In light of the importance of the cultural self and of the language that so closely represents that self, teachers should present standard English to students as an addition or complement to their home language or dialect. Equally important, students need to accurately perceive the intent of and benefits of this policy. Failure in both these regards results in the all-too-familiar occurrence of minority students giving less than an all-out effort to the acquisition of standard English.

Differences between home and school communicative requirements. Regardless of the cause, for many minority students, discontinuities in the communicative requirements of home and school may have several negative effects on the learning process. Among these effects are the following:

• *Inadequate teacher/student verbal comprehension.* Language, the principal medium of educational exchange, may be the most important factor in determining learning outcomes. A good command of standard English facilitates learning in academic areas other than just English. Technical language of

Minority students and families may view the emphasis on learning standard English as a threat to the "cultural self."

Discontinuity between home and school in communication processes can impose limitations on minority and disadvantaged students' achievement.

▼

Inadequate mutual comprehension between teachers and students is related to differences in communication styles.

▼

individual academic disciplines often is lost on students, especially on low-income minority students, who do not even share the basic language of their teachers and textbooks (standard English). For example, Orr (1987) presented anecdotal evidence that black-English-speaking students have difficulty understanding high school algebra as presented by their teachers and textbooks. Not only do teachers and students have great difficulty communicating about the troubles students have with the subject, but teachers often misunderstand and judge incorrect the responses students give to verbal problems, because the responses, though correct, are phrased in black English. The description in Profile 5 of how Jerome copes with his assignments (translating his answers from black to standard English) shows to what extent communicative difficulties negatively affect academic performance.

• *Inadequate teacher/student comprehension of social interactional patterns.* Patterns of social interaction vary considerably among different cultures and subcultures. Examples of social-interactional patterns that may vary include conversational styles and routines, establishment and maintenance of eye contact between conversants of different status, and establishment and maintenance of appropriate physical distance between conversing individuals. Even the appropriateness of social aggression varies considerably—behavior considered to be healthy assertiveness in one culture or subculture may be viewed as distasteful aggression in another.

Most minority children are socialized initially in exclusively minority subcultures, where nonstandard English is the norm. The mismatch between the patterns of social interaction considered appropriate in their subculture and those patterns considered appropriate in the standard-English-speaking mainstream culture may place many minority students at a disadvantage in school. A factor that may

Profile 5

JEROME—A Student

Jerome is a 10th-grade student in a medium-sized school. He is described by his mathematics teacher, who also runs the extra-curricular precollege program, as "bright, a hard worker, and very likely to succeed." The first two descriptors are understatements; the latter is an oversimplistic assessment.

I meet with Jerome, as with many other students, in a room provided on the spur of the moment by the program staff, who are not present during our discussion. Initially, Jerome provides the kinds of laudatory statements about the program I have learned to expect—it has exposed him to so many new things, the staff is wonderful and caring, and so on.

Throughout this initial stage of the interview, his speech is somewhat halting, lacking in spontaneity. He appears to be selecting his words very carefully, and I assume he is simply trying to say the right things, just in case the program's funding may be affected. However, as the interview progresses and he gradually lets down his guard, I realize that at least in part, his lack of spontaneity is due to a struggle with the use of standard English.

At that point, I ask him to just be himself. To put him at ease, I tell him a little about my own non-standard-English background. He becomes very involved, turning the tables to interview me with lots of questions about how I have overcome the language barriers and what obstacles I have encountered. In the process, I learn a lot about him.

Jerome is from an economically disadvantaged family living in the local "projects." His mother, the head of the household, never completed high school; neither did his older brother. Consequently, Jerome cannot rely on either of them for assistance with his homework. He has to be self-sufficient in solving problems encountered in the process of completing assignments.

The alternatives of studying with peers or seeking their help are not as readily available as might be hoped. Jerome feels he is an anomaly among his same-age friends in the projects. He believes he is seen as a nice but somewhat stupid kid for believing that he can make it academically or that his making it academically will translate to economic success. As is true of many minority youths in similar situations, Jerome

isolates himself to get his schoolwork done. The amount of self-isolation must be considerable, since he estimates that it takes him twice the expected time to complete assignments, both because he has no assistance and because he has to complete them first in black English and then translate them to standard English.

Despite these efforts, Jerome's grades have sometimes fallen below a B average. I gathered from our discussion that he continually feels he is only a step away from failure. Fortunately, he does not believe failure would be entirely the result of his lack of ability or effort. He believes some teachers are racially prejudiced. Among these, he includes teachers who associate his use of black English with lack of intellectual ability. Unfortunately, Jerome does not feel he has a single ally among the program staff, which at his school is composed almost entirely of whites. He feels they are well-meaning but just do not "understand" him the way a black person would.

Asked if he is going to make it, Jerome is optimistic. So am I.

exacerbate the problem is that knowledge about social interaction is often maintained at a subconscious level. Often, only with deliberate effort does this knowledge become available for conscious inspection and analysis. Hence, while teachers and students may generally dislike some intangible aspect of each other's behavior, they may find it difficult to verbalize, analyze, and effectively resolve conflicts that result from the mismatch of cultural standards of social interaction.

Heath's (1982) observation of adult-child linguistic interaction in a poor southern black town provides an example of the possible academic consequences of cultural differences in social interactional patterns: Adult blacks in the town generally did not ask children any questions to which they (the adults) already knew the answer. Imagining that same child in a school setting, where adults typically *do* ask many questions to which they (the adults) already know the answers, provides some idea of the problems encountered by some minority children. Heath's study is of a small town in one region of the country. Most likely, there are many more differences, varying region by region, that have not yet been studied or even discovered (Slaughter & Epps, 1987).

• *Negative teacher-evaluation of student academic performance.* As previously described, literacy is the product of social interactional exchanges between teacher and student, who jointly construct the knowledge the child is to acquire. A major aspect of this interactive process is continuous evaluation of what is learned, through informal judgments and standardized and nonstandardized tests. In fact, the evaluative aspect of the process is so major that it sometimes, perhaps too frequently, takes on a life independent of its intended purpose.

In evaluative interchanges, as described by Campbell (1986), the student's correct style of pre-

A mismatch between students' and teachers' cultural standards of social interaction can be overcome only with considerable effort and understanding.

▾

sentation of what is considered to be valid knowledge within the school is very important, perhaps
even more important than the knowledge itself. In
this regard, many teachers appear to equate use of
nonstandard English with limited intellectual ability, poor attitude towards school, and low motivation. The results can be disastrous when minority
students, whose initial socialization does not provide the valued style of presentation, are evaluated.
Moreover, as Cook-Gumperz (1986) and others have
pointed out, the evaluative histories of students
may be self-perpetuating, going on to affect the
subsequent acquisition of knowledge and demonstration of that acquisition.

How socially adept students are in presenting what they have learned is likely to affect how they are evaluated.

IN SUMMARY   The ability of minority students to acquire effective communication skills has been amply
demonstrated by their acquisition and expert use of the
language and dialects of various subcultures. Therefore,
the failure of many minority students to acquire middle-
class, standard-English literacy skills may be due primarily to social-psychological factors, including the attempt to maintain the integrity of minority cultures in
the face of a perceived desire by the majority culture to
eradicate them. Changing this perception should be of
great concern to educators, because empirical evidence
shows that ineffective communication between minority students and teachers may hamper the learning
process and, in particular, may affect the way students
are perceived and evaluated by teachers.

Thus far, discussion has focused on the factors
proposed as key to the academic achievement of minority youth: knowledge about specific fields, effective
problem-solving strategies, motivation, and effective
communication skills. In the following chapter, discussion focuses on the features of the ideal intervention
program that would enhance the academic performance
of minority students by circumventing or removing
obstacles to their development.

ENDNOTES

1. Perhaps the most negative explanation is the view expressed by Jensen (1969). From that perspective, the underrepresentation of minorities in professions such as those with a mathematics or science base is a logical outcome of their genetically determined lower intellectual ability. However, on the basis of empirical evidence, there are at least three basic problems with the argument.

First, a disproportionately high percentage of minorities are economically disadvantaged. It is therefore important to clearly separate the effect of race and the effects of socioeconomic factors in studies of racial differences in IQ performance. As Hetherington and Parke (1986) pointed out, this is not frequently done. When it is, social class differences in intellectual performance are consistently found to be associated with language differences between the classes (Golden & Birns, 1976).

Second, the long-term reliability of scores obtained on IQ tests is much lower than can be expected for genetically determined characteristics. Empirical evidence (e.g., Honzik, MacFarlane, & Allen, 1948) indicates that scores can change one or more standard deviations over a period of years. Hence, intelligence, at least as defined psychometrially, must be subject to environmental experiences, as Ginsburg (1972) suggested. Additionally, the construct validity of IQ tests is questionable in light of their frequently poor correlation with other indications of intelligence, such as creativity. Moreover, the possible cultural bias of many of the tests is a serious threat to their content and construct validity.

Third, when intelligence is defined in nonpsychometric terms, performance of minorities is not lower than that of whites. The operative structures of thinking described by Piaget do not differ in African Americans and whites (Ginsburg, 1972, 1986). The methods of selecting and classifying information *may*, in general, be different for African Americans and whites, as Hale-Benson (1986) proposed on the basis of Cohen's (1969), Hilliard's (1976), and others' work. However, both of these methods are logical, intelligent, and valid ways of processing information.

Chapter FIVE

The Components of an Ideal Intervention Program

As MORE AND MORE STUDIES of the educational process are carried out, it becomes increasingly clear that academic success is affected by a number of factors other than student ability (Slaughter & Epps, 1987), including student affective characteristics (Bloom, 1982), family economic status (Moore, 1982; White, 1982), and ethnicity (Ogbu, 1978). One traditional view of education holds that only those children whose behavior and lifestyles conform to the routines associated with school can be considered educable. As discussed earlier, such a view often results in the exclusion of low-income and minority children from full participation in the educational system, and this contributes substantially to their remaining at the lower social strata of their birth. This is an educational situation like that which Freire (1970) described as typical in Third World countries. Rather than *excluding* certain members of society, education in a democracy should, as Freire suggested, help all students to critically evaluate themselves and their society and provide them with the tools for improving both.

From an educator's point of view, it is probably easier to instruct those who are bright according to one's definition of "brightness" and who are similar to, rather than different from, oneself in terms of social, cultural,

_____ 5 _____

Academic success may elude minority students because of such non-academic factors as different ways of communicating or behaving.

▾

Educators must be responsive to students' unique characteristics (due to differences in cultural or individual backgrounds) *and* maintain high standards.

▾

Interventions should be based on what is known about fostering minority or disadvantaged students' motivation to stay in school and learn.

▾

and linguistic background. The hallmark of a true educator, however, is the ability to provide instruction that responds to the unique characteristics of individual learners, including those learners who are socially, culturally, and linguistically different. Simultaneously with this, as Gay (1988) and Slaughter and Epps (1987) pointed out, the effective educator should be able to maintain high standards.

From the first day of school, educators, if they are to be successful, must operate differently with children from different familial and social backgrounds. At present, however, the knowledge base—both the research and theory—that educators could use to help them operate effectively with diverse groups is inadequate. Nonetheless, some changes in the educational process, some *interventions*, can be based on what is already known. These changes require broadening the definition of education to include a number of functions not traditionally considered to be within its purview. The heavier burden placed on schools is one that they, with the assistance of government and the private sector, must assume if they are to successfully fulfill their mission of fashioning a learned American citizen out of every student, regardless of the student's economic status or ethnic background.

It goes without saying that to acquire an interest in school, to develop motivation to learn, and to master basic academic skills, young people must be physically and mentally present in the classroom. In other words, they must be discouraged from becoming dropouts. Because the high dropout rate of minority high school students probably results from the cumulative effect of years of alienation from school, the earlier that educational intervention can occur, the better.

It seems clear that intervention as early as preschool, especially intervention of the proper kind, has merit, since specific high-quality preschool programs have been found to have long-lasting effects—both social and academic ones extending into adolescence and early adulthood (Berrueta-Clement, Schweinhart,

Barnett, Epstein, & Weikart, 1984). Intervention that offers older (third- and fourth-grade) students the same kinds of support and stimulation provided by high-quality preschool programs could be beneficial as well, since at this point in school, the specific academic-achievement effects of some Head Start programs and other preschool programs for low-income children have been observed to level out (McKey et al., 1985). Later intervention, such as the 12 extracurricular precollege programs discussed in this report, may be especially important for students who have not attended pre-school programs. Summaries of the 12 programs, presented in the next 21 pages, reveal that each of these programs has several components that exemplify ways to advance the academic achievement of disadvantaged and minority students. This chapter will next develop a model of the "ideal intervention program"—one that contains *all* of the key components for advancing academic achievement.

The Key Components Leading to Academic Achievement

On the basis of what is known about minority students' achievement and development, it is possible to list the components—in terms of methods for achieving certain goals—that extracurricular precollege programs should adopt to improve students' academic achievement. The goals and methods can be grouped under the previously described four essential characteristics for academic success. However, such a separation of program components for analytical purposes is an artificial one, since their interrelationships are strong and complex; many of the methods we will propose are useful for achieving several different goals. Therefore, we will discuss each method, or ideal-program component, in terms of a variety of possible functions. How some or all of the 12 extracurricular precollege programs

The goals and methods of an ideal intervention program can be delineated.

Continued on page 93

PROGRAM SUMMARIES

Boulder, Colorado

American Indian Science and
Engineering Society (AISES)

Stated objectives:
To significantly increase the number of American Indian scientists and engineers in the nation and develop technologically informed leaders within the Indian community; ultimately, to be a catalyst for the advancement of American Indians as they seek to become self-reliant and self-determined members of society

Program structure:
AISES begins working with Indian students as early as elementary school to strengthen their educational background in mathematics and science. At the high school and college levels, AISES provides scholarships, mentoring support, and leadership training to further prepare Indian students for successful science and engineering careers. AISES also provides a career placement service for students entering the work force or wanting to change jobs. At the precollege level, students join local chapters at each school. Each chapter selects its own officers and decides on meeting times. The AISES chapters provide student tours, peer tutoring, science fairs, and so on.

Participation:
AISES participants represent various Indian tribes as well as various interests. Many students are from low-income families. Students are admitted to the program in the seventh grade and remain in it until high school graduation. To be admitted to the program, a student must (1) be tribally enrolled or have some degree of American Indian tribe bloodline, (2) be in the top half of the class and have an interest primarily in mathematics or engineering, (3) maintain a 2.5 GPA, and (4) be recommended by a mathematics or science teacher.

General activities:
To improve knowledge and communication
  • Reading and writing experiences
  • Being tutored
  • Tutoring others
  • Hands-on experiences
  • Leadership-skill training—a particularly strong component of the program
  • Service learning (Many of the science projects undertaken by students include some form of community service. In addition to the knowledge gained, students also learn to give something back to the Indian community.)

To improve problem-solving strategies
  • Hands-on projects, particularly through science fairs

To increase motivation
  • The AISES National Conference, an annual event that is held in a different major city in the fall of each year (More than 1000 Indian and non-Indian students and professionals from major U.S. corporations, government agencies, and academic institutions participate. This is the focal point of all the AISES program activities and has grown to become a major national event for corporations seeking to identify Indian students for recruitment.)
  • *Winds of Change*, a quarterly full-color magazine that portrays successful role models for Indian

youth and disseminates information on educational opportunities and on AISES activities.

- Math and science clubs
- Role models (including correspondence between Indian professionals and program participants)
- Personal counseling

Summer program:
For 7th- through 12th-grade students, a 2- to 4-week math- and science-based summer program provides academic enrichment and a college experience. Each year, approximately four of these regional programs are held throughout the country.

Teacher training:
AISES conducts various teacher-training programs to improve the quality of mathematics and science education in Indian elementary and secondary schools, so Indian students are better able to qualify for entrance into colleges of science and engineering and other math- and science-based fields. Training, which lasts from 1 to 5 weeks, includes science content, methodology, curriculum development, and cultural integration with Indian culture.

Parent involvement:
The level of parent involvement varies by tribe but is generally low. Parent involvement in the summer program is made difficult by the fact that students come from all over the country. However, the fact that parents are willing to let their children leave home is viewed as a strong measure of their involvement. AISES plans to develop workshops to help parents become more effective advocates for their children.

Assistance with college admission:
Information on college admissions is

provided during the annual AISES National Conference described earlier.

Financial assistance:
The AISES scholarship program helps talented and deserving American Indian students meet the financial demands of going to college. During the 1990–91 academic year, $250,000 worth of scholarships were awarded.

Boulder, Colorado

American Indian Upward Bound Science and Self-Determination Program at the University of Colorado at Boulder (AIUB)

Stated objectives:
To prepare high school students—primarily, but not only, those with an interest in science, engineering, mathematics, computers, and other technical areas—for college

Program structure:
AIUB is funded by a grant from the U.S. Department of Education. Unlike most precollege programs, AIUB consists mainly of a summer component and has monthly contact with participants during the academic year. Individual participants' involvement with the program usually extends over a 3-year period and consists of summer activities that occur in a planned, 3-year sequence. A student's program participation usually starts the summer after ninth grade and continues until high school graduation.

Participation:
Participants, who come from various middle-western states, including Colo-

rado, New Mexico, Oregon, South Dakota, Wisconsin, and Wyoming, are from small-town high schools with largely Native American populations. They tend to be high or potentially high achievers, mostly from the top quartile of their classes. Most are from low-income families and many are the first in the family to attend college.

Program admission is based on teachers' recommendations, a student's written essay, and grades (although a specific GPA cutoff is not used). A principal criteria is "potential for preparing for college." A large number of students are turned away each year, owing to lack of program resources.

General activities:

To improve knowledge and communication

- Courses in science, mathematics, computers, college preparatory writing, and Indian studies
- Educational field trips
- Tutoring by undergraduate and graduate students
- A test-taking skills workshop and a tutorial computer program for American College Test (ACT) preparation
- Time-management skills, provided through a workshop and through real-life experiences that "teach responsibility" (For example, when it departs on time without them, participants learn the negative effects of being late for the bus to a field trip.)
- Curriculum guidance, to assure that students take the required courses to gain admission to college
- Monthly homework assignments during the academic year, at students' home schools

To improve problem-solving strategies

- Hands-on problem-solving activities (such as a field biology course)

To increase motivation

- Role models
- Personal counseling (Once a week students meet with a counselor in groups of about 15 to discuss personal problems, homesickness, and so on.)
- Motivation, achieved in part by setting high goals and providing considerable verbal praise
- Dealing with racial prejudice, discussed as part of the Indian studies class (Prejudice is not generally experienced by most students while they are in the majority at Indian schools.)

Summer program:
Students spend 6 weeks each year at a Summer Institute on the campus of the University of Colorado at Boulder. Each subsequent year a student participates, the course content becomes more similar to that of college courses.

Teacher training:
There is no specific training component.

Parent involvement:
Though parent involvement is very limited, families do make considerable sacrifices to allow participants to attend the Summer Institute. For example, attendance at the Summer Institute means that a participant is not available for home chores; also, most families must arrange for their child to travel to the program from out-of-state.

Assistance with college admission:
Program staff assist students.

Financial assistance:
All students receive financial aid to attend the Summer Institute. The cost of the trip to Boulder is not covered, however. Financial aid for college is also available through various organizations. Program staff provide students with schedules for applying for financial aid, and they also follow up with individual students to make sure applications are completed.

Chicago, Illinois

Chicago Area Health and Medical Careers Program (CAHMCP)

Stated objectives:
To identify, recruit, and support (academically and financially) minority students who are capable of and interested in pursuing careers in the "MODVOPPP" professions: medicine, osteopathy, dentistry, veterinary science, optometry, pharmacy, podiatry, and public health

Program structure:
The program is coordinated by the Illinois Institute of Technology (IIT) in cooperation with seven Chicago-based medical schools. Program activities are conducted on the campuses of these medical schools, of IIT, and of local colleges and universities. CAHMCP is funded by state and federal agencies and by private corporations and foundations, and it has its own budget, director, and staff.

CAHMCP provides enrichment and advanced study related to the standard high school curriculum, especially in science and mathematics. Stu-

dents in 7th through 10th grades participate in the Young Scientists Program. This enrichment program provides students with four consecutive year-long (academic year plus summer) components, with the first component beginning in the fall of 7th grade. The 7th-grade component is designed to encourage and support students' high-level performance in science fair competitions. It includes advising for the science fair and a 4-week-long science day camp in the summer. The 8th-grade component combines laboratory-based activities with weekly workshops on technical writing, statistics, and "forensics" (effective communication of and successful "selling" of research). The 9th-grade component focuses on the use of graphics to communicate scientific and technical information. The 10th-grade component introduces and familiarizes students with "energy physics" and its various applications; it includes instruction in general physics and hands-on physics projects.

In the junior and senior years, successful graduates of the Young Scientists Program can take college-level mathematics and science summer courses in one or more of the following areas: calculus, precalculus, chemistry, and physics. The courses are taught by college professors and health-profession doctoral students who are former CAHMCP participants. The credits earned for these courses are transferable to 4-year colleges and universities.

Participation:
About half the participants have parents who are professionals. The other half are from lower-income backgrounds. Most of the students stand in the top quartile of their class, "definitely the brightest," in the words of

one staff member. In the early grades, more males than females are recruited because, as a staff member explained, "too many bright males are lost out of the system by sophomore year." Recruitment, based on academic performance, scores on standardized tests, and recommendations of teachers and counselors, targets students who are talented and interested in science.

General activities:
To improve knowledge and communication
- Enrichment classes in mathematics and science, including English (technical writing and "forensics"), as part of the Young Scientists Program
- Academic counseling
- Being tutored by others (when needed)
- Tutoring others
- Hands-on experiences (such as nature walks)

To improve problem-solving strategies
- Conducting experiments and writing laboratory reports
- Developing science projects

To increase motivation
- Role models, including an earlier generation of program participants working with students currently in the program
- Discussion of racial issues as part of the summer program. (Minority health-profession students and practitioners relate what it means to be a minority student at various institutions.)

Summer program:
The summer component is particularly strong in this program. Though involved with the students all year, the program does much of its work through the summer portion of the

Young Scientists Program. In addition, many participants take 4-week courses in the summers following their junior and senior years of high school. A placement exam determines which of the three levels of each course a student is assigned to. At each course level, students are challenged on the basis of their entrance skills.

Teacher training:
Program staff assist sixth- through eighth-grade teachers who feel they are not well prepared to teach science. However, there is no formal teacher-training component.

Parent involvement:
Regarding interest in their children, program parents are said to be "very involved," though not in a formal way.

Assistance with college admission:
The program networks with a local college-placement agency and directly with colleges and universities across the nation to assist students with placement and retention of students in their undergraduate programs. It also provides students with information on what different professions involve.

Financial assistance:
Students find out about funding for college through the college and university network just mentioned.

Denver, Colorado

Colorado Minority Engineering Association, Inc. (CMEA)

Note: CMEA is based on the California MESA model, but it has modified the basic model to suit unique needs of Colo-

rado students, many of whom reside in rural areas. In general, individual school districts and school advisors seem to have considerably more autonomy than do those in the California MESA model.

Stated objectives:
To provide educational support services to the Hispanic American, African American, Native American, and disadvantaged students of Colorado, in order to increase the number of these underrepresented minorities in the fields of engineering, science, and technology

Program structure:
CMEA is a statewide program. The director for each of 19 school districts served by the program reports to the statewide MESA director. To have a CMEA chapter, a district school must offer higher-level mathematics and science courses and a foreign language course. A program advisor (one of the teachers) at each school within a district (which may mean as many as 26 schools) reports to the district director but appears to be rather autonomous in the day-to-day administration of the program. At the school visited, the advisor received no class-release time, and program direction was added to the teacher's other responsibilities. Advisors receive a handbook and training that consists of an annual one-day statewide workshop detailing program procedures. Additional training of advisors occurs at the district level.

Participation:
In comparison with their peers, students in CMEA are described as "high achievers." The program serves low- and middle-income Hispanic, African, and Native Americans. A sizeable group of participants are Hispanic Americans from rural areas. Participants must maintain a 3.0 GPA. CMEA does accept students with a lower GPA (they are called MESA associates) and assists them in raising it.

General activities:
To improve knowledge and communication
- Enrollment in a higher-level mathematics or science class each semester
- Enrollment in a foreign-language course (for high school participants)
- Mathematics and English tutoring, both for participants' consolidation of basic skills and for their acceleration
- Training in test-taking skills

To improve problem-solving strategies
- Hands-on problem-solving activities

To increase motivation
- Incentives such as certificates and calculators awarded every year at honors assemblies (Special pins and tee-shirts are also given to students.)
- Counseling by advisors, including peer counseling (about grades, peer problems)
- Exposure to role models (including speakers and tutors)
- Informal career counseling in the form of exposure to career fields (This aspect of the program seemed particularly strong, ranging from taking trips to the Air Force Academy to interacting with a robot.)
- Discussions of how to deal with racial discrimination, which are built into interaction with role models

Summer program:
Summer enrichment programs in mathematics and science are held at the University of Colorado at Denver and at Boulder. Students attend these programs 4 hours a day for 11 days and are engaged in robotics, computer science, and rocketry. They also visit such sites as commercial research laboratories.

Teacher training:
There is no specific training component.

Parent involvement:
The program offers a special night for parents twice per semester, invites parents to accompany student trips, and holds parent activities with speakers. An estimated 40% of parents participate in these activities. Attendance is highest in rural areas.

Assistance with college admission:
Students make one trip per semester to a local university to converse with admissions staff. Local universities provide assistance with the application process, as do program staff.

Financial assistance:
Local universities provide scholarships. Through CMEA's Incentive Awards Program, junior and senior high school students earn "points" based on GPA, standardized test scores, extracurricular activity participation, and CMEA participation. The points translate into dollars that can be used for college. Three major Colorado universities currently provide matching funds for these incentive awards. While CMEA's incentive awards are only for the first year of college, the universities' matching funds are provided each year until graduation, for a maximum of 5 years.

Detroit, Michigan

Detroit Area Pre-College Engineering Program (DAPCEP)

Stated objectives:
To increase the number of minority students pursuing science/engineering degrees

Program structure:
Rather than being part of the school system, DAPCEP is a supplementary program that impacts curriculum by influencing teachers through a teacher-training program and curriculum development. Program offices are at a university. Three representatives from the Detroit Public School System serve on DAPCEP's board and on each of its standing committees. The Detroit Public Schools contribute to the program's funding. DAPCEP provides Saturday and summer enrichment components as well as intervention services for students during the academic year.

Participation:
DAPCEP serves over 3,700 students, primarily in middle school. Though open to students of all races, the program primarily serves African, Hispanic, and Native Americans. For admission, participants must have a 2.0 grade-point average. Popularity of the program in the community means that about twice as many students apply as can be admitted.

Prospective participants attend one of three Saturday open houses held during the year, where they are informed about the program and complete application forms. Participants are selected from the available pool on the basis of three criteria: (1) personal information on their applications—grades, school attendance, hobbies; (2) transcripts; and (3) teacher recommendations. DAPCEP tries to include a representative sample of both sexes and of different schools within the district. Most students remain in the program for an average of 3 years.

General activities:
To improve knowledge and communication
- Curriculum guidance to maintain students on a math/science track
- In-school program (consisting of science projects, tours of companies, motivational activities)
- Saturday morning enrichment classes at DAPCEP universities (in algebra, linear algebra, trigonometry, precalculus, calculus) to prepare students for college-level work
- Summer programs at DAPCEP Universities (See "Summer program.")
- Free tutorial program

To improve problem-solving strategies
- Hands-on problem-solving activities (such as a project for a science fair each year)

To increase motivation
- Activities such as films that create an awareness of career possibilities and portray minority role models
- Role models (minority professionals and college students who interact with program participants, give motivational presentations, or supervise activities)
- Personal counseling (on an informal basis)
- Informal peer-support groups that alleviate achieving students' feelings of isolation
- A summer of employment in industry for graduated high school seniors to give them experience in

their chosen fields and an opportunity to earn money before starting college
- Some scholarships for college and assistance with the college application process—information about requisite tests, for example, and career counseling on an informal basis

Summer program:
Summer programs at DAPCEP Universities (4–6 weeks each) offer students skills-intensification courses in mathematics, science, computer science, communication skills. Another summer program objective is to make students aware of what college life is like. Several different summer programs are offered: three 4-week programs for 8th- and 9th-graders, three 6-week programs for 10th-graders, and one 6-week program for 11th-graders.

Teacher training:
The teacher-training workshop is a very important aspect of the program. Teachers receive training in mathematics and science, including training in research methods. They are also taught new instructional methods by university professors, which results in teachers being more knowledgeable about subject matter and having improved mentoring skills. Certified mathematics and science teachers, as well as ones teaching those subjects without having any formal training for it, voluntarily participate in the training workshop.

Parent involvement:
Parent involvement, particularly parents' working as allies to keep students working, is seen as very important. To guarantee a minimal level of parent involvement for every student,

parents must sign up for some kind of participation when their child applies for program entrance. The amount and duration of parent involvement varies from one activity to another. It is higher for some activities (such as award banquets and open houses) than for day-to-day program activities.

Assistance with college admission:
DAPCEP provides assistance with the admissions process. Parents are provided with information about college application and financing.

Financial assistance:
DAPCEP assists students to locate available scholarships.

Boston, Massachusetts

Massachusetts Pre-Engineering Program for Minority Students, Inc. (MASSPEP)

Stated objectives:
To increase the number of African American, Hispanic American, and Native American students who successfully complete 4 years of high school mathematics through precalculus; to increase the number of such students who successfully complete 4 years of high school science, including chemistry and physics; to provide these students with scientific and technical career information and exposure for college and career decision making; to bring college/university, industry/business, public school, government, and foundation resources together to support achievement and motivation in science and mathematics for African American, His-

panic American, and Native American students; "to create a climate where students believe they can be successful at learning and preparing for math- and science-based careers"

Program structure:
Each high school has a three-member team composed of mathematics/science teachers, one of whom is team coordinator. Members of the team receive a stipend, with the coordinator's stipend being larger. Team members are selected by the local school principal in coordination with the MASSPEP director. MASSPEP provides professional development and technical assistance for the team members. For example, it provides curriculum resources, including college research laboratories and industry contacts for role models or field trips. Specific utilization of the resources is the responsibility of the team.

The group of MASSPEP students at each school meets with the team for one 90-minute period each week; students receive academic credit for this participation. (One coordinator said her group met for approximately 2 ½ hours each week.) MASSPEP also sponsors a Saturday Science Laboratory for grades 6–8.

Participation:
Participants are African American, Hispanic American, and Native American students in Boston and Cambridge public middle schools and high schools. Most students are from low-income families, and many have parents who lack high school diplomas. MASSPEP targets students who have high interest and ability in science and mathematics, with an emphasis on the high-interest qualification. Most participants earn grades of B and C.

General activities:

To improve knowledge and communication

- Laboratory projects linking mathematics and science and engineering design topics (at middle school level)
- Tutoring and study-skills assistance in science and mathematics
- Visits to laboratories, research centers, and manufacturing facilities

To improve problem-solving strategies

- Independent and group science research and engineering design projects
- Mathematics and science competitions

To increase motivation

- Academic counseling
- Role models as speakers and mentors
- Career education and exposure
- Awards and incentive programs

Summer program:

A 6-week summer program for high school students provides academic enrichment in mathematics, physics, chemistry, and communication skills involving scientific and technical material. Academic classes are conducted during the mornings. These include scientific and technical investigations organized around themes (applied mathematics, chemical engineering, engineering design). During the afternoons, students do independent study; participate in minicourses such as photography, biotechnology, and electronics; and participate in sports. In the evenings, they attend presentations by visiting professors, scientists, and engineers.

Teacher training:

Professional development and technical assistance is provided to teachers through hands-on workshops offered once each month during the academic year.

Parent involvement:

Parents must come to an initial meeting in order for students to be involved in the summer program.

Assistance with college admission:

Information received from colleges and universities is provided to MASSPEP central staff, so they may inform students.

Financial assistance:

MASSPEP does not have its own fund but helps to locate funding sources for college scholarships and aid.

Berkeley, California

Mathematics, Engineering, and Science Achievement Program (MESA, CA)

Stated objectives:

To increase the number of students from ethnic groups historically underrepresented in math- and science-related professions who complete a 4-year university degree in a math- or science-based field

Program structure:

MESA California is a large statewide program with an extensive administrative structure. At the state level, there is a director, who is assisted by a senior staff that includes executives on loan from corporations. These executives are in charge of various administrative, programmatic, research and development, or fundraising activities. MESA also has local directors for college and precollege programs in various cities served by the program. Finally, there are MESA advisors in the schools. All funding for the operation of the program comes from the California State Legislature, from corporate donations, and from foundations.

The MESA model has been adopted by 14 other states, including Washington, Colorado, Oregon, New Mexico, and North Carolina. Though other states' programs are not directly under California MESA's control, it does maintain information about them.

Participation:
MESA serves African American, Native American, and Mexican American (as well as other historically underrepresented Latino American) students in grades 4–12 and in college throughout California. Participants are from low- and middle-income backgrounds.

MESA accepts students who have interest and aptitude (aptitude is measured by a standardized mathematics test in the case of students who join MESA for the first time in high school, but elementary and junior high students are not tested). Though MESA is officially not aimed at students who are having difficulty in academic areas, counselors often recommend students who are perceived as bright but are having difficulty in school.

General activities:
Note: The combination of specific activities in which students participate varies from one local program to another. Thus, *other local programs' activities may vary somewhat from the following list of general activities, which is based on programs visited in the Berkeley area.*

To improve knowledge and communication
- A required 4 years of mathematics, of English, and of foreign language in high school (These are prerequisites for acceptance to the California public higher education system.)
- Enrichment of oral and written communication skills (In addition to 4 years of English, participants must take workshops that stress the importance of technical writing. There is also an annual essay contest, which is part of MESA Day, an annual gathering of all the programs.)
- Strengthening in mathematics and science through special MESA courses offered for high school credit
- Being tutored by others
- Tutoring others
- Training in test-taking skills
- Time-management, addressed "to some extent" in a Leadership Conference held in the summer
- Hands-on experience, such as model bridge construction

To improve problem-solving strategies
- Problem solving in which students compete at activities like model bridge construction, rocket construction

To increase motivation
- Field trips, incentive awards, and "recognition awards" (not necessarily money) offered for outstanding performance (Additionally, MESA maintains high visibility as an incentive to membership.)

• Student assumption of responsibility for success (Program staff believe that working hard to maintain grades is motivational and character-strengthening for high-school-level participants.)
• Minority role models (industry representatives, college-student tutors)
• Activities that build self-esteem (Students' ability to speak extemporaneously, for example, is fostered in small groups.)

Summer program:
A summer workshop for junior high and high school students includes academic instruction as well as exposure to high school and college life, respectively.

Teacher training:
Mathematics and science teachers voluntarily participate in training that (1) increases their knowledge of subject matter, (2) increases their facility with using hands-on curricula, (3) sensitizes them to the needs of minority students, and (4) helps them combat subject-matter phobia in students. In addition, the Berkeley directors encourage tutors and teachers to socialize more with students outside of the academic area—to attend baseball or basketball games, for example—so they can better relate to their students.

Parent involvement:
Contact with parents begins as part of the application and orientation process, when parents must respond to some questions on the application form. It seems that some parents maintain ongoing contact with the organization, but many do not. Parents in the Berkeley program are often informally advised by the staff about how to intervene with the public schools on their children's behalf.

Assistance with college admission:
MESA provides curriculum counseling to direct students into courses necessary for college admission; information about application, tests, and financial aid; and workshops about the college admission process. Career counseling is also provided.

Financial assistance:
Funding to attend college is provided through industry and colleges.

Seattle, Washington

Mathematics, Engineering, and Science Achievement Program (MESA, WA)

Note: The Washington MESA follows the basic structure of the California MESA. The population targeted for intervention, the focus and pattern of intervention, are the same. As in California, before graduating, participants in the program are required to take 4 years of mathematics, 4 years of English, and 4 years of a foreign language. Participants also have special MESA classes whose credits can be applied towards graduation. Salient features of Washington MESA are listed below.

Stated objectives:
To increase the number of students from ethnic groups historically underrepresented in math- and science-related professions who complete a 4-year university degree in a math- or science-based field

Program structure:
MESA Washington is a statewide program with a director and full-time assistant director. They are supported by the Board of Directors, whose members include leaders from industry, the state university, and the school board. The statewide program is divided into four main centers (Seattle, Tacoma, Yakima Valley, Spokane), each with two full-time staff persons. Finally, there are MESA advisors in the schools.

Participation:
Students in the program are African, Hispanic, and Native Americans from all levels of socioeconomic backgrounds. They participate in MESA while in middle and high school. While they are students who have high aptitude and interest and would most likely graduate from high school, they would probably not enter the college preparatory track for a science- or math-based career on their own. According to one staff member, MESA is "aiming for kids who will succeed at algebra, even though they [the students] may not know they will."

General activities:
To improve knowledge and communication
   • Laboratories in computers, mathematics, and science (with study materials integrated across laboratories) through which students learn to generate and test hypotheses

To improve problem-solving strategies
   • Same laboratories just described

To increase motivation
   • For high school participants, an incentive award of $49 that is given to students who quarterly maintain a 3.3 average in mathematics, science, and English; at the middle school level, such student rewards as calculators and family passes to science museums (to get the whole family involved)
   • Field trips to industry

Summer program:
There is a 5-week summer program. At the high school level, the program centers around physics and building structures (such as bridges). At the middle school level, the program centers on three labs—a computer lab, a mathematics lab, and a science lab, with study material integrated across labs. By the end of the program, students are generating and testing hypotheses.

A unique feature of the Seattle MESA center is a summer program for seventh- and eighth-grade girls. It is similar to the main, coeducational summer program in duration and in the extensive use of computers. However, the teachers, teaching assistants, and students are all females (African, Asian, Hispanic, and Native Americans, as well as whites). Connected with this program is an annual conference for women, where girls can interact with other girls with math/science interests, as well as with women with math/science careers.

Teacher training:
All MESA participating teachers are mathematics/science teachers. MESA pays for teacher substitutes, so MESA teachers may attend monthly seminars, during which they learn more about the applied side of their fields; about children's developmental patterns and learning styles; and about ethnic differences in study habits, in patterns of interaction with professors, and so on. MESA Washington also works with mathematics and sci-

ence teacher organizations to present new instructional strategies and materials to teachers.

Parent involvement:
At the high school level, parent groups are described as "very active." In general they hold two or three activities per year. "Family" mathematics programs are also held to get the entire family involved. At the middle school level, parent participation is low.

Assistance with college admission:
Starting in sophomore year, students are required to investigate and select colleges. Then they compose resumes and look at college application forms. They are also required to visit a college in their area. Scholastic Aptitude Test (SAT) workshops are offered on five Saturdays during the academic year. The workshops include practice problems, timed tests, and a test-sophistication component.

Financial assistance:
Approximately $100,000 worth of college scholarships from industry are awarded each year.

Philadelphia, Pennsylvania

Philadelphia Regional Introduction for Minorities to Engineering, Inc. (PRIME)

Stated objectives:
To increase the number of minorities and women graduating from college in engineering and other mathematics- and science-based professions, including medicine, pharmacy, allied health, computer science, actuarial science, accounting, and banking

Program structure:
PRIME serves students in six school districts in Philadelphia and surrounding counties, including the Camden School District (New Jersey). Each school has a PRIME team, which consists of a group of volunteers—teachers, counselors, and sponsoring representatives from industry. Beyond initial contacts, each school is responsible for setting up its own links with a sponsoring industry.

The team conducts program activities early in the morning, during lunch hour, or after school. Some team members get release time or a small monetary compensation, but many (probably most) do not. As an incentive for program participation, one teacher, for example, received a 45-minute preparation period, but no monetary compensation.

Participation:
PRIME serves "bright" middle school, junior high school, and senior high school students in the Philadelphia and Camden public schools. Student participants are African, Hispanic, and Native Americans from low- and middle-income families. A group of PRIME students encountered at one specialized high school were mainly from middle-class backgrounds and had parents with college degrees. However, these few students were described by staff members as more affluent than the typical PRIME student.

Program admission requires that students be earning A and B grades. To remain in the program, they must maintain at least an overall B average, with at least a B average in both their mathematics and their science courses. They must also take a mathematics and a science course each year, participate in PRIME activities, and be interested in pursuing a math- or science-based career.

To identify potential PRIME participants, all the elementary school records of students feeding into a middle or junior high school served by PRIME are evaluated. Parents of students thus identified as potential participants are sent letters and application forms. It sometimes happens that students with less-than-adequate elementary school grades but good teacher-recommendations are invited to participate.

General activities:
To improve knowledge and communication

- Curriculum guidance, including an attempt to place participants in a "good" magnet school or neighborhood school that has strong mathematics/science programs and demands academic excellence
- A PRIME-developed mathematics/science curriculum, which is provided to teachers
- Classroom visits by industry representatives, who demonstrate real-life applications of concepts learned in school
- Saturday Tutorial and Enrichment Program (STEP) for students in grades 9–12 who want enrichment or skill-strengthening in mathematics or science (STEP meets every other Saturday, and STEP teachers regularly communicate with students' classroom teachers.)
- PRIME students tutoring non-PRIME students (an informal component)
- Encouragement of student enrollment in an elective, test-taking skills course offered by the public schools

To improve problem-solving strategies

- Hands-on problem-solving activities

To increase motivation

- Role models (minority professionals from business and industry who work in the schools once a month)
- Field trips to businesses, industry, science museums

Summer program:
Compared with most of the other programs, PRIME seems to place a much stronger emphasis on its summer program. The sequential summer program has been elaborately designed to provide students with a broad exposure to math- and science-based professions. Students attend for 4 consecutive years, starting in the post-eighth-grade summer. The first year focuses on mathematics and computers at Temple University. The second year focuses on communications and computers at the University of Pennsylvania. The third and fourth years provide a choice of focusing on engineering science, pharmacy and allied health sciences, or actuarial science. The fourth year is residential. Students are pretested on mathematics and communication skills during the first day of the summer program and are assigned to class sections on the basis of their performance. Participants also receive advance teaching of the subjects they will take the following fall.

Recently the summer program was extended to include a reading program for seventh-grade students, which is housed at the University of Pennsylvania. It aims at enhancing students' reading comprehension and analytical skills. Similar programs are conducted at New Jersey colleges in the Camden area.

Teacher training:

There is a summer teacher-training program. Teachers are familiarized with content for high-level courses, as well as with new teaching methods. Staff members say many teachers admit to having had only one course in science during their training and to experiencing anxiety over teaching it.

Parent involvement:

Parents are somewhat involved. PRIME has a college relations coordinator who meets one-to-one with graduating seniors and their parents to "walk them through" the college application process.

Assistance with college admission:

PRIME provides a college relations coordinator, as just described, who assists students and parents in finding potential scholarship sources, financial aid packages, and loans. This coordinator has established informal support teams at several campuses in the state to help facilitate PRIME students' transition to college life.

Financial assistance:

One staff member proudly remarked: "We've never had a PRIME student who failed to go to college due to lack of funds." The funds come from outside sources.

Pittsburgh, Pennsylvania

Pittsburgh Regional Engineering Program (PREP)

Stated objectives:

To motivate students to take the courses needed to be admitted to engineering programs

Program structure:

PREP is primarily motivational. Beginning in the seventh grade, students are engaged in a set of activities aimed at motivating them to perform well academically and to take the courses that are necessary for college admission in math- and science-based fields.

One teacher from each school participating in the program acts as a PREP sponsor. PREP essentially functions as an extracurricular activity, with the frequency of meetings varying by school. On average, groups meet six or seven times per academic year.

Participation:

Most participants are African Americans from low-income families, and their parents have no college experience. Participants, who first join while in middle school, are good students, but not all are A or B students. One teacher described them as "competitive—not the ones you are going to have to fight to do things."

There are no grade requirements for joining the program. Recommendations from mathematics teachers or counselors are usually the main criterion. To remain in the program, high school (but not middle school) students must enroll in mathematics courses.

General activities:

To improve knowledge and communication

- Required student enrollment in high school mathematics courses; also encouraged enrollment in an advanced English course

- Field trips to local universities and industries
- Tutoring of others (informal component)
- Sponsored "talks" about time-management, organization, and so on

To improve problem-solving strategies
- Hands-on activities (acid rain studies, battery construction, wheel-axle-gear activities) to increase understanding of chemical, electrical, and mechanical engineering
- Participation in the hands-on components of other programs (PREP sends a few students to other programs for this purpose.)

To increase motivation
- Guest speakers and role models
- Mentoring/counseling
- Provision of calculators and instruction in calculator use

Summer program:
The summer program was dropped because of lack of funds. Presently some participants are placed with other summer programs at several universities in the surrounding area. Also, PREP encourages and pays for students to take college courses for high school credit.

Teacher training:
Except for an annual orientation meeting for the teachers who will serve as PREP sponsors, there is no specific teacher-training component.

Parent involvement:
A letter is sent to parents when students first join the program. Parents are also invited to some activities. However, parent involvement appears to be very low.

Assistance with college admission:
College assistance is not a structured part of the program. However, it is available as a service of the Pittsburgh Public Schools, and PREP encourages the use of this service.

Financial assistance:
Students are provided with information about sources of financial aid for college.

Rochester, New York

Program for Rochester to Interest Students in Science and Math (PRIS²M)

Stated objectives:
To substantially increase the number of Rochester City School District students, particularly minority students, who can advance their mathematics, science, and communication skills enough to pursue careers in engineering and science-related fields

Program structure:
According to a staff member, the program is viewed by the schools as an "after-school science club." This must be an understatement, given that between 1978 and 1981, the program developed a New York State award-winning science curriculum that was eventually adopted by the Rochester School District.

PRIS²M's model is a "team" approach. Each of the schools served by the program has a team of 60–80 students (about 20 per grade level, in grades 7–12). The "teams" meet on a regular basis that varies from school to school. At some schools, the team meets daily; at others, weekly; and at others, bi-weekly. The focus of the team is to build a positive academic support group in which students help one another and feel a sense of family.

Pivotal team roles are played by the "coaches" of the team and by the "PROS." Each team has two coaches, regular school teachers (often mathematics or science teachers) whom PRIS²M provides with small stipends, and when necessary, with substitute teachers. In return, the coaches (1) serve as official representatives for the program at the school; (2) assist in the selection of students for the team; (3) provide direction and opportunities for meaningful and rewarding involvement of PROS, parents, and students; (4) evaluate student development, counsel students, and intervene with those students failing to meet the standards set for team participation. Also, the coaches make effective use of activities developed by PRIS²M staff, such as student visits to local companies, museums, or college campuses. Activities vary from school to school.

PROS are professionals (usually persons from racial/ethnic minorities) from local businesses and industry who volunteer to help the program in several capacities: as mentors, tutors, career counselors, science/math consultants, and escorts for visits to companies or for cultural activities. A set of PROS assists each team. The business and industry professionals in this program seemed to be more actively involved than those in any of the other programs.

Participation:
PRIS²M serves 7th- through 12th-graders in Rochester public schools. This includes a large number of minority students from low- and middle-income families. Participants range from children of doctors and lawyers to children "at risk" and disadvantaged. Most participants are African American. In terms of GPA, there is a good mix among participants. Most minority students who are doing well academically are in the program, but many program participants do not have good academic records. In the words of one staff member, the program has "kids who have always been teachers' pets and kids whom everybody has kept away from."

Students who score at the 50th percentile or better on the California Achievement Test (CAT) or who are recommended by a teacher are invited to participate. However, students whose parents request that they participate or who themselves request to participate are also admitted, even if they do not meet other criteria. Participants must take at least one mathematics and one science course each semester of high school. They are also required to take "Regents" courses, which are more challenging and demanding than regular courses. To remain in the program, they are asked to maintain at least a 2.5 grade-point average, which is also required for participation in the field trips to local businesses and industry.

General activities:
To improve knowledge and communication
• Activities that reinforce academic skills (science fair projects for competition, student bowl competition among schools)
• Instruction in specific skills related to academic performance (workshops on verbal/written

communication, time-management)
- Tutoring by others
- Tutoring others

To improve problem-solving strategies
- A special PRIS²M-developed curriculum, which was adopted by the public schools

To increase motivation
- Membership on the "team"
- Role models/relationship with PROS
- Leadership training
- Workshop on developing positive attitudes
- Information about different professions
- Paid summer internship in industry

Summer program:
About 40–50 students experience a paid 8-week summer internship with local business and industry. Also, high school juniors and seniors attend a 1-week summer orientation at the Rochester Institute of Technology, a local college. The orientation is residential and includes minicourses in calculus, physics, creative writing, and computers. A similar program for junior high students is of 2-week duration, with the first week held at Monroe Community College, and the second week held at Clarkson University. The program will expand to 4 weeks in summer 1992.

Teacher training:
There is no specific training component.

Parent involvement:
Parents develop and conduct the Four Year Workshop, a workshop given each year for students entering PRIS²M for the first time. The workshop familiarizes students with the programs and points out the important milestones in high school. Also each year, PRIS²M offers parents a tour of local colleges.

Assistance with college admission:
PRIS²M provides tutoring for the Scholastic Aptitude Test (SAT), information about the college admissions process, and assistance for students in applying for college

Financial assistance:
The PRIS²M Kodak Scholarship is awarded to one student each year. Funded by the Eastman Kodak Company, it covers all college expenses for 4 years. The Freddie Thomas Foundation also funds a $1,000 scholarship each year for a total of 4 years. In addition, PRIS²M provides information on available college scholarships.

Atlanta, Georgia

Southeastern Consortium for Minorities in Engineering (SECME)

Stated objectives:
To increase the supply of minority engineering graduates by implementing a program of early identification and intervention that prepares students to enter and complete college studies in engineering, mathematics, and science

Program structure:
SECME is a consortium composed of 69 public school systems, 28 college and university engineering departments, and 65 corporations in eight southeastern states. The program provides broad guidelines for participat-

ing schools, in which it is an extracurricular activity.

In the SECME model, most of the activities that other programs assign to special program staff are performed by students' regular classroom teachers. An attempt is made to provide teachers with a broad range of teaching strategies, so they may fulfill these program roles. Each school has a SECME "team," which consists of one or more mathematics teachers, science teachers, and language arts teachers, as well as a counselor and the principal. The team meets on a regular basis (once a week at some schools, once every other week at other schools) to plan and implement activities.

Participation:

All students are encouraged to participate, but SECME targets students who are African, Hispanic, and Native Americans from both urban and rural school districts. They are not top students, but neither are they students needing remedial help. Middle-class participants are the exception.

Recruiting is the responsibility of the coordinator at each school, but SECME provides broad criteria: a combination of good test scores and a good grade-point average, enrollment in mathematics and science courses, and teacher recommendations. SECME does not encourage the use of test scores for cutoff, but individual school systems may. For many years, SECME has served students in grades 6–12. Recently it extended its services to fourth- and fifth-graders.

General activities:

To improve knowledge and communication
- Improved training of teachers (indirect method)

To improve problem-solving strategies
- Improved training of teachers (indirect method)
- Hands-on classroom activities (such as robot or transistor construction)

To increase motivation
- Public promotion of the consortium through holding SECME days, having students wear SECME tee-shirts, and so on
- Role models, professionals from industry, business, and academia, many of them from Atlanta, where successful minority role models abound
- Incentives such as rewards, public recognition

Summer program:

See "Teacher training."

Teacher training:

A 12-day Summer Institute for Teachers is held yearly, with a different member engineering university being used as the campus each summer. The training emphasis seems to be as much on affective as on cognitive domain. (Recently, for example, a multicultural component was added.) Teachers spend two thirds of institute time in classes pertaining to the various disciplines. These classes are taught by college professors in each field, many of whom are of national reknown. The goals of the Summer Institute for Teachers are to enrich their understanding of subject matter, to help them develop more hands-on applications for students, to provide them with an understanding of what engineers do, and to facilitate teacher/engineer and teacher/teacher networking.

The other one third of institute time involves such activities as bringing in minority engineering students to talk about what they needed from high school to be successful in college. Teachers also hear presentations by former students who have succeeded despite specific obstacles (for example, poor grammar).

Parent involvement:
Parental support varies from school to school. It is encouraged by the SECME model, but getting parents involved is very difficult, in part because, parents say, their children do not want them to get involved. To increase parent involvement, a new "family" component was recently added, whereby "family members" are asked to serve as chaperones and to otherwise become involved in program activities whenever possible.

Assistance with college admission:
At the summer training institute for teachers, there is a session on helping students with the college application process.

Financial assistance:
Universities and corporations belonging to SECME offer scholarships. In addition, SECME is connected to a country-wide network of people who identify students for scholarships in engineering.

Continued from page 71

exemplify each component will also be considered.

Based on the research presented in earlier chapters, Table 5.1 on the next page summarizes the ideal program we propose.[1] Obviously students are the ultimate beneficiaries of each method described in Table 5.1. However, students often benefit indirectly from changes in schools and from changes in parental behavior. Therefore, the following discussion of ideal-program components from the table is organized according to the *primary* target of the recommended change: the schools, the students, or their parents.

Based on what is known about minority youth and what is exemplary in existing intervention programs, changes must occur for schools, students, and parents.
▼

Program Components Involving Changes for Schools

Component 1: Advanced Courses

Program Needs

For many minority students, acquisition of knowledge about mathematics and science is limited because schools in poor neighborhoods typically do not offer advanced courses in these subject areas. Ideally, in part because they offer greater challenges, advanced courses should help to develop students' problem- solving strategies. Also, the mere existence of advanced courses can be a source of motivation for some students.

Exemplary Programs

As a prerequisite for program participation by a school, several of the extracurricular precollege programs—the Denver-based Colorado Minority Engineering Association, Inc. (CMEA), for one—insist that the school establish advanced courses. Almost all the programs participating in this study steer their students either subtly or not so subtly into the higher-level mathematics and science courses. The Chicago Area Health and Medical Careers Program (CAHMCP), for example, provides the option of students receiving college-level credit for

Many programs strongly advocate or provide advanced course work, especially these:
CMEA
CAHMCP
PREP
DAPCEP
MESA, CA
▼

Table 5.1

Components of the Ideal Intervention Program

Goals	Methods
Knowledge of specific fields	
Improved knowledge in math, science, or other subjects	• Advanced courses • Improved laboratories & resources • Hands-on problem-solving exercises • Lessons & practice in using different learning styles • Multidimensional screening procedures to identify high potential • Teacher/staff training & retraining • Tutoring for & by students • A professional support-group to work with teachers & students
Improved study & time-management skills	• Coaching in study & time-management skills
Improved performance on standardized IQ & achievement tests	• Coaching in test-taking skills
Placement in math/science track	• Training of counselors for improved precollege guidance & counseling
Maintenance & improvement of knowledge over summer recess	• Residential summer classes (college)
Effective problem-solving strategies	
Improved problem-solving strategies	• Hands-on problem-solving exercises • Advanced courses
Self-awareness about preferred methods of processing information	• Lessons & practice in using different learning styles
Knowledge & use of alternative methods of processing information	• Lessons & practice in using different learning styles
Improved performance on standardized IQ & achievement tests	• Coaching in test-taking skills

Table 5.1 (continued)

Components of the Ideal Intervention Program

Goals	Methods
Motivation	
Improved motivation for academic achievement	• Hands-on problem-solving exercises • Curriculum modification to reflect minority contributions • Interaction with role models • Assistance with college admission/financial aid • Exposure to professionals in work settings • Residential summer classes (college) • Teacher/staff training & retraining • Partnership between parents & schools/teachers
Enhanced academic, racial/ethnic, & personal self-esteem	• Curriculum modification to reflect minority contributions • Interaction with role models • Group & personal counseling (as needed) • Restructuring of schools
Resiliency to racism/discrimination	• Discussions about racism/discrimination • Establishment of a peer support-group • Group & personal counseling (as needed)
Perception on the part of students that college is affordable	• Assistance with college admission/financial aid • Training of counselors for improved precollege guidance & counseling
Effective communication skills	
Cultural literacy	• Partnership between parents & schools/teachers
Situationally appropriate use of standard or nonstandard English	• Remediation/enrichment in communication skills (including learning standard English as a second language)
Improved mutual communication between students & teachers	• Teacher/staff training & retraining • Lessons & practice in using different learning styles • Partnership between parents & schools/teachers • Restructuring of schools
Acquisition by minority students of standard English	• Remediation/enrichment in communication skills (including learning standard English as a second language)

some courses taken in the senior year. Another approach is taken by the Pittsburgh Regional Engineering Program (PREP), which encourages high school students to take college courses for high school credit and pays their tuition. Some programs do even more than encourage students to take existing school or college courses. They create their own classes, or train teachers, or do both. The Detroit Area Pre-College Engineering Program (DAPCEP), for example, provides students with enrichment classes in such subjects as algebra and trigonometry. The classes, conducted on Saturday mornings at local universities by university faculty, are intended to give students an edge in their regular school courses. DAPCEP summer programs have a similar focus.

In California, participants in the Mathematics, Engineering, and Science Achievement (MESA, CA) program are required to take 4 years of math, 4 years of English, and 4 years of a foreign language in high school. Additionally, they participate in workshops on communication, including technical writing.

Washington State MESA and CAHMCP offer unique, challenging summer components.

▼

The Washington State MESA program, at the middle school level, offers a unique summer component that may be at the forefront of intervention techniques—using laboratories in computers, mathematics, and science, together with study material *integrated* across laboratories. In these laboratories the students learn to generate and test hypotheses.

Students in Chicago's Young Scientists Program (part of CAHMCP) and Boston's MASSPEP actively engage in math and science technical investigations.

▼

In addition to providing college credit for some advanced courses, as we have already mentioned, Chicago CAHMCP provides enrichment classes in mathematics and science (including technical writing), opportunities to tutor and be tutored, and, perhaps most important, the Young Scientists Program, offered for students in grades 7 through 10. In the summer these students perform experiments and write laboratory reports, and during the regular school year they work on science projects. In the summer, they attend courses taught by college professors, and each student is appointed a research advisor from a pool of graduate students and upper-level undergraduates. Summer courses essentially include the content of Illinois Institute of Technology freshman courses.

Interesting features of the Massachusetts Pre-Engineering Program for Minority Students, Inc. (MASSPEP), in Boston, are the independent and group science-research projects in which students are engaged. In these projects, technical investigations are organized around such themes as applied mathematics.

Component 2: Improved Laboratories and Resources

Program Needs

When advanced mathematics and science courses are offered by schools in poor neighborhoods, the conditions of school laboratories and other educational resources are often substandard. State-of-the-art or approximately state-of-the-art equipment is necessary to overcome the traditional abstract presentation of information.

The importance of this component has become very clear to the author in his capacity as liaison between a college and a local high school attended primarily by economically disadvantaged black and Latino students. When the college "adopted" the high school in an attempt to help improve the academic performance of students, one of the first and strongest requests made by high school staff was for donation, by the college, of its old laboratory equipment. Use of the college laboratory facilities was also requested.

Exemplary Programs

Perhaps because of their relationships with institutions of higher education, many of the extracurricular precollege programs seem to provide adequate laboratory facilities for the students they serve. However, even the programs with the most resources are severely limited in the number of students they can accept. As a result, many students in need are not served. Overall, the previously described integrated computers, math-

Washington State MESA students experience learning that is integrated across computer, mathematics, and science laboratories.

ematics, and science laboratories of the Washington State MESA program stand out as exemplary.

Component 3: Hands-on Problem-Solving Exercises

Program Needs

Providing students with practical applications of classroom-presented information and with experiential, hands-on kinds of activities helps them see class content as relevant to the real world, which likely results in increased interest in learning. The hands-on approach used in the programs typically takes the form of bridge construction or rocket construction-and-launching projects. (As an example of the former, students must build a bridge capable of supporting a specified amount of weight but limited by guidelines for dimensions and construction materials.) These types of projects occur one or more times during the academic year and summer, usually as part of science fairs in which students from different schools or communities compete. Nature walks are another typical hands-on experience.

Exemplary Programs

Several programs are outstanding in their incorporation of this component. The Washington State MESA summer program, in which middle school students learn to generate and test hypotheses, deserves praise, as does the California MESA program, which provided the basic MESA model. (An example of a hands-on problem-solving exercise from the California program is a teacher's surreptitious removal of one component from a rocket-assembly kit, which forced students to figure out which component was missing and what role it served.) The Chicago CAHMCP Young Scientists Program is similarly praiseworthy. As previously stated, MASSPEP, in Boston, has its students conduct group and independent science research and engineering design projects. In Pittsburgh, PREP attempts to improve students' understanding of chemical, electrical, and mechanical engineering with hands-on activities that

Hands-on problem-solving activities are key elements in these programs:
CAHMCP
MASSPEP
MESA, CA
MESA, WA
PREP
PRIME
SECME
▾

include the study of acid rain, battery construction, and wheel-axle-gear functions, respectively. All five of these programs aim to provide students with more-than-average competence and a distinct advantage over students who lack similar experiences.

The Philadelphia Regional Introduction for Minorities to Engineering (PRIME) and the Southeastern Consortium for Minorities in Engineering (SECME) in Atlanta tackle the problem-solving component by placing an emphasis on modifying the traditional curriculum to make it more experiential. PRIME and SECME try to modify the method of instruction by retraining classroom teachers, largely through teacher workshops conducted in the summer. Additionally, PRIME has developed its own curriculum, which it provides to classroom teachers.

Component 4: Lessons and Practice in Using Different Learning Styles

Program Needs

As discussed in an earlier section of this report, Hale-Benson (1986) and others argued that differences exist in the ways blacks and whites tend to process information. They also argued that the traditional educational system favors the analytic reasoning strategies of whites, placing blacks at a disadvantage. One implication of their argument is that students who happen to be relational reasoners should be assisted to understand and recognize the analytic method of reasoning. Moreover, all teachers and students should be aware of both styles of reasoning and of the situations in which each may be particularly useful.

Many black students use the relational-analytical reasoning distinction to explain, post facto, problems they initially encountered at predominantly white universities. Some say, for example, that professors have discounted some of their oral or written arguments because the arguments did not follow analytic expectations. An early understanding of reasoning differences by both students and teachers may help to clarify such sources of difficulty and facilitate the mutual accommodation of both types of reasoners.

Exemplary Programs

Individual members of the staff of several programs know about the learning styles issue. However, the Washington State MESA program stands out as one that seems to approach the problem in a systematic way: In a workshop, teachers learn about the different learning styles and about how to accommodate them.

Washington State MESA offers systematic workshops for teachers to develop approaches for accommodating diverse learning styles. ▾

Component 5: Multidimensional Screening Procedures to Identify High Potential

Program Needs

At present, performance on standardized tests, despite their numerous problems, factors most heavily in the identification of gifted and talented students (Subotnik, 1989). However, this identification method, according to Baldwin (1987), overlooks many minority students who, though they have high intellectual ability, perform poorly on the tests. As long as this testing practice is continued, culturally different and economically disadvantaged children will continue to be underrepresented in traditional programs for the gifted and talented and overrepresented in special education programs.

The demise of standardized tests is unlikely because they have been used substantially in the past and because an entire industry has built up around them. Still, Baldwin (1987), Hilliard (1976), Subotnik (1989), and many others have argued that for assessing ability in minority students, the use of standardized tests should be replaced by the use of multidimensional screening procedures that incorporate input from parents, peers, observational data, and so forth. Only then, perhaps, will minority talent be adequately identified.

In addition to information from testing, assessment of students' abilities should include input from parents and peers, as well as information from teachers' observations. ▾

Exemplary Programs

Though most of the programs studied use multidimensional screening procedures, no program exemplifies this component. In an effort to identify talented students who may not be identified by standardized test scores and grades, program admissions personnel do often seek additional input from teachers and counselors. This use of flexible admissions criteria is commendable, since in contrast to standardized tests, flexible criteria give students the benefit of the doubt. However, flexibility is not without its drawbacks.

One major drawback is that the validity and reliability of admissions judgment may be compromised. For example, in discussions with program staff, it was not always clear which specific groups of students—high achievers, talented low achievers, and so forth— were being targeted, nor was it clear whether the participants selected would have been admitted to the programs again, were they to undergo the admissions process a second time. Many program staff actively working with students tend to view these reliability and validity issues as concerns only of measurement experts. However, program staff, if they are to adequately meet students' needs, also need to have a clear understanding of *whom* the program is targeting.

Another drawback is that reliance on teacher and counselor recommendations as a complement to or substitute for grades or standardized test scores may simply be replacing one form of bias with another. Without adequate training, teachers and counselors are likely to overlook students whose talents are not obvious, and they may recommend only students whose classroom behavior is consistent with their expectations of talented students—namely, students who are articulate and outgoing.

Component 6: Teacher/Staff Training and Retraining

Program Needs
Teachers and other staff need the following types of training or retraining:

- *Training in mathematics and science.* State-of-the-art equipment and higher-level courses were previ-

The programs do use multidimensional assessment approaches to identify high-potential students, but no program exemplifies this ideal.

Reliability and validity issues must be seriously considered in employing flexible program admission criteria.

ously proposed as keys to students' acquisition of knowledge in mathematics and science. Such equipment and courses, however, can only be effective when teachers are sufficiently knowledgeable—when they know the equipment well enough to guide others in how to use it and when they can teach the content of higher-level courses in a way that demystifies it. The supply of such teachers is limited. A common occurrence in schools is one where the art, English, or social studies teacher is recruited to teach mathematics or science. Such teachers are clearly deserving of inservice training in the subject areas they must teach. Many teachers specifically trained in mathematics or science could also use inservice training to update their knowledge as well as to improve their pedagogical skills.

Teachers need training/retraining in
- Advanced mathematics and science
- Innovative pedagogy
- Identification of student talent
- Career development techniques
- Financial-aid guidance.

• *Training in innovative pedagogy.* For many already well-trained teachers, the application of new technology (such as microcomputers) to the classroom, as well as the constantly growing store of new knowledge about the development of children's thinking and information-processing strategies, requires further pedagogical training.

• *Training in nonprejudiced identification of talented minority students.* The proposed changes in the educational system will be largely wasted if counselors and teachers are not knowledgeable of and effective in combating their own prejudices about minorities. Counselors and teachers should be trained to look beyond standardized test scores to identify talents that may not be readily displayed by students. Counselors and teachers are a crucial link in achieving the goal of guiding more minority high school students into mathematics and science academic tracks.

• *Training in career guidance and financial aid options.* Knowledge about general factors that affect the academic performance of minority students should also be a part of teacher and counselor training. Additionally, knowledge about the various professions that have a mathematics or science base should result in improved career guidance of students. Finally, knowledge about college financial aid and about how to effectively communicate aid information to parents should be part of counselor training.

• *Training in multicultural education.* Minority students are the numerical majority in several large urban school districts (like New York City's). Many school districts and states will be populated primarily by racial/ethnic minorities in the next 10 to 15 years. The teaching force, which is largely white and middle-class, is unlikely to change dramatically in its racial composition, given current enrollment trends in teacher-training programs nationally (American Council on Education, 1988; Paige, 1987). Consequently, teachers and staff must learn to accommodate a culturally diverse student body.

Accommodating minority students requires some knowledge of their home life and of how it interacts with school life. Therefore, training in multicultural education (Gay, 1988), as part of teacher-training programs and inservice training, is important. This type of training should occur in considerable depth and over an extended period of time if, as Gay recommended, teachers are to develop an understanding of the role of cultural diversity in the general learning process, as well as in specific academic subjects.

At a minimum, the training of teachers in multicultural education should include the following categories proposed by Gay (1987):

1. Theory of multicultural education, including an understanding of what multicultural education is and is not. This knowledge is important because, in practice, multicultural education is frequently reduced to learning about foods, dress, and the most obvious cultural differences, while

Teachers need multicultural training/retraining that includes such topics as
- **Communication styles**
- **Values**
- **Educational philosophy**
- **Pedagogical skills**

▼

more subtle and important cultural differences that may affect learning are ignored. The differences that teachers ought to study include communication styles, values orientation, learning styles, socialization patterns, and interaction patterns.

2. Philosophy of multicultural education as it relates to philosophy of American education.

3. Pedagogical and methodological skills.

Teachers need training/retraining in accommodating black English and other minority languages.

• *Training about black and other nonstandard English.* While conducting a teacher workshop on the psychological development of black children, the author developed an appreciation for what a slow and difficult process it may be to change attitudes about nonstandard English. The teachers were assigned a chapter by Labov (1970). In it, he translates the verbal arguments of a black-English speaker, regarding the existence of God, into standard English. He then compares them with those of a standard-English speaker, to highlight the similarity of content and degree of abstractness. After reading the chapter, a white teacher in the workshop said: "You know, I have been in school for years, and I have heard most of this before, that black English is grammatical, and all that stuff. But I never *really* believed it until I read this chapter."

There was nothing magical about the chapter or about this author's instructional technique. Perhaps the teacher's work in previous classes and her experience over the years were somehow catalyzed into synthesis by the workshop and by that chapter, in particular. The point is, a variety of methods aimed at changing teachers' knowledge of and responsiveness to linguistic differences are necessary.

Exemplary Programs

Most of the extracurricular precollege programs visited conduct some amount of teacher training or retraining. However, seven programs stand out as exceptional in their implementation of one or more of the subcategories of the teacher-training component. Six of them—the California and Washington State MESA programs, PRIME in Philadelphia, SECME in Atlanta, DAPCEP in Detroit, and AISES (American Indian Science and Engineering Society) in Boulder—provide teachers with mathematics and science training through summer sessions or academic year workshops.

PRIME's and DAPCEP's summer teacher-training programs serve teachers whose formal training in science is limited or who experience anxiety over teaching science. Teachers are familiarized with the content and with new instructional methods for high-level courses.

SECME has a large teacher-training summer component. It brings together teachers and university faculty from mathematics and science departments, as well as from departments of education. In so doing, the program is able to impact not only content but also pedagogy. In addition to having features similar to this, both California and Washington State MESA programs incorporate information about the needs of minority students. The Washington State MESA program also incorporates a component that improves teachers' knowledge of child development patterns and learning styles. DAPCEP's mathematics and science workshops for teachers include training in research methods.

AISES includes in its teacher-training program a unique component on multicultural education to help teachers integrate the sometimes opposing views of Western science and Native American cultures. It is worth noting that there are numerous tribes of American Indians, all with different cultures and belief systems. Consequently, teachers are helped to accommodate intertribal cultural differences, as well.

An alternative to summer teacher-training programs is offered by a seventh program, Boston's MASSPEP, which provides professional development and technical assistance to teachers through monthly workshops during the academic year.

In one or more areas of teacher training, there are many exemplary programs:
AISES
DAPCEP
MESA, CA
MESA, WA
PRIME
SECME
▾

While most programs offer teacher training in the summer, MASSPEP provides teacher training and technical assistance throughout the school year.
▾

Component 7: A Professional Support-Group to Work With Teachers and Students

Program Needs

All mathematics and science teachers, particularly those not formally trained in these subjects, should have at their disposal a network of industrial and academic professionals who are willing to work with them to make the study of mathematics and science more interesting and full of active involvement for students.

Exemplary Programs

In Philadelphia, PRIME brings minority professionals from business and industry into the schools on a monthly basis to work with students and simultaneously serve as role models. Perhaps the best example of how to bring professionals, teachers, and students together is provided by the Program for Rochester to Interest Students in Science and Math (PRIS^{2}M), a primarily motivational program in upstate New York. PRIS^{2}M is managed by a team at each school. The team is composed of a mathematics or science teacher, a professional from local industry, and the students. The team approach of PRIS^{2}M can provide the kind of interaction between experts and novices (students) that facilitates students' knowledge acquisition and development of problem-solving strategies. Although a considerable amount of such interaction now occurs, there is potential for even further development of this interaction between students and professionals. During its long history in the Rochester area, PRIS^{2}M has developed a New York State award-winning curriculum, which has been adopted by the Rochester Public Schools. Ideally, the PRIS^{2}M model for involving industry professionals in education should have widespread adoption.

> Mechanisms for teacher training and support from industry and university professionals are exemplary in PRIME and PRIS^{2}M.

Component 8: Curriculum Modification to Reflect Minority Contributions

Program Needs

Widely used textbooks do not accurately or consistently

describe the role of minorities in the broad scope of American history (Alter et al., 1989). Almost everyone has heard about Martin Luther King, Jr., and George Washington Carver. However, countless other contributions by minorities are not typically blended into the quilt of American history as presented in textbooks.

One way of motivating students to achieve in school is to encourage them to feel that they belong there. As discussed previously, feelings of belonging are often undermined in many minority students by the lack of similarity between their subcultures and those aspects of the dominant culture deemed worthy of study and emulation at school. The introduction of new textbooks with a more multicultural approach and, until those books are produced and distributed, the teacher's own interjection of new, multicultural materials are two ways of dealing with this problem.

Until more textbooks include a multicultural approach, teachers should provide this input, as is done in most of the 12 science and math programs.

Exemplary Programs

Because they are extracurricular and confined to specific subject areas, the precollege programs discussed here are generally not able to bring about or exemplify the widespread kinds of changes in school curricula that we are talking about. However, most programs attempt to set a good example by implementing some curriculum changes in their own area of intervention (for example, discussing contributions of minority scientists during summer science classes).

Component 9: Remediation/Enrichment in Communication Skills

Program Needs

Without mastery of appropriate levels of skill in reading, writing, and speaking, a student's school success is virtually impossible. Some teachers in the public schools of New York City, which are overwhelmingly composed of children from culturally diverse and economically disadvantaged backgrounds, have said that they are very happy to have a student who is reading only a year below actual grade level. A minority student who reads *at* grade level, according to them, is often considered gifted. This is not acceptable.

A program designed to enhance the achievement of minority students in mathematics and science must provide any needed remediation and enrichment in basic skills. This is no simple task, given the complexity of the learning problems of many minority students. For example, students who have been taught inappropriate strategies for decoding text, as Collins (1986) suggested, are likely to have to unlearn them before acquiring new ones.

Constructively dealing with bilingualism is crucial. For instance, some educators have suggested that standard English should be taught as a second language to speakers of black English or other nonstandard forms of English. This suggestion is worthy of much consideration.

Exemplary Programs

Students in the California and Washington State MESA programs are required to take 4 years of English and to participate in workshops on communication. In California, the workshops include technical writing and oral communication. Students in the CAHMCP program in Chicago develop technical writing skills, as well as skills for orally presenting and defending their research. The development of skills for analyzing and comprehending written text is the special focus of summer reading programs for seventh grade students that are offered by PRIME in Philadelphia and Camden, New Jersey. Hosted at local colleges and universities, the programs involve reading novels and discussing their plots.

Component 10: Restructuring of Schools

Program Needs

Urban schools tend to be large and impersonal, limiting the opportunities for teachers and students to become familiar with each other and to develop positive long-term relationships. In the absence of such relationships,

---

Math and science programs must provide students with reading and communication remediation and enrichment. Exemplary programs in this respect are these:

CAHMCP
MESA, CA
MESA, WA
PRIME
▾

it is easy for teachers and students from different cultural and economic backgrounds to develop and maintain stereotypic attitudes about each other. To combat this problem, two strategies that are currently being implemented in various places across the country with varying degrees of success are recommended. First, is the restructuring of the schools into subdivisions that allow teachers and students to interact in smaller units, thereby increasing their opportunities to become familiar with each other. Second, as suggested by Comer (1980), is providing opportunities for extended teacher-student relationships by allowing students to remain with the same teacher over several years in an activity, area of study, or homeroom. The resulting long-term relationships are likely to facilitate the instructional process. In such a design, potential teacher-student personality clashes could be resolved on an individual basis by the reassignment of students and the transfer of teachers who are not able to successfully function in this type of setting. Restructured schools might also facilitate establishment of the partnership between parents and teachers that will be described later.

Some program features point to the need for school-restructuring strategies, such as developing smaller units within large schools, allowing certain teachers to stay with students over several years, developing teacher-parent partnerships.

Exemplary Programs
Because they are extracurricular, the precollege programs under discussion are not usually in a position to change school structure in any other way than by being exemplars of key components for improving academic achievement.

Component 11: Residential Summer Classes

Program Needs
As previously discussed, summer classes are important because they may prevent the decline in knowledge and the decline in academic work habits that often occur over a student's summer of inactivity. Residential summer classes at a local college or university may attract students to higher education by giving them a taste of college life and dispelling fears of attending college, which are felt especially by those who are the first in the

Residential classes and summer programs offer unique experiences and opportunities. Exemplary programs are

AIUB
CAHMCP
DAPCEP
MASSPEP
MESA, CA
MESA, WA
PRIME
▾

family to attend college. Additionally, as discussed in connection with peer support-groups in Chapter 4, the camplike atmosphere of residential summer classes may provide feelings of self-worth, may enhance development of leadership skills, and may increase motivation in students from backgrounds not particularly rewarding of academic prowess.

Exemplary Programs

All but one of the precollege extracurricular programs include the summer component as one (not necessarily the principal one) of several major activities throughout the year. The only exception, the American Indian Upward Bound Science and Self-Determination Program (AIUB) in Boulder, Colorado, has primarily the summer component.

Some of the exemplary summer components have already been discussed in previous contexts and thus will only be briefly mentioned here. These include components of the CAHMCP in Chicago, the California and Washington State MESA programs, Philadelphia's PRIME, and Detroit's DAPCEP. Notable additions here are the summer programs of Boulder's AIUB and Boston's MASSPEP. The AIUB summer program includes test-taking-skill training, weekly personal counseling sessions, and a number of other activities. MASSPEP has a 6-week residential summer program of morning classes (including scientific investigations) followed by afternoons dedicated to independent study, taking minicourses such as photography, hearing noted speakers, and participating in sports.

Another exemplary summer program, and one of the most elaborate ones, is provided by PRIME. It includes a sampling of experiences in a broad range of mathematics- and science-based professions. The summer experiences are sequential. Starting in the post-eighth-grade summer, students attend programs for 4 consecutive years. One sample of students spent the first summer focusing on mathematics and computers at Temple University and the second summer focusing on communication and computers at the University of Pennsylvania. The third summer and fourth summer (which is residential) offered one of three choices: engineering science; pharmacy and allied health sciences; or actuarial science. To maximize learning, students are pretested on the first day of each summer, and instruction groups are designed to fit the knowledge levels of individual students.

Component 12: Partnership Between Parents and Schools/Teachers

Program Needs

Knowledge in any field is highly dependent on the learner's active participation in its construction. Improved communication between parents and schools (or teachers) can lead to their jointly encouraging (and when necessary, enforcing) students' class attendance, class participation, and completion of homework. Potentially, improved parent-school communication can also lead to reducing the amount of time students spend being entertained by commercial video and audio media and concomitantly increasing the amount of time spent in more intellectually challenging activities.

The partnership advocated here is not of the type recently adopted in the Chicago schools. In that public school system, parents have virtually taken control of school decision making, almost the opposite of the traditional parent role as nonparticipant observers. Systems such as Chicago's have historically failed, perhaps because, as Leslie and Springen (1989) argued, they place too heavy a burden on parents who lack the necessary training and experience of school personnel. The criticism may be particularly applicable to many schools in poor neighborhoods, where parents who are already overburdened with the struggle against poverty, crime, and drugs may have little energy or know-how to take charge of the schools.

Parents can and should become considerably more involved in their children's education. One way of fos-

Parents can be more than bystanders in their children's education. As partners with schools and teachers, they can make many contributions— helping with homework, acting as resources for multicultural information or as resources in running the schools.

tering involvement is to invite parents to be more than casual bystanders of the educational process. Parents are potentially one of the best sources of information regarding other cultures. Schools should use parents' expertise to provide inservice training for teachers who lack such knowledge (Comer, 1980). Parents can also be a valuable additional resource for improving the day-to-day running of school. They can serve as proctors, assist with field visits, and so on. Simultaneously, teachers can help parents acquire achievement-promoting behaviors, such as those described by Clark (1983), and teachers can conduct workshops, as they do in Head Start programs, to enhance parents' education and skills.

Adequately structured, these programs may help dispel many preconceptions that middle-income, nonminority teachers have about minority and low-income parents. Teachers are likely to find the parents to be a lot more concerned about their children than one might imagine. Simultaneously, parents are likely to feel more competent and willing to discuss their children's education with teachers.

Exemplary Programs

Creating a partnership between parents and schools is a task that obviously requires the concerted effort of parents, teachers, and school administrators. While staff of the intervention programs can, at best, only facilitate this task, they can and should encourage the involvement of parents in their own intervention programs as well as in the regular school programs. While staff of most of the precollege extracurricular mathematics and science programs strongly express a belief in the need for more parental involvement, they are also quite self-critical about their inability to elicit high levels of parental involvement. Many admit that their best efforts have failed to procure involvement from more than a small group of parents. They generally point out that parental involvement is an area earmarked for considerable work in the immediate future.

Moreover, some program staff give the impression

> With parent participation in the schools, there is greater teacher-parent communication and support of children's education. For this component, programs worthy of mention are MESA, CA, and PRIS²M.
>
> ▾

that they simply do not feel parental involvement is a crucial issue. A few admit that they are not concentrating on parents. Instead, they rely on staff to engage in a kind of proxy parenting. Compared with parents, staff doing proxy parenting are usually closer to students in age and other demographic variables. They are also well educated and familiar with the academic system and its red tape.

Although proxy parenting helps students whose parents simply do not exhibit interest in their children's academic performance, programs should expend all efforts to get parents involved. Lack of parental involvement may take a toll even on apparently independent-minded adolescents who seem to be so involved with their peers that they do not want their parents to visit the school.

Although no program stands above all the others for how it fosters a parent-school partnership or for how it increases the level of parental involvement in program activities, the California MESA program is worthy of mention for its staff's involvement with parents. MESA, CA, staff serve not only as sources of information about the school system but also as motivational coaches or "cheerleaders" for parents in their dealings with the schools. PRIS^{2}M, in Rochester, also deserves mention for the unique way it involves parents in program activities. Parents of students in PRIS^{2}M develop and conduct an annual workshop for students entering the program. The workshop provides students with a description of the milestones of their upcoming high school years and familiarizes students with PRIS^{2}M's program.

IN SUMMARY Several ideal-program components imply changes for schools in poor neighborhoods— changes that can bridge the gap between the home and school experiences of many students and provide an academic preparation similar to that provided in suburban public schools and in private schools. Of unquestionable importance among these school changes are improved facilities and class offerings for advanced study. To make the best use of such improvements, schools should provide teacher training and retraining in multicultural education and in pedagogical skills that facilitate development of students' critical thinking and problem-solving ability. They should also establish support groups of industry professionals to work with teachers. Given the importance of effective communication skills as a foundation for education, both schools and intervention programs should also provide activities for remediating or enriching the communication skills of minority students.

Program Components Involving Changes for Students

Component 1: Coaching in Test-Taking Skills

Program Needs

High scores on standardized tests of achievement are tickets to college, particularly to the more prestigious colleges. However, minority high school graduates have a decreased probability of acceptance to the most prestigious colleges because, in general, their scores on standardized tests of achievement are lower than those of whites.

Until multidimensional screening procedures are implemented nationally, other strategies should be utilized to help improve minority students' performance on standardized tests. Empirical evidence indicates that classes designed to train students in test-taking skills can improve performance on standardized tests of aptitude (Slack & Porter, 1980) and achievement (Bangert-Drowns, Kulik, & Kulik, 1983). They are a viable and cost-effective way of dealing with the problem.

According to Johnson (1987), the training method has worked at the Gainesville branch of the University of Florida. Students who are admitted but were unable to achieve the required Scholastic Aptitude Test (SAT) entrance scores must take a computer-based, self-paced, test-taking sophistication course. Most are subsequently able to achieve a passing score.

Exemplary Programs

A well-structured test-sophistication component is provided by 2 of the 12 precollege programs. Having such a component in the programs may be unnecessary, because most of the programs have selected participants who are already good test-takers. AIUB in Boulder has devised its own test-taking skills workshop. It includes the use of a microcomputer software package as a tutorial for the American College Test (ACT). Washington MESA provides SAT workshops on five Saturdays during the academic year. The workshops include practice problems, timed tests, and general guidelines for taking standardized tests.

Component 2: Coaching in Study and Time-Management Skills

Program Needs

Certainly by high school (when students are expected to be more autonomous) but perhaps as early as elementary school, many students need assistance in developing skills for studying, managing time, and keeping on task. Students may spend a lot of time studying and doing homework. However, if they are not using effective study strategies, managing their time properly, and remaining actively engaged on task, the amount of time invested may have little positive impact on their performance, according to Bloom (1974) and others.

Exemplary Programs

Most programs include some amount of coaching in time-management and study skills, particularly as part of the residential summer component. However, these are usually informal, ancillary benefits derived from other formal program components, not unique strategies systematically incorporated into programs. No program stands out as exemplary for this component.

Students' test-taking skills can be enhanced by coaching, as shown especially by AIUB and MESA, WA.

Most programs include some study and time-management coaching for students, but no program stands out for this component.

Component 3: Tutoring for and by Students

Program Needs

Having knowledgeable students tutor their peers is another method for helping students to acquire knowledge of mathematics and science. Peer tutors, being close to their students in developmental level, may readily diagnose and remedy learning problems. As suggested by Kinsler's (1990) empirical findings, and by the maxim "In order to teach, one has to first learn," students who receive remediation might also benefit from tutoring younger students. Besides fostering knowledge acquisition, tutoring others may improve the self-esteem of tutors. A recent ABC news report included a description of a program that has potential high school dropouts tutoring elementary school children. As a result, not only have the tutors remained in high school; many of them now plan on college.

Exemplary Programs

Most programs provide some form of subject-area tutoring, in particular, PRIME, through its STEP program.

A few programs incorporate a limited amount of voluntary tutoring *by* program participants. However, none seem to systematically provide their participants with a supervised experience in tutoring others. Most programs provide tutoring *for* participants. Exemplary among these is PRIME, in the Philadelphia/Camden area, which has a Saturday Tutorial and Enrichment Program (STEP) for students in grades 9 through 12. STEP classes, which meet every other Saturday, allow students to consolidate or enrich their knowledge of mathematics and science. Most important, as a strategy for maximizing the benefits of the tutoring experience, teachers in the STEP program regularly communicate with students' classroom teachers about individual students' relative strengths and weaknesses.

Component 4: Exposure to Professionals in Work Settings

Program Needs

The knowledge students acquire from experiencing a

profession in its real-life setting can be a strong motivator for academic success. The development of problem-solving strategies for dealing with the world of work and the development of more effective communication skills may be added benefits of this component.

Exemplary Programs

As a result of established relationships with industry, most of the programs are able to secure summer employment for a limited number of students. Rochester's PRIS²M and Detroit's DAPCEP seem to be particularly adept at doing so. For example, DAPCEP's summer "bridge employment" program provides high school seniors with jobs in their chosen fields during the summer between finishing high school and beginning college. Similarly, each year, 40–50 PRIS²M students acquire experience working with professionals in paid 8-week internships with local businesses.

Component 5: Interaction With Role Models

Program Needs

From the perspective of social-learning theory (Bandura, 1986) and other views, students will imitate the behaviors of persons they perceive as warm, powerful, and similar to themselves. Low-income minority teenagers find too few academic and professional role models in their neighborhoods. Hence programs to enhance minority achievement should provide such models.

All programs include role models from the same ethnic and cultural backgrounds as the students served. In fact, many staff members seem to be of the opinion that providing ethnically and culturally appropriate role models is sufficient. It is not. The age of role models, their gender, and any other characteristics that facilitate the students' perception of similarity are also important. In fact, according to a staff member of one program, in her program, age and gender seem to be *as* crucial as racial/ethnic background.

Exemplary Programs

The California MESA program has been especially suc-

Students gain unique problem-solving skills from real-life professional settings. Exemplary programs:
DAPCEP
PRIS²M
▾

Programs should include role models students can readily identify with—program "graduates" and minority professionals from science and engineering, both male and female.
▾

All the programs have some variation of role model contact that can be emulated. Especially exemplary are these programs:
AISES
CAHMCP
DAPCEP
MESA, CA
MESA, WA
PRIME
PRIS²M
SECME
▾

cessful in providing role models. It has been particularly adept at involving as role models earlier generations of students who have successfully completed the program and gone on to college. They return to work with students currently in the program. Virtually bombarding students with minority role models, Chicago's CAHMCP also has an exemplary role-model component; like California MESA, it enlists the assistance of former program participants who have gone on to college.

AISES, one of two programs in Boulder for American Indians, has been exemplary in its use of role models to increase motivation. At an annual AISES National Conference, American Indian students are able to talk with American Indian scientists and engineers about issues of concern (for example, how to incorporate tribal ceremonies into nontribal settings, establish relationships with professionals, and even correspond with professionals during the year).

A similar annual conference, held by MESA Washington, focuses exclusively on girls. The annual conference, as well as a summer program exclusively for seventh- and eighth-grade girls, allows female students to interact with female scientists, mathematicians, and engineers. This strategy is worthy of consideration by other programs because it counters a major problem of our educational system and society: Jointly, women of all ethnic groups make up roughly half the pool of talent from which scientists and engineers must come for the balance of this century (Task Force on Women, Minorities, and the Handicapped in Science and Technology, 1989). Moreover, girls obviously have the potential to succeed at subjects such as mathematics, because until they reach adolescence, girls perform similarly to boys and demonstrate similar interest and effort in these subjects. However, by young adulthood, women are significantly outnumbered by men in math- and science-based careers (National Research Council, 1989; Task Force on Women, Minorities, and the Handicapped in Science and Technology, 1989).

As suggested by the National Research Council (1989), the perception that mathematics and science careers are for men must be included among the various reasons for girls' declining interest in mathematics and science as they get older. Such a perception is encouraged, if not engendered, by the dearth of female role models available to junior and senior high school girls. As long as females in general, and minority females in particular, have few role models in mathematics and science, girls with potential to contribute to these fields will not be challenged to develop their potential.

The Atlanta branch of SECME has taken advantage of that city's large number of minority professionals to provide numerous role models for its students. Rochester's PRIS^{2}M, whose primary focus is motivational, seems to do a similarly outstanding job of providing role models, and often, long-term relationships develop between role models and students. Industry professionals on the team apparently do develop supportive relationships with students.

In Philadelphia, PRIME brings minority professionals from business and industry into classrooms once a month. These professionals assist with instruction and simultaneously serve as role models. Detroit's DAPCEP uses a different approach—producing its own films to create an awareness of career possibilities in mathematics and science while motivating students by portraying role models.

Component 6: Personal Counseling and Discussions About Racism

Program Needs

Students ill-prepared to expect and deal with racism may be easily discouraged when they encounter it on campus or elsewhere. Minority students should know about the history (including recent history) of race relations in America. They should also have effective strategies for dealing with racism, particularly in educational settings. Frank discussions with older students and adults are one method of accomplishing this goal. Personal counseling regarding racism and other issues should also be available for students who need it.

Exemplary Programs

Most programs provide discussions about racism on an *ad hoc* basis, as the need is perceived. However, the methods are not systematically incorporated in any program. Boulder's AIUB is the only program that includes systematic personal counseling. This may be in response to the needs of its participants, who come from various states and therefore are more likely to experience homesickness and other personal problems.

Component 7: Establishment of a Peer Support-Group

Program Needs

Frequently, inner-city minority students who succeed academically find they must do so on their own. They may be isolated and unpopular because peers view them as acting "white." Jerome, the self-isolated 10th-grader described in Profile 5 (in Chapter 4), is a good example of a student in need of a support group. The establishment of a formal or informal peer support-group in a program is one means of combating this type of isolation.

Exemplary Programs

Peer support is a by-product of most of the programs. An exemplary program, however, is PRIS²M, in Rochester, where school "teams" build support groups that encourage students to help one another and that provide students with a sense of belonging.

Component 8: Assistance With College Admission/Financial Aid

Program Needs

The cost of college tuition and room and board can be discouraging to anyone. So can the complex bureau-

Students are often in need of information or counseling about dealing with racism. Boulder's AIUB systematically includes personal counseling for students on a wide range of issues.

As students strive to excel in inner-city schools, they need peer support. Rochester's PRIS²M program is exemplary in providing this.

cracy of the financial aid system. These can be doubly threatening to minority students from an economically disadvantaged background who are the first in the family to attend college. The cost may seem prohibitive, the system, unfathomable. It is therefore important that as early as possible, students and their parents perceive that they can overcome these difficulties, that financial aid is available, and that it is sufficient.

In their sophomore and junior years of high school, students should begin to take steps in seeking admission to college and seeking financial aid. One of these steps, for example, would be talking to local admissions officers. Also, parents should be strongly encouraged to get involved in the process.

Programs like those featured in recent news accounts, where wealthy individuals "adopt" economically disadvantaged elementary or high school classes, guaranteeing students tuition if they are admitted to college, should be effective. State and federal government, corporations, and foundations should be encouraged to replicate such highly desirable programs.

Exemplary Programs

Not surprisingly, no precollege extracurricular program has sufficient funds of its own for providing financial aid. Though, in general, they seem to be doing an effective job of putting their participants in touch with sources of funding, this may not be enough. Several programs do an exemplary job of assisting with college admission.

For instance, besides providing curriculum counseling to direct students into courses necessary for college admission, California's MESA provides workshops about the college admissions process, including information about application, tests, and financial aid. The Washington State MESA program also has an exemplary procedure for assisting students with college admission. At different points in their tenure with the program, students are required to research various colleges, visit an area college, look at college application

Students and classes need information and direction for planning college admission processes. Exemplary programs in this respect are these:

AIUB
CAHMCP
CMEA
DAPCEP
MESA, CA
MESA, WA

forms, and try their hand at composing the dreaded essays about why they want to go to college. In addition, as stated earlier, Washington MESA, as well as AIUB in Boulder, provides workshops for passing college entrance exams.

The Philadelphia (PRIME), Chicago (CAHMCP), and Detroit (DAPCEP) programs have set up informal networks with a few universities, not only to help place their students but to help guarantee their *retention* in college. In addition, a PRIME coordinator meets with seniors and their parents to "walk them through" the admissions process.

In Denver, CMEA arranges trips to local universities, so their students may converse with admissions officers. They also provide assistance with composing the admissions essay. CMEA has developed an Incentive Awards Program that provides financial assistance for students and also attempts to increase their motivation to succeed academically. Under this program, junior and senior high school students earn points based on their grades, standardized test scores, and participation in extracurricular activities (including CMEA). For each point earned, students are awarded money to be used for college tuition and fees for the first year of college. Three major Colorado universities provide matching funds for these monetary awards. The matching funds are provided each year until the student graduates, for a maximum of 5 years.

In addition to providing a small number of scholarships specifically for students in its Rochester program, PRIS²M provides tutoring for the Scholastic Aptitude Test and offers parents tours of local colleges. As part of its focus on teachers as the vehicles for change, Atlanta's SECME trains teachers to provide assistance to students in the college application process. In addition, as part of a large network that includes universities and corporations, SECME is able to advise students about available scholarships offered by other members of the network.

Denver's CMEA has an Incentive Awards Program for the first year of college tuition and fees. Other programs with exemplary financial aid components:
PRIS²M
SECME

IN SUMMARY   To foster academic achievement, many changes in the academic and social environment of minority students are needed. Coaching in study and test-taking skills; coaching in time-management; exposure to work settings and interactions with positive role models; and frank discussions of racism are perhaps foremost among the recommended changes. Students may also need peer support, tutoring opportunities, and introduction to the college-entrance process. The following section considers recommendations for increasing parental involvement in education.

Changes for Parents

One ideal-program component discussed under those involving changes for schools—a partnership between parents and schools/teachers—implies that changes for schools and for students should be accompanied by changes for parents. However, some of the most important parental change should occur long before children are in precollege intervention programs.

Bloom (1980) argued that parents, as the first and most consistent figures in children's lives, play a very important early role in children's later academic performance. Bronfenbrenner's (1979) ecological model suggests that parental influences are particularly important during early childhood, when much of the foundation for school success may be laid. Although entrance to school marks the beginning of a lengthy *formal* apprenticeship in which children are inducted into the literacy of the prevailing society, the apprenticeship actually begins *informally* at home, with parents, other adults, and peers (Cook-Gumperz, 1986; Santmire, 1987).

For children who speak nonstandard English, particularly black English, the impact of the difference between formal (school) and informal (home) literacy apprenticeships can be substantial and even negative. Schools generally assume that standard English is the language children use (or should use) to represent im-

The parent-child learning apprenticeship requires input from educators, so the match between home and school, especially in literacy, can be facilitated.

ages to themselves and that children are ready to acquire concepts in this language. As discussed earlier,
black-English-speaking children taught on the basis of
this assumption often acquire a poor, unintended understanding of what teachers say (Orr, 1987). The negative impact may be less for minority children whose
primary language is not a dialect of English (for example, for Spanish-speaking children). As Santmire
(1987) suggested, with such children, teachers are not as
likely to assume they are ready to acquire concepts in
standard English.

The dissimilarity between the school and home
literacy of minority children may also affect children's
development of what Erikson (1963) labeled autonomy,
initiative, and industry. According to Santmire (1987),
because the home language they use to communicate
needs and to negotiate with adults in having those
needs met often does not work at school, minority
children may often feel they have a lack of control of
their environment. As a result, they may be less willing
to initiate the kinds of investigative activities from which
children would usually learn about the world.

The problems just described are not the fault of
parents or schools. They are the results of a society in
which multiple cultures try to function in harmony
while maintaining their uniqueness. However, it may
be primarily up to schools, working with federal, state,
and local agencies, as well as with the private sector, to
assist minority and economically disadvantaged parents in giving their preschool children the skills crucial
to academic success.

According to Piaget (1983), the knowledge children
construct at home, prior to first attending school, is
largely the result of a proclivity to actively, spontane-
ously, and simultaneously engage in the assimilation of
and accommodation to environmental experiences.
School knowledge is similarly constructed. From a
Piagetian perspective, the motivation to learn comes
mainly from within the child. However, parents and
other adults can play the supporting role of providing

the scaffolding for children's construction of knowledge (Santmire, 1987). In this regard, Slaughter and
Epps (1987) argued that parents, particularly mothers,
help preschool children's development by being verbally responsive to their verbal behavior and by setting
clear, firm, consistent standards for behavior.

Stevens (cited in Slaughter & Epps, 1987) found that
poor, single mothers, when they lack the emotional
support of an extended family, are less likely to engage
in the behaviors just described. Unfortunately, minority
communities have large numbers of poor, single mothers who lack the support of an extended family, and
their numbers may increase as inner cities continue to be
the habitat of mainly the underclass. Social policy at the
local, state, and federal levels must be adjusted to assist
these mothers with the needed resources that extended
families once provided. Programs that benefit preschool
children may appear to be costly. However, they are
indeed cost-effective when the long-term consequence
of failure to implement them is considered in terms of
educational remediation, welfare, judicial, and most
important, human costs (Berrueta-Clement et al., 1984).

SUMMARIZING THIS CHAPTER   The following are the
ideal-program components discussed in this chapter in
connection with the 12 model programs in our study.
Components involving changes for schools are these:

1. Advanced courses
2. Improved laboratories and resources
3. Hands-on problem-solving exercises
4. Lessons and practice in using different learning
styles
5. Multidimensional screening procedures to identify high potential
6. Teacher/staff training and retraining
7. A professional support-group to work with teachers and students
8. Curriculum modification to reflect minority contributions

**For low-income
families, early intervention
programs can contribute
to children's lasting
learning that results from
the parent-child process.**

9. Remediation/enrichment in communication skills
10. Restructuring of schools
11. Residential summer classes
12. Partnership between parents and schools/teachers

Components involving changes for students are these:

1. Coaching in test-taking skills
2. Coaching in study and time-management skills,
3. Tutoring for and by students
4. Exposure to professionals in work settings
5. Interaction with role models
6. Personal counseling and discussions about racism
7. Establishment of a peer support-group
8. Assistance with college admission/financial aid

In the next chapter, we describe the overall impressions of extracurricular precollege programs that we have formed from our study of model programs.

ENDNOTES

1. It is worth noting that many of the components considered here, which are conceptually based, were also found by Gordon et al. (1987) in their survey of precollege engineering programs (including some of the programs described in this report).

Chapter SIX

Summary and Concluding Remarks

FAILURE TO EDUCATE MINORITY YOUTH will undermine the welfare of the nation. Only in recent years has this realization exploded upon the national consciousness. The realization has sparked a renewed desire, reminiscent of that of the 1960s, to find what works and to implement it. Examples of what works do not abound, however. Over the last 10 years, the limited availability of federal funds for basic and applied research on minority adolescent development and achievement has not been without consequence.

Fortunately, during those same years, individuals, corporations, and foundations with vision have created and maintained some extracurricular precollege programs for minority students. Twelve of them—all of which emphasize mathematics and science—have been examined for this report. Such programs have not all come into being through selfless acts. Indeed, in many instances, the real vision may have been derived from demographic predictions of a future work force shortage. This does not detract from the great benefits society, in general, and minority students, in particular, have derived from the programs.

A staff member of one model program used the term *poverty industrial complex* to describe his perception

---

6

In the national search for educational methods to match tomorrow's needs, individuals and organizations launched the 12 precollege programs we have studied.

that most intervention programs create jobs more for the sake of creating jobs than for the sake of helping poor children. There are indeed instances where programs are motivated this way, but an overwhelming majority of staff in the programs are truly dedicated persons who want to, and usually do, make a difference in minority children's lives. The breadth and depth of that difference vary from program to program, and from time to time within programs. Unfortunately, because of the unavailability of hard evaluative data, it is impossible to say how much they vary.

What *can* be said, on the basis of interviews with staff at all levels of programs, is that *there is far too much variation in how staff conceptualize and implement program components.* Some staff, at all levels of programs, are relatively up-to-date on psychological and educational research and clearly think through the major issues. These persons are knowledgeably deliberate in the steps they take. There are also staff, however, who need a better focus on the range of factors involved in fostering the development and academic achievement of their students.

Program staff at every rung of the ladder—pro-

> **Without systematic evaluation research, it is hard to know how programs are succeeding in making a significant difference in students' lives.**
>
> ▼

Profile 6
RAUL—A District
Program Director

Raul is the director of a mathematics and science extracurricular program for an entire school district in a medium-sized city. He has been on the job a couple of years and seems to know it well. He believes the qualifications that got him the job—a bachelor's degree in a science field and a couple of years' teaching experience—were necessary, but

not sufficient, for him to be successful. The amount of training he received after being hired, he describes as "minimal." Many of his present job skills have been acquired through trial and error and through sharing information with other directors he has met.

Raul is very committed to his job, the most important aspect of which, he believes, is to help minority students to succeed. He knows, fairly well, the teachers who serve as ad-

visors in each of over a dozen schools. He also knows a large number of students in those schools and tries to keep in touch with them weekly.

Raul's job can easily be hindered by red tape at any of several levels, including the state, school district, school, and classroom level. Even the program in which he works has its own red tape. However, Raul appears to see this as a mere obstacle to be overcome. There is a certain amount of indepen-

gram directors, district directors, teachers who serve as program advisors—can make or break a program, at least for some students. Given this fact, it seems that in general, *too little time and effort is expended in staff selection and training*. For example, the question "How do you select the best teacher to serve as advisor for the program?" was asked of many interviewees. Across the country, the most common responses were, "I ask the principal" or "I look for the person who is already doing too much." Similarly, the "learn on the job" training of some middle-level directors is exemplified by the minimal training of Raul, the district program director described in Profile 6. Further complicating matters is the belief held by many program staff that the qualities of a "good staff member" are inborn and cannot be instilled by training.

Perhaps the gravest danger to the programs is at the highest level. As one director stated, "We need to get away from the one man/woman running the program, which could die with that person." He would like to see support for extended internships (with the programs) for young people who decide they want to direct or staff these programs.

Without identification of the key components for effective programs, a solid basis for staff hiring and training is lacking, and program success becomes a function of who leads the program.

dence and rebelliousness (of the constructive variety) that he brings to the tasks. He recounts with glee a number of instances in which he "beat the system" from within, to the benefit of his charges.

I leave the interview with Raul with the distinct impression that despite the overall strength of a given program (and his is a strong, well-structured one), success depends largely on having a local director like him, one who is able to translate pro-gram policy into everyday practices. Such directors help to motivate teachers and advisors, as well as students.

I also leave the interview with some concern over the selection and training of the people who fill important program roles. In Raul's case, the process has worked quite well. However, given the apparently insufficient planning that has gone into the process, it could just as easily have gone awry. Insufficient atten-tion to leader selection and training does not seem to be an unusual occurrence in the field of minority intervention programs. Another school-district-wide director, in another program, said that his training consisted of a one-day "familiarization talk." Similar stories are told by staff in other programs, in other parts of the country.

The programs are, in general, doing an effective job. Certainly, each of the programs considered in this report has, to some degree, most of the ideal-program components described in the previous chapter. Unfortunately, across programs, we see these components designed and implemented with varying degrees of thoroughness and thus varying degrees of probability of success. Empirical evidence and evaluation research about the overall effectiveness of programs or the effectiveness of individual components within programs is very limited. After years of existence, many of the programs are only now beginning to keep track of their students—an attempt that cannot produce the best type of evidence. Moreover, some programs are tracking in the most rudimentary ways, simply maintaining tallies of the current educational and occupational status of former students.

Financial resources for much-needed systematic evaluation research are limited.

The lack of hard evidence is understandable. *Faced with limited resources and annual, biannual, or even monthly struggles to secure funding, programs have little time or money to divert to program evaluation.* Nor do they have the requisite expertise. To paraphrase one director, "Staff are so busy trying to keep the program going, they don't have time to do evaluation." His comment was echoed by most other directors.

Without the evidence of systematic evaluation studies, many of the programs will lose funding, hampering further program development. The very existence of some programs may be threatened. In times of budgetary constraints at federal and state levels and fiscal conservatism in the private sector, in order to secure funding, programs are being asked to demonstrate that they work. Compared with quantitative and qualitative evaluation, simple anecdotal evidence is the cheapest and most common means of demonstration, but it is falling into disfavor. More systematic data collection, however, is difficult and expensive. *Programs are caught in a vicious circle. To secure funding, they must prove they are effective, and to prove they are effective, they must secure funding.*

Part 1 of this book has set forth a theoretical framework for evaluating programs, a framework that is a first step in assisting the programs. We have presented and theoretically justified the key components of programs aimed at enhancing the achievement of minority students. However, determination of whether an individual program works cannot be based simply on a count of how many key components the program has. More extensive evaluation is necessary.

Furthermore, determining *whether* programs work is probably not the issue. We all know that most programs work to some extent; we do not need a study to tell us that. *We need a national evaluation study that enables us to further improve programs.* This would mean a study of several of the major programs to determine the effectiveness of each of the components described in this report, as well as the effectiveness of other components that may be of interest to program staff as well as psychological and educational researchers. The cost-effectiveness of such a national evaluation study would be measured not just on the basis of how it helps the students in the specific programs studied. It would be measured on the basis of how it helps programs and students in general by providing national visibility for effective strategies for improving the academic achievement of minority students.

Launching a national evaluation study may be more easily said than done. Most directors and program staff seemed leery about any evaluation involving outside "experts." This is not an unusual attitude regarding summative evaluation, since so much usually depends on its outcomes. However, the kind of evaluation proposed here is *formative*, not merely summative (Gronlund, 1985). It is intended to assist programs to improve existing components, drop unnecessary ones, and possibly add new ones. It is not intended to merely render a final judgment about program effectiveness.

An additional benefit of a formative evaluation may be to increase the currently limited contact be-

A national study of programs (including formative and summative evaluation approaches) is called for.

tween program staff and academicians in such fields as psychology and education, who can help them do a better job. In their report to the National Action Council for Minorities in Engineering (NACME), Gordon et al. (1987) criticized programs in this regard. This author independently arrived at a similar conclusion. For example, most of the programs are housed on university campuses; yet on several occasions, while visiting such programs, the author was astonished to find program staff completely unaware of the host university having a resident scholar whose work is quite pertinent to their endeavor. In a sense, staff are not to blame. Academicians tend to write for an inner circle of peers and to fail to disseminate their work to a wider audience that could derive practical benefit from it.

One way of dealing with the problem was suggested by the same director quoted earlier regarding the need for extended internships for prospective program directors. He suggested having a computer network bulletin board accessible to each program and staffed by persons who are up-to-date on theory, research, and applications. Via such a network, programs could obtain new information as well as share it among themselves.

Another conclusion of this study, independently arrived at and consistent with the Gordon et al. report, is that overall, the programs select the most easily identified high-potential students. As Gallagher (1985) said about the identification of gifted and talented, students in general, we tend to identify as talented those students who are obedient, attractive, and socially adept, while missing those who are talented but shy, bored, less popular, and often, of a lower socioeconomic level. Any kind of program works most easily with the former group; by primarily selecting them as participants, chances of program success are kept very high. We do not mean to deny the important service that extracurricular precollege programs provide to that group. However, in the interest of fairness, as well as in the interest of the real needs of the nation, the latter group—

Mechanisms that could enhance program development are a computer network linking programs, a system of staff internships, use of flexible methods for identifying the less-obvious high-potential students.

Programs must move beyond involving mainly the students with the most obvious high potential to involving the less easily identified talented students.

the less easily identified talented students—must definitely be assisted in greater numbers.

IN SUMMARY   Systematic evaluation of existing programs, including assessment of the effectiveness of their specific components, is important because their successful intervention strategies hold the potential for application in schools across the country. A long-term goal of the evaluation should be examination of the use of intervention program methods with talented disadvantaged and minority students who are not succeeding academically. Part 2 of this book addresses the question of what form systematic evaluation of programs might take.

Part TWO

Research Models and Results: Studies of the High/Scope Institute for IDEAS

SHERRI ODEN
ZHENKUI MA
DAVID P. WEIKART

Chapter SEVEN

The High/Scope Institute for IDEAS

PART 1 OF THIS BOOK—which described and analyzed 12 mathematics/science intervention programs—
ended with a statement of the need for a national evaluation of existing intervention programs for young people
from disadvantaged and minority backgrounds. The
goal of this evaluation would be two-fold—further fine-
tuning of existing model programs, and subsequent
widespread development of "programs that work."
Part 2 provides a model for the systematic evaluation
that is needed; its chapters describe the quantitative
and qualitative research on yet another intervention
program—the High/Scope Institute for IDEAS.[1]

The High/Scope intervention program differs
in some ways from the 12 programs described in Part 1.
For example, though High/Scope's program, like the
others, includes improving high school students' performance and motivation as they relate to science and
mathematics, it also has a wider scope than this. Therefore, before launching into a description of the empirical research, we trace the history of the program and
subject it to the same scrutiny undergone by the programs considered in Part 1.

**To fine-tune existing
and future programs for
talented disadvantaged
and minority youth, we
need to systematically
describe, analyze, and
evaluate program models.
Two empirical studies of
the High/Scope model
may lead the way.**

History of the High/Scope Institute for IDEAS

The Original Camp Program

Today's High/Scope program for talented disadvantaged high school students has its roots in the High/Scope summer camp program for talented teenagers, which David and Phyllis Weikart began over 28 years ago. The camp program, with its informal educational activities designed to engage and develop the talents and skills of promising high school students of varied economic levels, over the years drew teen participants from across the country and abroad. Its unique approach matched the needs and interests of adolescent learners by emphasizing the cognitive processes through active experiences and hands-on projects. This High/Scope camp approach has served as a program model in the design of other camp programs—the Kamehameha Schools in Hawaii and the Aga Khan Foundation U.S.A. camps serving Ismaili youth (camps like these now exist in the U.S., Canada, and the United Kingdom).

Tailoring the Camp Program for Disadvantaged Students

The current High/Scope intervention program for disadvantaged teenagers—the subject of the empirical study we are about to describe—grew out of a version of the High/Scope camp program that staff, about 10 years ago, specifically tailored to the needs of disadvantaged high-potential adolescents. This "custom-tailoring" of the program so it would serve disadvantaged teenagers came about with the encouragement and support of the Crawford, Ogemaw, Oscoda, and Roscommon (COOR) Intermediate School District in northern Lower Michigan.

The economy of the region of Michigan encompassed by the COOR Intermediate School District is dominated by agriculture, tourism, local government, and some light manufacturing, but many families in the

High/Scope's adolescent program—the High/Scope Institute for IDEAS—is an outgrowth of a 28-year-old camp program that engages talented teenagers in active learning.

About a decade ago, the High/Scope Institute's program was "custom-tailored" to serve disadvantaged high-potential students from rural areas of northern Lower Michigan.

region have low incomes due to unemployment, under-
employment, disability, and other factors. The COOR
Intermediate School District's review of students in its
high schools in the late 1970s found that a surprisingly
large number of talented low-income students, though
they had seventh- and eighth-grade achievement test
scores above the 75th percentile, did not perform up to
their potential in or beyond high school. Moreover, a
disproportionate number of these low-income high-
potential students ended up below their economically
more-advantaged peers in both postsecondary education and career achievement. Thus the COOR Intermediate School District initiated a planning process with
High/Scope to develop an intervention program—
modeled on the High/Scope summer camp program
—specifically for low-income, small-town and rural
teenagers. The school district staff hoped that such a
program would succeed in getting more of these young
people to go on to postsecondary education.

Since 1981, when this program was initiated, students from northern Lower Michigan have been recruited in their sophomore or junior year of high school
to participate in the month-long camp program, which
is held during the month of May. As in the original
High/Scope camp program, the emphasis is on participants' cognitive development in the context of
hands-on activities. Their "active learning" experiences
include not only science and mathematics but also the
humanities and applied technology and arts (in the
form of work projects). The processes emphasized
throughout camp learning experiences include individual initiation, planning, cooperation, and creative
problem solving. The program also includes exploration of career and postsecondary education opportunities.

In the residential camp environment, away from the
familiar settings of home, neighborhood, school, and
popular youth culture, students become a part of
an interdependent peer atmosphere. Through supportive interaction with counselors and program directors,

**The High/Scope Institute
for IDEAS has always
focused on mathematics,
science, humanities,
and applied technology
and arts.**

Participants in High/Scope's Institute live, learn, and work in a camp setting, where supportive staff emphasize problem solving, peer cooperation, and exploration of careers.

▾

Of U.S. teenagers living in poverty, 60% are white and 36% are black, though blacks represent only 16% of all U.S. teenagers.

▾

In 1987, the High/Scope program extended its recruitment to include both rural white students and urban black students.

▾

they can make positive strides in both self-esteem and achievement motivation.

From its start in 1981, until 1987, High/Scope's Institute for IDEAS recruited its participants as we have described—from lower-income rural and small-town, predominantly white, communities in northern Lower Michigan. Since, at that time (and even presently) about 60% of all U.S. teenagers (12- to 17-year-olds) living at or below the poverty line were white (U.S. Bureau of the Census, 1986; U.S. Bureau of the Census, 1990a), High/Scope's program chose an important population to address. However, in recent years the High/Scope program has addressed an even wider population by expanding its recruitment area to create a more diverse ethnic mix among participants.

Recruitment From Inner-City Detroit

Even though black U.S. teenagers (12- to 17-year-olds) represent 16% of all U.S. teenagers, they account for nearly 36% of all teenagers living in poverty (U.S. Bureau of the Census, 1986; U.S. Bureau of the Census, 1990a). Not surprisingly, then, the High/Scope Institute for IDEAS—the residential program for disadvantaged, talented teens—extended recruitment to include black students from Detroit's public schools. This came about in 1987, when at the request of the COOR Intermediate School District, the High/Scope Foundation expanded the adolescent program to have a multi-ethnic focus, so participants would have better preparation for the educational and occupational challenges of a diverse society.

The High/Scope IDEAS Program Today

Since students from the Detroit Public Schools responded positively to the initial invitation to attend the High/Scope camp program for high-potential teenagers, the program is now being offered regularly to

Detroit students. This ethnic diversification has enabled the program to include components aimed at fostering positive understanding and interaction between campers from the two seemingly disparate backgrounds. However, the main features of the program have remained the same, and these are presented in the remainder of this chapter, when we scrutinize them in relation to the components of an ideal intervention program, as outlined in Part 1. To draw together all the elements of the present Institute program, we also present on pp. 142–145 a program summary, like those drawn up for the other 12 intervention programs (on pp. 72–92).

The empirical results presented in the chapters following this one are, first, the results of a longitudinal study conducted with the 1982 and 1983 cohorts of former campers 5 years after their participation in the High/Scope intervention program. (This would be the High/Scope camp program when it served disadvantaged rural and small-town students with high potential.) Second, we present results of a more recent evaluation of the High/Scope Institute for IDEAS. This 1990 evaluation, which took place when the program had expanded to serve a more ethnically diverse population, reveals that except for racial differences, the two groups of disadvantaged students served—the white, rural and small-town teens and the black, urban teens—are highly similar to each other in family background.

High/Scope's Intervention Program— How It Measures Up to the Ideal

Part 1 of this book listed four characteristics essential for students' academic achievement: (1) *knowledge of one or more specific fields*, (2) *effective problem-solving strategies*, (3) *motivation*, and (4) *effective communication skills*. It also discussed obstacles that minority students face in relation to developing these characteristics. Some of the

Continued on page 146

Now, with its diverse participants, the High/Scope Institute for IDEAS has a new aim—fostering positive understanding and interaction between black and white teenagers.

One study focuses on participants from the High/Scope camp program of the early 1980s. The other focuses on the 1990 camp cohort, a more diverse group of high-potential teenagers.

PROGRAM SUMMARY

Clinton, Michigan

High/Scope Institute for IDEAS

Stated objectives:
To foster students' motivation, confidence, and skills for the pursuit of higher education by addressing goals in (1) personal development; (2) achievement motivation through educational and career focus; and (3) social-cognitive development in planning, experimenting, and creative problem solving; within these major goal areas, to work on five specific process objectives for participants:

- Developing a more positive attitude towards academically oriented learning in science, mathematics, humanities, and the arts
- Developing orientation and motivation towards postsecondary education and training
- Developing greater self-esteem, personal initiative, and leadership ability
- Improving the ability to work cooperatively
- Developing ability to learn, interact, and build relationships in a diverse group of participants who are from different ethnic/cultural and regional communities

Program structure:
The program, which is residential and month-long, takes place in late spring each year at the High/Scope Camp and Conference Center in Clinton, Michigan. Staff include a director, an assistant director, and a group of young-adult counselors (some of whom are former campers) who are upper-level college students, recent college graduates, or graduate students with various fields of expertise. The director and assistant director have a minimum of 5 years of program staff experience. Counselors receive a week of advance training in instructional methods that utilize active participation and group processes—an approach that emphasizes "thinking-based achievement" as opposed to "routinized skills," as recommended by the Commission on the Skills of the American Workforce (National Center on Education and the Economy, 1990). This approach is very unlike the more formalized, teacher-directed instructional method used in most high school classrooms. Periodic staff meetings also add to the counselors' understanding of program methods and goals.

The 45–55 program participants, most of whom attend a single session of the program in their freshmen, sophomore, or junior year of high school, range from 14 to 16 years of age. Each year a few former participants are invited to return and serve as senior campers.

Financial support for the program includes Job Training Partnership Act (JTPA) funds from Michigan's Region 7B Employment and Training Consortium. It also includes funds from several Detroit-area foundations (Matilda R. Wilson Fund, The Skillman Foundation, and Detroit Edison Foundation, among others). The rationale for the provision of JTPA funds is that job training should include supporting higher education outcomes, rather than just short-term skill training for low-paying, limited jobs.

Participation:
The program serves low-income, high-

potential adolescents from rural northern Lower Michigan and, since 1987, also from urban Detroit (about 25 participants from each area). JTPA guidelines are used to determine low-income eligibility (whether family income is at the federal poverty threshold). Students who are from low-income families and have scored (in grades seven through nine) in the top quartile on at least one subtest of a national standardized achievement test make up the eligible pool. (For Detroit participants, the family economic backgrounds are more varied, with most, however, being from low-income families.) At the time of program enrollment, because many participants are students who have low aspirations or are not achieving up to their potential, participants' grades may range from low to very high.

Administrators, counselors, and teachers from the school districts and the JTPA office, after working together to identify eligible students who would seem most likely to respond well to the program, set up group sessions at which the program director from High/Scope describes the program and encourages students to attend. Students (with their families) make their own decisions about whether or not to participate. The month-long release time required for their participation is arranged in cooperation with their schools districts.

General activities:
The major program components include *instructional activities*, *project-oriented activities*, and *group-process enhancement*. A new program component beginning in 1992, *youth services activities*, will facilitate students' involvement in service activi-

ties upon returning to their schools and communities.

The *instructional activities* can take the form of "workshop" sessions in both small-group and individual time slots (students can make their own choices among these time slots). In a given week, groups of 4–8 campers sign up with a staff member for 2–18 hours of instruction on a topic. In the workshop sessions, application of concepts is stressed; students are not graded; and staff act as resources and guide student exploration through careful questioning that allows students to discover "answers" through experimentation. Students schedule, plan, execute, and present their work to their peers. Field trips (to museums, plays) are another type of instructional activity. Instructional activities cover a variety of academic areas: natural and physical sciences, computer operations, mathematics, writing, music, drama, art, and folk dance.

The *project-oriented* activities include (1) work projects and (2) evening programs. Group "work projects" involve program participants in physical labor and applied technology or arts, as several students, together with a staff member, cooperate in constructing a permanent contribution to the camp (a potter's wheel, a solar panel, a bridge, an observatory, a trout pond). The students plan the work project, including effective use of time, materials, tools, and skills. Through such projects, campers learn that work is difficult and often requires steady determination and cooperation.

The "evening programs" include a weekly musicale (an evening of short student-developed performances in song, dance, reading, or drama) and student presentations (of outcomes of their workshop or work project efforts). Also, once each week, a council is held, wherein students gather around a fire and reflect on such topics as obstacles to achievement, peer pressure, or goal setting.

The component of *group-process enhancement* pervades all program activities. Projects are designed so that everyone's effort is needed. Group composition is regularly mixed to give all students maximum exposure to many different participants. While friendships are encouraged, cliques and romances are discouraged. Cooperative effort and behavior is supported and encouraged; negative, exclusive, competitive behavior is discouraged. Activities include new challenges and successes for everyone, and this promotes a common bond among participants.

In summary, the program includes these general activities:

To improve knowledge and communication
- Application of knowledge from academic areas that makes facts and concepts meaningful to students
- Presentation of newly gained knowledge
- Exposure to active learning and problem solving
- Exposure to educational and cultural events and institutions
- Opportunities to gain a greater understanding of options for the future (college, vocational/technical postsecondary training)
- Practice in ways to communicate more clearly

To improve problem-solving strategies
- Cooperative effort, which can be more efficient than individual or competitive approaches and can promote a variety of prosocial behaviors

- Staff guidance and support that models problem-solving behaviors

To increase motivation
- Discussion and sharing activities in which students learn to identify ideas, feelings, attitudes, and goals
- Peer-group work and socialization
- Challenges and leadership opportunities appropriate to participant age and ability level
- Young-adult counselors who are positive and supportive and act as role models
- Opportunities to exercise respect for individual differences in personality and background (with no negative comments accepted or tolerated)

Summer program:
Unlike most intervention programs, which take place after school or on Saturdays and may or may not have a summer session, this program is an intensive month-long residential program taking place in late spring.

Teacher training:
High/Scope Foundation staff, together with camp staff, have begun a cooperative training program with Detroit secondary school faculty. The training, which consists of workshops on "students' active learning" and "class organization for student leadership," challenges educators using traditional teacher-directed educational methods to reform their schools.

Parent involvement:
Staff meet with parents prior to the camp session. Also, on a visitor day midway through the session, parents are encouraged to come and learn about their teenagers' experiences.

Assistance with college admission:
Field trips are taken to nearby universities to see classrooms, libraries, bookstores, dormitories, and a financial aid officer. Also, a "college night" evening program is provided to discuss postsecondary education options, whether academic or vocational/technical, in college or in the military. Focus is on financing, admission, course loads, testing, time-management, and dealing with success or failure. Staff

also talk informally with individuals about personal, educational, and career goals.

Financial assistance:
Participants meet with a financial aid officer and receive individual counseling with staff on planning for future educational expenses. At camp, participants also receive peer counseling on interviewing for and keeping jobs.

Continued from page 141

disadvantaged and minority students participating in High/Scope's camp program may face many of the same or similar obstacles. The major obstacles discussed in Part 1 are these:

- A strict reliance on standardized test scores for identification of high-potential students
- The predominantly abstract nature of typical classroom instruction and subject matter
- Teachers' lack of focus on individual learning styles
- The absence of role models for achievement
- The absence of peer support for academic achievement
- A lack of parent and student knowledge about college admission and financial aid
- Inadequate advising and counseling
- Teachers' low expectations for disadvantaged or minority students' achievement
- Inadequate teacher-student communication
- The curriculum's lack of a multicultural view

Components

IDEAL PROGRAM

Involving Changes for Schools

1. Advanced courses
2. Improved laboratories and resources
3. Hands-on problem-solving exercises
4. Lessons and practice in using different learning styles
5. Multidimensional screening procedures to identify high potential
6. Teacher/staff training and retraining
7. A professional support-group to work with teachers and students
8. Curriculum modification to reflect minority contributions
9. Remediation/enrichment in communication skills
10. Restructuring of schools
11. Residential summer classes
12. Partnership between parents and schools/teachers

Involving Changes for Students

1. Coaching in test-taking skills
2. Coaching in study and time-management skills
3. Tutoring for and by students
4. Exposure to professionals in work settings
5. Interaction with role models
6. Personal counseling and discussions about racism
7. Establishment of a peer support-group
8. Assistance with college admission/financial aid

In Part 1, consideration of students' obstacles led to a listing of components—goals and methods—of the ideal intervention program (see Table 5.1 on page 94). Organized according to whether they involve changes for schools or changes for students, these components are summarized again on these pages (see insert).

The 12 programs reviewed in Part 1, when measured against the components of an ideal intervention program, each proved to be exemplary with respect to some but not all of the 20 components listed here. High/Scope's adolescent program likewise addresses some of the components more thoroughly than others. For descriptive purposes, we now examine the High/Scope program in the light of each component:

Components Involving Changes for Schools

Component 1: Advanced courses; Component 2: Improved laboratories and resources. Workshop activities and projects in the High/Scope program are designed to challenge students to use higher-level, advanced thinking skills. Adequate science laboratory settings and other resources are developed according to the requirements of the projects that the students and program staff decide upon. The staff, referred to as counselors, are all upper-level college students and recent college graduates. Their fields of expertise include a variety of areas, such as physics, biology, dance, photography, mathematics, dramatic arts, music, and computer science.

Component 3: Hands-on problem-solving exercises; Component 4: Lessons and practice in using different learning styles. The High/Scope program is especially strong in regard to these components. The program provides continual hands-on, or active, learning and discovery experiences in a workshop context. Experience with different learning styles is readily fostered in the camp's informal learning atmosphere: Individual participants' see their unique contributions as highly valued in the program's small-group problem-

We first apply the *ideal-program components* from Part 1 in describing the High/Scope program.

▾

A strong feature of the High/Scope program is its "hands-on" problem-solving process, which pervades both academic and nonacademic activities.

▾

solving activities covering a range of subject areas—science, mathematics, writing, and the arts.

Component 5: Multidimensional screening procedures to identify high potential. The selection process for the High/Scope program is flexible. Economically disadvantaged students who tested in approximately the upper quartile on at least one subtest of a standardized national achievement test in middle or junior high school are considered eligible. Students' actual grades at the time of their acceptance into the program may range considerably, from low to very high. Some students with low or mixed grades (and perhaps problem behavior) are recommended by teachers or counselors because they seem to have potential for considerably higher achievement.

Component 6: Teacher/staff training and retraining; Component 7: A professional support-group to work with teachers and students. Program staff include a director, an assistant director, and a group of counselors who are upper-level college students, college graduates, and graduate students trained in various academic specialties, including mathematics and science. The counselors receive 5 days of training by High/Scope Foundation staff prior to the program. Also, staff meetings are conducted throughout the program to enhance the counselors' understanding of program goals and methods and to give feedback on communication and problem-solving approaches used by counselors. With the aim of supporting the same kinds of learning processes in the schools that students engage in at High/Scope's camp, for the past 2 years, High/Scope Foundation and camp staff have provided workshops to Detroit secondary school teachers. The major topics of these workshops are "students' active learning" and "class organization for student leadership." (See Component 10: Restructuring of schools.)

Component 8: Curriculum modification to reflect minority contributions. Since the High/Scope program's "curriculum" is not a traditional one in the sense of a body of knowledge being transmitted to

The High/Scope Institute's selection process identifies talented low-income students by their upper-quartile achievement test performance and by teacher recommendations. Low grades or problem behavior do not necessarily eliminate a student from consideration.

As an outgrowth of the Institute for IDEAS, High/Scope collaborates with Detroit public school teachers to conduct workshops emphasizing students' active learning and classroom leadership.

students by their textbooks or teachers, this component does not apply in the same way as it might apply to a school. However, because of the active nature of the High/Scope program, students observe "live" the contributions of counselors and campers from diverse cultural backgrounds. Participants are particularly encouraged to offer one another instruction as well as support for their contributions.

Singing, folk dancing, and evening programs provide a history of shared experiences for everyone. At the same time, students and staff are encouraged to share their various views, interests, and experiences, so everyone can appreciate the unique individual contributions that result from participants' diverse cultural backgrounds.

Component 9: Remediation/enrichment in communication skills. In workshops, students practice ways to communicate more clearly, especially in social-situation problem solving, in relating to parents and peers, and in securing and sustaining employment. Program participants also practice leadership communication skills by taking on responsibilities in the operation of the program.

Component 10: Restructuring of schools. As an offshoot of the camp program, the High/Scope Foundation, working with Detroit secondary school faculty, recently began a cooperative training program consisting of teacher workshops on "students' active learning" and "class organization for student leadership." The training encourages educators to depart from traditional, teacher-directed methods of instruction and to turn towards the active-participation, problem-solving approach that is used by staff in the High/Scope intervention program.

Component 11: Residential summer classes. The program takes place in the late spring for one month in an attractive residential camp setting that includes adequate space for participants and staff to live, learn, and work together.

Component 12: Partnership between parents and

schools/teachers. This has not been a major focus of the program. There are communications between parents and staff, and there is a visitor day, when parents are encouraged to come and learn about the experiences their children are having.

Components Involving Changes for Students

Component 1: Coaching in test-taking skills; Component 2: Coaching in study and time-management skills. Students and staff participate in a "college night," in which test-taking and time-management skills are examined in group and individual discussion contexts. The issues that arise are further pursued by the counselors in their informal discussions with students.

Component 3: Tutoring for and by students; Component 4: Exposure to professionals in work settings. There is no formal tutoring component. However, as they interact one-to-one and in small groups with counselors who have had recent college education, the students further develop their academic skills. On field trips to universities and colleges, in particular, students interact with professionals in those settings. Contact with industry professionals is not a regular feature of the program.

Component 5: Interaction with role models. In their informal leadership roles, the counselors model new ways for students to think about themselves, to develop their potential, and to seek various career paths. In addition to camp counselors serving as role models, several rural and urban campers from the previous spring's camp attend the program as "senior campers." Students' opportunities for interaction with role models occur naturally in program activities, particularly in such activities as the individual and small-group discussions where campers and counselors consider such topics as striving for independence, goals for the future, and ways to reach one's goals.

Component 6: Personal counseling and discussions about racism. Time is set aside in the program

The Institute's informal academic activities, social activities, work projects, field trips, and group and individual counseling provide students with continuous opportunities for learning from role models—counselors, senior campers, fellow campers.

for individual and group discussions about obstacles to achievement. As participants learn to trust one another and the counselors, they reveal their goals and their perceptions of the obstacles they face, including discrimination and prejudice. Counselors and fellow-participants provide individual and group peer support, respectively, along with practical suggestions for coping with discrimination and prejudice.

Component 7: Establishment of a peer support-group. This is an especially strong component of the High/Scope program. Cooperative learning and teamwork foster peer support in the "workshop" sessions that are oriented towards academic content. Also, in their applied technology or applied arts "work projects," students experience peer support as they work together to design and construct some permanent contribution to the camp setting—a walking bridge, a gazebo, a stage-lighting system, a wall mural.

Groups are regularly mixed so a student's coworkers vary. As a result, the students have as much exposure as possible to working and interacting with everyone in the program. Although friendships are encouraged, exclusive cliques are not. In peer groups, cooperative group effort and positive behaviors are supported and encouraged, and negative, exclusive, and competitive behaviors are discouraged. Students tend to form a common bond from living and participating in challenging new activities together in a setting that is free from the trappings of popular youth culture—television, radio, movies, and fast foods.

Component 8: Assistance with college admission/ financial aid. As mentioned earlier, a "college night" provides students and staff with a chance to discuss career and college plans and strategies, including financial aid strategies, for reaching these goals. There are also college campus tours to nearby universities, where students see classrooms, labs, libraries, and dormitories and visit with a financial aid officer.

Overall, the High/Scope program taps nearly all the components of the ideal intervention program out-

An especially strong feature of the program is the supportive peer atmosphere. In noncompetitive academic workshops and other activities, students experience cooperation and mutual support for achievement behaviors.

Another strength of the IDEAS program is its setting, which is free of popular youth culture— television, radio, fast food, and so forth.

lined in Part 1, and it is especially strong with regard to some components. However, thus far we have provided only one kind of qualitative information about the High/Scope program—information such as one might obtain by interviewing and observing program staff and participants. To give a more complete picture of the program's impact, we now turn to a quantitative study of program effectiveness, a longitudinal study of former participants in the High/Scope program.

A Follow-Up Evaluation Study

The next six chapters of Part 2 present a study comparing how young adults who attended the High/Scope adolescent intervention program compare, 5 years later, with young adults who have highly similar backgrounds and ability but never attended such a program. As noted in Part 1 of this book, those who determine the future direction of our country's educational programs need evaluation research data on existing intervention programs for talented disadvantaged students. The longitudinal study presented in the following chapters can perhaps serve as a model for this much-needed research.

High/Scope's longitudinal study of its IDEAS program may serve as a model for much-needed research on programs for disadvantaged high-potential youth.

▼

A Brief Summary of the Study

The purpose of the evaluation was to examine how former High/Scope campers compared, as young adults, to noncampers of similar age, family background, and talent. As a first step, to achieve a comparison group, former campers were matched with same-age young adults who as adolescents had been eligible to attend the High/Scope program but did not. (This eligibility, as described in detail elsewhere, was based on low income and high achievement test scores.)

Data collection consisted of interviewing both the "camper" and the "noncamper" groups approximately 5 years after the former's High/Scope experience. Interview questions included collecting additional family background data from both groups. Several major aspects of young adulthood and background were surveyed in the evaluation: family background; educational status; employment status; income and other economic resources; marital and offspring status; economic difficulty; problem behavior (including delinquency); role models and other sources of influence; attitudes about personal causation and achievement; and future plans and aspirations.

It was expected that compared with the young-adult noncampers, the young adults who had attended the High/Scope camp as teenagers would be making more positive progress in higher education—that they would (1) have attained a higher educational level, (2) have a higher current educational status, and (3) have more plans for further education. All major variables were examined to provide an explanatory model of factors related to the disadvantaged talented student's pursuit of higher education.

How We Proceed

In the next chapter, we explain the longitudinal study method. This is followed by an analysis of the comparability of the camper and noncamper groups in Chapter 9. Chapters 10 and 11 examine campers' and noncampers' current status indicators, such as education, military service, marital/offspring status, employment, and financial difficulties. Chapter 12 looks at various sources of influence from family, school, and other experiences.

As will become clear from the data presented in Chapters 9 through 12, the major finding of this 5-year follow-up of former High/Scope campers is that the majority of them—73% of the camper group versus 55% of the comparison group—go on to postsecondary education. What accounts for such outcomes? Chapter 13 attempts to answer this question by using the data from earlier chapters to derive a causal model that explains

In a 5-year follow-up, the longitudinal study found that 73% of campers, versus 55% of noncampers, had completed some post-secondary education. The study also examined the factors that led to this outcome.

▾

High/Scope's 1990 program evaluation adds a qualitative examination of how the IDEAS program's processes affect participants.

———— · ————

how variables act together as positive factors or negative factors to determine students' later educational outcomes.

In Chapter 14 we present an evaluation of the 1990 High/Scope program—a study of one program cohort before and after their camp experience. We look at participants' family and school backgrounds, their perceptions of the program experience, and the impact of the program on their other-ethnic-group relationships and their future educational plans. The 1990 study produced both quantitative and qualitative data.[2] Among the latter are participant case studies based on interviews. The young people and the aspirations portrayed in these profiles add an important human dimension to our research.

ENDNOTES

1. High/Scope's residential program for teenagers has been named the High/Scope Institute for IDEAS to convey the program's emphasis on Initiative, Diversity, Expectations, Achievement, and Service.

2. There has been considerable discussion in educational research about the merits of quantitative versus qualitative approaches (Shulman, 1988; Jacob, 1987). The research (on 12 model programs) presented in Part 1 used qualitative approaches—observations from field notes, interviews, and case studies, and analysis of program features. The High/ Scope longitudinal study (Chapters 8–13) used mainly quantitative methods—achievement test scores, frequency data from categorical levels, and average ratings from scales— along with some qualitative data, particularly concerning subjects' role models and influential experiences. The 1990 High/Scope program evaluation (Chapter 14), used more qualitative data, collected from observations and in-depth interviews, but also included quantitative data collected from participant questionnaires.

Chapter **EIGHT**

The Study Method

THIS CHAPTER DESCRIBES the interview instrument used in the longitudinal study of the High/Scope Institute for IDEAS. Study methods are then specified, including data collection, subject selection and location, and interview training and procedures. The chapter concludes with a brief summary of data coding, which is described in greater detail in the Appendix.

The Interview Instrument

As mentioned earlier, data collection consisted of interviewing the camper and noncamper groups. The 263 questions and response items in the interview instrument[1] are based mainly on the goals of the High/Scope program (p. 142) and on other subject background and attitudinal factors to be discussed in this chapter.

The content areas for the interview questions about the subjects are these:

1. *Family background* from childhood through high school, including education, employment, family composition, household type, and perceptions of parental attitudes
2. *Current family status*, including marital status, number of offspring, residence (parental home or elsewhere)

The interview with study subjects pertained to school and family background, current educational status, employment and economic situations, marital status, attitudes, and future aims.

▼

3. *Experiences and achievement* in education, work, and the community, including such experiences as delinquency or criminal activity

4. *Sources of economic support,* including self, family, government

5. *Attitudes* towards self, work, education

6. *Perceived sources of influence*, including family, school, and other experiences

7. *Future goals and plans*

Over half the instrument's questions reflect content from areas 1–4. These questions, and also some questions dealing with areas 5–7, were designed using methodology developed and employed with adolescents and young adults over the last 10 years in High/Scope's long-term studies assessing the effectiveness of educational programs. Over the years, the content and focus of items, the formats, and the survey methods have been designed based on the following: reviews of relevant theoretical and empirical research; pilot work conducted specifically for various High/Scope studies; findings obtained from ongoing research at High/Scope; and consultation with the University of Michigan Institute for Social Research (ISR), which has developed methodology and research on adolescence and transitions to adulthood.

The High/Scope studies used as a basis for this study's methods include a follow-up assessment of High/Scope Perry Preschool children as teenagers and young adults—at ages 15, 19, and 28 years (Berreuta-Clement, Schweinhart, Barnett, Epstein, & Weikart, 1984)—and a follow-up assessment of former High/Scope Head Start children as young adults. Included in each of these studies is a sequence of questions on locus of control of success—on whether positive outcomes are perceived by subjects to come from internal or external sources. These questions are derived from the study instrument for the Monitoring the Future study, a national longitudinal survey of youth in the United States, which is a continuing study at the University of

> **Interview questions were largely based on previous research with adolescents and young adults done by High/Scope and by other researchers.**
>
> ▾

Michigan Institute for Social Research (e.g., Bachman, Johnston, & O'Malley, 1986).

What role attitudes and expectancies play in causing outcomes is unclear, but evidence indicates that changes towards more-optimistic attitudes and expectancies can result in constructive behavioral change. This relates to our interest in whether High/Scope program objectives influenced campers' later situations and behaviors, particularly their obtaining higher education, being employed, having aspirations, and making related plans for the future. Therefore, in addition to the questions derived from other studies, we constructed questions on subjects' achievement motivation and self-esteem, including questions about setting high goals, solving problems, and being persistent. The format for these questions and the rating scales for subjects' responses are based on research by Harter (1982). The content of these questions is based on the goals of the High/Scope program. (To have a clear basis for these newly constructed questions, we ascertained the objectives of the High/Scope Institute for IDEAS from High/Scope's annual reports about the program and from discussions with present and previous camp leaders.) The questions seek to determine whether gains in education, for example, may be associated with specific types of achievement attitudes, role models, or peer relations.

For the present study, the "role model" questions adapted from previous High/Scope studies were modified to ask subjects about several behaviors related to program goals (for example, persisting at a task, working cooperatively with others). Subjects were asked to identify any persons or experiences influencing them in a major way in connection with each of these behaviors.

To evaluate comprehensibility of the interview questions, we first conducted an interview with approximately 50 pilot subjects and subsequently refined the interview questions. The resultant interview instrument, with newly developed and revised items, was then used with approximately 20 additional pilot

Questions on subjects' attitudes about their achievement were modified from previous studies to reflect the High/Scope camp program goals.

▼

The interview also queried subjects about sources of influence—role models and other experiences— on achievement-related issues.

▼

subjects, and this led to a final revision of the content and format of the interview questions.

Method of Data Collection

Interviews were conducted by telephone.

▾

A survey employing the interview instrument was the major methodology used to gather the data. A survey may be administered by subjects filling out a questionnaire or by an interviewer filling out a form while asking questions from a questionnaire. In the latter case, with most populations, the interview may be conducted by telephone. With populations or individuals who have substantial difficulties in comprehension or establishing rapport, interviews are typically conducted in person. However, since the subjects in the present study were known to be high achievers on standardized academic tests, we expected that this study's subjects would have little or no difficulty with comprehension on the telephone. This certainly proved to be the case; interviewers found little or no difficulty in communication or comprehension, and all interviews were conducted by telephone. Though participation in the camp program was not revealed as the reason for the telephone call, the majority of subjects were very receptive to being interviewed.

Selection of Subjects for the Camper Study Group

Program-eligible subjects were low-income, high-potential students recommended by school staff. Their grades ranged from low to high.

▾

The *camper group* of study subjects were selected from a pool of former students from 16 schools in the COOR Intermediate School District and surrounding areas. All members of this pool had been determined eligible to participate in the High/Scope camp program according to the following criteria:

   • *They had been identified as low-income.* Job Training Partnership Act program guidelines were used to identify students as being from "low-income families," as determined by the federal poverty threshold or as indicated by their eligibility for enrollment in the National School Lunch Program (NSLP) or in some other federal, state, or local public-assistance program.

• *They had been identified as having high potential.* They had scored, in the later grades of middle or junior high school, in the top quartile of at least one mathematics or reading subtest of a national standardized achievement test, specifically the *California Achievement Test, Iowa Test of Basic Skills, Stanford Achievement Test,* or *Metropolitan Achievement Test.*

• *They had been recommended by school staff as being able to profit from the camp program.* Students whose behavior or attitudes were very problematic were either not recommended or not encouraged to participate unless their school staff thought they could respond constructively to the program.

• *Their high school grades were not necessarily indicative of their potential.* The eligible pool of students had grades at the time of enrollment that ranged from low to very high grades.

During their high school careers, students who met all four of these program eligibility criteria were initially invited to informational meetings with the High/Scope Camp director and school district staff. Not all eligible students enrolled in the program. Some students, though invited, did not attend the informational meetings, and others who did attend did not follow through with enrollment. There were a variety of reasons for their non-enrollment, including the camp having space limitations and students having other commitments or competing interests.

The pool of camp-eligible students (including campers and noncampers) were from the high schools' graduating classes of 1983, 1984, 1985, and 1986 (subjects were considered to be members of a year's graduating class

For a variety of reasons, not all eligible students enrolled in the High/Scope camp program.

Ninety-two subjects from the 1982 and 1983 High/ Scope camp program cohorts formed the *program study group.*

▾

regardless of whether they had persisted until graduation). In all, 92 students from these classes participated in the camp program in either 1982 ($n = 43$) or 1983 ($n = 49$). The 1982 camp cohort included 6 campers who had returned from the 1981 camp to serve as senior campers, but these individuals are not included in the 43 campers just cited for 1982. Of the 1982 camp cohort, 7 (5 males and 2 females) are campers who returned as senior campers in 1983; all 7 participated in the study and are counted in the 43 members of the 1982 cohort. Of the 49 members of the 1983 cohort, 2 male and 2 female campers returned to serve as senior campers in 1984. The combined cohorts of 43 and 49 campers from 1982 and 1983, respectively, will hereafter be referred to as the *camper study group* ($n = 92$).

Selection of Subjects for the Comparison Study Group

Great care was given to selecting, from the pool of former students who were camp-eligible, a comparison group that was highly similar to the camper group. First, the names of the camper study group and the potential comparison subjects were placed on their respective lists and each identified as to gender, school, and graduation cohort (for example, male, Roscommon High School, 1984 graduation cohort). This was done to achieve the same balance of males and females within each graduating class for the camper group and the comparison group. Students who had attended camp were matched with noncampers (with respect to gender, school, and graduation cohort) except in a few cases where, for example, the pool contained only one or no noncampers for a particular school in a given year. In these cases, noncampers with closely matching characteristics were selected from another area high school.

Next, within each block of students (for example, all those identified as male, Roscommon High School, 1984 graduation cohort), reading and mathematics achievement test percentile scores were used to organize the student names so students matching each other most closely on scores were placed next to each other on the lists. To select the comparison group subjects, in each same-gender, -school, and -cohort block, the noncamper student whose reading and math achievement test scores were closest to that of a given camper subject was matched with that camper. With only a few exceptions, the percentile scores of a matching camper and noncamper were each within only a few points of the average of the two students' scores. Whenever any additional noncamper also matched scorewise with a camper, such a noncamper was also included in the comparison group. When a camper had reading and math scores that were quite discrepant, a noncamper with similarly discrepant reading and math scores was matched with that camper whenever possible.

For some campers, because of school testing schedules or policies, no test scores were available. Matching noncampers for such campers were selected randomly from across the range of pool students within that camper's school or within a school that was considered to be comparable.

It should be noted that although the camper and noncamper subjects appear to be well matched, because camp participants were not randomly selected, we cannot entirely rule out potential *self-selection* factors. That is, there may have been something different, to begin with, about students in the camper group and students in the pool of potential comparison subjects. For example, those who attended camp may in some way—in family background, personality, or motivation—differ from those camp-eligible students who (1) were invited but chose not to attend the camp information seminar, (2) attended the seminar but decided they did not want to go to camp, (3) were invited but could not participate in camp because of such conflicts as being on a sports team, having a part-time job, or lacking parental permission. Self-selection bias is a common

> The *comparison study group* comprised 104 young adults who had been camp-eligible as teenagers. They matched program subjects with respect to gender, high school, graduation cohort, and achievement test scores.

limitation in the study of any program that is primarily designed not to conduct a research study, but to serve particular needs of its participants. For the High/Scope Institute for IDEAS, which is such a service-providing program, random selection of participants is not feasible or desirable.

The finally determined study subject groups included 196 subjects from the 1983–1986 high school classes from 16 schools. This included 92 former campers from the 1982 and 1983 camp cohorts ($n = 43$ and $n = 49$, respectively) and 104 noncampers.

Procedures for Subject Location and Initial Contacts

Locating subjects approximately 2–3 years after high school required using a variety of strategies.

▼

A number of strategies were employed to try to locate the former students who were now 2 or 3 years out of high school. For campers, it was approximately 5 years since they had participated in the High/Scope IDEAS program. Subject location and subsequent interviewing took place over a 3-year period. The strategies and sources used to find the former students, their parents, their spouses, or other relatives were these:

- Regional, local, and state telephone directories and operators
- School lists obtained by the COOR Intermediate School District, with last-recorded addresses and telephone numbers of the students' parents
- Addresses and telephone numbers provided from the Michigan State Bureau of Driver and Vehicle Records
- Forwarding addresses provided by the United States Postal Service
- Letters and postcards sent to the former students or to their parents
- Letters forwarded to the students by their parents, in cases where parents were unwilling to provide student addresses or telephone numbers

• Letters inviting students or their parents to make a collect call to interviewers for further information about participation
• Letters sent to students that included either stamped return postcards or envelopes with forms requesting the student to give an address, telephone numbers, and best times to call
• Interviewed students who were willing to give information about the whereabouts of former classmates
• Calls or visits by a High/Scope staff member (a former camp counselor) to local schools and communities to develop contacts (with parents and with a few former students)

Five interviewers were contracted specifically for the project, and after interviewer training, they attempted to locate subjects by calling telephone numbers provided from the sources just mentioned. School-record address and telephone lists provided the main basis for initiating contacts with the former students. From their homes, the interviewers called the former students at various day and evening times. When addresses were available, postcards giving a brief description of the study were mailed to the interviewees prior to the telephone contact.

Minimizing Bias

To avoid any association of the survey with High/ Scope—to minimize study bias—interviewers presented the study as a survey being conducted by a research foundation (referred to in all communications as the Survey of Michigan Youth Center) with the endorsement of the COOR Intermediate School District. Furthermore, for approximately 80% of interviews, the interviewers themselves were not aware of the camper or noncamper status of the subject prior to the interview. As interviewers worked with researchers to locate and interview the majority of subjects interviewed from each group and to achieve a balance in numbers of

To minimize potential bias in subjects' responses, we used procedures to prevent study subjects from relating the High/Scope research division (in Ypsilanti, MI) to the camp program (in Clinton, MI).

▼

subjects from each camper cohort, the interviewers did become conscious of the group status of some individuals. This did not appear to be a problem, since the interviewers were not informed about the specific aims of the study. Interviewers were instructed not to refer to a subject's group status in talking with the subject before or during the interview.

Subject Location and Response Rates— Problems and Strategies

Locating and contacting former students was more difficult than anticipated. Even where the school supplied 1- and 2-year-old addresses and telephone numbers of former students, many of these addresses proved to be out-of-date and provided no leads to follow. School personnel were not in a position to devote the time and effort needed to trace former students through family, friends, and associates. However, several school counselors and Region 7B's Employment and Training Consortium in Michigan provided additional help in tracing subjects.

While most of the students were found to still be living in or very close to their original towns, many were living elsewhere in Michigan or out of state— attending college or serving in the military or living with a spouse in the military. Others had merely moved to a town neighboring their original town. The subjects hardest to find were those who either were not in close contact with their families or were living with someone on a temporary basis.

One High/Scope Foundation research assistant helped by calling and setting up interview appointments with subjects who had been especially difficult to schedule for an interview. To facilitate this scheduling, the research assistant sent follow-up letters written on High/Scope stationery. Of those who finally were interviewed, 8 campers and 11 noncampers received these follow-up letters about the Survey of Michigan Youth.

Locating subjects in the northern Lower Michigan region in their young adult years presented many more obstacles than expected.

As previously mentioned, another High/Scope Foundation staff member, a former camp counselor, used his contacts, making visits and calls to former school staff and others in the local communities and calling or visiting parents and a few camper and noncamper subjects. In this way, he was able to obtain telephone numbers and addresses for the interviewers to pursue. In a few cases, he had to identify himself and his workplace, using his own and High/Scope's name, rather than just mentioning the Survey of Michigan Youth and the COOR Intermediate School District. In these cases, he was instructed to simply say that he was helping out in the location of former students from the school district for the High/Scope Foundation's research division, which conducts various studies. Of the study subjects who were eventually interviewed, this staff member directly or indirectly helped to find 21 out of 66 campers (32%) and 17 out of 64 noncampers (27%).

Interviewers indicated that although some subjects did make a direct link between the interviews and the High/Scope Educational Research Foundation (located in Ypsilanti, Michigan), they did not appear to link the survey project to the camp program (located in Clinton, Michigan). Interviewers felt that most subjects were very candid and confident that their answers would be coded and not made available to anyone other than the researchers, who would separate respondents' names from their interview forms, per standard survey procedure.

To achieve representativeness of the camper and noncamper samples, all subjects in each study group—camper and noncamper—needed to be pursued to ensure sufficient and comparable proportions for each group. Although the noncamper group was somewhat overenrolled to assure a sufficient number of subjects, it was necessary to interview a roughly equal number of "hard-to-get" students in both groups, and it was important to interview a majority of each study group.

Of the 92 campers in the 1982 and 1983 camp cohorts, 1 had recently died, reducing the camper study

The goal was to locate similar proportions of the two study groups—including similar proportions of "hard-to-get" subjects. Of the camper group, 81% were found; of the noncamper group, 84% were found.

group to 91. Of these 91 camper subjects, 74 (81%) were directly or indirectly located and 17 (19%) were not located. Of those 74 located, 1 (1%) directly refused to be interviewed; 7 (9%) could not be scheduled for an interview or were not reachable (after over 12 telephone calls and various letters), or their parents would not facilitate our communication with them; and 66 (89%) were interviewed. Out of the entire camper study group ($n = 91$), 73% were interviewed.

Of the 104 comparison study group subjects, 1 had recently died, reducing the sample to 103. Of these 103 subjects, 87 (84%) were directly or indirectly located and 16 (16%) were not located. Of those 87 located, 10 (11%) directly refused to be interviewed; 13 (15%) could not be scheduled or were not reachable to schedule, or the parents would not facilitate our communication with them; and 64 (74%) were interviewed. Out of the entire comparison study group ($n = 103$), 62% were interviewed.

The main difference here is not in the two location rates (81% for campers versus 84% for noncampers) but in the two response rates for those located (89% of the located camper group and 74% of the located noncamper pool). Of those subjects located who were hard to reach or hard to schedule for an interview, a greater percentage of campers than noncampers finally agreed to be interviewed; there was only 1 direct refusal in the camper group, compared with 10 in the noncamper group. Many other comparison subjects did not refuse outright but would consistently fail to be home at the scheduled times.

The awareness of some camper subjects that the High/Scope Foundation was conducting the study may have had some kind of influence on their willingness to be interviewed. This may have been particularly the case among those interviewed towards the end of the study, when the High/Scope Foundation staff member did location work or when High/Scope Foundation stationery was used. The somewhat higher camper response rate may indicate a desire to cooperate with a

It was important to interview comparable proportions of the located campers and the located noncampers. For the campers, this was 89%; for the noncampers, 74%.

High/Scope project, which could also have affected the candidness of camper subjects' responses in interviews. Still, greater willingness to be interviewed could also be an indication that in general, campers were in more positive life situations than noncampers. At the same time, if being in a positive life situation makes one more willing to be interviewed, the noncampers' lower response rate could have acted as an advantage to the comparison group, since those noncampers who were willing to be interviewed could *also* have been ones with positive life situations.

To further address such potential bias issues, we also conducted statistical analyses of the data on key variables (that is, education, employment, public assistance use, and criminal activity) on the last 10% of subjects interviewed, which was the "hard-to-get" group. The results indicated that these latter interviewees were not significantly different from the rest of the sample on any of these variables.

After being interviewed, subjects received a $15 check in the mail as compensation for completing the interviews, and this incentive appeared to be positively received by both camper and noncamper subjects.

Interviewer Training and the Interview Procedure

Five interviewers, who had been hired for the project on a part-time basis, interviewed subjects by telephone from their homes. These interviewers were trained by one of the researchers, using a manual developed for the interview. First, in individualized training sessions, interviewers practiced a script explaining to subjects the purpose of the study. Acceptable digressions from this script, in response to a subject's questions, were part of the training and were listed in the manual for interviewers. Interviewers also participated in role play with interview questions and responses and conducted prac-

Although the somewhat higher response-rate from campers may indicate more cooperation from campers than noncampers, data analysis results indicate the response-rate difference did not have a major effect on results.

▼

High/Scope hired five part-time interviewers to conduct the telephone interviews out of their homes.

▼

In their training, interviewers learned how to locate subjects by telephone, inform subjects about the study and its procedures, and conduct interviews.

▾

Interviewer training involved use of a training manual, role play, and pilot interviews.

▾

tice interviews with pilot subjects. The researcher provided individualized supervision and gave feedback on the interviewers' tape-recorded practice interviews. In particular, the researcher reviewed the tape-recorded practice interviews for accuracy, objectivity, voice quality, and pacing.

At the conclusion of training, interviewers were given lists of study subjects to contact and invite to be interviewed. Using all the available location information, the interviewers telephoned subjects, made inquiries, and tried to interview each subject at the initial call or made arrangements to interview the subject at another time.

Before asking subjects to be interviewed, interviewers explained that the purpose of the interview was to learn more about the current lives of young adults and about how their previous school experiences may have contributed to their present life situations—their jobs, educational activities, and economic resources. The interviewers also informed subjects of the confidentiality procedures: that respondents' names would be separated from interview forms, that only researchers would see the data, and that study identification numbers would be used. Interviewers returned completed interview forms to High/Scope to be checked by one of the researchers for clarity and consistency of procedure and to be processed for data coding and analysis.

Data Coding and Analysis

In all, 1107 variables were directly derived from responses to the 263 interview questions. To develop the variable codes, researchers listed all responses from approximately 40 subjects to determine a set of category codes that would represent the range of subjects' responses. They then used these data, along with other anticipated responses, to develop the final category codes. A coding manual specifying all interview questions, corresponding variables, and coding options was developed, along with a computer data-entry program. In a separate study of 25% of the coded and entered data, the accuracy of coding and data entry was found to be in the 95%–99% range. Finally, routine, standard checks were made in cleaning the data throughout data analyses by checking for out-of-range or miscoded values for each variable.

SUMMARIZING THIS CHAPTER   The methods employed in this longitudinal follow-up study included (1) an *interview* based on the goals of the High/Scope program and previous research on youth; (2) methods of *subject selection* that matched campers and noncampers according to demographic factors and achievement test scores; and (3) subject *locating, contacting, and interviewing techniques* designed to minimize subject self-selection biases. In all, approximately two thirds of both program group and comparison group subjects were interviewed in the follow-up study.

In the next five chapters, we present our analyses of the interview data, beginning with analyses of subjects' family background characteristics in Chapter 9. Our analyses are presented for two purposes—to describe the long-term outcomes of the High/Scope program and to suggest a model for examining the effectiveness of programs for talented disadvantaged youth.

For data analysis purposes, researchers developed a manual for coding study subjects' interview responses.

—————— • ——————

ENDNOTES

1. The interview instrument is available from the authors upon request.

Chapter NINE

The Study Sample: Background Comparability of Campers Versus Noncampers

THE INITIAL PHASE of the longitudinal study data analysis was to examine the comparability of the camper and noncamper study groups on a number of variables where we expected them to be highly similar. Although these variables are typical ones employed in looking at group comparability, we will discuss how they are especially relevant to our study of educational outcomes. We looked at

1. *Comparability of sample sizes*—first, with respect to campers versus noncampers; then, for the camper sample subgroups, with respect to gender, high school class year, and age at time of interview; and then, for the camper sample, with respect to years since attending the 1982 or 1983 camp programs
2. *Comparability of mathematics and reading achievement test percentile scores*
3. *Comparability of family household factors*, including subjects' birth order and the composition of the households subjects grew up in
4. *Comparability of family socioeconomic factors*, including parents' education and employment, and families' additional sources of income (from relatives and public assistance)

9

At the study's outset, the camper and noncamper groups were examined for background comparability.

Table 9.1

**Male and Female Camper
and Noncamper Final Sample**

Group	No. (%) of Campers	No. (%) of Noncampers	Total
Males	31 (47%)	34 (53%)	65 (50%)
Females	35 (53%)	30 (47%)	65 (50%)
Total	66 (100%)	64 (100%)	130 (100%)

Comparability of Sample Sizes

Campers Versus Noncampers

The subjects who were interviewed, the final study sample ($N = 130$), consisted of nearly equal numbers in the camper ($n = 66$) and noncamper ($n = 64$) samples. As can be seen in Table 9.1, there were also comparable numbers of males and females [$\chi^2(1) = .49$, which is not a significant difference or a trend].[1]

Camp Cohorts

Of the camper sample, 34 (52%) attended the 1982 camp program and 32 (48%) attended the 1983 camp program, with comparable numbers of males and females within each camp cohort. This included 15 males and 19 females in the 1982 cohort, and 16 males and 16 females in the 1983 cohort.

Ages of Subjects

High school class year. Table 9.2 shows, in each sample, the numbers and proportions of subjects who belonged to each of the high school graduation classes (irrespective of whether they persisted until graduation). In addition to being from two different camp cohorts, camper subjects also attended camp at different ages, which resulted in a sampling from four high school class years.

Table 9.2 reveals a nonsignificant trend of more campers being from the later high school class years and more noncampers being from the earlier high school class years [$\chi^2(3) = 7.60, p < .10$]. To create two class-year groups for later comparisons with other variables, we combined the numbers of subjects in class years 1983 and 1984 and compared them with the numbers of subjects in the 1985 and 1986 class years. This grouping also yielded a nonsignificant class-year trend [$\chi^2(1) = 3.07, p < .10$].

Ages at time of camp enrollment and time-interval since camp. Table 9.3 shows the ages of subjects for each

Table 9.2

High School Class Year Membership of Groups

High School Class Year	No. (%) of Campers by Camp Cohort			No. (%) of Noncampers
	1982	1983	Total	
1983	6 (18%)	—	6 (9%)	2 (3%)
1984	12 (35%)	4 (13%)	16 (24%)	29 (45%)
1985	15 (44%)	13 (41%)	28 (42%)	23 (36%)
1986	1 (3%)	15 (47%)	16 (24%)	10 (16%)
Total	34 (100%)	32 (100%)	66 (100%)	64 (100%)

camp cohort at the time they were participating in camp. Table 9.3 data yields no significant differences in age distribution between the two camp cohorts at the time of camp participation. Comparing 14- plus 15-year-old, 16-year-old, and 17- plus 18-year-old subjects yielded no significant differences [$\chi^2(2)$ = .50, nonsignificant].

For the campers who were interviewed (n = 66), we also considered the amount of time since their camp enrollment. For those in the 1982 camp cohort, the time-interval range since camp was 4 to 7 years, with an average of 5.03 years. For campers in the 1983 camp cohort, the range was 3 to 7 years, with an average of 4.75 years. There were no significant differences between groups for the time-interval since camp.

Ages of subjects at time of follow-up. Next we examined the ages of subjects in the camper versus noncamper groups at the time of their interviews. Table 9.4 indicates the age distributions for the campers from both camp cohorts and for the noncampers. For the 1982 and 1983 camp cohorts combined, the exact age at time of interview ranged from 18.9 to 25.2 years, with an average of 21.0 years (SD = 1.45). For noncampers, the range was from 19.1 to 24.1 years, with an average of 20.9 years (SD = 1.15). The overall median was 20.8 years (SD = 1.30). The nonparametric two-sample median test on these data indicated no significant difference between the camper and noncamper groups.

When considering ages (exact age at time of interview) of subjects according to gender, we found that for male campers, the range in age was 19.2 to 23.7 years, with an average of 20.9 years (SD = 1.17). For female campers, the range was from 18.9 to 25.2 years, with an average of 21.2 years (SD = 1.67). For male noncampers, the range was from 19.2 to 24.1 years, with an average of 20.8 years (SD = 1.10). For female noncampers, the range was from 19.1 to 24.0 years, with an average of 21.0 years (SD = 1.22). For each group, the nonparametric two-sample median test for males versus females indicated no significant difference for age.

> Subjects from both groups were interviewed at an average age of 21 years.

Table 9.3

Campers' Ages at Time of Institute Enrollment

No. (%) of Subjects by Age

Camp Cohort	14 yr	15 yr	16 yr	17 yr	18 yr	Total
1982	0 (0%)	11 (32%)	13 (38%)	9 (27%)	1 (3%)	34 (100%)
1983	2 (6%)	11 (34%)	11 (34%)	8 (25%)	0 (0%)	32 (100%)
Total	2 (3%)	22 (33%)	24 (36%)	17 (26%)	1 (2%)	66 (100%)

Table 9.4

Ages of Subjects by Group at Time of Interview

No. (%) of Subjects by Age

Group	Age 18	Age 19	Age 20	Age 21–23	Age 24 or more	Total
1982 camp cohort	1 (3%)	8 (24%)	10 (29%)	12 (35%)	3 (9%)	34 (100%)
1983 camp cohort	0 (0%)	8 (25%)	9 (28%)	15 (47%)	0 (0%)	32 (100%)
Camper total	1 (1%)	16 (24%)	19 (29%)	27 (41%)	3 (5%)	66 (100%)
Noncamper total	0 (0%)	19 (30%)	16 (25%)	26 (42%)	2 (3%)	63 (100%)

Note. One noncamper's interview date was not available.

Comparability of Mathematics and Reading Scores

Achievement test scores were used as part of the criteria for identifying students from low-income families as talented, and therefore eligible for the High/Scope IDEAS program. Low-income students who had at least one subtest percentile score (in mathematics or reading) in the upper quartile were included in the camp-eligible pool. As noted in the previous chapter, across the various schools, several different standardized achievement tests had been used to obtain the scores. For some students in the camp-eligible subject pool, no achievement test scores were available to the researchers. In the final study sample, 49 campers (74%) had available scores from both reading and mathematics subtests, 42 noncampers (66%) had available mathematics subtest scores, and 43 noncampers (67%) had available reading subtest scores. The mean and median percentile test scores for these subgroups are shown in Table 9.5.

The two-sample median test indicated no significant differences between groups on reading subtest percentile scores ($Md = 79$) or mathematics subtest

Table 9.5

Achievement Test Scores—Mean, Standard Deviation, and Median

Group	Reading			Mathematics			Combined		
	M	*SD*	*Md*	*M*	*SD*	*Md*	*M*	*SD*	*Md*
Campers	77.71	15.97	79.0	83.02	10.67	82.0	80.37	10.78	80.5
Noncampers	79.33	12.56	79.0	83.38	13.21	87.0	81.33	8.45	82.5

Note. For campers, $n = 49$ for reading and mathematics, and for noncampers, $n = 42$ for mathematics and $n = 43$ for reading.

percentile scores (Md = 86). For female campers, reading scores ranged from 46 to 99, with an average of 78.7, and math scores ranged from 51 to 98, with an average of 81.1. For male campers, reading scores ranged from 42 to 99, with an average of 76.4, and math scores ranged from 68 to 98, with an average of 85.6. For female noncampers, reading scores ranged from 44 to 97, with an average of 80.7; their math scores ranged from 62 to 99, with an average of 85. For male noncampers, reading scores ranged from 48 to 98, with an average of 78.2; their math scores ranged from 33 to 98, with an average of 81.9.

The two-sample median test indicated no significant differences for reading scores between male and female campers ($Md = 79$), and for math, there were also no significant differences (Md = 82). For noncampers, there were no significant differences between males and females (Md, reading = 79; Md, math = 87). For the campers and noncampers combined, there was a non-significant trend for a gender difference on the median test at a level of $p < .11$ for math scores, where more females than males fell below the combined-group median of 86. When we examined high school class cohorts, years '83/'84 versus years '85/'86, for reading and math scores, first for campers and then for noncampers, we found no significant differences for high school class cohorts.

On the two-sample median test with reading and math scores, the group medians yielded no significant differences at, below, or above the median for campers, noncampers, or high school class cohorts. For campers, the median test indicated no significant differences among the high school class cohorts on reading and math scores at, below, or above the median. For the noncamper high school class cohorts, there was a trend bordering on significance ($p < .056$) indicating that the '85/'86 class cohorts had higher mathematics scores than the '83/'84 class cohorts.

Both groups had average scores in the upper quartile on standardized mathematics and reading achievement tests.

IN SUMMARY Campers were very comparable to noncampers on several critical variables, including age at time of interview, high school class cohort, and mathematics and reading percentile scores.

Comparability of Family Household Factors

When considering family household factors, we looked at the following: subject's birth order, number of members in subject's household, and household structure (number of parents in household).

Birth Order of Subjects

Table 9.6 shows the distribution of subjects according to *birth order*. This variable was of interest because some research indicates that birth order is related to educational achievement, primarily that greater achievement

Table 9.6

Distribution of Subjects by Birth Order

Birth Order	No. (%) of Campers	No. (%) of Noncampers
1st-born	23 (35%)	22 (34%)
2nd-born	15 (23%)	18 (28%)
3rd-born	8 (12%)	7 (11%)
4th-born or later	20 (30%)	17 (27%)
Total	66 (100%)	64 (100%)

is seen in first-born or only children (e.g., Adams & Phillips, 1972).

The birth orders are fairly well distributed in the study sample, with about one third of the sample being first- born, about one third being second- or third-born, and the others being later-born. The sample contained just 1 only child, a camper. There was no significant difference in birth order for campers versus noncampers.

Size of Parental Household

Large family-size is a factor that may contribute to economic difficulty: In 1983, the U.S. poverty rate for families with 1 or 2 children was about 15%, while families with 3 or 4 children had a 28% poverty rate, and families with 5 or more children had a 56% poverty rate (U.S. Congressional Research Service & U.S. Congressional Budget Office, 1985). Therefore, determining study subjects' household sizes was of interest to us, since family economic conditions can have an impact on children's educational outcomes.

The camper and non-camper groups had similar distributions for household composition factors.
▾

Table 9.7 concerns the number of children in the households study subjects grew up in. The largest family-size for campers was a 10-child family, whereas for noncampers, the largest was a 6-child family. Maxi-

Table 9.7

Distribution of Subjects by Number of Children in Parental Household

| Group | \multicolumn{4}{c}{Number of Children in Household} | |
	1–2	3–4	5–6	7 or More	Total
No. (%) of campers	22 (33%)	26 (39%)	12 (18%)	6 (9%)	66 (100%)
No. (%) of noncampers	21 (33%)	33 (52%)	10 (16%)	0 (0%)	64 (100%)

mum family-size was larger for the camper subjects, and camper families appeared to have more children overall. However, we combined the higher two categories in Table 9.7 into one category—families with 5 or more children—resulting in 3 levels of family size. Then the comparison of campers versus noncampers on these 3 levels indicated no significant difference or trend [$\chi^2(2) = 3.11$, nonsignificant].

Household Structure

It is important to examine household structure, because a number of studies have found that one-parent households, often referred to as single-parent families or households, are subject to economic and other related difficulties (Duncan, 1984; McLoyd & Wilson, 1990). Tables 9.8 and 9.9 show the numbers of subjects who at important points in their lives had one or both parents in the household.

There were no significant differences or trends for household structure in the subjects' early and elementary years (Table 9.8) or in their teenage years (Table 9.9). Comparing two-parent versus one-parent households, chi-square tests indicated no significant differences or trends between campers and noncampers.

It is interesting to note in Table 9.8 that although some increase occurred in one-parent households across subjects' childhood years, most households remained stable. However, by the time subjects were teenagers (Table 9.9), 30% of both camper and noncamper households had become one-parent households.

There were a few cases in which, although a subject lived in a single-parent household, additional adults lived in the household. There were 2 subjects in the noncamper group who at age 5 had 1 adult, in addition to the parent, in the household. Among age-5 campers, 1 subject had 1 additional adult, 1 subject had 2 additional adults, and 1 subject had 3 additional adults in the household. Only 1 subject in the noncamper group and 2 subjects in the camper group had an additional adult

As young children, most study subjects lived in two-parent households. By the time they were teenagers, 30% of their families had become single-parent families.

Table 9.8

Household Structure: Early and Elementary Years

Group	No. (%) With Both Parents	No. (%) With Mother Only/Other	Total
Age 5			
Campers	60 (91%)	6 (9%)	66 (100%)
Noncampers	59 (92%)	5 (8%)	64 (100%)
Elementary years			
Campers	55 (83%)	11 (17%)	66 (100%)
Noncampers	56 (87%)	8 (13%)	64 (100%)

Note. The "other" category refers to 1 camper who had no father or mother in the household but had 2 grandparents, and to 1 noncamper whose mother had an unrelated adult living in the household.

Table 9.9

Household Structure: Teenage Years

Group	No. (%) With Both Parents	No. (%) With Mother Only	No. (%) With Father Only	No. (%) With Other	Total
Campers	45 (68%)	18 (27%)	2 (3%)	1 (2%)	66 (100%)
Noncampers	44 (69%)	16 (25%)	3 (5%)	1 (2%)	64 (100%)

Note. The "other" category refers to 1 camper who lived with 2 grandparents but no parents, and to 1 noncamper who lived with 1 unrelated adult.

in the household during the elementary school years. For the teenage years, only 1 additional household adult was reported per group, and 1 camper reported 2 additional adults.

IN SUMMARY The ranges in total household sizes, including all members, adults and children, are shown in Table 9.10. The frequencies and proportions of household sizes for each group are similar, and there are no

Table 9.10

Distribution of Subjects, Across Ages, by Number of Household Members

Group	Number of Household Members				
	2–3	4–5	6–7	8 or More	Total
Age 5					
No. (%) of campers	7 (11%)	29 (44%)	19 (29%)	11 (17%)	66 (100%)
No. (%) of noncampers	4 (6%)	35 (55%)	18 (28%)	7 (11%)	64 (100%)
Elementary years					
No. (%) of campers	3 (5%)	30 (45%)	21 (32%)	12 (18%)	66 (100%)
No. (%) of noncampers	1 (2%)	35 (55%)	21 (33%)	7 (11%)	64 (100%)
Teenage years					
No. (%) of campers	9 (14%)	31 (47%)	16 (24%)	10 (15%)	66 (100%)
No. (%) of noncampers	8 (12%)	39 (61%)	12 (19%)	5 (8%)	64 (100%)

significant differences or trends. However, there appears to be more of a tendency for campers than for noncampers to come from the largest households. This may indicate that campers' families had fewer economic resources or more household stress, and as mentioned earlier, these factors can affect educational outcomes for children.

Comparability of Family Socioeconomic Factors

Since we did not have information about income levels of subjects' parents, we examined several variables to assess areas of potential socioeconomic differences. We have already examined in this chapter some variables relevant to family economic level or need. These were the variables relating to household composition. Other income-relevant variables to be examined next include educational levels of subjects' parents, the employment and occupations of parents, families' use of public assistance, and families' use of other economic assistance.

Educational Background of Subjects' Mothers

Maternal educational background was a variable of interest to us because the education of the mother is often found to be an important factor affecting the level of a child's educational achievement (U.S. Congressional Budget Office, 1987). Looking at less-than-high-school, high school, and postsecondary educational levels, in a comparison of campers versus noncampers, we found no significant differences or trends in mothers' educational levels. In Table 9.11, we see that approximately 90% of study subjects' mothers at least graduated from high school, and this includes nearly 24% of all the mothers having achieved at least some level of college education.

Educational levels of subjects' parents were similar for the two study groups.

▾

Table 9.11

Educational Background of Subjects' Mothers

Highest Level Achieved by Mother	No. (%) of Campers	No. (%) of Noncampers
Less than high school	8 (12%)	7 (11%)
High school	41 (62%)	43 (67%)
Postsecondary technical/vocational, or some college	4 (6%)	2 (3%)
2 years college	9 (14%)	8 (13%)
4 years college	4 (6%)	4 (6%)
Total	66 (100%)	64 (100%)

Educational Background of Subjects' Fathers

We were also interested in fathers' educational backgrounds; in households where the father has at least some education beyond high school, we would expect to find more ability to provide economic resources and educational role models for children. Table 9.12 presents the educational levels of fathers of subjects in the study sample.

A somewhat higher proportion of noncamper fathers than camper fathers had at least some postsecondary education. However, in comparing the camper versus noncamper distributions for fathers with less than high school, high school, some postsecondary education or college, and college degrees, no significant difference or trend was found [$\chi^2(3) = 5.60$, $p < .15$].

Employment of Fathers

For noncampers' fathers, years of employment during the subject's lifetime ranged from 0 to 18 years, with an average of 10.7 years ($SD = 6.71$); for campers' fathers, years of employment ranged from 0 to 18 years, with an average of 7.73 years ($SD = 6.88$). The median test indicated that this was a significant difference ($Md = 9.0$, $p < .01$). A chi-square test was also administered by grouping the number of years employed into these categories: never, 1–3 years, 4–6 years, and so on, up to 16–18 years. It appeared that fewer noncamper fathers never worked (14% of noncamper fathers versus 29% of

Table 9.12

Educational Background of Subjects' Fathers

Highest Level Achieved by Father	No. (%) of Campers	No. (%) of Noncampers
Less than high school	23 (40%)	16 (26%)
High school	23 (40%)	34 (56%)
Postsecondary technical/ vocational, or some college	4 (7%)	0 (0%)
2 years college	3 (5%)	3 (5%)
4 years college	4 (7%)	6 (10%)
Graduate education	1 (2%)	2 (3%)
Total	58 (100%)	61 (100%)

camper fathers) and more noncamper fathers than camper fathers worked a greater number of years. This was a nonsignificant trend indicating, again, greater years of employment for noncamper fathers [$\chi^2(6) = 12.44$, $p < .10$].

As previously discussed, in both camper and noncamper groups, single-parent households, predominantly ones headed by the mother, did not occur to any extent until the subjects were in their teen years, and there was no significant difference between groups in this incidence. This is important to mention, since the data reported here about fathers' employment include even subjects who had no father present in the household. If a subject knew the employment status of his or her nonresident father, that data was included in the variable, even if it was unclear whether the father had contributed to the economic resources of the household. If a subject did not know his or her father's employment status, preferred not to mention it, or said the father was deceased, that data was not included in the variable.

Table 9.13 shows the types of jobs held by fathers in their employment history. The job types in Table 9.13 are presented in descending order, going from highest-paying (at the top) to lowest-paying. These job types were classified according to the U.S. Bureau of the Census (1971) occupational classifications. The Appendix further discusses the definitions and combinations of occupations used here. Comparing campers and noncampers for types of first jobs of fathers, we find no significant differences. Subsequent job totals indicate the numbers of fathers who moved on to hold second, third, and even fourth and fifth jobs. Overall, camper fathers held 111 jobs. Noncamper fathers held 104 jobs.

Examination of the overall numbers of jobs of fathers reveals that the jobs classified in the *professional* through *transportation* categories were 70 out of the 111 jobs for camper fathers (63%) and 86 out of the 104 jobs for noncamper fathers (84%). *General labor* through *other* kinds of jobs included 41 out of the 111 jobs for camper fathers (37%) and 18 out of the 104 jobs for noncamper

Table 9.13

Job Types of Subjects' Fathers

Job Description	No. (%) of Campers Reporting Father's:				No. (%) of Noncampers Reporting Father's:			
	1st Job	2nd Job	3rd Job	4th/5th Job	1st Job	2nd Job	3rd Job	4th/5th Job
Professional/ managerial	9 (15%)	7 (22%)	1 (11%)	2 (22%)	10 (16%)	5 (15%)	3 (33%)	0 (0%)
Sales/ secretarial	1 (2%)	1 (3%)	0 (0%)	1 (11%)	4 (7%)	4 (12%)	2 (22%)	0 (0%)
Skilled crafts/operative & transportation	33 (54%)	12 (37%)	2 (22%)	1 (11%)	35 (57%)	19 (58%)	4 (44%)	0 (0%)
General labor/office/ factory cleaning	8 (13%)	8 (25%)	5 (56%)	3 (33%)	9 (15%)	1 (3%)	0 (0%)	0 (0%)
Food service/ sales work	2 (3%)	0 (0%)	0 (0%)	0 (0%)	1 (2%)	1 (3%)	0 (0%)	0 (0%)
Health aide/ personal assistant	1 (2%)	0 (0%)	0 (0%)	0 (0%)	0 (0%)	1 (3%)	0 (0%)	0 (0%)
Guard/personal cleaning/clerical	6 (10%)	2 (6%)	1 (11%)	2 (22%)	0 (0%)	2 (6%)	0 (0%)	1 (100%)
Other	1 (2%)	2 (6%)	0 (0%)	0 (0%)	2 (3%)	0 (0%)	0 (0%)	0 (0%)
Total	61 (100%)	32 (100%)	9 (100%)	9 (100%)	61 (100%)	33 (100%)	9 (100%)	1 (100%)

fathers (17%). This pattern of jobs suggests an economic advantage for noncampers. However, the data were not sufficient to directly assess this pattern, because some subjects may not have indicated changes in job levels when their fathers moved up but stayed at the same place of work. We also know that subjects' recollection and awareness of their parents' jobs varied.

Employment of Mothers

Of noncampers, 19 out of 63 (30%) reported mothers never working outside the home; 1 subject did not know for sure. Of campers, 19 out of 57 (33%) reported mothers never working outside the home; 9 did not know for sure. The mothers' occupations in Table 9.14 are also presented in descending order, going from the highest-paying (at the top) to the lowest-paying.

The majority of the camper mothers appeared to be in the lower-paying jobs, whereas the majority of the noncamper mothers were in the higher-paying jobs. However, when we combined the occupational levels in Table 9.14 into 4 levels, there were no significant differences between groups.

As with the fathers' jobs, we can get some further indication of the difference between camper and noncamper mothers' jobs by combining job classifications. The number of mothers' jobs classified in the *professional* through the *transportation* categories were 43 out of the 112 jobs for camper mothers (38%) and 52 out of the 87 jobs for noncamper mothers (60%). *General labor* through *other* jobs included 69 out of 112 for camper mothers (62%) and 35 out of 87 for noncamper mothers (40%). When we compare these two groupings of job classifications for campers versus noncampers, we find a higher level of jobs for noncamper mothers. This finding is another indication of economic advantage for noncampers, although the data were not sufficient to directly assess the levels and changes, because of limited subject recollection and awareness, as was the case with fathers' jobs. It also appears that fewer noncamper than camper mothers were employed. This may be related to the tendency for more-highly-paid positions among noncamper fathers, but there is no direct evidence on this.

Greater parental employment gave noncampers some economic advantage over campers.

Other Sources of Economic Support

Relatives. Subjects were asked if any relatives gave the family money in times of economic difficulty. It is interesting that while 11 subjects in the total study sample did not know, 10 campers (compared with 4 noncampers) indicated that they *had* received help from relatives.

Public assistance and welfare use. Subjects were asked how often their families had used public assistance or welfare. Table 9.15 shows the extent of family

Table 9.14

Job Types of Subjects' Mothers

Job Description	No. (%) of Campers Reporting Mother's:				No. (%) of Noncampers Reporting Mother's:			
	1st Job	2nd Job	3rd Job	4th/5th Job	1st Job	2nd Job	3rd Job	4th/5th Job
Professional/ managerial	4 (9%)	1 (4%)	2 (12%)	2 (10%)	4 (9%)	3 (12%)	0 (0%)	0 (0%)
Sales/ secretarial	11 (23%)	7 (25%)	5 (29%)	3 (15%)	18 (40%)	5 (19%)	5 (42%)	3 (75%)
Skilled crafts/operative & transportation	4 (9%)	3 (11%)	1 (6%)	0 (0%)	9 (20%)	4 (15%)	1 (8%)	0 (0%)
General labor/office/ factory cleaning	6 (13%)	3 (11%)	0 (0%)	0 (0%)	0 (0%)	2 (8%)	1 (8%)	0 (0%)
Food service/ sales work	8 (17%)	2 (7%)	1 (6%)	2 (10%)	7 (16%)	9 (35%)	2 (17%)	0 (0%)
Health aide/ personal assistant	8 (17%)	3 (11%)	2 (12%)	1 (5%)	4 (9%)	2 (8%)	2 (17%)	1 (25%)
Guard/personal cleaning/clerical	4 (9%)	6 (21%)	3 (18%)	1 (5%)	3 (7%)	0 (0%)	0 (0%)	0 (0%)
Other	2 (4%)	3 (11%)	3 (18%)	11 (55%)	0 (0%)	1 (4%)	1 (18%)	0 (0%)
Total	47 (100%)	28 (100%)	17 (100%)	20 (100%)	45 (100%)	26 (100%)	12 (100%)	4 (100%)

The noncampers also reported less family use of public assistance.

▾

use of welfare during the subjects' elementary school years. Significantly more campers than noncampers reported frequent use of welfare in their families during the elementary school years [$\chi^2(2) = 8.63, p < .05$.].

Table 9.16 shows family welfare use during subjects' teenage years. Here, there is a different pattern between groups than in the earlier years, but there is not a significant difference or a trend between campers and noncampers. Therefore, at the time of the camp experience, the teenage years, the economic situations of the groups were comparable. Even so, the pattern does suggest an economic advantage for the noncamper group. Correlations between frequency of family welfare use in the elementary school years and in the teen years were significant—for campers, $r = .68$; for noncampers, $r = .65$; for the combined groups, $r = .67$; $p < .001$. This indicates that in general, those families who had economic difficulty in subjects' early years also tended to have economic difficulty in the subjects' teenage years. The magnitude of the correlation, however, indicates that families did some shifting between

Table 9.15

Family Welfare Use During Subjects' Elementary School Years

Extent of Welfare Use	No. (%) of Campers	No. (%) of Noncampers
Never	38 (58%)	49 (77%)
1–4 times	14 (21%)	12 (19%)
Frequently	14 (21%)	3 (5%)
Total	66 (100%)	64 (100%)

categories of need from subjects' elementary to teen years.

It is important to further consider the life circumstances of those families who used public assistance or welfare during the subjects' teenage years. In particular, we examined welfare use and parents' employment in single-parent versus two-parent households. Among campers whose families were on welfare at some point during the subjects' teenage years, 13 out of 34 campers (38%), compared with 10 out of 22 noncampers (45%), came from single-parent households. Comparing campers versus noncampers, we found no significant differences or trends for the number of single- versus two-parent households using welfare or for the number of employed versus unemployed families using welfare.

Regarding parental employment among families using welfare during subjects' teenage years, 16 out of 34 campers (47%), compared with 13 out of 22 noncampers (59%), had one or more employed parents. Across these groups, 14 out of 23 parents (61%) in single-parent households were employed, a slightly greater proportion of the noncamper group (7 out of 10) than of

Table 9.16

Family Welfare Use During Subjects' Teenage Years

Extent of Welfare Use	No. (%) of Campers	No. (%) of Noncampers
Never	32 (48%)	42 (66%)
1–4 times	20 (30%)	12 (19%)
Frequently	14 (21%)	10 (16%)
Total	66 (100%)	64 (100%)

the camper group (7 out of 13). It is interesting that for two-parent households, 15 out of 33 of both groups combined (45%) reported having an employed parent—6 out of 12 noncamper households and 9 out of 21 camper households. There was no significant difference in the number of employed parents in single- versus two-parent households using welfare.

One further question to consider is whether the single-parent households were more likely than two-parent households to use welfare. To address this question, campers and noncampers from families that used welfare were combined and compared with those never on welfare. Of the 39 single-parent households, 23 (59%) had been on welfare, compared with 33 out of 90 two-parent households (37%), indicating a significant difference [$\chi^2(1) = 5.51$, $p < .05$]. Overall, approximately 60% of single parents nevertheless were employed.

The use of public assistance at some point in families' lives is probably the clearest indicator of economic differences between the groups, because it indicates households are living at the poverty threshold. However, a one-to-one correspondence between need and use should not be made, since some welfare-eligible families may have opted not to use welfare. Also, families differed in the amount of back-up economic resources they had from other family members. The greater use of welfare may mean fewer economic resources, especially for younger families. Welfare use may imply a different attitude towards being on welfare, towards education, and towards employment. In later sections, we will examine the potential relationship between family use of welfare and the subject's own use of welfare.

SUMMARIZING THIS CHAPTER Camper and noncamper groups were highly comparable on all major variables, thus allowing for further comparisons between groups regarding later educational achievement and other life outcomes. However, since we found a statistical trend (more years of employment among

Except for the noncampers' slight economic advantage, the two study groups were highly comparable—in achievement test scores, family background, age, and gender.

noncamper fathers) and one significant difference (more-frequent welfare use among campers' families), there was some suggestion of economic advantage for the noncamper group. Economically related background variables are thus included and examined in subsequent analyses of campers' and noncampers' educational outcomes. We would expect that campers' educational outcomes 5 years after the High/Scope program would be undermined or hampered, compared with those of the noncampers, because of the economic advantage in the noncampers' backgrounds. In the next chapter, we begin to analyze the subjects' educational outcomes.

ENDNOTES

1. In the analyses presented in Chapters 9 through 15, we report findings to be statistically *significant* (typically on two-tailed tests) when the obtained probability levels are $p < .05$ (we sometimes even specify $p < .01$ or $p < .001$, when obtained). We report findings to be *nonsignificant trends* when the probability levels are in the range $.05 < p < .10$. Conventional procedures for nonparametric and parametric statistical tests were employed. For a discussion of specific nonparametric tests, see Siegel (1956).

Chapter TEN

Life Choices—
Education, Military

THE MAJOR FINDING of the longitudinal study of
the High/Scope Institute for IDEAS program is that
significantly more of the students from the High/Scope
program—73% of campers versus 55% of noncampers—
went on to higher education. The present chapter is an
in-depth exploration of this finding.

We begin with an examination of the educational
status of camper and noncamper subjects at the time of
interview—the educational levels they had attained, the
degrees they had earned, their enrollment situations
and major areas of study, and their long-term educational plans. Then, in this chapter and the next, we look
at the life situations of subjects—whether they were in
military service, whether they were married, how many
children they had, what employment they had found,
and what economic resources and difficulties they had.
All these life-situation factors are considered as they
relate to subjects' educational status.[1]

Educational Status of Subjects

High School Completion or the Equivalent

As shown in Table 10.1, the high school dropout rate was
2% for campers and 8% for noncampers (1 camper and

Subjects' choices—
education, the military—
were considered in relation
to their life situations—
marriage, employment,
economic resources.

▾

Most of the study's high-potential subjects (over 95% in each study group) completed high school or the GED equivalency.

▾

5 noncampers). Two of the noncamper dropouts subsequently passed the high school equivalency exams (the General Educational Development Tests—GED). By the time of interview, the rate of high school or GED completion was 98% for campers and 95% for noncampers.

The high school/GED completion rate reported here was high for the overall sample, indicating that in general, subjects' abilities and motivation did carry them at least through a high school level of education. Their rates of high school dropout (meaning the campers' 2% and the noncampers' 8%) were in the same range as rates for the study subject population—specifically, as the reported rates from the 1983–84 Michigan Department of Education (cited in Verway, 1987) for these northern Lower Michigan counties: Arenac, Clare, Crawford, Gladwin, Iosco, Ogemaw, Oscoda, and Roscommon. As shown in Table 10.1, the noncamper dropout rate was above the average across these northern Lower Michigan counties, whereas the camper dropout rate was below the average. Since both camper and noncamper groups have above-average academic ability as indicated by their achievement test scores, this finding about the noncamper dropout rate was somewhat unexpected.

It should be noted that the average northern Lower Michigan dropout rate cited here is comparable to that of other nonurban areas in north-central regions of the United States (Chronicle of Higher Education, 1991).

Table 10.1

**1983–84 High School Dropout Rates
for Region and Study Sample**

Average Regional Rate	Camper Rate	Noncamper Rate
6%	2%	8%

The first real challenge for talented, low-income students living in areas such as these is reaching at least a high school education. Then, going beyond into some technical or academic education is another challenge, but a real possibility, as this study's results show.

When asked the reason for dropping out of high school, no subjects who had dropped out indicated pregnancy, finding school work too hard, advice from others, failing grades, school expulsion, economic problems, family moves or illness, psychological problems, or drug or alcohol addiction. The only reasons given included having a negative feeling towards school, getting married, or having a personal illness or injury.

Education Paths Beyond High School

The decisions that a young person makes within 1 or 2 years after high school in terms of education, marriage and family, and employment may well set a life course (U.S. Bureau of the Census, 1989; Spanard, 1990). First we look at study subjects' decisions regarding education, as shown in Table 10.2 on the next page.

The overall picture of educational attainment of campers versus noncampers by the time of their interviews is shown in Table 10.2. The data for the two *postsecondary education* categories in the table show that significantly more campers (73% versus 55% for noncampers) went on to postsecondary education $[\chi^2(1) = 4.58, p < .05]$. Explanation of what is included in each of these postsecondary categories follows:

Among the postsecondary education reported by subjects, it was sometimes difficult to determine whether subjects were taking courses leading to a 2-year or 4-year degree. Thus, in Table 10.2, we make this distinction: The *postsecondary education* category *vocational/technical/college* includes subjects who pursued education at a postsecondary vocational or technical school, a military college, or a community college and subjects who had only 1 year of undergraduate courses at a 4-year college or university. The category *college*

However, significantly more campers than noncampers (73% versus 55%) went on to obtain some postsecondary education.

▼

Table 10.2

Educational Attainment at Time of Interview

Highest Level Attained	No. (%) of Campers			No. (%) of Noncampers		
	Males	Females	All	Males	Females	All
Secondary education						
Less than high school	0 (0%)	1 (3%)	1 (2%)	2 (6%)	1 (3%)	3 (5%)
High school or equivalent	11 (35%)	6 (17%)	17 (26%)	14 (41%)	12 (40%)	26 (41%)
Secondary total	11 (35%)	7 (20%)	18 (27%)	16 (47%)	13 (43%)	29 (45%)
Postsecondary education						
Vocational/ technical/college	11 (35%)	16 (46%)	27 (41%)	12 (35%)	8 (27%)	20 (31%)
College	9 (29%)	12 (34%)	21 (32%)	6 (18%)	9 (30%)	15 (23%)
Postsecondary total	20 (65%)	28 (80%)	**48 (73%)**	18 (53%)	17 (57%)	**35 (55%)**
Total of secondary & postsecondary	31 (100%)	35 (100%)	66 (100%)	34 (100%)	30 (100%)	64 (100%)

Note. Subjects with only 1 year of college are counted under *vocational/technical/college*, whereas those with 2 years or more of college are counted under *college*. Because of rounding of percentages, not all columns total 100%.

includes subjects who clearly were not engaged in short-term postsecondary training—those who had 2 or more years of courses at a 4-year college, who had a completed college degree (2- or 4-year), or who had university graduate courses.

Subjects who took courses that were offered through the military or their place of employment but held at colleges were counted under either *vocational/technical/college* or *college*, as appropriate. The few subjects who took only on-the-job training courses at work or in the military and subjects who took only adult continuing education courses at night school or at a high school were *not* counted under *postsecondary education*.

In comparing the distributions of campers and noncampers at four levels of education, as they are shown by the four categories in Table 10.2, we found no significant differences for males and females within or between groups.

A closer look at Table 10.2 data about the postsecondary educational attainment for campers and noncampers indicated no significant differences in the camper versus noncamper proportions at the *vocational/technical/college* versus the *college* level. There were also no significant differences for males and females within or between groups. When we compare the numbers of campers and noncampers who attended different levels of postsecondary education, we find that out of the postsecondary education subgroup, 27 of 48 campers (56%) attained the *vocational/technical/college* level, compared with 20 out of 35 (57%) for noncampers. Of campers with postsecondary education, 21 out of 48 (44%) attained the *college* level, compared with 15 out of 35 (43%) for noncampers.

From an examination of the data on which type of postsecondary school the study subjects first attended (not including data on those starting postsecondary education in the military), we found that approximately 59% of each group—campers and noncampers—began their studies at a 4-year college or university. Also, we would expect that among the 41% of each group who began their studies at vocational/technical schools or community colleges, there were some eventual transferees to 4-year institutions. Where students begin their higher education is influenced by many considerations, including their economic situations and the

On-the-job training courses at work or in the military and adult continuing education courses were not counted as postsecondary education.

Most subjects' postsecondary education was at a college or university. Only a few chose a vocational or technical school for their higher education.

Nearly 60% of subjects going on to higher education began their studies at a 4-year college or university.

types of careers they aspire to. Therefore, we will later examine students' major areas of study, plans for future education, and economic resources.

For a closer examination of the study subjects' educational attainments, we organized data according to the three after-high-school paths shown in Table 10.3. This table shows the distributions of campers and noncampers according to their choices of the following three paths:

Path A: High school only. The *high-school-only* subjects (n = 47, including 18 campers, 29 noncampers) had not completed more than a high school education at the time of interview. This includes the 4 subjects who did not complete high school and the 43 who did graduate but never pursued any further formal education. In the *high-school-only* group, it was common for subjects

Table 10.3

Subjects According to Paths Beyond High School

Path	No. (%) of Campers			No. (%) of Noncampers			Campers & Noncampers
	Males	Females	All	Males	Females	All	
Path A: High school only	11 (35%)	7 (20%)	18 (27%)	16 (47%)	13 (43%)	29 (45%)	47 (36%)
Path B: High school→ vocational education	0 (0%)	3 (9%)	3 (5%)	2 (6%)	1 (3%)	3 (5%)	6 (5%)
Path C: High school→ college	20 (65%)	25 (71%)	45 (68%)	16 (47%)	16 (53%)	32 (50%)	77 (59%)
Total	31 (100%)	35 (100%)	66 (100%)	34 (100%)	30 (100%)	64 (100%)	130 (100%)

to have experienced some kind of general orientation or specially tailored on-the-job training in their employment or in the military. This kind of training was not considered as formal education and was also not unique to this group, since the majority of those who attained postsecondary education levels were also employed— a point that will be explored in Chapter 11.

Path B: High school followed by vocational education. As shown in Table 10.3, the *high school → vocational education* group consists of only a few subjects (*n* = 6, including 3 campers, 3 noncampers) who clearly had pursued some formal vocational/technical education beyond high school. Included in the 6 are 3 campers (all females), and 3 noncampers (2 males and 1 female). For 2 of these campers and 2 of these noncampers, the training had already resulted in their certification. Also, 1 camper was in school pursuing more training, and 1 camper was still working towards a certificate. The subjects' vocational/technical education was short-term and usually included several courses and supervised experiences for credits. The certificates obtained were for such specialties as word processing, mechanics, computer operations, cosmetology, and dental hygiene. Some of the 6 subjects who pursued such specialty training also mentioned that they were receiving or had received on-the-job skill training at their place of employment.

Path C: High school followed by college. The *high school → college* group (*n* = 77, including 45 campers, 32 noncampers) shown in Table 10.3 includes all subjects, both males and females, whose postsecondary education was at any degree-granting college and who had any number of years of college. Of Path C campers, males represented 44% and females represented 56%. Of Path C noncampers, males and females each represented 50%. There were no significant differences for gender within or between Path C campers and noncampers.

Table 10.4 shows the overall study sample and the proportions of the campers, of the noncampers, and of

Three educational paths were used to differentiate subjects' educational choices:

A. High school only
B. High school followed by vocational education
C. High school followed by college

"Post-secondary subjects" were considered to be those following path B or path C.

▾

A few postsecondary subjects studied vocational or technical specialties— word processing, dental hygiene, cosmetology—at certificate-granting institutions. Most, however, attended degree-granting institutions.

▾

Table 10.4

**Educational Paths Beyond High School:
Campers Versus Noncampers**

Group	No. (%) of Campers	No. (%) of Noncampers	No. (%) of Total Sample
Path A: High school only	18 (38%)	29 (62%)	47 (100%)
Path B: High school → vocational education	3 (50%)	3 (50%)	6 (100%)
Path C: High school → college	45 (58%)	32 (42%)	77 (100%)

the total sample for each path. The percentages presented here, because they are based on the rows, reveal the camp program's contribution to each path. Of those taking Path A, the *high-school-only* group ($n = 47$), campers represented 38%, whereas noncampers represented 62%. Of those pursuing *postsecondary education* by taking either Path B or C (Paths B and C groups combined, $n = 83$), 58% were campers and 42% were noncampers. The contribution of campers versus the contribution of noncampers to the total sample's frequency of subjects following these paths (Path A versus Paths B and C combined) was significantly different [$\chi^2(1) = 4.58$, $p < .05$].

Postsecondary Subjects' Major Areas of Study

As indicated earlier, the major areas of study in Path B were specialized, leading towards such vocations as cosmetology, dental hygiene, mechanics, and computer operations. For Path C, subjects reported a wide range of

Those many post-secondary subjects attending college—campers and noncampers alike—chose a wide range of study areas, such as education, business, health, humanities, science, mathematics, and vocational/technical majors.

Table 10.5

Distribution of Path C Subjects by Major Areas of Study

Group	No. (%) in Vocational/ Technical	No. (%) in Education/ Business/ Health	No. (%) in Engineering/ Computer Science	No. (%) in Humanities/ Science/ Social Science	No. (%) in Other	Total Path C Subjects
Campers	10 (22%)	11 (24%)	7 (16%)	8 (18%)	9 (20%)	45 (100%)
Noncampers	7 (22%)	11 (34%)	3 (9%)	6 (19%)	5 (16%)	32 (100%)

Note. Other was used to count subjects who were undecided about a major area of study or whose program did not fit into one of the major categories.

major areas of study, as shown in Table 10.5. Because there was a considerable spread across areas, males and females were combined to allow comparisons between campers and noncampers.

A question to consider is whether campers and noncampers may have differed in the kinds of major areas they selected to study in college. However, there were no significant differences in campers versus noncampers with respect to their major areas of concentration [$\chi^2(4) = 1.40$, nonsignificant]. It might be expected that since more campers than noncampers went to college, college-going campers would have exhibited a high proportion of students concentrating on vocational subjects. However, this was not the case; campers and noncampers were distributed similarly over a wide range of areas of study.

Continuation and Completion of Postsecondary Education

We next examine how far subjects who chose Paths B or C (postsecondary education) had pursued their education. We look at, in particular, their continuing enrollment and their degree completion. We considered that

The majority of campers and noncampers reporting some completed post-secondary education were enrolled in college at the time of the interview.
▾

Although more campers than noncampers had already obtained some college education, similar proportions of both groups were enrolled in college at the time of the interview.
▾

the age of a subject at the time of interview would affect how much education he or she had completed—that those who had been the longest time out of high school would probably have completed the most higher education. However, this was not an issue in the study, because the average and the median ages at the time of interview were each nearly 21 years, for campers as well as for noncampers (M = 20.9 years; Md = 20.8 years). Age was not a significant difference, as noted in Chapter 9.

Of those in the Path B group (subjects with vocational/technical education), 4 subjects out of 6 had completed a certificate or vocational/technical degree. The 4 subjects included 2 female campers, and 1 male and 1 female noncamper. As shown in Table 10.6, the Path C group (subjects with some college education) can be broken into three groups: (1) subjects who were not currently enrolled in college and had no completed degree; (2) subjects who were currently enrolled in college but had no degree; and (3) subjects who had 2- or 4-year degrees completed (some of whom were also currently enrolled in college.)

Table 10.6 shows a somewhat greater proportion of Path C noncampers currently in college or with a completed degree—23 out of 32 noncampers (72%), compared with 29 out of 45 campers (64%)—but this was not a statistically significant difference [$\chi^2(1)$ = .47]. There were no significant differences between either camper males and females or noncamper males and females in frequency of current enrollment or completion of college. Across groups, there were no significant differences between the proportions of males (67%) and females (68%) who were counted under *currently enrolled/ no degree* or *2- or 4-year degree completed*.

Plans for Future Education

Having educational plans is an indicator of how much one recognizes the value of education, and it can also be a predictor of future education, especially if one has already begun higher education. Table 10.7 shows data

Table 10.6

Path C Subjects, Continuation and Completion of College

Group	No. (%) of Campers			No. (%) of Noncampers		
	Males	Females	All	Males	Females	All
Not currently enrolled/no degree	7 (35%)	9 (36%)	16 (36%)	5 (31%)	4 (25%)	9 (28%)
Currently enrolled/ no degree	12 (60%)	13 (52%)	25 (56%)	11 (69%)	9 (56%)	20 (63%)
2- or 4-year degree completed	1 (5%)	3 (12%)	4 (9%)	0 (0%)	3 (19%)	3 (9%)
Total	20 (100%)	25 (100%)	45 (100%)	16 (100%)	16 (100%)	32 (100%)

Note. Currently means at the time of interview. Degrees included 3 female noncampers with 2-year degrees, 1 male and 1 female camper with 2-year degrees, and 2 female campers with 4-year degrees. Because of rounding of percentages, not all columns total 100%.

Table 10.7

Number of Subjects Who Plan Further Education

Group	No. (%) of Campers			No. (%) of Noncampers		
	Males	Females	All	Males	Females	All
No plans	16 (52%)	7 (20%)	23 (35%)	9 (26%)	13 (43%)	22 (34%)
Plans for more education	15 (48%)	28 (80%)	43 (65%)	25 (74%)	17 (57%)	42 (66%)
Total	31 (100%)	35 (100%)	66 (100%)	34 (100%)	30 (100%)	64 (100%)

Significantly more camper females (80%) than noncamper females (57%) reported to interviewers that they had plans for future postsecondary education.

▾

obtained when interviewers asked subjects if they planned to pursue any further education and what type of education they would pursue.

Overall, majorities of both campers and noncampers indicated they planned to pursue more education (65% of campers and 66% of noncampers), with no significant differences or trends between campers and noncampers. There was a significant difference between male and female campers, with a greater percentage of females (80%) than males (48%) planning further education [$\chi^2(1) = 7.24$, $p < .05$]. Also, significantly more camper females (80%) than noncamper females (57%) planned further education [$\chi^2(1) = 4.13$, $p < .05$]. There were no other significant differences or trends.

When subjects who plan further education have already begun to pursue their education, that gives more credibility to their intentions. Table 10.8 breaks down the planners and nonplanners according to their present educational paths. Comparing, within Path A (high school only), the campers versus noncampers *with plans* versus *with no plans* yielded no significant differences. Likewise, within Paths B and C (postsecondary education), the same kind of comparison yielded no significant differences. However, when we compared, within campers, Path A subjects versus Paths B and C subjects *with plans* versus *with no plans*, we found significantly more planning among the postsecondary group [$\chi^2(1) = 11.04$, $p < .001$]. Among campers in the *high-school-only* group, the plans for further education included the following: to finish high school (1 subject); to pursue more technical education (1), to pursue a 2-year degree (2), and to pursue a master's degree (2). Among campers in the *postsecondary* group, the plans for further education included these: to pursue a 2-year degree (5 subjects); to pursue a bachelor's degree (16); to pursue a master's degree (12); and to pursue a doctoral-level degree (4).

Also, within noncampers, in a comparison of Path A versus Paths B and C subjects *with plans* versus *with no plans*, we found significantly more planning among

Table 10.8

Comparison of Present Paths and Plans for Future Education

Group	No. (%) of Campers			No. (%) of Noncampers		
	Males	Females	All	Males	Females	All
Path A: High school only						
With plans	0 (0%)	6 (86%)	6 (33%)	8 (50%)	5 (38%)	13 (45%)
With no plans	11 (100%)	1 (14%)	12 (67%)	8 (50%)	8 (62%)	16 (55%)
Total	11 (100%)	7 (100%)	18 (100%)	16 (100%)	13 (100%)	29 (100%)
Paths B and C: Postsecondary						
With plans	15 (75%)	22 (79%)	37 (77%)	17 (94%)	12 (71%)	29 (83%)
With no plans	5 (25%)	6 (21%)	11 (23$)	1 (6%)	5 (29%)	6 (17%)
Total	20 (100%)	28 (100%)	48 (100%)	18 (100%)	17 (100%)	35 (100%)

the *postsecondary* than among the *high-school-only* noncampers [$\chi^2(1) = 10.17$, $p < .01$]. Among the noncampers in the *high-school-only* group, the plans for further education included these: to pursue some technical education (1 subject); to pursue a 2-year degree (4); to pursue a bachelor's degree (7); and to pursue a master's degree (1). It should be noted that 1 Path A noncamper had just enrolled in postsecondary education but had not yet completed any course work. Among noncamper *postsecondary* subjects, plans for further education included the following: to pursue a bachelor's degree (22 subjects); to pursue a master's

Significantly more of the postsecondary than of the high-school-only group said they had plans for future postsecondary education.

▾

degree (6); and to pursue a doctoral-level degree (1). Although there was no significant difference in the *numbers* of Paths B and C campers versus noncampers with plans for further education, there did appear to be *more-ambitious* educational plans among the campers.

Summary: Postsecondary Education Level and Enrollment/Completion

In Table 10.9, a summary table, subjects with vocational/technical higher education (Path B) and college higher education (Path C) are looked at as one postsecondary education group and distributed according to their enrollment and degree-completion status at time of interview. These postsecondary subjects make up 73% of campers and 55% of noncampers. Also in Table 10.9, we see what proportions of subjects did not take the postsecondary education path, 27% of campers and 45% of noncampers.

As shown in Table 10.9, subjects who were enrolled in higher education courses at the time of interview but had not yet completed a degree included 39% of campers and 31% of noncampers. (A few subjects who had completed degrees were also enrolled, but they are not included in these *currently enrolled* percentages.) These camper and noncamper rates of current enrollment are comparable to a national average of approximately 39% of white high school graduates enrolled in college in 1989, which included young adults aged 18 to 24 years from all levels of economic backgrounds (American Council on Education, 1991). Since our subjects are from low-income backgrounds, it is also relevant here to look at college enrollment rates nationally for low-income groups. In 1985, for young white adults aged 18 to 24 who were either living with their parents or economically dependent on them and whose parents had incomes under $10,000, college enrollment was about 16%; for those whose parents had incomes from $10,000–$20,000, it was about 25% (U.S. Bureau of the Census, 1987).

Table 10.9

Subjects' Postsecondary Education Status at Time of Interview

Group	No. (%) of Campers	No. (%) of Noncampers	No. (%) of Study Sample
Currently enrolled/ no degree	26 (39%)	20 (31%)	46 (35%)
Completed voc./tech. certificate, or 2-yr or 4-yr degree	6 (9%)	5 (8%)	11 (8%)
Previously enrolled/ no degree	16 (24%)	10 (16%)	26 (20%)
Total with postsecondary education	48 (73%)	35 (55%)	83 (64%)
Total never enrolled in postsecondary education	18 (27%)	29 (45%)	47 (36%)
Total	66 (100%)	64 (100%)	130 (100%)

Note: Currently enrolled refers to enrollment at the time of the subject's interview.

An important subgroup here are those who had some postsecondary education but were not enrolled in postsecondary courses at the time of interview. This subgroup included 24% of campers, compared with 16% of noncampers. The majority of these postsecondary "dropouts" indicated that they did plan to return to complete their studies: Of the 16 campers who had dropped out of postsecondary education, 6 were in the military, and 4 of these campers planned further education; of the 10 noncampers, 1 noncamper was in the military and also had further plans for education.

Out of the 48 campers with postsecondary education, 32 (67%) were still enrolled or had already completed degrees. The other 16 of the 48 campers (33%) had permanently dropped out or were simply not enrolled at the time of interview. Out of the 35 noncampers with

Of those postsecondary subjects who were not enrolled in college at the time of the interview, the majority reported having postsecondary education plans for the future.

postsecondary education, 25 (71%) were still in school or had completed a degree, and 10 (29%) had permanently dropped out or were simply not enrolled at the time of interview. (We should add that for the nondegreed campers or noncampers who reported "not presently enrolled," their non-enrollment was not due to their being interviewed during the summer or other breaks.) Campers and noncampers were not significantly different in their rates of current enrollment or degree completion. In general, therefore, for both campers and noncampers, the majority of study sample subjects (57 out of 83, or 69%) who did start down the path of college education appeared to have pursued completion of that education into their young-adult years.

Obstacles on the Path to Completion of Higher Education

It is relevant to compare our data with the High School and Beyond study (National Opinion Research Center, 1986a). The national samples for the High School and Beyond study were first surveyed as high school sophomores and seniors in 1980. Most recently, the same samples were interviewed about 3–5 years after their high school graduations. The research revealed that of the 1980 seniors, over 50% had been enrolled in some form of postsecondary education at some point since high school. Although there was generally much less postsecondary education among the subgroups with low socioeconomic status (SES), there were somewhat better rates among low-SES subjects with high cognitive test scores in high school. In general, this overall national rate of postsecondary education is comparable to the rate of the noncamper group (55%) in the present longitudinal study. When it is compared with the national figure of 50%, the camper group's higher postsecondary education rate of 73% even more clearly suggests the positive impact of the High/Scope Institute for IDEAS.

Our data are unclear about how many course

The noncamper rate of 55% of subjects obtaining some postsecondary education by age 21 is comparable to the national rate of 50%, whereas the camper rate of 73% is substantially higher.

credits the students who were currently enrolled in college were taking. We would expect some subjects to be part-time students, which is true for increasing numbers of students nationwide, especially for students beyond the first year of college. According to research reviewed by Spanard (1990), there are increasing proportions of part-time and "stop-out" students (former college students planning to go back to college). Except at the most selected colleges and universities, the traditional full-time students now represent only about 50% to 60% of college students. Going to school part-time, varying the timetable for taking courses, and engaging in off-on enrollment are all part of the new pattern for obtaining a college degree. In the present research, since the majority of postsecondary "dropout" subjects in both camper and noncamper groups indicated that they did plan to return to pursue a degree, they fit into the category Spanard referred to as "stop-out" students; they may need to pursue their education on a part-time basis when they do return.

> Nationally, part-time and "stop-out" college attendance (pursuing degrees off and on) is increasing, apparently because of students' economic difficulties.
>
> ▾

In one study by Wright and Spanard (cited in Spanard, 1990), the investigators conducted exit surveys of withdrawing college students. They found that 31% intended to return within 12 months, yet after 30 months, only 13% had returned, with the rest citing economic reasons and family responsibility reasons that made reentry difficult. However, this does not mean that the nonreturnees will not reenter at a later time. According to a 1988 nationwide survey conducted by the College Board (cited in Spanard, 1990), 45% of college students enrolled today are over 25 years old, with the over-25s consisting of nearly equal numbers of full-time and part-time students. From the High School and Beyond study data discussed earlier, of the 1980 high school seniors interviewed 4 years later (at about age 22), only about 23% had completed the 2-year college degree, the 4-year college degree, or the postsecondary certificate for which they had originally enrolled. The survey of the same sample 2 years later (at about age 24) found that by then, about 37%

> Research shows that today, to complete their degrees, many students of all ages attend college beyond the traditional 4-year period.
>
> ▾

had completed their degrees (National Center for Education Statistics, 1989). Economic limitations appear to have played a large role in whether and how students pursued an interrupted, off-and-on path of postsecondary higher education.

Military Service of Subjects

Military service can provide young adults with expanded opportunities— for education or training, and employment.

For many young people, military service, with its variety of educational and employment experiences, provides an economically feasible and independent way to pursue education and training; it can thus provide a bridge to the future, a transition into adulthood. The young people in our longitudinal study sample went into the military at various points, including right after high school, after working, or after enrolling in postsecondary courses for a while.

Of the entire study sample, 14 subjects were in the military at some point. This included 12 (18% of) campers (which was 23% of camper males and 14% of camper females) and 2 (3% of) noncampers (which was 6% of noncamper males and 0% of noncamper females). Out of the 66 subjects in the camper sample, 5 (8%) were serving in the military at the time of the interview (13% of camper males and 3% of camper females). Of the 64 subjects in the noncamper sample, only 1, a male, was serving in the military at the time of interview (this was 3% of noncamper males). Overall, a significantly greater proportion (86%) of the subjects who ever served in the military were former campers [$\chi^2(1) = 7.67, p < .01$]. The national High School and Beyond study (National Opinion Research Center, 1986a) provides figures for comparison. That study found that about 7% of white former 1980 seniors (11% of males and 2% of females) had served in the military sometime during the 4 years after high school graduation. Camper male and female rates in the present study exceeded those rates, whereas noncamper male and female rates were more comparable to the national rates.

It is important to note that 12 of the 14 subjects who were in the military at some point had also completed some postsecondary courses. Recall that in the earlier section on Educational Status of Subjects, those in the military who were enrolled in college-level courses at a civilian or military college were counted in the postsecondary education group (Paths B and C). However, subjects in the military who were taking only on-the-job courses were not included in the postsecondary group.

A look at the total group with military service reveals that few of the high-school-only group took this route. Only 1 camper male and 1 noncamper male, and no females, with high-school-only education (Path A) served in the military. Though military service affords a way for such young adults to gain further skills, education, or employment, they did not seek this opportunity.

In contrast, for Paths B and C subjects, the postsecondary education subjects, we see a pattern of (1) entering the military, perhaps in order to obtain higher education, and in fact pursuing that education, (2) going into the military after having already taken some college or other postsecondary training, or (3) entering the military first and pursuing education afterwards. The data do not reveal the reasons for subjects going into the military, nor do they reveal the relationship between military service and education as perceived by the subjects in their planning.

Of those in the military at the time of interview, 3 camper males and 1 camper female had some previous postsecondary education and were not at the time taking higher education courses in the military. The other 2 subjects, 1 camper male and 1 noncamper male, were from the Path A, high-school-only, group and were not in any college-level education in the military at the time of the interview. Among the 8 subjects (7 campers and 1 noncamper) who had been in the military previous to the interview, all were from either Path B or C, the postsecondary education group. It was not always

Most of the study subjects with military service were former High/Scope Institute participants. The campers' military service rate exceeded the national averages for males and females.

Most of the study subjects who reported serving in the military also reported obtaining some postsecondary education— before, during, or after their military service.

clear when subjects had obtained their education—whether before, during, or after their military service—but all three patterns were found among the subjects with a record of military service.

SUMMARIZING THIS CHAPTER   So far we have shown that significantly more camper than noncamper subjects had attained postsecondary education. For the entire study sample (campers and noncampers) at the time of interview, the majority of those who had chosen the postsecondary paths were either currently enrolled in courses or had a certificate or a 2- or 4-year degree completed. Compared with all study sample subjects who had chosen the high-school-only path, significantly more of all postsecondary subjects (camper and noncamper, enrolled and not enrolled) had plans for more education. Also, significantly more campers than noncampers had a record of military service.

In the following chapter, we examine subjects' life situations—marital status, employment status, and economic resources. To better understand the key factors related to pursuing higher education, we compare the life situations of subjects who settled for high-school-only and of those who did not.

ENDNOTES

1. The longitudinal study's interview questions were current, retrospective, and prospective, which are methods that have been employed in life span and longitudinal studies (see Belsky & Isabella, 1985; Vasta, 1979). The data were analyzed for linkages between subjects' current life situations and their past experiences and future directions. This basic research approach is a life course analysis with particular emphasis on subjects' key life events—academic achievement and behavior adjustment in high school; participation in the High/Scope program; and transition into young adulthood in education, employment, and family formation. This kind of research approach has been proposed as especially relevant for studying adolescence (Entwisle, 1990; Leigh & Loewen, 1987).

Chapter ELEVEN

Life Situations—
Marriage, Children,
Economic Resources

OFTEN, WHEN YOUNG ADULTS get married, the likelihood that they will begin or complete higher education decreases. There is an inverse relationship between their plans to obtain postsecondary education and their marital status (National Opinion Research Center, 1986b). For couples married or living together, starting a family at a young age is likely to further divert the young adults' time and resources from higher education. Thus, efforts to discourage marriage and parenthood at a young age are one of the objectives of many educational intervention efforts. In this chapter, we examine the potential relationships between early marriage, parenthood, economic resources, and the educational paths of the young adults in the longitudinal study.

Marriage, Children, and Educational Paths

Subjects' Place of Residence

Today, when cohabitation of young adults may precede or take the place of marriage, a young adult's place of

Early marriage or cohabitation may lessen the likelihood that a young adult will go on to postsecondary education.

▼

residence is tied in with his or her marital status and economic situation. For this reason, we considered whether or not subjects still lived in their parents' households. We learned that of campers, 19 subjects (29%) lived in their parents' households, and 47 (71%) lived in their own households; of noncampers, 26 (41%) lived in their parents' households and 38 (59%) lived in their own households. (Subjects who were college students were counted as living in the parental household unless they lived on their own or with a spouse or roommate 12 months of the year.) There were no significant differences or trends between campers and noncampers on the number of subjects living in the parental household at the time of interview.

According to analyses of 1988 national census data (U.S. Bureau of the Census, 1989), approximately 54% of 18- to 24-year-olds, including those away at college for part of the school year, live with their parents. In the present study, the noncamper group appeared to be closer to the national rate of 54% of young adults still living at home, but both campers and noncampers appeared to be more likely than average U.S. young adults to go out to live on their own. We will examine factors that may be related to this pattern as we examine marital status, childrearing, and economic situations of the campers and noncampers, including both those who have pursued postsecondary education and those who have not.

Marital Status

Table 11.1 shows the data obtained from asking subjects about their marital status. Overall, significantly more males than females (71% versus 46%) had remained *single*, not cohabiting [$\chi^2(1) = 8.11$, $p < .01$]. The 1988 national rates for young white adults aged 20 to 24 years who are *single*, never married, are approximately 76% for males and 59% for females (U.S. Bureau of the Census, 1989). In the present research, comparing the distribution of three groups of subjects—*single* (never

---

Compared with a national rate of 54%, a greater percentage of study subjects were living on their own by age 21.

▼

At interview time, significantly more male subjects than female subjects were still single— they had never married and were not cohabiting with a spouse-equivalent.

▼

Table 11.1

Marital Status of Campers and Noncampers

Group	No. (%) of Males			No. (%) of Females		
	Campers	Noncampers	All	Campers	Noncampers	All
Single (never married)	18 (58%)	28 (82%)	46 (71%)	15 (43%)	15 (50%)	30 (46%)
Married	5 (16%)	3 (9%)	8 (12%)	11 (31%)	11 (37%)	22 (34%)
Cohabiting (living with a spouse-equivalent)	7 (23%)	2 (6%)	9 (14%)	8 (23%)	3 (10%)	11 (17%)
Separated or divorced	1 (3%)	1 (3%)	2 (3%)	1 (3%)	1 (3%)	2 (3%)
Total	31 (100%)	34 (100%)	65 (100%)	35 (100%)	30 (100%)	65 (100%)

married); "ever married" (combining *married* and *separated/divorced*); and *cohabiting* (living with a spouse-equivalent)—we found a significant difference indicating that fewer campers than noncampers remained *single* [$\chi^2(2) = 6.40$, $p < .05$]. For campers versus noncampers, when we compared the number of subjects who were *single* (never married) with those who were "ever married" (combining, this time, *married*, *cohabiting*, and *separated or divorced*), we found a significant difference [$\chi^2(1) = 3.95$, $p < .05$]. One half (50%) of campers, compared with the majority (67%) of noncampers, had remained *single*.

Also, significantly more noncampers than campers had remained single.

The proportion of campers cohabiting (23%) was nearly 3 times the proportion of noncampers cohabiting (8%) at the time of interview. If we also include cohabitation as single status, the percentages that remained

The rate of unmarried couples cohabiting has been steadily increasing nationally, and about 60% of such couples do eventually marry.

▼

single would be more similar for campers and non-campers: 81% of camper males and 66% of camper females, compared with 88% of noncamper males and 60% of noncamper females. If, however, we include cohabitation as married status, the marital rate would be 39% of camper males and 54% of camper females, compared with 15% of noncamper males and 47% of noncamper females.

The U.S. Bureau of the Census (1989) data indicate that from 1970 to 1980, there was a continuous increase in unmarried-couple households. Furthermore, the majority of cohabiting couples, about 70%, were childless, and an estimated 60% of these cohabiting young adults do eventually marry (U.S. Bureau of the Census, 1989). It seems that cohabiting may indicate either a transition to marriage or a way to remain unfettered by responsibilities of marriage.

Because gender is a particularly important factor in considering marital status, we next looked at Table 11.1 data for gender patterns in marital status—looking at males for campers versus noncampers, and at females for campers versus noncampers. Examining the distribution of the four marital-status indicators—*single, married, cohabiting,* and *separated or divorced*—we found no significant differences or trends between camper versus noncamper males or between camper versus noncamper females. There was also no significant difference between male versus female campers. Interestingly, however, a significant difference *was* found for noncamper males versus noncamper females, with more noncamper males having remained *single* [$\chi^2(1) = 7.57, p < .01$].

The data are insufficient for evaluating why we found this just-mentioned male-female difference among the noncampers, or why we found the earlier-mentioned camper-noncamper difference (more *married/cohabiting* campers). One possibility is that delaying setting up a household of one's own may be indicative of a stable parental household or economic help from parents. In troubled parental households or ones that offer little economic help, young adults may more readily go out to live on their own, even if it turns out to be economically or educationally less advantageous in the long run.

Marital Status Related to Educational Paths Since High School

We next consider whether marital status is related to the educational paths taken by subjects since high school. In particular, we look at whether single subjects had pursued more education than other subjects had. Table 11.2 distributes *single* and *married/cohabiting* subjects by educational paths.

High-school-only versus postsecondary subjects. There were no significant differences in marital status for campers or noncampers between Path A and Paths B and C combined. In a comparison with other sub-

Table 11.2

Educational Paths and Marital Status

| Educational Path | No. (%) of Campers | | | | No. (%) of Noncampers | | | |
| | Single | | Married/ Cohabiting | | Single | | Married/ Cohabiting | |
	M	F	M	F	M	F	M	F
Path A	6 (33%)	1 (7%)	5 (38%)	6 (30%)	12 (43%)	5 (33%)	4 (67%)	8 (53%)
Paths B and C	12 (67%)	14 (93%)	8 (62%)	14 (70%)	16 (57%)	10 (67%)	2 (33%)	7 (47%)
Total	18 (100%)	15 (100%)	13 (100%)	20 (100%)	28 (100%)	15 (100%)	6 (100%)	15 (100%)

Note. M = males; F = females. Path A = high school only; Paths B and C = postsecondary education. The *single* group contains only single, never-married, not-cohabiting subjects; all others are included in *married/cohabiting*.

Single female campers appeared to be especially likely to go on to post-secondary education.

▼

groups, female campers in Path A (high school only) versus Paths B and C (postsecondary education) exhibited some interesting nonsignificant trends: (1) Comparing *single* female versus *single* male campers between educational paths indicated a nonsignificant trend of more *single* female campers going on to postsecondary education ($p = .07$, Fisher's exact test). (2) Comparing educational paths for *single* versus *married/cohabiting* female campers also indicated a nonsignificant trend of more *single* female campers going on to postsecondary education ($p = .10$, Fisher's exact test). (3) Comparing camper versus noncamper *single* females between educational paths indicated a nonsignificant trend of more camper *single* females going on to postsecondary education ($p = .08$, Fisher's exact test).

Table 11.2 data indicate that solid majorities of both *single* and *married/cohabiting* female campers went on to postsecondary education (93% and 70%, respectively). This contrasts somewhat with noncamper *single* females (67% of whom went on to higher education), as well as with noncamper *married/cohabiting* females (47% of whom went on to higher education).

Next, we look marital status separately for each educational path.

High-school-only subjects. Table 11.3 distributes high-school-only subjects according to whether they were *single* or *married/cohabiting*. In the high-school-only group (Path A), campers versus noncampers were not significantly different in marital status. However, comparing all males versus all females yielded a statistically significant difference [$\chi^2(1) = 6.18$, $p < .05$]: The majority (67%) of high-school-only males, compared with less than a third (30%) of high-school-only females, remained *single*. This means that of Path A females, 70% were *married/cohabiting*.

For campers within the high-school-only group, comparing males versus females yielded a borderline trend indicating more *married/cohabiting* female campers ($p = .11$, Fisher's exact test). For noncampers within the high-school-only group, comparing males versus

Most high-school-only males and most post-secondary males were single. The pattern was different for female subjects.

▼

Table 11.3

Path A (High-School-Only Education) and Marital Status

Marital Status	No. (%) of Males			No. (%) of Females		
	Campers	Noncampers	All	Campers	Noncampers	All
Single	6 (55%)	12 (75%)	18 (67%)	1 (14%)	5 (38%)	6 (30%)
Married/ cohabiting	5 (45%)	4 (25%)	9 (33%)	6 (86%)	8 (62%)	14 (70%)
Total	11 (100%)	16 (100%)	27 (100%)	7 (100%)	13 (100%)	20 (100%)

Note. The *single* group contains only single, never-married, not-cohabiting subjects; all others are included in *married/cohabiting.*

females yielded a significant difference: The majority of noncamper males (75%) remained *single*, whereas only 38% of the noncamper females remained *single* [$\chi^2(1) = 3.95, p < .05$].

It is interesting that the majority of males with high-school-only education remained *single*, whereas a majority of their female counterparts were *married/cohabiting*. With so many high-school-only female subjects married or cohabiting by 20 or 21 years of age, we might expect that female subjects would be less likely than male subjects to pursue further education and more likely than male subjects to begin childrearing. Not just the high-school-only males, but males across both educational levels (high-school-only and postsecondary) appear to have remained single longer than their female counterparts, as we discuss next.

Postsecondary education subjects. Overall, of 83 subjects with some postsecondary education, 63% (52) were single and 37% (31) were married or cohabiting (no table). In Path B, vocational/technical education, only 1

Although at age 21 the majority of high-school-only female subjects were married/ cohabiting, only about half of postsecondary female subjects had this status.

(a camper female) out of 6 study subjects had married, and none had children. Next, we look at the marital status of those who had completed some college (Path C, Table 11.4), first among males, campers versus noncampers, and then among females, campers versus noncampers.

Overall, in this more highly educated group, there was a borderline trend showing more campers than noncampers *married/cohabiting* [$\chi^2(1) = 2.70, p < .11$]. Comparing males versus females, we find the majority of males (72%) were *single*, whereas approximately one half of females (51%) were *single*, which was a nonsignificant trend [$\chi^2(1) = 3.56, p < .10$]. A simple majority of the camper males, compared with the vast majority of noncamper males, remained *single*, which was a nonsignificant trend ($p = .07$, Fisher's exact test). Comparing male and female noncampers reveals that significantly more male than female noncampers had remained *single* (88% versus 56%). However, the female

> At the time of interview (age 21), married/cohabiting status was more common among camper subjects than among noncamper subjects.

Table 11.4

Path C (College Education) and Marital Status

Marital Status	No. (%) of Males			No. (%) of Females		
	Campers	Noncampers	All	Campers	Noncampers	All
Single	12 (60%)	14 (88%)	26 (72%)	12 (48%)	9 (56%)	21 (51%)
Married/ cohabiting	8 (40%)	2 (12%)	10 (28%)	13 (52%)	7 (44%)	20 (49%)
Total	20 (100%)	16 (100%)	36 (100%)	25 (100%)	16 (100%)	41 (100%)

Note. The *single* group contains only single, never-married, not-cohabiting subjects; all others are included in *married/cohabiting.*

campers and noncampers were very comparable (as indicated by the lack of significant differences or trends), with approximately half *married/cohabiting* in each group.

IN SUMMARY   Compared with their noncamper counterparts, campers (both genders combined) were *married/cohabiting* at a higher rate (47% versus 28%). Concerning marriage, in the higher-education group (Path C), gender made a difference among noncampers, with just 2 out of 16 male noncampers (12%) *married/ cohabiting*, compared with 7 out of 16 female noncampers (44%). Also, 24 out of 45 campers (53%) were *single*, and 23 out of 32 noncampers (72%) were *single*. In other words, staying *single* was more related to pursuing college for noncampers than it was for campers.

Marital Status, Childrearing, and Pursuit of Higher Education

Next, we consider the question of whether marital status and childrearing relate to subjects' pursuit of higher education—particularly to whether they stay in school. We first look at those subjects who were enrolled in postsecondary courses or had completed degrees at interview time versus those who had begun but then dropped out of postsecondary education.

Marital status. Table 11.5 gives data regarding the marital status of subjects with some college education, and it groups those subjects according to whether or not they continued their pursuit of higher education. The major finding here is that remaining single is related to whether subjects continue or complete higher education. Comparing *single* versus *married/cohabiting* and *enrolled/degreed* versus *not enrolled* for campers and noncampers combined yielded a significant difference [$\chi^2(1) = 6.89, p < .01$]. Of *enrolled/degreed* subjects, 37 out of 52 (71%) were *single*, and 15 out of 52 (29%) were *married/cohabiting*. For *not enrolled* subjects, 10 out of 25 (40%) were single, and 15 out of 25 (60%) were *married/ cohabiting*.

Although somewhat less true for campers, being single appeared to be more likely among postsecondary-educated study subjects.

Table 11.5

Postsecondary Subjects (Path C) Enrolled/Degreed Versus Not Enrolled

Group	No. (%) of Campers			No. (%) of Noncampers		
	Males	Females	All	Males	Females	All
Enrolled/degreed						
Single	10 (77%)	9 (56%)	19 (66%)	10 (91%)	8 (67%)	18 (78%)
Married/ cohabiting	3 (23%)	7 (44%)	10 (34%)	1 (9%)	4 (33%)	5 (22%)
Total	13 (100%)	16 (100%)	29 (100%)	11 (100%)	12 (100%)	23 (100%)
Not enrolled						
Single	2 (29%)	3 (33%)	5 (31%)	4 (80%)	1 (25%)	5 (56%)
Married/ cohabiting	5 (71%)	6 (67%)	11 (69%)	1 (20%)	3 (75%)	4 (44%)
Total	7 (100%)	9 (100%)	16 (100%)	5 (100%)	4 (100%)	9 (100%)

Note. Those subjects who have completed degrees include: 1 male camper, 1 female camper, and 2 female noncampers, all of whom are single; 1 male camper, 3 female campers, and 2 female noncampers, all of whom are married. Subjects who have completed a degree or are enrolled are combined. The *single* group contains only single, never-married, not-cohabiting subjects; all others are included in *married/cohabiting*.

The pattern was one of more *enrolled/degreed* subjects remaining *single*, and more *not enrolled* subjects being married. For males, this pattern involved a nonsignificant trend $[\chi^2(1) = 3.19, p < .10]$, whereas for females, the pattern involved a significant difference ($p = .05$, Fisher's exact test). For males, 20 out of 24 (83%) who were *enrolled/degreed* were *single*, whereas 6 out of 12 (50%) of those males who had dropped out were *single*. For females, 17 out of 28 (61%) who were *enrolled/*

degreed were *single*, while 4 out of 13 (31%) of those who had dropped out were *single*.

The majority of *enrolled/degreed* camper males (10 out of 13, or 77%) were *single*, whereas the majority of *not enrolled* camper males (5 out of 7, or 71%) were *married/ cohabiting*, which was a significant difference ($p = .05$, Fisher's exact test). There were no significant differences like this, however, among camper females, enrolled or not. It is interesting that camper females were able to continue or complete their education even though they were married or cohabiting. There were no significant differences or trends within male noncampers or within female noncampers, since majorities of both of these subgroups who were in school had remained single.

The overall pattern is that remaining in school to complete one's education is related to remaining single, especially for males and especially for camper males, but less so for camper females, 44% of whom were married or cohabiting while in college.

Early family formation. Childrearing, in the teenage years and in young adulthood, is an especially challenging responsibility and can subsequently frame a young person's decisions regarding education and employment. Thus, the study subjects' experiences with early parenthood were of interest to us.

Just 1 female in each group—campers and noncampers—gave birth to a child before the age of 18. Through age 17, the childbirth rate for the female campers and noncampers combined ($N = 65$) was about 3%. This is comparable to the 1985 national rate of 3% for 15- to 17-year-olds, according to data presented in *Youth Indicators 1991* (National Center for Education Statistics, 1991). Also, if we look at the childbirth rate for camper and noncamper females at ages 18 and 19, we find there were 3 children born to females in each group. This is a rate of 5%, which is somewhat less than the 1985 national rate of 8% (National Center for Education Statistics, 1991).

According to longitudinal data from the High School

While degreed/enrolled subjects tended to be single, this was less true for camper females; 44% of the latter were married/ cohabiting while enrolled in college.

The childbirth rate for female subjects was less than or comparable to the national rate for their age cohort.

and Beyond study (National Opinion Research Center, 1986b), study subjects' somewhat lower childbirth rates may be related to their high academic skills and educational aspirations. According to a Children's Defense Fund (1990) report, across black, Hispanic, and white females, those young women who have low academic achievement and employment expectations are most likely to begin early parenthood.

We next examine early family formation of both males and females, including the years beyond age 20 (no table). In looking at numbers of subjects who had children, we found no significant difference or trend between campers and noncampers. At the time of interview, a significantly higher percentage of females (25%), compared with males (9%), had children [$\chi^2(1) = 5.47$, $p < .05$]. These rates for females and males are comparable to data from the national High School and Beyond study (National Opinion Research Center, 1986b), which found that approximately 21% of females and 13% of males had children approximately 4 years after high school.

More female than male campers were parenting, and the difference was significant.

▼

In our comparison of male and female campers, more female campers had children—11 out of 35 females (31%) versus 3 out of 31 males (10%) [$\chi^2(1) = 4.65$, $p < .05$]. This is in contrast to noncampers, who showed no significant difference between males with children (3 out of 34, or 9%) and females with children (5 out of 30, or 17%).

Both campers and noncampers with children tended to be married or living with a spouse-equivalent. Among single campers, just 1 out of 33 (3%) had a child, whereas among married campers, 13 out of 33 (39%) had children [$\chi^2(1) = 13.06$, $p < .001$]. For noncampers, this comparison also was significant, with no single noncampers having children but 8 out of 21 married noncampers (38%) having children [$\chi^2(1) = 15.40$, $p < .001$, Yates' correction]. Only a few subjects had more than one child.

With one exception, both male and female subjects with children were married or cohabiting.

▼

Examining the numbers of subjects with children and without children for the high-school-only versus postsecondary groups (Path A versus Paths B and C) yielded no significant differences for the overall sample or within and between any subgroups—campers, noncampers, males, or females. Out of all 22 study subjects (campers and noncampers, all paths) with children, 12 subjects (55%) reported having some postsecondary higher education, which suggests that there was some potential for these subjects with children to complete higher education. However, only 1 of the subjects reporting some postsecondary education (a female camper) had completed a degree (2-year), and only 2 of these subjects (1 female camper and 1 male noncamper) were enrolled in college at the time of interview.

Next in this chapter, we will continue to examine the roles of marital status and childrearing as we look at the economic resources of study subjects. We will look for relationships between subjects' educational paths and their employment, their financial help from parents and student aid, and their reliance on public assistance.

Relationships Between Employment and Education

Table 11.6 shows the overall employment picture for campers versus noncampers.

Overall, 75% (97) of all 130 study subjects were *employed* at the time of the interview, with no significant differences or trends between any groups, including campers versus noncampers, camper males versus females, noncamper males versus females, and males versus females. It should be noted that subjects who were in the military at the time of the interview were counted as *employed*. The employment rates shown in the study sample data are comparable to the estimated national rate of employment for white adults approximately 2 years after high school, which is 70% (National Opinion Research Center, 1986b). Though there were

The majority of study subjects (75%) were employed—a rate comparable to national rates for this age group.

Table 11.6

Employment Status of Campers Versus Noncampers

Status	No. (%) of Campers			No. (%) of Noncampers		
	Males	Females	All	Males	Females	All
Employed	24 (77%)	26 (74%)	50 (76%)	24 (71%)	23 (77%)	47 (73%)
Unemployed	7 (23%)	9 (26%)	16 (24%)	10 (29%)	7 (23%)	17 (27%)
Total	31 (100%)	35 (100%)	66 (100%)	34 (100%)	30 (100%)	64 (100%)

significantly more campers with some postsecondary education, the rates of employment for campers and noncampers are the same, suggesting a commitment of campers to education *and* economic self-sufficiency.

Types of Occupations

Table 11.7 shows the distribution of campers and noncampers according to 7 levels of occupations. The job types in Table 11.7 are listed in descending order, going from highest-paying (at the top) to the lowest-paying. The Appendix further discusses the definitions and combinations of occupations used here.

When we combine the 7 levels of occupations in the table into 3 levels (*professional–sales*, *skilled trade–transportation*, and *laborer–service*), the distributions are significantly different, with more noncampers in the higher-paying types of jobs [$\chi^2(2) = 6.47$, $p < .05$]. Since we know that more campers took postsecondary courses, this may account for their having low-pay jobs—possibly part-time ones to help finance their education. This may explain, for example, the greater number of campers in food service jobs, where the largest difference is observed. We look next at the nature of jobs held—whether employment was full-time or part-time for subjects.

It is important to consider employment and other economic resources in relation to the other aspects of the subjects' lives. Knowing whether or not a person is enrolled in school, is married, and has children, in particular, provides a more complete basis for interpreting the role of employment and unemployment in young-adult lives. A few subjects who had just enrolled in a university, college, or vocational/technical school and had not yet completed any courses were not included as *enrolled/degreed* in the previous section on education, and they were not counted as having any postsecondary

Perhaps because so many campers were pursuing or planning to pursue post-secondary education, at age 21 a considerable number of them had what seemed to be short-term, low-pay jobs.

Table 11.7

Occupations of Employed Subjects

Occupation Type	No. (%) of Campers	No. (%) of Noncampers
Professional/ managerial	3 (6%)	5 (11%)
Clerical/sales	14 (28%)	20 (41%)
Skilled trade	3 (6%)	5 (11%)
Machine operator/ transportation	6 (12%)	6 (13%)
Laborer	10 (20%)	8 (17%)
Food service	11 (22%)	0 (0%)
Cleaning/service	3 (6%)	3 (6%)
Total	50 (100%)	47 (100%)

education in earlier chapters. However, in the remainder of this chapter, since we are interested in considering the economic resources of students currently enrolled, these subjects are included in the *in-school* group for subsequent analyses.

Hours of Employment

Within campers and within noncampers, the number of hours that subjects were employed varied according to whether they were enrolled in postsecondary school or not. Of the 97 employed subjects, 13 (13%) had a second job—6 campers and 7 noncampers. Of these 13 two-job holders, 3 campers and 3 noncampers were also in school. Hours worked per week was selected as the point of comparison. The minimum hours worked per week was 12 for camper males and 7 for camper females. Among subjects working two jobs, the maximum worked in *job one* was 65 hours per week, and in *job two*, 40 hours per week. For such subjects, their hours for the two jobs were combined to arrive at a total number of hours per subject. For the 50 employed campers, the average number of hours worked per

Table 11.8

Weekly Hours of Employment for Campers and Noncampers

| Hours per Week | No. (%) of Campers | | | No. (%) of Noncampers | | |
	In School	Not in School	All	In School	Not in School	All
Part-time: 1–30 hr	10 (53%)	6 (19%)	16 (32%)	9 (60%)	2 (6%)	11 (23%)
Full-time: 31+ hr	9 (47%)	25 (81%)	34 (68%)	6 (40%)	30 (94%)	36 (77%)
Total	19 (100%)	31 (100%)	50 (100%)	15 (100%)	32 (100%)	47 (100%)

week was 37.26 (SD = 16.99), and for the 47 employed noncampers, the average was 37.45 hours (SD = 16.42). To look at the distribution of weekly hours employed, we split hours employed into two categories, *1–30 hours*, considered as *part-time*, and *31 or more hours*, considered as *full-time* (see Table 11.8).

Employment and Current Educational Enrollment

Campers versus noncampers. Looking at those who were in school, among campers and noncampers (Table 11.8), we find the pattern is essentially the same in each group, with more *in-school* subjects working *part-time* and more *not-in-school* subjects working *full-time* or near *full-time* [$\chi^2(1)$ = 5.99, p <.01, for campers; $\chi^2(1)$ = 13.60, p <.001, for noncampers, Yates' correction]. Even though a somewhat greater proportion of campers than noncampers were currently *in school*, there were no significant differences between the campers and noncampers in *part-time* versus *full-time*, as shown here.

Males versus females. Significantly more employment was found among *not-in-school* male campers and among *not-in-school* noncampers than among their respective *in-school* counterparts (p = .01, Fisher's exact test; p = .01, Fisher's exact test, respectively). For camper females, however, in a comparison of hours worked by *in-school* and *not-in-school* subjects, there were no significant differences or trends. This suggests that camper females worked a considerable number of hours even when enrolled in school. For noncamper females, comparing *in school* and *not in school* yields a significant difference, with more employment for those females *not in school* (p = .02, Fisher's exact test).

To further compare males and females, campers and noncampers, and *in-school* versus *not-in-school* groups, exact hours of employment per week was subsequently treated as a continuous variable, with separate *t*-tests conducted. The results of the analysis of hours of employment treated as continuous data re-

There were no significant differences between campers and noncampers in numbers holding part-time jobs versus full-time jobs.

▼

In general, in-school subjects worked fewer hours than not-in-school subjects did. An exception were the in-school and not-in-school female campers, who worked similar hours.

▼

flect no significant differences between campers and noncampers.

Overall, as expected, *in-school* subjects worked significantly fewer weekly hours than did *not-in-school* subjects. *In-school* subjects worked an average of 26.59 hours weekly (SD = 14.68), whereas *not-in-school* subjects worked an average of 43.16 hours weekly (SD = 14.68), [$t(95)$ = 5.30, $p < .001$]. For all males, whether in school or not, M = 39.69 hours (SD = 18.22), whereas for all females, M = 35.06 hours (SD = 14.74). The median test indicated that the median was 40 hours worked, with an average rank of 53.8 hours for males (n = 48) and 44.3 hours for females (n = 49), which is not a significant difference.

Employment/Education and Other Life-Situation Factors

We next group subjects according to four groups with respect to employment and education: *employed/in school, employed/not in school, in school only, employed/ not in school*. Other life-situation factors, such as marriage, childrearing, and economic resources, are then examined for each of these four groups. The various combinations of employment and education status at the time of interview are described for male and female campers and noncampers in Table 11.9.

From Table 11.9, we can see that the majority of subjects in school were employed. Among campers, 19 out of the 26 in school (73%) were employed, and among noncampers, 15 out of the 21 in school (71%) were employed. There were no statistical differences between distributions of campers and noncampers in the table's four employment/education groups. Among the 14 camper females who were in school, 12 (86%) were also employed, compared with a rate of 7 out of 12 (58%) for camper males, which was a borderline trend (p = .13, Fisher's exact test). However, on the distributions of the four employment/education groups, there were no significant differences or trends for camper males versus

The life situations of the vast majority (85%) of study subjects fell into one of these categories:

- **Employed and in school**
- **Employed but not in school**
- **In school only**

It is interesting that only 10% of subjects were able to attend school and yet not be employed.

Table 11.9

Distribution of Subjects by Employment and Postsecondary Enrollment

Status	No. (%) of Campers			No. (%) of Noncampers		
	Males	Females	All	Males	Females	All
Employed/ in school	7 (23%)	12 (34%)	19 (29%)	8 (23%)	7 (23%)	15 (23%)
Employed/ not in school	17 (55%)	14 (40%)	31 (47%)	16 (47%)	16 (53%)	32 (50%)
In school only	5 (16%)	2 (6%)	7 (11%)	4 (12%)	2 (6%)	6 (9%)
Unemployed/ not in school	2 (6%)	7 (20%)	9 (14%)	6 (18%)	5 (17%)	11 (17%)
Total	31 (100%)	35 (100%)	66 (100%)	34 (100%)	30 (100%)	64 (100%)

Note. Because of rounding of percentages, not all columns total 100%.

camper females. There was also no significant difference for males versus females overall.

Of campers, about 87% of subjects are accounted for by the first three groups in Table 11.9: they are *employed/ in school, employed/not in school,* or *in school only.* Of noncampers, about 82% of subjects are accounted for in these three groups. Similar levels of campers and noncampers were in the group *unemployed/not in school.*

It is interesting to note here that among campers, 13 (20%) indicated that they augmented their economic resources with occasional jobs, such as babysitting or mowing lawns. Of noncampers, 9 (14%) indicated they took occasional jobs.

Employment/education and marital status. Next we consider the economic resources of those in different life situations. Table 11.10 summarizes the different life situations of subjects, distributing them according to marital status and employment/education status. Several decisions were made to distribute subjects for the table. *Married/cohabiting* in Table 11.10 includes 3 divorced persons (1 camper female, 1 noncamper female, and 1 noncamper male), each with a child, because they may have been receiving aid from former spouses. A divorced camper male with no children was treated as *single*.

Within camper and noncamper groups, there were no significant differences in the distribution of *single* versus *married/cohabiting* subjects across the four employment/education groups. Overall, 32 campers (48%) and 43 noncampers (67%) were *single* and had no children (of *single* camper subjects, only 1—a female who was working and not in school—had a child). Among campers, looking at the four basic employment/education groups as shown in Table 11.10, we find a nonsignificant trend for *single* versus *married/cohabiting* camp-

Table 11.10

Employment, Education, and Marital Status

Marital Status	No. (%) Employed/ in School	No. (%) Employed/ Not in School	No. (%) in School Only	No. (%) Unemployed/ Not in School	Total
Campers					
Single	13 (39%)	13 (39%)	5 (15%)	2 (6%)	33 (100%)
Married/ cohabiting	6 (18%)	18 (55%)	2 (6%)	7 (21%)	33 (100%)
Noncampers					
Single	14 (33%)	18 (42%)	4 (9%)	7 (16%)	43 (100%)
Married/ cohabiting	1 (5%)	14 (67%)	2 (9%)	4 (19%)	21 (100%)

ers [$\chi^2(3)$ = 7.45, $p < .10$]. Combining some of the sub-groups in Table 11.10, we see that the differences be-tween these groups appear to be that more *single* camp-ers were in school and several more *married/cohabiting* campers were neither working nor in school. For *single* campers, the majority were *employed/not in school* or *employed/in school* (approximately 78%). Of *married/co-habiting* campers, the same was also true, with 73% *employed/not in school* or *employed/in school*. Among noncampers, the four patterns in Table 11.10 also indi-cated a nonsignificant trend for *single* versus *married/ cohabiting* subjects [$\chi^2(3)$ = 6.45, $p < .10$]. Majorities of *single* noncampers (73%) and *married/cohabiting* noncampers (72%) were *employed/not in school* or *em-ployed/in school*. Only one married noncamper worked and went to school.

IN SUMMARY   The majority of sample subjects—in-cluding campers and noncampers, married or single— either worked or combined working with being en-rolled in postsecondary education. It is interesting that only 13 subjects (10% of the sample) were in school and not working, while 20 subjects (15%) were neither em-ployed nor in school. Presumably, few subjects had sufficient funds to go to school without working. Eco-nomic issues such as this will be examined next.

Employment/education and childrearing. Of the *married/cohabiting* subjects with a child, only 2 (1 camper and 1 noncamper) were part of the *in-school-only* group. The other *married/cohabiting* subjects with children were 7 campers and 5 noncampers who were in the *employed/ not-in-school* group and 5 campers and 2 noncampers who were in the *unemployed/not-in-school* group.

The distribution of campers and noncampers in the *unemployed/not-in-school* group included 2 male and 7 female campers and 6 male and 5 female noncampers. No males in this group had children, whereas 5 out of the 7 camper females, and 2 out of the 5 noncamper females, had children. A total of 7 out of 12 females in

Of those study subjects in the unemployed, not-in-school group, the majority of females had children and were married or cohabiting.

this small subgroup (*unemployed/not in school*) had children, and these were all married or living with a spouse-equivalent—an indication of a potential source of economic support.

Employment/education and student or parental aid. For many young adults, whether they stay in school or not is at least partly a function of whether or not their parents can or will provide some form of economic aid, such as paying for all or part of tuition, providing housing for the young adults at home, or paying for their housing at school and buying their clothes. In particular, young adults who marry or have children may lessen the likelihood that their parents will provide economic resources or direct aid to help them stay in school. For those young adults working in low-income jobs or having a child and thus not being able to work, some families provide enough economic assistance to help their children make the transition to adult responsibilities; other families do not help in these situations, simply because they think it is best for the young adult to learn independence. Still others, however, not only cannot help their children financially but also need their children to work and help *them* financially.

Our data were not sufficient to determine to what extent subjects relied on parental aid. However, the majority of study subjects (83%) enrolled in postsecondary education indicated that they were receiving some financial aid from parents, school, or both (no table). Of 26 *enrolled campers*, 12 (46%) received aid from one source (parents or school), 7 (27%) received aid from both sources (parents and school), 7 (27%) received no aid from any source. Of the 21 *enrolled noncampers*, 13 (62%) received aid from one source, 7 (33%) received aid from both sources, and 1 (5%) received no aid from any source. Comparing campers versus noncampers for *some aid* versus *no aid* yielded a borderline trend [$\chi^2(1) = 2.62$, $p < .13$, Yates' correction]. Apparently, a somewhat greater proportion of campers than noncampers relied on their own resources to finance postsecondary education.

Compared with in-school noncampers, in-school campers had fewer sources of financial aid (from parents or school).

Employment/education and public assistance. Another potential source of financial support for young
adults is public assistance, such as Aid to Families With
Dependent Children (AFDC), food stamps, Medicaid.
Thus, we considered the number of campers and
noncampers on public assistance at the time of interview and prior to that point. Subjects were asked a
number of questions about various types of public
assistance. A few subjects noted that they had received
public assistance of some type but did not specify the
type. Others indicated specific types of public assistance they had received, including unemployment insurance, Medicaid, social insurance benefits, and other
forms of aid.

Subjects who received welfare in the form of AFDC
or food stamps (only a few received just food stamps)
are of particular interest. A comparison of all campers
($n = 66$) and all noncampers ($n = 64$) with regard to how
many received this welfare (no table) revealed 9 campers versus 2 noncampers, which is a significant difference [$\chi^2(1) = 4.64, p < .05$]. Of the 9 campers on welfare,
4 were also employed at least part-time, whereas neither of the 2 noncampers on welfare was employed. Of
the 9 campers and 11 noncampers who were *unem-
ployed/not in school*, 5 campers versus 2 noncampers
were on welfare, a nonsignificant trend ($p = .10$, Fisher's
exact test).

A focus on unemployed/not-in-school subjects.
We next examined the life circumstances of those 20
study subjects (9 campers and 11 noncampers) who
were *unemployed/not in school*. As pointed out earlier, for
females in this subgroup, 10 out of 12 did have the actual
or potential economic resources of a spouse. In contrast,
only 1 male in this subgroup was married or had a
spouse-equivalent. These *unemployed/not-in-school*
subjects represent 14% of campers (mainly females) and
17% of noncampers (but with no significant gender
difference for noncampers).

There were no significant differences between campers and noncampers in the educational levels of *unem-*

Few subjects received
AFDC or food stamps.
Though 9 of these subjects
were campers, 4 out of the
9 were also employed.

Subjects with the least
economic independence
had the least education.

Table 11.11

Distribution of Unemployed/Not-in-School Subjects by Educational Level

Group	No High School	High School/ Equivalent	Voc./Tech./ 1 yr College	2 yr or More College
Unemployed/not-in-school subjects	3 (75%)	9 (21%)	6 (13%)	2 (6%)
Other subjects	1 (25%)	34 (79%)	41 (87%)	34 (94%)
Total	4 (100%)	43 (100%)	47 (100%)	36 (100%)

ployed/not-in-school subjects. Table 11.11 shows the distribution of subjects in this subgroup according to educational level. From Table 11.11, it is clear that subjects with the least economic independence had the least education.

As noted in the previous section on public assistance, there was a nonsignificant trend for more *unemployed/not-in-school* campers than noncampers to be receiving welfare. Of the 5 camper females who were *unemployed/not in school* but were on welfare, 1 was *single* with no child, and 4 each had a child. Of these 4 subjects, 1 was married, 1 divorced, and 2 cohabiting with spouse-equivalents. Of the 2 *unemployed/not-in-school* noncampers on welfare, the male noncamper was *single*, without children, and the female noncamper was *married*, with a child. Of subjects *unemployed/not in school*, an additional 3 campers (2 females and 1 male) and 3 noncampers (all females) indicated that they had at some point since high school received some form of public assistance (social insurance benefits, unemployment insurance, or Medicaid). Of the remaining subjects without jobs and not in school, there were 3 single male noncampers and 1 cohabiting female noncamper, none of whom had children.

SUMMARIZING THIS CHAPTER   Our analysis of marriage, children, and economic resources in this chapter
revealed that significantly more noncampers than campers had remained single, not cohabiting. Nevertheless, there were more campers in postsecondary school,
and campers were employed at the same rates as
noncampers. Given that campers' backgrounds showed
greater economic disadvantage, we would expect them
to have more economic difficulty in young adulthood,
and we did see some indicators of this. For example, we
found that compared with in-school noncampers, fewer
in-school campers had student aid or economic assistance from parents. We also found that a small number
of study subjects were receiving AFDC and food stamps,
and this involved significantly more campers than
noncampers. But, of those receiving this public aid,
more campers worked, at least part-time.

Overall, we saw campers making considerable efforts to overcome their economic difficulties through
education and employment. Given this, we would expect campers to have the greater long-range economic
potential. In the next chapter, we look at the influences
in campers' and noncampers' lives that may have led to
their life situations at the time of interview.

Chapter TWELVE

Influences Related to Educational Level

THUS FAR, this 5-year follow-up study of program and comparison subjects has shown that a significantly greater proportion of program subjects went on to postsecondary education. As pointed out in Chapter 6, although it is useful to show that the High/Scope Institute for IDEAS "worked" in this way, an evaluation should also provide direction for future program development. Therefore, in this chapter, we examine the various past and continuing influences on subjects that led to the educational levels of campers versus noncampers. The influences we look at are these: recognition for achievement in high school, attitudes towards education and achievement, problem behavior in high school, and role models and life experiences.

Recognized Achievement and Attitudes

We first examine the relationship between subjects' recognition for achievement in high school and their pursuit of postsecondary education.

High School Recognition

Subjects were considered to be *recognized achievers* in high school if they reported having been on the dean's

A program's educational outcomes should be examined in relation to other influences—past and present—such as subjects' high school achievement and economic resources.

list, having received any scholarships, or having received any academic awards. As shown in Table 12.1, similar numbers of campers and noncampers were *recognized achievers*; there were no significant differences between the two groups. Out of the 66 campers, 32 (49%) received recognition for academic achievement in high school; this compared with 29 out of 64 noncampers (45%). Also, we found no significant gender differences within or between groups. Out of the 35 female campers, 19 (54%) were *recognized achievers* in high school; this compared with 15 out of 30 female noncampers (50%) being recognized for academic achievement. Male *rec-*

Table 12.1

High-School-Recognized Achievers and Educational Level

High School Status	No. (%) of Campers		No. (%) of Noncampers	
	Males	Females	Males	Females
Recognized achievers				
Postsecondary	10 (77%)	16 (84%)	13 (93%)	12 (80%)
No postsecondary	3 (23%)	3 (16%)	1 (7%)	3 (20%)
Total	13 (100%)	19 (100%)	14 (100%)	15 (100%)
Others				
Postsecondary	10 (56%)	12 (75%)	5 (25%)	5 (33%)
No postsecondary	8 (44%)	4 (25%)	15 (75%)	10 (67%)
Total	18 (100%)	16 (100%)	20 (100%)	15 (100%)

Note. With the exception of 3 campers and 3 noncampers, *postsecondary* refers to *college.*

ognized achievers included 13 out of 31 campers (42%) and 14 out of 34 noncampers (41%). Among campers, 81% of recognized achievers went on to postsecondary education, while among noncampers, 86% of *recognized achievers* went on; this was not a significant difference or trend.

The most important finding concerns how many campers were not recognized for academic achievement in high school but did go on to postsecondary education. As shown in Table 12.1, of campers who had not received academic recognition (*others*), the majority (65%) nonetheless did go on to postsecondary education, whereas only a minority (29%) of their noncamper counterparts (*others*) went on. This was a statistically significant difference [$\chi^2(1) = 9.06$, $p < .01$]. Thus it appears that for campers—whether male or female—the High/Scope program had a unique impact on nonrecognized achievers. Perhaps if they had not participated in the High/Scope camp program, only a minority of these low-income students would have gone on to postsecondary education.

Attitudes Towards Education and Achievement

Not only recognition from others but also students' own attitudes towards education and achievement are potential influences on whether or not they choose education after high school. Thus we also examined subjects' attitudes towards high school and achievement in general.

Attitudes towards high school. The first attitudinal variable to be considered is subjects' ratings of their satisfaction with their last year of high school. Table 12.2 shows the overall camper and noncamper distributions for attitudes towards their last year of high school. Among campers, 56 out of 66 (85%) were *fairly satisfied* or *very satisfied* with their last year of high school; this compared with 51 out of 64 noncampers (80%), which was not a significant difference.

Of the nonrecognized achievers (with no academic honors in high school), significantly more campers than noncampers (65% versus 29%) went on to postsecondary education.

Table 12.2

Subjects' Attitudes Towards Last Year of High School

Attitude	No. (%) of Campers		No. (%) of Noncampers	
	No Postsecondary	Postsecondary	No Postsecondary	Postsecondary
Very dissatisfied	1 (6%)	3 (6%)	5 (17%)	0 (0%)
Dissatisfied	3 (17%)	3 (6%)	3 (10%)	5 (14%)
Fairly satisfied	8 (44%)	26 (54%)	12 (41%)	13 (37%)
Very satisfied	6 (33%)	16 (33%)	9 (31%)	17 (49%)
Total	18 (100%)	48 (100%)	29 (100%)	35 (100%)

When we examined the relationship of subjects' 4 levels of attitudes (from *very dissatisfied* to *very satisfied*) to whether they went on to *postsecondary* education, we found no significant differences or trends among campers versus noncampers. Thus, overall, subjects' attitudes about their last year of high school did not appear to be related to whether or not they continued their education beyond high school.

We next looked at all satisfied study subjects— combining those who were *fairly satisfied* and *very satisfied* and then comparing campers versus noncampers for *postsecondary* education versus *no postsecondary* education. We found that 42 out of 56 campers (75%), compared with 30 out of 51 noncampers (59%), went on to *postsecondary*, which was a nonsignificant trend $[\chi^2(1) = 3.17, p < .10]$. This nonsignificant trend indicates that among those study subjects who were in any way satisfied with their last year of high school, there was some tendency for more campers than noncampers to continue their education beyond high school.

Next, we compared *very dissatisfied* subjects versus *dissatisfied* subjects for *postsecondary* versus *no postsecondary*, first for campers and then for noncampers. For campers, we found no significant difference or trend. Thus, for dissatisfied campers, the level of their dissatisfaction with their last year of high school was not related to whether or not they continued their education; 6 out of the 10 campers (60%) who were at all dissatisfied still did go on to *postsecondary* education. However, among noncampers, 5 of the *8 dissatisfied* subjects versus none of the *5 very dissatisfied* subjects went on to *postsecondary* education, which was a significant difference ($p = .04$, Fisher's exact test). Overall, 5 out of 13 (38%) of the *very dissatisfied* or *dissatisfied* noncampers went on to *postsecondary* education.

Finally we compared *dissatisfied* campers versus *dissatisfied* noncampers for *postsecondary* versus *no postsecondary* and found no significant difference. However, when we compared *very dissatisfied* campers versus *very dissatisfied* noncampers for *postsecondary* versus *no postsecondary*, we found the *very dissatisfied* campers were more likely to go on to higher education (Fisher's exact test, $p = .05$).

Since the vast majority of study subjects felt positive about their last year of high school, it was difficult to assess the impact of the High/Scope program on students' attitudes about their last year of high school. However, we can make some inferences about the program's impact on students' receptivity to the idea of education beyond high school: When looking at study subjects who were *fairly satisfied* or *very satisfied* with the last year of high school, we found a nonsignificant trend of more campers versus noncampers going on to postsecondary education. It is also interesting that among the subjects who were *very dissatisfied* with their last year of high school, students chose against postsecondary education unless they had participated in the High/Scope camp program. These findings suggest that even when talented disadvantaged students

Of subjects who reported being very dissatisfied with high school, significantly more campers than noncampers went on to postsecondary education.

▾

feel negative about high school, their receptivity to higher education can be positively affected by an intervention program. Next we examine subjects' attitudes about themselves and their educational aspirations.

Attitudes about locus of control and achievement motivation. As described in Part 1 of this book, such attitudes as high self-esteem and feelings of personal causation (positive beliefs about *locus of control*) are involved in students' motivation for achievement. These attitudes are important for students' development of such behaviors as risk taking, persisting at a task, and striving for excellence. For this reason, our general descriptive findings on such attitudinal data are next reported and discussed (also see the Appendix).

Subjects were asked to rate themselves on a series of 5-point attitudinal scales connected with 16 items about their perception of the *locus of control* of events. For example, several items like this one were designed to assess whether a subject felt that personal planning or chance had a greater effect on events: *Every time I try to get ahead, something or somebody stops me.* A more positive response to this item is to disagree, since agreeing indicates a perception that success is outside of one's personal control. The scale for this item ranged from 1–5, from *disagree* to *agree*.

High positive ratings (that is, ratings tending towards personal control of success) were found for both campers and noncampers, including males and females. The average median score across campers was 4.37, and across noncampers, 4.29. The mean score across campers was 4.26 ($SD = .41$), and across noncampers, 4.24 ($SD = .36$). The statistical tests indicated no significant differences between groups or between genders.

A set of 4-point attitudinal scales specifically designed to assess subjects' *achievement motivation* was also administered. In connection with these scales, subjects were asked to consider each of 23 items and to rate how well an item did or did not apply to them (1 = *not true of you*, 2 = *somewhat true of you*, 3 = *true of you*, 4 = *very true of you*). The following sentences are sample items:

On the average, study subjects in both the program and the comparison group had a strong sense of personal causation and achievement motivation.

(1) *I feel I can go into many different types of work and succeed.* (2) *If I see I may just fail or flop at something, I get eager to do something else.* The items connected with these 4-point scales were found to have sufficient internal consistency. The average median score was 3.09 for campers and 3.07 for noncampers, with no statistical differences found between campers and noncampers or between genders on the two-sample median test.

Although the statistical analyses on the attitudinal data about locus of control and achievement motivation provided no significant differences overall between campers and noncampers, males and females, this data will be used in Chapter 13 to further examine indirect links to the major variables.

IN SUMMARY   Thus far we know that lacking high academic achievement and recognition in high school and being dissatisfied with high school can be limiting factors in talented disadvantaged students' higher education choices unless programs like High/Scope's intervene. Next we look at what limitations are imposed by students' problem behaviors.

Problem Behaviors

A lack of positive influences in young people's lives may lead them into a pattern of problem behavior, which in turn may direct them away from academic achievement during and after high school. For example, some research has indicated that negative influences from family and friends contribute to adolescents' problem behaviors (such as illegal substance use) (Hundleby & Mercer, 1987), and national data indicate that young people who commit juvenile and criminal offenses also tend to achieve low educational levels (U.S. Department of Justice, 1983).

Considering the importance of problem behaviors to our educational concerns, we examined behavioral difficulties reported by subjects. It was expected that more campers than noncampers in the 5-year follow-up study would have experienced some problem behaviors, since in several cases, high school counselors had specifically encouraged some troubled young people to sign up for the camp program, feeling it could help them turn their lives around.

Frequencies of Problem-Behavior Incidents

Subjects answered a series of 18 questions about a range of problem behaviors, including incidents of physical fighting, shoplifting, stealing, vandalism, using illegal substances, being suspended or expelled from high school or work, and being arrested. Subjects were asked to indicate how frequently they were involved in such incidents and to describe them (see the Appendix). The frequencies are shown in Table 12.3. Using Table 12.3 data, we found no significant differences in the distributions of campers versus noncampers according to frequencies of problem-behavior incidents [$\chi^2(7) = 6.57$, nonsignificant].

It is encouraging to note that according to Table 12.3, 23% of campers and 31% of noncampers reported never having experienced any of the problem behaviors in question. Furthermore, an additional 27% of campers and 20% of noncampers had experienced only 1 or 2 problem behaviors (shoplifting an inexpensive item as a child, having a fight, and using marijuana were among the most frequent of these behaviors). Thus, for approximately 50% of both camper and noncamper groups, problem behaviors were rare or nonexistent.

We next looked at per subject frequencies of the problem-behavior incidents, comparing campers and noncampers. For campers the average score was .32 ($SD = .41$), and for noncampers the average score was .22 ($SD = .23$); so both groups averaged between 0 and 1 for per subject frequency of problem-behavior incidents. On the two-sample median test, there were no statistically significant differences or trends between campers

Problem behaviors (fighting, shoplifting, getting suspended from school) were nonexistent or rare for about 50% of study subjects.

There were no significant differences between campers and noncampers in frequencies of problem-behavior incidents.

Table 12.3

**Distribution of Subjects by Frequencies
of Problem-Behavior Incidents**

Frequency of Problem-Behavior Incidents	No. (%) of Campers	No. (%) of Noncampers
None	15 (23%)	20 (31%)
1–2	18 (27%)	13 (20%)
3–4	9 (14%)	9 (14%)
5–6	7 (11%)	8 (13%)
7–8	4 (6%)	5 (8%)
9–12	4 (6%)	6 (9%)
13–19	5 (7%)	3 (5%)
20 or more	4 (6%)	0 (0%)
Total	66 (100%)	64 (100%)

and noncampers or between males and females (within or between groups).

Types of Problem-Behavior Incidents

To examine numbers of subjects with various types of problem behaviors, we looked at problem-behavior incidents divided into these categories: (A) *suspension or expulsion from high school* for behavior problems;

(B) *minor delinquency* (such as getting into fights, shoplifting, vandalizing school property); and (C) *serious delinquency* (such as car theft, robbery). We then looked at subjects' incidents of police arrest, dividing the incidents according to whether subjects experienced a *first arrest* before or after age 18. Finally, we looked at another category of problem behavior—use of *marijuana* and *other illegal substances.*

From Table 12.4, which shows problem behaviors divided into the categories A, B, and C just mentioned, we can see that although the minor problem behaviors (categories A and B) predominated, there were also some study subjects with serious delinquent behavior (category C). We found no significant differences between campers and noncampers for categories A–C. There were, however, some significant gender differences for certain categories, which will be explained next, under discussion of each category.

A. Suspension or expulsion from high school. Table 12.4 data indicate that a significantly greater proportion of males (19 out of 65, or 29%) than of females (9 out of 65, or 14%) had ever experienced *suspension or expulsion from high school* [$\chi^2(1) = 4.55, p < .05$]. Among campers, there were significantly more camper males (13 out of 31, or 42%) who had ever been suspended or expelled; this compared with 5 out of 35, or 14%, for camper females [$\chi^2(1) = 6.34, p < .05$]. Although there were more camper males (13 out of 31, or 42%) than noncamper males (6 out of 34, or 18%) who had ever been suspended or expelled, the difference was not significant, nor was it a trend. There were no other significant differences.

B. Minor delinquency. Table 12.4 data also show that there was a nonsignificant trend for more males (38 out of 65, or 58%) than females (28 out of 65, or 43%) to have experienced *minor delinquency* [$\chi^2(1) = 3.08, p < .10$]. There were no significant differences between male and female campers for *minor delinquency*, but there was a significant gender difference in this category for noncampers, with more males (20 out of 34, or 59%) than

There were no significant differences between campers and noncampers in the types of incidents they reported—school suspension, minor delinquency, or serious delinquency.

▾

Significantly more males (29%) than females (14%) had been suspended or expelled from school.

▾

Table 12.4

Types of Problem Behaviors

Type of Incident	No. (%) of Campers Reporting Incident	No.(%) of Noncampers Reporting Incident
A. Suspension or expulsion from high school		
Some incidents	18 (27%)	10 (16%)
No incidents	48 (73%)	54 (84%)
Total	66 (100%)	64 (100%)
B. Minor delinquency		
Some incidents	36 (55%)	30 (47%)
No incidents	30 (45%)	34 (53%)
Total	66 (100%)	64 (100%)
C. Serious delinquency		
Some incidents	11 (17%)	8 (13%)
No incidents	55 (83%)	56 (87%)
Total	66 (100%)	64 (100%)

Note. The data presented here indicate how many subjects reported that they had ever experienced an incident. Table data do not indicate subjects' total frequencies of incidents.

females (10 out of 30, or 33%) having experienced *minor delinquency* [$\chi^2(1) = 4.16$, $p < .05$]. There were no other significant differences.

Compared with female subjects, male subjects reported somewhat more minor delinquency; they reported significantly more serious delinquency.

▾

There was no significant camper/noncamper difference in numbers of first arrests after age 18. However, as expected, significantly more campers (mostly males) had at some time been arrested by police.

▾

C. Serious delinquency. From Table 12.4, we can also see that there were significantly more males (14 out of 65, or 22%) than females (5 out of 65, or 8%) who reported *serious delinquency* [$\chi^2(1) = 4.99$, $p < .05$]. For male versus female campers, 8 out of 31 males (26%), compared with 3 out of 35 females (9%), had participated in *serious delinquency*, a nonsignificant trend [$\chi^2(1) = 3.52$, $p < .10$]. There were no other significant differences.

Arrest by police. Table 12.5 contains data about campers' and noncampers' arrests for problem behavior before and after reaching age 18. From the table, we can see that there was a significant difference between campers and noncampers in total number of first arrests reported. Among campers, 14 out of 66 (21%) had been arrested by police; this compared with 5 out of 64 (8%) for noncampers [$\chi^2(1) = 4.67$, $p < .05$].

When we looked at the arrest data to compare males and females (no table), we found that the number of study subjects who had ever been arrested were predominantly males. Overall, a significantly greater proportion of males than females had experienced police arrest, 17 out of 65 males (26%) versus 2 out of 65 females (3%) [$\chi^2(1) = 13.87$, $p < .001$]. Among campers alone, there were also significantly more males than females who had experienced police arrest, 12 out of 31 males (39%) versus 2 out of 35 females (6%) [$\chi^2(1) = 10.71$, $p < .01$]. Also among noncampers, more males (5 out of 34, or 15%) than females (0 out of 30, or 0%) had experienced arrest, a nonsignificant trend [$\chi^2(1) = 2.96$, $p < .10$, Yates' correction]. Finally, a significantly greater proportion of camper males than noncamper males had been arrested [$\chi^2(1) = 4.84$, $p < .05$], but there were no significant differences between camper versus noncamper females.

Generally, we could not determine whether problem-behavior incidents had occurred before or after subjects' camp participation, because we did not ask subjects to provide dates for most incidents. But since we did inquire about the ages at which subjects were

Table 12.5

Subjects' Incidence of First Arrest by Police

Incident/ Time	No. (%) of Campers Reporting Incident	No. (%) of Noncampers Reporting Incident
First arrest at age 17 or younger		
Yes	9 (14%)	3 (5%)
No	57 (86%)	61 (95%)
Total	66 (100%)	64 (100%)
First arrest at age 18 or older		
Yes	5 (8%)	2 (3%)
No	61 (92%)	62 (97%)
Total	66 (100%)	64 (100%)

Note. The data presented here indicate how many subjects
reported experiencing a first arrest in each time period. Table data
do not indicate subjects' total frequencies of arrest incidents.

first arrested by police, we were able to divide first-
arrest incidents into the two categories shown in Table
12.5, *at age 17 or younger* and *at age 18 or older*. (We chose
age 18 as the dividing point because campers reached
age 18 after attending camp, and also, age 18 is when
illegal activity typically moves from juvenile into criminal jurisdiction.)

Table 12.5 shows that the vast majority of subjects in
both groups (86% of campers and 95% of noncampers)
were never arrested before age 18, and there were only
very small percentages of both groups indicating first
arrests after reaching age 18 (8% of campers and 3% of

noncampers). Of campers, 9 (14%) reported a first arrest before age 18; this compared with 3 noncampers (5%), which is a nonsignificant trend [$\chi^2(1) = 3.11$, $p < .10$]. Just 5 additional campers (8%) and 2 additional non-campers (3%) reported first arrests after reaching age 18, which is not a significant difference or trend.

When we examined the per subject frequency of arrests across ages (no table), we found that subjects who were first arrested before age 18 did not specify dates for their subsequent arrests. We do know that out of the 14 campers reporting first arrests, 5 had multiple arrests (this includes 2 campers who were each arrested twice after reaching age 18; of the other 3 multiple-arrest campers, 1 was arrested twice, 1 was arrested 3 times, and 1 was arrested 6 times, but *when* these subsequent arrests occurred—whether before or after the subjects reached age 18—is unclear). No noncampers had multiple arrests.

Subjects who had been arrested were asked how much time they spent in jail. Of those arrested, only a few had committed offenses that were serious enough to require spending time in jail. However, as expected, we did find that several more campers than noncampers had serious problem behaviors before age 18; for both groups there were few first arrests after subjects reached age 18.

Use of illegal substances. We next considered the problem behavior of using illegal substances other than alcohol or tobacco. [We did also consider separately subjects' use of tobacco and alcohol and found no significant differences or trends with regard to their use. Study subjects' overall 23% rate of daily smoking was somewhat less than the 30% national rate of "smokers" among 20- to 24-year-olds. Likewise, study subjects' overall 85% rate of alcohol use was under the national rate of 90% (U.S. Bureau of the Census, 1990b).]

The U.S. Bureau of the Census (1990b) provides relevant national rates of illegal substance use excluding alcohol and tobacco use: In 1988, approximately 56% of 18- to 25-year-olds reported having used marijuana;

> Subjects' arrests were for acts of minor delinquency, and very few resulted in subjects' spending time in jail.

approximately 20% reported having used other illegal substances, such as cocaine, heroin, hallucinogens. Table 12.6 provides data about camper and noncamper use of illegal substances.

From the data in Table 12.6, we found no significant differences between campers (47%) and noncampers (48%) who reported *ever* using *marijuana*. There were also no significant differences or trends for gender. There was a significant difference between campers and noncampers on use of *other illegal substances*, with more campers (23%) than noncampers (6%) reporting they had used *other illegal substances* [$\chi^2(1) = 7.07, p < .01$]. Between males and females in general, and within

Subjects reported rates of tobacco and alcohol use that were comparable to national rates. This was also the case for marijuana use.

Table 12.6

Use of Illegal Substances

Use	No. (%) of Campers Reporting Use	No. (%) of Noncampers Reporting Use
Marijuana		
Ever	31 (47%)	31 (48%)
Never	35 (53%)	33 (52%)
Total	66 (100%)	64 (100%)
Other illegal substances		
Ever	15 (23%)	4 (6%)
Never	51 (77%)	60 (94%)
Total	66 (100%)	64 (100%)

Note. Illegal substances excludes alcohol and tobacco.

camper and noncamper groups, there were no significant differences in use of *other illegal substances*.

For gender between groups (no table), there was a significant difference between male campers (9 out of 31, or 29%) and male noncampers (3 out of 34, or 9%) who reported use of *other illegal substances* [$\chi^2(1) = 4.40$, $p < .05$]. Although female campers outnumbered female noncampers in reporting use of *other illegal substances*, we found no significant differences between female campers (6 out of 35, or 17%) and female noncampers (1 out of 30, or 3%) who reported use of *other illegal substances* [$\chi^2(1) = 1.93$, nonsignificant, Yates' correction].

While the campers' 23% rate of using *other illegal substances* appears to be comparable to the national rates cited earlier for young adults, the noncampers' rate of 6% is considerably lower. It is not clear why this might be the case. We do know that to begin with, compared with the noncamper group, the camper group included several more subjects with problem behaviors, and the greater illegal substance use by campers may be a part of that pattern.

IN SUMMARY   Overall, campers did not differ from noncampers in frequency or types of problem-behavior incidents, except in more first arrests before age 18 and greater use of illegal substances. Problem incidents subjects did report most likely occurred primarily during the high school years. Males experienced more problem-behavior incidents than females did. A small number of campers, predominantly males, experienced behavior that was problematic to the point of serious delinquency, primarily before 18 years of age. However, few subjects spent time in jail.

One would expect that for young people in general, problem behavior might be negatively related to the pursuit of higher education. In fact, of those 15 campers with no self-reported problem behaviors, 11 (73%) went on to postsecondary education. For noncampers, the comparable statistic is 13 out of 20, or 65%. However, it is also noteworthy that 4 (36%) of the 11 campers who

Significantly more campers than noncampers reported having at some time used other illegal substances, but the camper rate was no greater than national rates for their age cohort.

had the most serious problem behaviors (*serious delin-quency*) did go on to postsecondary education; this compared with 1 (17%) of the 6 noncampers with *serious delinquency.*

Influences From Parents, Role Models, and Experiences

For adolescents, their parents, teachers, friends, and experiences, as well as their own personal values, inter-ests, and confidence can all influence motivation to achieve academically. We now focus on the study sub-jects' perceptions of how parents, other role models, and experiences influenced their lives. The frequency and categories of these kinds of influences were examined in relation to subjects' educational levels at the time of interview.

Parent Expectations and Support

To assess parent influence, interviewers asked subjects how much their parents valued their education and what their parents did to foster it. Table 12.7 lists 6 categories of parent support and shows how many subjects reported receiving each category of support. Across categories, the only significant difference be-tween campers and noncampers was in the category *encouraged graduation from high school*, with more noncampers perceiving that their parents were highly supportive in this respect [$\chi^2(1) = 10.23, p < .01$].

Subjects were also asked to rate their parents spe-cifically regarding the degree of parent emphasis on homework, as shown in Table 12.8. There were no significant differences between campers and noncampers on parent encouragement of homework [$\chi^2(3) = 2.61$, nonsignificant]. Majorities of both groups reported that parents encouraged homework *sometimes* or *frequently*— 67% for campers and 74% for noncampers.

Subjects also reported on their parents' expecta-

Significantly more noncampers than campers perceived parental expectations for their graduation from high school.

▾

Table 12.7

Subjects' Perceptions of Parent Support for Achievement

Categories of Parent Support	No. (%) of Campers	No. (%) of Noncampers
Valued education	15 (23%)	14 (22%)
Involved selves in school/homework	9 (14%)	7 (11%)
Gave encouragement	13 (20%)	18 (28%)
Encouraged persistence	14 (21%)	17 (27%)
Encouraged graduation from high school	11 (17%)	27 (42%)
Other	17 (26%)	16 (25%)
Total responses indicating support	79	99

Note. Percentages are based on $n = 66$ for campers and $n = 64$ for noncampers. Columns of percentages do not total 100%, since a given subject could name more than one type of support.

In both study groups—camper and noncamper—about 55% reported their parents expected them to go on to postsecondary education.

tions about what they (the subjects) would do after high school (no table). Categories included *no expectations* and expectations for *a job*, for *military service*, for *vocational/technical training*, or for *2-year or 4-year college or university*. Expectations were similar for both groups. Of campers, 26 (39%) perceived their parents as having *no expectations*; this compared with 22 of the noncampers (34%) perceiving their parents as having *no expectations*. Of campers, 36 (55%) perceived their parents as expecting some postsecondary education (*vocational/technical training* or *college*); this was not significantly different from noncampers, of whom 36 (56%) perceived parent

Table 12.8

**Subjects' Perceived Parent Encouragement
of Homework**

Degree of Encouragement	No. (%) of Campers	No. (%) of Noncampers
Hardly at all	17 (26%)	12 (19%)
Just a little	5 (8%)	5 (8%)
Sometimes	9 (14%)	5 (8%)
Frequently	35 (53%)	42 (66%)
Total	66 (100%)	64 (100%)

Note. Because of rounding of percentages, columns do not total 100%.

expectations for some postsecondary education. It is interesting that 56% of the noncampers reported parent expectations for postsecondary education, since that was approximately the same percentage of noncampers who went on to postsecondary education.

Parent Expectations Related to Educational Level

Table 12.9 shows how we examined the connection between low parent-expectations and subjects' going on to *postsecondary education* (including *college* and, for 3 campers and 3 noncampers, postsecondary *vocational/technical training*). We found a relationship similar to that found for high school achievement recognition and postsecondary education:

Among noncampers, 10 out of 27 (37%) perceiving

Table 12.9

Parent Expectations and Student Current Educational Level

Student Current Educational Level	No. (%) of Campers by Parent Expectations		No. (%) of Noncampers by Parent Expectations	
	Low	High	Low	High
Postsecondary education	20 (69%)	28 (76%)	10 (37%)	25 (68%)
No postsecondary education	9 (31%)	9 (24%)	17 (63%)	12 (32%)
Total	29 (100%)	37 (100%)	27 (100%)	37 (100%)

Note. Low parent-expectations indicates *no expectations* or expectations for *a job; high* parent-expectations indicates expectations for *military service, vocational/technical training,* or *2-year or 4-year college or university.*

Significantly more campers than noncampers reporting low parent-expectations nevertheless went on to postsecondary education.

▼

low parent-expectations (*no expectations* or expectations for *a job*) went on to *postsecondary education*; this compared with 25 out of 37 (68%) who perceived *high* parent-expectations, which is a significant difference [$\chi^2(1) = 5.87, p < .05$]. Among those campers with *high* parent-expectations, 28 out of 37 (76%) went on to *postsecondary education*. The majority of campers with *low* parent-expectations, 20 out of 29 (69%), also went on, which is not a significant difference. Thus we found no significant differences or trends within campers for parent expectations and *postsecondary education*. Among all subjects whose parents had *low* expectations, significantly more campers than noncampers went on to *postsecondary education* [$\chi^2(1) = 5.73, p < .05$]. These findings indicate that unlike their noncamper counterparts, even the High/Scope campers whose parents did not expect much of them went on to higher education.

Family Relations and General Expectations

The perceptions that students hold in their minds about their parents' attitudes and expectations can have a major influence on students' motivation and achievement. Therefore, we considered how subjects rated their relationships with their families and how they rated their families' overall perceptions and expectations. Subjects responded to the following questions, using the described 3-point rating scales:

- **Family relations:** *How have you been getting along with your family, the one you grew up in?* [1(low) = *not too good, hardly get along at all*; 2(medium) = *get by fair with them*; and 3(high) = *get along with them*]
- **Family Perceptions:** *How does your family feel about how you are doing?* [1(low) = *not doing anything worth much*; 2(medium) = *getting by okay*; 3(high) = *doing great*]
- **Family Expectations:** *Are you turning out to be the kind of person your family expected you to be?* [1(low) = *not doing as well*; 2(medium) = *doing about the way they expected*; 3(high) = *doing better than they expected*]

For each of these questions, Table 12.10 shows the frequencies per rating for campers and noncampers. There were no significant differences or trends for gender within or between groups. There were no significant differences between camper and noncamper ratings in the areas of *family relations* and *family perceptions*. However, in the area of *family expectations*, 92% of noncampers (versus only 77% of campers) perceived that their families saw them as turning out *about the way they expected* (a medium rating) or *better than expected* (a high rating) [$\chi^2(1) = 5.41$, $p < .05$]. This significant difference may indicate that noncamper families communicated higher satisfaction than camper families did. In general, it would appear that campers perceived their parents to be less supportive or less positive towards them.

Table 12.10

Subjects' Perceptions About Families

Type of Question	No. (%) of Camper Ratings				No. (%) of Noncamper Ratings			
	Low	Medium	High	Total	Low	Medium	High	Total
Family relations	2 (3%)	9 (14%)	54 (83%)	65 (100%)	0 (0%)	11 (17%)	53 (83%)	64 (100%)
Family perceptions	2 (3%)	34 (52%)	30 (45%)	66 (100%)	4 (6%)	30 (48%)	29 (46%)	63 (100%)
Family expectations	14 (23%)	32 (53%)	14 (23%)	60 (100%)	5 (8%)	48 (77%)	9 (15%)	62 (100%)

Note. Because of rounding of percentages, not all rows total 100%.

Table 12.11

Frequency of Stressful Problems

Number of Stressful Problems	No. (%) of Campers	No. (%) of Noncampers
0	30 (45%)	32 (50%)
1	16 (24%)	18 (28%)
2	14 (21%)	13 (20%)
3 or more	6 (9%)	1 (2%)
Total	66 (100%)	64 (100%)

Note. Because of rounding of percentages, columns do not total 100%.

Sources of Family Stress

Next we considered sources of family stress, a factor that can influence the degree to which parents are supportive of their children's aspirations. Family stress was indicated by subjects' responses to a question asking if they had any really difficult family events or experiences while they were growing up. Stress has been found in some research to result from family economic difficulty and family dysfunction—such situations as parents getting a divorce, parents engaging in alcohol or substance abuse, or parents engaging in physical or sexual abuse.

Analyzing the data in Table 12.11, we found no significant differences between campers and non-campers on their numbers of stressful experiences. About half of the subjects in each group, however, experienced 1 or more stressful family problems.

About half of the study subjects reported one or more very stressful problems in their family backgrounds—parental divorce, alcoholism, abuse.

Influences From Role Models and Experiences

Although role models are frequently mentioned as important in the lives of children and adolescents, except for experimental studies of modeling, there is little research on the topic. Recently, however, as pointed out in Part 1 of this book, there has been an interest in providing student and adult mentors in programs for disadvantaged youth.

The interviews developed for this longitudinal evaluation included several questions in which subjects were asked to name persons or experiences that had an influence on them—positive or negative—in certain areas of their development. The areas of development had to do with 4 achievement behaviors researchers derived from the goals of High/Scope's camp program. High/Scope goals, as described in Chapter 7, helped young people develop the following achievement behaviors:

- *Working cooperatively* with others
- *Reflectivity*—thinking things through and plan-

ning, rather than reacting impulsively to situations
• *Persistence*—working at a problem or task until completion
• *Excellence*—striving to do one's best in work or school

These 4 achievement behaviors were built into the interview questions that asked subjects whether some person or experience had been an influence in their lives. Subjects named influential persons or experiences related to each of these 4 behaviors and explained how each person or experience was influential in helping them develop the particular behavior.

The descriptive examination of the role models and experiences included 3 major variables: *number of subjects* with influential role models or experiences; *number of influences* per behavior; and *number of different types of influence* (for example, whether a parent, teacher, or experience) per behavior.

Campers reported 246 influences that had an impact on their lives, compared with the 211 reported by noncampers. Few subjects in either group named negative influences. For campers, the total number of influences per subject ranged for 0 to 12, with *Md* = 3.00. For noncampers, the total number of influences per subject ranged from 0 to 11, with *Md* = 3.00. For the overall sample, campers and noncampers combined, *Md* = 3.00. The two-sample median test indicated a nonsignificant trend of more camper influences above the combined median, as indicated by an average rank of 69.60 for campers, versus an average rank of 61.27 for noncampers (*p* < .11).

We should explain that the overall median of 3.00 influences per study subject was not a result of extreme scores from a few subjects: Of campers, 3 indicated they had not been influenced regarding the 4 behaviors by any role model or experience; this compared with 5 of the noncampers. Subjects could name up to 12 influences—3 influences for each of the 4 behaviors. Approximately 1–2 influences were named per achieve-

Campers reported more influences related to achievement behavior than noncampers did.

▾

ment behavior by all subjects who named influential persons or experiences. Table 12.12 shows the distributions of influences—role models or experiences—across all 4 behaviors for campers and for noncampers. The frequency of influences is normally distributed for both campers and noncampers, which means that the difference in total influences for campers and noncampers (246 versus 211) is not the result of a few extreme scores.

Number of influences per achievement behavior. Next, these data were examined with the number of influences per behavior as the basis of comparison between the camper and noncamper groups.

Table 12.12

Distribution of Subjects' Influential Role Models/Experiences by Frequency of Influence

No. of Influences Reported per Subject	No. (%) of Campers Reporting	No. (%) of Noncampers Reporting
0	3 (5%)	5 (8%)
1–2	17 (26%)	23 (36%)
3–4	32 (48%)	25 (39%)
5–6	10 (15%)	5 (8%)
7–8	3 (5%)	5 (8%)
9 or more	1 (2%)	1 (2%)
Total	66 (100%)	64 (100%)

Note. Because of rounding of percentages, columns do not total 100%.

Table 12.13 shows how many influences were mentioned for each behavior by campers and by noncampers. There were no significant gender differences in the number of influences per behavior.

As mentioned earlier, there were few negative influences reported overall. Out of the total number of sources of influence reported by sample subjects (457 influences), only 34 (7%) were negative influences, and most of these (23 out of 34, or 68%) influenced subjects against *reflectivity* (no table). For example, some subjects said they were negatively influenced by the bad example of a parent, relative, friend, or teacher who was quick to respond angrily to situations. Although more negative influences were reported by campers (21) than by noncampers (13), we found no significant differences on the two-sample median test (*Md* = 0 for both groups). Furthermore, when reported negative influences were eliminated from the data, there was still a nonsignificant trend for more camper influences than noncamper in-

> **Over 80% of all influences subjects cited related to working cooperatively, persisting at tasks, and striving for excellence.**
>
> ▾

Table 12.13

**Distribution of Reported Influences
by Achievement Behavior**

Achievement Behavior	No. (%) of Influences Reported by Campers	No. (%) of Influences Reported by Noncampers
Working cooperatively	79 (32%)	57 (27%)
Reflectivity	43 (17%)	33 (16%)
Persistence	63 (26%)	53 (25%)
Excellence	61 (25%)	68 (32%)
Total	246 (100%)	211 (100%)

fluences on the two-sample median test ($p < .10$).

As Table 12.13 shows, although campers reported more influences overall than noncampers did, the percentages of total influences related to each behavior were quite similar for campers and noncampers. Influences for *working cooperatively* represented 32% of campers' influences and 27% of noncampers' influences. Influences for *excellence* represented 25% of campers' influences and 32% of noncampers' influences. Camper and noncamper percentages were virtually the same for *persistence* and also for *reflectivity*. Overall, subjects cited the fewest influences for *reflectivity*, which may indicate that (1) subjects had less need for help or direction with developing this behavior, or (2) having fewer resources for learning how to think before acting, subjects had more difficulty developing this behavior.

Types of influences. Table 12.14 indicates the different types of influences that subjects indicated for each behavior. The data in this table show that the patterns of types of influences were somewhat different for campers than for noncampers. For instance, though campers and noncampers cited similar total numbers of *role models*—212 for campers and 202 for noncampers—under the category of *role model*, the two groups' patterns for *type of influence* were dissimilar: On the one hand, campers cited fewer *family* role models than noncampers did; campers' *family* role models were 36% of 246 influences, whereas noncampers' *family* role models were 50% of 211 influences. On the other hand, compared with noncampers, campers cited more role models who were *friends* and *other adults* outside the family—21% of 246 influences, compared with 14% of 211 influences for noncampers. The two groups did cite *school staff* as role models with almost equal frequency (approximately 31%). Overall, 96% of noncampers' influences, compared with 86% of campers', were *role models*.

Another pattern difference occurs in the *experience* category. More *experience* influences were cited by campers—14% of all their influences, compared with just 4%

Compared with non-campers, campers cited fewer family role models but more influences from friends, other adults, and experiences.

▾

Table 12.14

Summary of Types of Influences

Type of Influence	No. (%) of Influences Cited by Campers	No. (%) of Influences Cited by Noncampers
Role model		
Family	88 (36%)	106 (50%)
School staff	73 (30%)	67 (32%)
Friends	34 (14%)	21 (10%)
Other adults	17 (7%)	8 (4%)
All role models	212 (86%)	202 (96%)
Experience		
School	7 (3%)	3 (1%)
Other	9 (4%)	6 (3%)
High/Scope camp	18 (7%)	—
All experiences	34 (14%)	9 (4%)
Total influences	246 (100%)	211 (100%)

Note. Percentages for each group—campers, noncampers—are based on the total influences across all 4 achievement behaviors, which could be up to 3 role models or experiences per behavior for each subject.

for noncampers. Since the *family* influences cited by campers were proportionately less (88, 36%) than those cited by noncampers (106, 50%), and since campers cited more *total influences*, it appears that some person or persons, or something in the campers' lives, more than made up for less influence from *family*.

Although noncampers would obviously not cite the High/Scope camp as an influence (as was done 18 times by campers, which was over half their total *experience* influences), we might expect noncampers to mention more other kinds of experiences instead. However, the noncampers' low percentages under the *experience* category suggest that they felt experiences were not very influential in their lives.

Types of influences for each behavior. Table 12.15 shows the total picture of the role model/experience types of influence, as related to each of the 4 behaviors. It also indicates how many influences were positive or negative for each achievement behavior. This table allows us to make some more-specific observations about campers and noncampers.

For *working cooperatively*, the camper and noncamper distributions of influences were somewhat different. (Given the nature of the data, with each subject being able to name up to 3 influences for each behavior, significance tests between campers and noncampers were not appropriate.) For noncampers, as observed earlier, 73% of influences for *working cooperatively* came from *family* and *school staff*, whereas for campers these two sources made up only 48% of influences for *working cooperatively*. For this same behavior, *working cooperatively*, similar proportions of influences from *friends* or *other adults* were reported by campers (24%) and by noncampers (25%). However, as we observed earlier, campers reported that more influences for *working cooperatively* came from the *experience* category (29% of all their *working cooperatively* influences, compared with just 2% for noncampers).

No differences were found between groups regarding influences for *reflectivity*. Regarding influences for

Table 12.15

Distribution of Types of Influences by Behavior

Type of Influence	No. (%) of Influences Cited by Campers for:				No. (%) of Influences Cited by Noncampers for:			
	Coop. Work	Reflec- tivity	Persist- ence	Excel- lence	Coop. Work	Reflec- tivity	Persist- ence	Excel- lence
Role Model								
Family	15 (19%)	16 (37%)	24 (38%)	33 (54%)	15 (26%)	14 (42%)	31 (58%)	46 (68%)
School staff	23 (29%)	11 (26%)	24 (38%)	15 (25%)	27 (47%)	6 (18%)	17 (32%)	17 (25%)
Friends	11 (14%)	10 (23%)	7 (11%)	6 (10%)	10 (18%)	7 (21%)	3 (6%)	1 (1%)
Other adults	8 (10%)	2 (5%)	3 (5%)	4 (7%)	4 (7%)	1 (3%)	0 (0%)	3 (4%)
Experience								
School	6 (8%)	0 (0%)	1 (2%)	0 (0%)	1 (2%)	1 (3%)	1 (2%)	0 (0%)
Other	6 (8%)	2 (5%)	1 (2%)	0 (0%)	0 (0%)	4 (12%)	1 (2%)	1 (1%)
High/Scope camp	10 (13%)	2 (5%)	3 (5%)	3 (5%)	0 (0%)	0 (0%)	0 (0%)	0 (0%)
Total influences	79 (100%)	43 (100%)	63 (100%)	61 (100%)	57 (100%)	33 (100%)	53 (100%)	68 (100%)
Negatives	3	14	1	3	1	9	0	3
Positives	76	29	62	58	56	24	53	65

Note. Subjects could name up to 3 influences per behavior. Because of rounding of percentages, not all columns total 100%.

persistence, a greater percentage of noncamper influences (58%) than camper influences (38%) were *family*
influences, while slightly more camper influences (54%)

than noncamper influences (38%) were from *school staff*, *friends*, and *other adults*. Regarding *excellence*, somewhat more noncamper influences (67%) than camper influences (54%) were from *family*. Compared with noncampers, campers cited somewhat less influence for *excellence* from *other adults* and more influence for *excellence* from *friends* and the *High/Scope camp* experience.

It is validating for the High/Scope Institute for IDEAS program goals that for the behavior of *working cooperatively*, campers indicated substantial influence coming from *role models* outside of school and home and from *experiences*, predominantly the *High/Scope camp* experience.

IN SUMMARY   The patterns for types of influences were different for campers and noncampers in the following ways: Campers tended to report more influences overall and, in particular, more influences from *other adults*, *friends*, and *experiences*. Also, more influences were reported by campers than by noncampers for the behavior of *working cooperatively* (many reported influences from the High/Scope camp experiences). Campers also seem to have encountered more extrafamilial role models for achievement. Perhaps campers who did not perceive their families as supportive sought more out-of-home models and influences. This interpretation does point to the importance of intervention programs providing *positive* alternative role models for disadvantaged and minority youth.

At the end of their interviews, subjects were asked about 9 types of extracurricular courses, programs, or experiences in which they might have participated either in or out of school. They were asked if any were especially helpful and how they were helpful. As discussed in Chapter 8, most campers were not aware that the interview was to evaluate the High/Scope program. Even so, many campers' responses to the last interview question gave some picture of the unique impact the High/Scope experience had on them. Of campers, 49

The High/Scope Institute's influence was noted by campers especially in connection with learning to work cooperatively.

(74%) named High/Scope camp as especially helpful and specified how it had been helpful (see insert). It appears that the camp experience broadened their outlook, making them receptive to seeking additional experiences and models.

SUMMARIZING THIS CHAPTER Compared with noncampers, campers reported lower parent-expectations and parent-support, which perhaps increased their need for additional or alternative role models and experiences. For campers who had not received high recognition for academic achievement in high school, who were very dissatisfied with high school, who had serious problem behaviors, who did not sense much parent expectation for their achievement, it appears that the camp program—with the role models and satisfying experiences it could provide—filled a gap. Without the camp experience, they might have been like noncamp-

---

There's Really Nothing You Can't Do . . .

The following are quotes obtained from six former campers when they were asked to describe whether some extracurricular course, program, or experience had been an influence in their lives. Though unaware that the interview was to evaluate the High/Scope adolescent program, they volunteered these remarks:

• "Camp High/Scope, it was. It built up your self-esteem. It taught you to respect yourself and that you are just as good as everybody else."

• "Definitely High/

Scope camp. No doubt about it. It has to be one of the biggest influences on me. How? Very positively. I learned a lot about being more tolerant. And accepting and listening to what other people have to say, trying to find alternative ways of working things out, compromising."

• "Yeah, High/Scope. It's really hard to say how it helped. It was such a big influence on me. My life right now probably would be totally different if I hadn't gone there."

• "From High/Scope I just learned to be more independent and make decisions on my own. I mean, instead of other people's

convictions, they were mine. "

• "The program that I went through called High/Scope, that taught me to work my problems all the way out thoroughly. "

• "The High/Scope camp showed a person that there's really nothing you can't do—you know, whatever you want to do, you can do it. And if it's failing the way you're doing right now, well then, you must be going about it the wrong way. No matter how hard something is, you can always get it accomplished; you just have to go about it a different way."

ers who, even when they did experience recognition or satisfaction in high school, met their parents' modest expectations and did not go on to higher education.

Next, the influences discussed in this chapter, along with some family background factors (from Chapter 9) and economic factors (from Chapter 11) will be presented in an empirically based model of causal factors.

Chapter THIRTEEN

A Model of Major Paths to Postsecondary Education

WE HAVE SO FAR REPORTED the longitudinal study data on subjects' current educational status, employment, and life circumstances, and we have descriptively explored family, school, and other background factors that may influence the various paths that young people take after high school. In this chapter, with the goal of developing a general model of major paths that lead to postsecondary education among talented disadvantaged students, we employ correlational and path analyses on the longitudinal data. We present the results of the correlational analyses first, followed by the path analyses.

Correlational analysis provides a descriptive assessment of the extent to which any two variables covary (for example, it may reveal that higher levels of school achievement correlate with higher-level paths of postsecondary education). Going beyond correlational results, path analysis techniques allow us to construct explanatory models. These models include all major variables and statistical assessments of the strengths of paths from the major variables that, if combined, will lead to one or more specific outcomes (for example, one conclusion might be that a path of high levels of school achievement combined with a path of high parent-

We employed path analyses to develop an explanatory model of influences leading to subjects' educational levels.

expectations is likely to be a positive path towards postsecondary education). Within a given model, we thus expect to find various alternate paths leading positively or negatively towards a particular outcome. Such path models are helpful as we try to interpret data. Sometimes researchers propose and examine a variety of path models to determine the most plausible explanations of the data collected.

To be examined in the path analyses of major factors leading to postsecondary education, we selected variables based on findings from the previous research on disadvantaged youth presented in Part 1, the descriptive analyses presented in earlier chapters of Part 2, and the correlational analyses on the longitudinal data, which are presented next. The proposed major influence variables are subjects' (1) backgrounds (primarily their parents' education, their family economic difficulty, their parents' expectations and support, and their role models and influential experiences), (2) recognized achievement in high school, (3) personal economic difficulty, (4) problem behavior, and (5) marital status.

Correlations of Major Influence and Education Variables

We began by analyzing the intercorrelations of the 3 educational status variables—*educational level* (ranging from less than high school to graduate school), *current enrollment* (postsecondary), and *educational plans* (for further postsecondary education). This was followed by analyses of correlations between the proposed influence variables and the educational status variables. The influence variables were also intercorrelated, and these intercorrelations are presented in the Appendix.

For both campers and noncampers, significant intercorrelations were found between the educational status variables. (See the Appendix for specific variable scoring used for these analyses.) **For campers,** the correlations between *educational level* and *current enrollment*

The path analyses variables were selected from previous research and from descriptive analyses in the present research.

The key educational status variables—*educational level, current enrollment,* and *educational plans*—were found to be substantially intercorrelated.

($r = .39$) and between *educational level* and *educational plans* ($r = .76$) were statistically significant ($p < .01$); the correlation between *current enrollment* and *educational plans* ($r = .40$) was also significant ($p < .01$).

The pattern of correlations **for noncampers** was similar to that found for campers. For noncampers, the correlations between *educational level* and *current enrollment* ($r = .58$) and between *educational level* and *educational plans* ($r = .61$) were significant ($p < .01$); the correlation between *current enrollment* and *educational plans* ($r = .53$) was also significant ($p < .01$).

The high-magnitude, significant intercorrelations of the 3 educational status variables in both study groups indicate that these variables have considerable validity as indexes of subjects' postsecondary educational status. Current enrollment seems to have the weakest relationship to the other educational status variables, which suggests that some other factors (such as economic factors) may be more strongly related to whether or not students are enrolled at any given time.

We next examine the correlations between these educational status variables and the variables that we propose as major influences in subjects' pursuit of postsecondary education. Table 13.1 shows the correlations between the 3 educational status variables and 6 of the proposed major influence variables.

Camper Correlations

As shown in Table 13.1, for campers, significant correlations included correlations between *recognized achievement* (in high school) and *current enrollment* (in postsecondary education) ($r = .37$, $p < .01$). A significant correlation ($p < .01$) was found between *role models/experiences* and *educational level* ($r = .33$, $p < .01$), as well as between *role models/experiences* and *educational plans* ($r = .28$, $p < .05$). The correlations between *problem behavior* and *educational level* ($r = -.32$) and between *problem behavior* and *educational plans* ($r = -.30$) were inverse and significant ($p < .01$, $p < .05$, respectively).

Proposed influences were
• **Recognized achievement**
• **Parent expectations**
• **Role models/experiences**
• **Problem behavior**
• **Marital status**
• **Personal economic difficulty**

For campers, we found significant correlations between two of the educational status variables and
• **Role models/experiences**
• **Recognized achievement in high school**

Table 13.1

**Correlations Between Educational Status
and Major Influence Variables**

Influence Variables	Educational Status Variables		
	Educational Level	Current Enrollment	Educational Plans
Campers			
Recognized achievement	.20	.37**	.20
Parent expectations	.04	.14	.19
Role models/experiences	.33**	-.06	.28*
Problem behavior	-.32**	.02	-.30*
Marital status	-.20	-.21	-.15
Economic difficulty	-.15	-.07	.00
Noncampers			
Recognized achievement	.64**	.42**	.25*
Parent expectations	.26*	.25*	.39**
Role models/experiences	.11	-.11	.08
Problem behavior	-.31*	.05	.01
Marital status	-.11	-.16	-.27*
Economic difficulty	-.26*	-.15	.04

Note. *$p < .05$; **$p < .01$, two-tailed tests. *Marital status* ranged
from *single* to *married/cohabiting*.

The results of these correlational analyses indicate
that camper subjects with higher levels of recognized
achievement in high school tended to attain and plan for

higher levels of education than did those with less or no recognized achievement. Also, camper subjects who reported higher levels of positive influences from persons or experiences also attained and planned for higher levels of education than did those with few positive influences from persons or experiences. On the negative side, the camper subjects with more problem behavior in high school tended to attain and plan for less education than did those with little or no problem behavior in high school.

For camper subjects, no other significant correlations were found between educational status variables and the proposed influence variables. The correlations between *parent expectations* and the educational status variables were nonsignificant. There was a pattern of inverse but nonsignificant correlations between *marital status* (ranging from single to married/cohabiting) and the educational status variables. The correlations between *economic difficulty* (subjects' own use of public assistance) and educational status variables revealed a pattern of inverse or zero-order, nonsignificant correlations. The nonsignificant correlations between these proposed influence variables and the educational status variables indicate that these variables were not related to campers' attainment of postsecondary education.

> We also found, for campers, significant inverse correlations between problem behavior and two of the educational status variables. ▾

Noncamper Correlations

Looking again at Table 13.1, we see for noncampers, significant correlations between *recognized achievement* and *educational level* ($r = .64, p < .01$), between *recognized achievement* and *current enrollment* ($r = .42, p < .01$), and between *recognized achievement* and *educational plans* ($r = .25, p < .05$). Significant correlations were also found between *parent expectations* and *educational level* ($r = .26, p < .05$), between *parent expectations* and *current enrollment* ($r = .25, p < .05$), and between *parent expectations* and *educational plans* ($r = .39, p < .01$). *Problem behavior* and *educational level* were inversely and significantly correlated ($r = -.31, p < .05$).

> For noncampers, we found significant correlations between the three educational status variables and
> • Parent expectations
> • Recognized achievement in high school ▾

Also for noncampers, we found significant inverse correlations between one educational status variable and
- **Problem behavior**
- **Marital status**
- **Economic difficulty**

Also for noncampers, *marital status* was significantly and inversely correlated with *educational plans* ($r = -.27, p < .05$). The correlations between *marital status* and *educational level*, and between *marital status* and *current enrollment* were also inverse, but nonsignificant. The correlation between *economic difficulty* and *educational level* was inverse and significant ($r = -.26, p < .05$), and the correlation between *economic difficulty* and *current enrollment* was also inverse, but nonsignificant; a near-zero correlation was found between *economic difficulty* and *educational plans*.

These correlations indicate that the noncamper subjects who had higher levels of recognized achievement in high school tended to also attain and plan for a higher level of education than did those with less or no recognized achievement. Also, those noncamper subjects whose parents had higher expectations of them tended to attain and plan for higher levels of education than did those whose parents had lower expectations of them. On the negative side, the noncamper subjects with more problem behavior in high school tended to attain and plan for less education than did those with little or no problem behavior in high school. Also, the noncampers who had more personal economic difficulty after high school tended to attain and plan for lower levels of education than did those with less or no economic difficulty after high school.

For noncampers, no significant correlation or pattern of correlations was found between *role models/experiences* and the educational status variables. This indicates that for noncampers, this variable was not related to pursuit or attainment of postsecondary education. Since noncampers' higher level of parent expectations was related to more educational attainment and planning, the influences that were unrelated to greater education were most likely those involving other adults and peers. No other noncamper patterns of correlations or significant correlations were found between the educational variables and the proposed major influence variables.

As mentioned earlier, we also examined the intercorrelations of the proposed major influence variables per se. Only a few significant intercorrelations were found, and these were for the noncamper group (see Appendix). This lack of intercorrelations indicates that the influence variables have the potential to have separate effects on postsecondary educational outcomes.

IN SUMMARY   The fact that we found significant correlations between the proposed influence variables and the educational status variables indicates that these variables may have some validity as causal factors. Since the campers had the additional influence of the High/Scope program, and since more campers than noncampers went on to postsecondary education, it is reasonable that between campers and noncampers, we found differences concerning which influence variables were significantly correlated with educational status.

In the next section, we present a model to further explain the effects of the proposed influence variables and the role of the High/Scope program.

Major Paths to Postsecondary Education

In examining how the proposed major influence variables affected postsecondary education level and plans, we conducted a path analysis on *educational level* (postsecondary) and *educational plans*—first for the noncampers and then for the campers. In each of these path analyses, each potential influence variable was examined to determine whether it advanced *educational level* (was a positive causal factor) or lessened *educational level* (was a negative causal factor). In addition to conducting path analyses with the major influence variables, we also conducted analyses to examine other variables that could affect subjects' *educational level* and *educational plans*. The impact of *current enrollment* is examined within the path analyses on *educational level* and *educational plans*.

> The correlational pattern between educational status variables and proposed influence variables was different for campers than it was for noncampers.

Figure 13.1

General Path Analysis of Educational Level and Plans

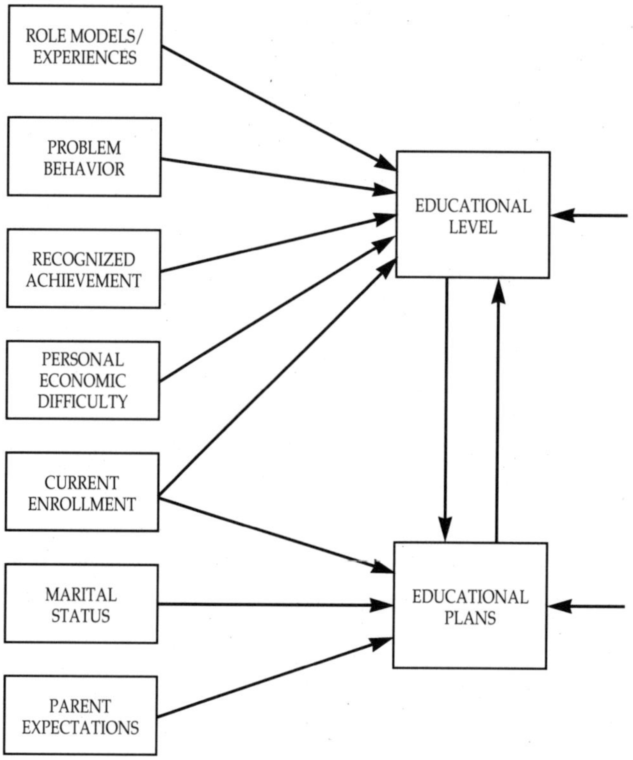

Note. The model is nonrecursive with standardized variables (two-stage least squares). See Table 13.2 for beta weights.

To first provide an overview of the results of our path analyses, a general model based on the results of the major path analysis is presented in Figure 13.1. (The results of other individual path analyses that we conducted, also to be discussed in this chapter, correspond to Figures A.1 and A.2 in the Appendix.) In the path analysis model in Figure 13.1, the arrows show the paths found to affect two educational status variables: the *educational level* that subjects had completed and their future *educational plans*. The arrows between these two educational status variables indicate that the two variable themselves were found to affect each other, as well.

A general path analysis model shows how key influence variables contribute towards subjects' educational levels and plans.

Table 13.2

**Path Analysis Coefficients of Educational Level
and Educational Plans**

Model Variables	Campers	Noncampers
A. Variables influencing educational level		
Educational plans	.34	.37
Current enrollment	.26	.21
Recognized achievement	.03	.38
Role models/experiences	.28	.04
Problem behavior	-.23	-.15
Economic difficulty	-.18	-.17
R^2 for educational level	.62	.70
B. Variables influencing educational plans		
Educational level	.82	.03
Current enrollment	.06	.41
Parent expectations	.15	.27
Marital status	.01	-.19
R^2 for educational plans	.61	.40

Note. This nonrecursive model is derived from a two-stage, least-square procedure; path coefficients (beta weights) are presented. See the Appendix for variable definitions and scoring.

Table 13.2 provides the path coefficients for the general path analysis model. As the coefficients indicate, the following paths depicted in Figure 13.1 were found to have positive effects on the *educational level* completed by subjects: influences from *educational plans, current enrollment* in postsecondary education, *recog-*

nized achievement in high school, and *role models/experiences.* Two paths were found to have negative effects on subjects' *educational level: problem behavior* and personal *economic difficulty.*

Three paths had positive effects on subjects' *educational plans: educational level* completed by subjects, *current enrollment* in postsecondary education, and *parent expectations* and encouragement. One path had a negative effect on subjects' *educational plans:* subjects' *marital status.*

The results of the Figure 13.1 path analysis are next examined more closely. First, we describe the findings of this major path analysis on *educational level* and *educational plans.*

Influences on Educational Level

For both study groups, problem behavior and personal economic difficulty were negative influences on the educational level attained.

▾

Part A of Table 13.2 indicates that **for both noncampers and campers,** the major factors that *negatively* affected the path to *educational level* (postsecondary) were *problem behavior* and personal *economic difficulty.*

The noncamper group provides a benchmark of the major positive and negative factors typically affecting the educational levels of talented but disadvantaged students who do not have program intervention:

▾

Major positive influences for noncampers
As shown in Part A of Table 13.2, **for noncampers,** the path analysis yielded the following **major positive influences** on postsecondary *educational level,* given in descending order of magnitude of path coefficients:
- *Recognized achievement* in high school
- *Educational plans* for future postsecondary education
- *Current enrollment* in postsecondary education

If we consider only the noncamper subjects' paths to postsecondary education, we realize that some disadvantaged high-potential students who had already been on a path towards postsecondary education when in high school did in fact go on to postsecondary education, even though they had no special kind of intervention. These students are the ones who were very high achievers in high school, had parents holding higher educational expectations for them, had little or no problem behavior during or since high school, and had rarely or never used public assistance since high school. Most of these students, at the time of interview, were enrolled in postsecondary education and were planning to complete a degree.

However, when we consider the camper subjects' paths, we realize that participation in the High/Scope Institute for IDEAS expanded the picture, allowing a greater number of talented, economically disadvantaged students to develop their potential for higher education. The path analysis for campers revealed that the *positive influences* leading to postsecondary education shifted as a result of the High/Scope program:

▾

Major positive influences for campers
For campers, the path analysis yielded the following **major positive influences** on postsecondary *educational level*, given in descending order of magnitude of path coefficients:

- *Educational plans* for future postsecondary education
- *Role models/experiences*, including High/Scope program influence
- *Current enrollment* in postsecondary education

Overall, **for campers,** 62% of the variance of educational level is explained by the path analysis model; **for noncampers,** 70% of the variance of educational level is explained by the path analysis model. This finding of less explained variance for campers versus noncampers is likely to be due to camp program variables that are not measured in the present study. Also, some background

Positive paths to non-campers' postsecondary educational levels included highly recognized achievement in high school.

▾

Positive paths to campers' postsecondary educational levels included influential role models and experiences.

▾

variables were not as influential for campers as for noncampers, owing to the influence of the camp program.

A path analysis to directly test the High/Scope program's effects on educational level showed that the Institute's influence was substantial and could offset negative influences.

To further assess the role of High/Scope program intervention, we developed a path analysis to directly examine the program's effect on educational level (see Figure A.1 in the Appendix). In this analysis, LISREL computer software (Jöreskog & Sörbom, 1989) was used to combine major factors, including *parents' education* and all the positive influences and negative influences we have just discussed. The analysis also separated out whether or not subjects had been in the High/Scope program. The *High/Scope program* contribution was found to be positive and had a path coefficient of .22—large enough to possibly offset the effect of negative influence, which had a path coefficient of -.29.

Influences on Educational Plans

The results of the major path analysis with respect to the level of further *educational plans* are shown in Part B of Table 13.2 (on p. 283).

Positive paths to non-campers' postsecondary education plans were
• Being presently enrolled in post-secondary education
• High parent-expectations

For noncampers, the positive factors, given in descending order of magnitude of path coefficients, were these: *current enrollment* in postsecondary education and *parent expectations* for subjects' postsecondary education. Subjects' *educational level* had little effect on their *educational plans*. A contributing negative factor was *marital status* (being married or cohabiting). For noncampers, 40% of the variance of *educational plans* is explained by the path analysis model, indicating that many other factors were not known.

A negative influence on noncampers' educational plans was being married or cohabiting.

In contrast, for campers, the path analysis accounted for 61% of the variance of *educational plans*. This path analysis revealed that **for campers,** the major positive factors, given in descending order of magnitude of path coefficients, were these: subjects' *educational level* and *parent expectations* for subjects' postsecondary education. While high *parent-expectations* did have a small positive effect on camper subjects' *educational plans,* their *marital status* contributed little to their *educational plans.*

Influence of Family Background Factors

It is useful to further examine the identified explanatory variables in light of subjects' background factors. To effectively alter and advance the educational paths of students who have potential but are not already high achievers and do not have strong parent-expectations and parent-support, intervention programs must help students overcome the difficulties or limitations that have been part of their backgrounds.

To more closely examine study subjects' backgrounds, a path analysis was conducted by combining camper and noncamper background data (see Figure A.2 in the Appendix). Four interrelated factors were examined: *parents' education, family economic difficulty, subjects' attitudes,* and subjects' *personal economic difficulty.* This path analysis revealed that subjects' *personal economic difficulty* since high school was related to the level of their *family economic difficulty* (parents' low employment and high use of public assistance). Furthermore, the level of *parents' education* was inversely related to *family economic difficulty* and subjects' *personal economic difficulty.* Subjects' *attitudes* were also found to be somewhat affected by their family backgrounds. The path analysis revealed that subjects' levels of personal *locus of control* and *achievement motivation* were inversely related to subjects' *personal economic difficulty* since high school.

The results of the subject background path analysis suggest that for talented disadvantaged students from families with the lowest educational and economic levels, both educational and economic attainment are likely to be seriously undermined. Since the primary source of influence for students who have no program intervention tends to be parent role models, it becomes increas-

For campers, there were no negative paths to postsecondary educational plans, but two positive paths were these:
- Having some postsecondary education
- High parent-expectations

A path analysis using subjects' background data revealed that personal economic difficulty was interrelated with the following:
- Parents' low educational level
- Family economic difficulty
- Low achievement motivation and low sense of personal locus of control

ingly clear that a particularly critical function of intervention programs is to broaden students' sources of influence.

SUMMARIZING THIS CHAPTER   Considering the results of the series of path analyses conducted, we can conclude that the High/Scope Institute for IDEAS effectively expanded the pool of disadvantaged students who went on to postsecondary education and planned to complete degrees. This pool, owing to the High/Scope camp program, came to include not only those talented students everyone would expect to go on to postsecondary education but also those talented students who had not been highly recognized in high school, did not experience high parent-expectations, may have married early, or may have at some point had to drop out of college.

The High/Scope participants reported that they were positively influenced by role models and various past experiences, and they cited the influences of the High/Scope program in particular. In contrast, for the comparison group, influences from role models and experiences had little significance, and fewer of this group who had not experienced the High/Scope program went on to postsecondary education.

The path analyses showed that program interventions (such as High/Scope's) can influence talented disadvantaged students to pursue higher education, even in the face of many obstacles.

Chapter FOURTEEN

1990 Evaluation of the High/Scope Institute for IDEAS

As RECOUNTED EARLIER, in 1987 the High/Scope Institute for IDEAS began to address a wider population that included both urban and rural, black and white participants. Therefore, in addition to conducting the longitudinal study, we wanted to look particularly at intergroup relationships in the current High/Scope program. This led to an evaluation of the 1990 program.

The 1990 evaluation, which was funded by the Detroit Edison Foundation, had three major goals: (1) to provide more description of and insight into the processes of the program, (2) to assess the effectiveness of program goals from the perspective of the participants, and (3) to identify areas for future program development.

Evaluation Methods

Information gathered in the 1990 evaluation concerned participants' family backgrounds, important influences in participants' lives, and participants' responses to the program. The evaluation was carried out in the program's camp setting—through administration of questionnaires to program participants and staff; observations of participants, activities, and staff; and interviews with par-

14.

The ongoing High/Scope Institute was evaluated during its 1990 program year to gain more insight into the key academic and social processes.

▾

ticipants and staff. A researcher administered a questionnaire to each participant at the beginning and the end of the camp program. The same researcher made observations throughout the 4 weeks of the camp program at various periods of the day and during each of the major activities. At the end of the program, this researcher interviewed 6 campers who in particular had been observed at various times throughout the program. The researcher who collected the data was not a part of the camp staff or of the program development staff.

Evaluation Instruments

The items contained in the participants' pre- and postcamp questionnaires had been developed for use in the longitudinal study of the Institute for IDEAS and in previous High/Scope evaluations. The precamp questionnaire, which was filled out by campers on the second day after their arrival at camp, contained

> • Questions about the campers' family backgrounds, role models, and other influential experiences
> • Questions (with rating scales) to assess campers' attitudes about achievement and locus of control
> • Questions about campers' attitudes and experiences in high school (including academic recognition)
> • Questions about campers' problem behaviors
> • Questions about campers' educational goals and expectations

The postcamp questionnaire, which was filled out by campers on the last day of camp, contained

> • Questions about campers' perceptions of the camp experience
> • Questions (with rating scales) to assess campers' evaluations of camp activities and events
> • Questions designed to assess any camp-enhanced changes in campers' peer relationships or attitudes towards different ethnic groups

The 1990 evaluation employed qualitative and quantitative methods to examine participants' interrelationships and responses to various program components.

▾

Specific study methods used were observations, interviews, and precamp and postcamp questionnaires.

▾

- Questions (with rating scales) to assess campers' attitudes about achievement and locus of control
- Questions about participants' future educational goals and expectations

Questions in the last two categories were identical to ones contained in the precamp questionnaire.

At the end of the program, staff were also asked to respond to a questionnaire that consisted of a set of open-ended questions asking them to describe how activities and events had an effect on them and on one or more campers.

Naturalistic Observations

One of the major aims of the 1990 evaluation was to gain a greater understanding of the campers' perceptions of and responses to the program experience. Towards this end, observations of campers were made on various days, at different times of the day, and in a cross section of activities and experiences. Because of the 24-hour-a-day, 7-day-a-week format of the program, only a limited number of campers could be focused on using such a naturalistic observation technique; so 6 campers were selected to be observed more closely than the others and to later be interviewed in depth. These 6, who were identified by the Institute director as representing a cross section of the high school students who typically come to the Institute, included 3 black and 3 white students; 3 were from northern Lower Michigan (2 males, 1 female), and 3 were from Detroit (2 females, 1 male). Staff-camper interactions, as well as peer interactions, were of particular interest in the observations.

Interviews

The in-depth interviews of the 6 selected campers were conducted the last week of camp and were recorded on audio tape for later transcription. The interviews lasted approximately 1 to 1½ hours and consisted of questions about each camper's home life, school activities, extra-

Interviews with students pertained to home life, school, friendships, future expectations, and perceptions of the Institute experience.

▾

The observations and interviews focused on a cross section composed of several Institute participants.

▾

curricular activities, relationships with friends and significant others, and goals for the future. Campers' feelings about their experiences in the High/Scope program were also explored, along with their perceptions of how the experiences had affected them. The researcher took care not to ask leading, biased questions. To encourage campers to express their own ideas, attitudes, and feelings, she asked many questions that were open-ended, that is, structured to allow for many kinds of responses. The researcher also informally interviewed some staff members during the 4-week program and took "field notes" of staff responses to students and activities.

Study Subjects

Institute participants were from both rural and urban areas and included almost equal numbers of African Americans and whites.

▾

The total number of participants in the 1990 High/Scope program was 46, including 25 (54%) from northern Lower Michigan high schools and 21 (46%) from Detroit high schools. The total of 46 participants included 29 females and 17 males; of the 46 participants, 26 (56%) were white, 19 (41%) were African American, and 1 participant had parents from India. Two of the 46 participants, both white and from rural areas, left halfway through the program: One, a female, left because of personal choice and the other, a male, was asked to leave because of behavior problems.

As these quotes from 4 individual participants indicate, campers were somewhat aware that their special abilities had caused them to be invited to participate in the program:

> 'Cause of art and science. 'Cause I was doing good in it. I didn't do good in art class because my teacher was stupid. But, like I can draw and stuff, and I can make stuff out of clay. I went to college last year for an art course. I did this sculpt thing . . . and a bunch of stuff. I got to come because I'm good at those things.

> I don't know. My grades . . . [stops talking and appears to be thinking] because of my grades, yeah. I have a 3.7 grade-point.

> I talked to Mr. _____, the coordinator of our school, to do

this. He said it's cause, ahh, three teachers recommended me. My algebra teacher, my English teacher, and my science teacher recommended me to come here. And then, like I got high test scores, when I was in the seventh grade, on one of the tests I took. He said that's why I came here.

Grade-point average. They told me it was for honor students. They said you have to have at least a three-point [3.0] to go.

While most campers saw an invitation to attend the Institute as a positive reward for a special skill or ability, a few campers saw it as a last chance to prove themselves.

The Campers—Observations, Interviews, and Profiles

There was considerable diversity among Institute participants. As already indicated, observations and interviews were conducted with 6 campers who seemed to represent a cross section of that diversity, in hopes of obtaining a greater understanding of the camp experience from the camper's point of view. In the observations and interviews, the researcher focused on the following processes, which are derived from the program's goals:

Through interviews and observations, researchers examined participants' responses to the program in light of the program's goals.

- Encouraging cooperative learning and positive relationships among campers in camp activities
- Providing campers with role models and experiences to foster personal initiative, leadership, and a positive attitude towards academically oriented learning and higher education
- Fostering campers' motivation for achievement—encouraging and supporting self-confidence, goal setting, planning, and persistence
- Aiding campers to view education as an ongoing enterprise
- Broadening campers' views of their future opportunities

Because the interactional processes between campers and staff produced gradual, subtle changes in campers' attitudes over a period of time, the nature of the
processes that led to particular changes proved to be
difficult to discern. For example, as would be expected,
campers did not identify with role models overnight.
Rather, staff became role models for campers over time,
as relationships developed and experiences were shared.

The observational data are useful for gaining a
greater understanding of program activities and for
gaining insight into the perspectives expressed by the
campers in their interviews. The observational data and
the interviews provide evidence of influences on campers from such activities as the musicale, special performances by the campers, the work projects, the workshops
led by campers, and the folk dancing.

For example, folk dancing, a program activity that
is designed to broaden campers' experience, was anticipated with great dread by many campers. Prior to the
first folk dance session, they believed that the sessions
would be "stupid" or "boring." However, by the end of
all the sessions, the majority of campers felt more positive about the experience. The following is an excerpt
from the observer's notes:

> Twenty-five campers and most of the staff are gathered
> into a large circle in the barn, watching their instructor
> demonstrate the next dance they are to learn. Camper
> John is standing next to staff member Flora, and while
> waiting, as the music is being cued, they begin modern
> dancing together, shimmying and bending at the knees.
> As the music starts, the instructor is announcing to the
> beat of the music, "In, in, in, in, heel." Members of the
> group attempt to move their feet to the music. Trying to
> focus their attention, the instructor adds the words, "Mix
> pickle, mix pickle, step forward."
> John is intently studying the instructor's feet as she
> demonstrates the dance twice. She has the group prac-
> tice, voicing encouragements and hints as they move in
> a giant circle around the floor. As they stop, she asks,
> "Who really has it and can show the rest of the group?"
> John and three other campers, one African American and
> two whites, volunteer together. Joining hands together
> with the instructor, who is at the head of the line, they

The observational data
show students' responses
to such program compo-
nents as the musicales,
council sessions, work
projects, workshops, and
folk dancing.

demonstrate the dance together. While it is not perfect, they are met with clapping and approval when they finish.

As indicated previously, the researcher took observational notes and tape-recorded an in-depth interview with each of 6 selected campers. Of the 6 campers, 3 were judged to represent 3 distinctly different types of program participants. Profiles of these 3 campers were developed by the researcher, using quotes from their interviews (with any potentially identifying information, such as their names or schools, excluded). The profiles also contain the researcher's introductory remarks, descriptions, and interpretations, which are based on her observations. The profiles provide insight into what kinds of students the program serves, what processes are inherent in the camp activities, how the camp experience is perceived by the participants, and how it has affected them.

From the interview information, narrative profiles of three different students were drawn up.

▼

YVONNE

Yvonne is an outstanding example of a bright, talented, and perceptive student from the city of Detroit. Living in the inner city, Yvonne, who is from an African American background, is a 14-year-old freshman at one of the more challenging public high schools. She has been an honor student all of her life and hopes to become an engineer:

Yvonne is a high-achieving student with a strong family relationship.

▼

> I have folders and folders [filled with academic awards] from kindergarten on up. I'm looking forward to getting more since I'm in high school.
> At school, my curriculum is chemical engineering. I take introductory physics, and I take German. I'm just telling you the sciences that are related to my curriculum. Then I take the regular classes—world history, algebra, and English.
> My high school is not a neighborhood school, because you have to take a test to get in there. It's one of the best schools in Detroit, and you have to maintain a certain average, which is a 2.0, but they're raising it for next year. I have a 4.0. . . . I'm pretty good in school.

She appears to have considerable self-awareness

and to have thought through her life goals:

> I want to be in any engineering field. Right now, I'm studying chemical engineering, but if I don't like it, I know there's so many engineering fields. I want to be in engineering because I love it. I want to work for Proctor and Gamble, because I get to work with people and products and stuff like that—like Tide and stuff, and I want to work on the market too. I want to work as a chemical engineer, because that's a field that's really gonna be opening up when I get out of college. They need more Americans and more minorities to get involved, too. Not just because of the money, but because I like it a lot. If I don't get into chemical engineering, I want to do something dealing with solar power, 'cause I'm crazy about solar power. As soon as I found out about it, I said, "Wow!" You know, really, it's an ancient method, but now people are really realizing that it makes a lot of sense and it saves a lot of money. The only thing is, it's hard for them to store it. That's what I want to work on.
>
> I'm not necessarily looking for a cure for cancer or anything like that with chemical engineering. I want to do something that's simple, that can be used every day, something almost anybody can use—like Tide or soap or Ivory.

"Very close" to her family, Yvonne was observed to spend a good portion of visitor day hand-in-hand or arm-in-arm with her mother, with the two of them deep in conversation. She says simply, "I love my family":

> I think my best friends are my parents, my family, because they understand me more than probably anybody ever will in their life. I'm friends with everybody, I have no enemies, but I don't have a particular best friend. I feel a best friend is someone I would really, truly give my life for.

Problem or delinquent behavior is not something Yvonne engages in. When questioned, "Have you ever been drunk or high or done anything 'bad'?" she replies, quite aghast, "Oh no! Bad? I swung on the medicine cabinet and broke it." Understandably, her parents place few rules and regulations on her at home:

> No rules. I watch my brother more than anything . . . you know. They know what we would do and what we wouldn't do. The only thing they have to get on us about is probably—not even my grades or nothing like that—

probably more like watching the house when they leave or being careful when we play. My mother's really worried about our safety. Any old thing makes her want us to be careful. "Make sure the stove is off . . .," you know, [she] gets on us about things like that [that are] really important. Not so much social things and peer pressure.

Yvonne is an active, eager participant in the camp activities, even though she was invited to attend only a few days before camp began. Arriving with little knowledge of the purpose of the camp program and not really knowing what to expect, she nevertheless became enthusiastically involved—volunteering to help build a solar panel to heat water in the art area, reading several of her poems aloud during a musicale, building a laser apparatus, and leading a workshop:

She enthusiastically recounts a workshop she taught at camp and a solar panel activity.

▾

> I taught pantomime, which was really fun—I had so much fun! [I had never done pantomime before coming to camp] but, I watched a lot of pantomimers. The people in my class, at first they didn't want to do anything, but after I did a couple of pantomimes, I had them rolling on the ground laughing. Then they really wanted to be a part of it, and we showed a presentation.
>
> I volunteered because I directed like a couple of workshops before, when I was real little, and I hadn't done it in a while. It was fun, because I liked letting people learn stuff and learning stuff at the same time. I don't like the power, or anything like that, because I didn't have much power at all—they were gonna do what they wanted to do—but I like working with people and want them to like to work with me, too.

Regarding the solar panel activity, she feels this:

> I like working with the people, and I liked the planning we did—the improvising we did, although we didn't finish the project. What I liked about it is that it was something I've never done before and I probably won't ever do again until I get grown or something. What I like was working on the roof—and the patience. I gained a lot of patience. Especially working with those people. I couldn't choose my group, and there was some people that I didn't get along with at some times. Then all of a sudden we'd have to work together, and we'd get a little sarcasm here and there. But that was about it, you know, we didn't argue. I liked having to deal with working out in the sun, right on top of the roof, and having to deal

with all the problems. I wish we could have finished it though .

Other activities during camp included a field trip to the University of Michigan and to a nearby city's art museum and zoo. Visiting the campus of the university for the first time definitely made an impression on Yvonne:

> We went to the art museum and we saw the nuclear reactor, which was really great!
>
> I learned that it's just a gigantic school. It's just the same thing [as high school] all over again—you're just older and it's a school, but you have more opportunities. And, it's just one more step you gotta go through before you hit, hit the real life. I saw that people there were really, really going for it. They were minding their business. They were serious—I guess they would be, 'cause they pay so much to get there. They work so hard to get there.

Yvonne also reports on a field trip and on her impressions of council sessions.

Council is an important component of the Institute's program. The purpose is to encourage campers to examine, share, and expand their feelings and self-knowledge. While not every council session seemed relevant to Yvonne's life experience, she feels that the camp experience as a whole and, in particular, at least one council session affected her:

> Well, being at camp, one area I've grown in is being with people. I didn't realize I could care about so many people at the same time and have them as a second family. I've never been close to so many people. It's like they're my brothers and sisters now. And that's one thing, and I've realized how much I could really miss a person. That's probably how I've grown. Oh, and patience and thinking before I move. 'Cause my father—well, when we had our council—when we talked about a certain topic, at the first council we had, I couldn't believe how many people were crying, because I didn't realize how, well, it was consideration (but I think it's tact is what it really was) and my father stressed that, and before, I was terrible in consideration and inconsideration.
>
> I wrote a letter to my parents after that council and told them I really understand what they were talking about now. I didn't realize how many people are . . . really have their feelings hurt, because they really opened themselves up that night. They told how they really felt about

certain topics like, "So and so said this to me, and I really, really felt badly and I started crying, tears were pouring . . ." I'm the type of person, I don't care what people say about me, and I don't realize that there's a lot of people who do. I learned a lot that night, and I think that's one thing a lot of people should think about—thinking before they do any action. I don't do it as much as I should. I've changed, I've really improved, but I can still improve in that area. I realize if I don't, I'm really gonna hurt some people, and I'm really gonna miss out on a lot of relationships with people.

Other council sessions, such as one on peer pressure, did not seem as pertinent to Yvonne:

I don't think [peer pressure] ever did exist with me. I was surprised by how many people, same thing with consideration and inconsideration . . . people brought up some interesting topics. I thought, well, it could be possible for me to get into peer pressure, 'cause it can come in all forms, good forms and bad. When I spoke about it, I just said that if it's good or bad, always keep in mind who you are and be frightened when anyone tries to change your mind. Realize what you really feel. Peer pressure can just cease, if you truly know who you are and if you really believe in yourself and you have pride in yourself. A lot of people are lacking a little bit of that, and then they get into that peer pressure trap—even if it's good or bad.

Campers perceived differences on many levels between the High/Scope program and school. The two learning experiences are compared by Yvonne:

In school it's learning, just like camp is, but in camp you learn to talk with your friends and you learn at the same time, but in school you can't do that, because there's so many people, the teachers have this time limit. I mean, you can't go back to your teachers, especially in my school, because I have [thousands], and that's a lot of students, and you don't get that much attention from your teachers.

In high school, everything's just like, very, very competitive at school, and that's not always good. You need to get away from that, and that's what this camp is. You need to be able to just work at your level. I know students that have parents who are really pushing them. I'm lucky though, 'cause I don't have that too much. At school everything's like, "Rush-rush- rush." The only thing you

She reflects on peer pressure and compares the High/Scope experience with her school experiences.

get is lunch, and some people don't even have lunch, because they have to take an extra class, or they're failing in this, or something like that. I'm lucky to have lunch when I went to the library. My school is kind of boring inside—it's really old and dusty, no fresh air, no trees, no exercise. I didn't have exercise 'cause I didn't have sports. But, I heard that the sports classes are like, "You have to do this"—none of that fun stuff, you know. "Five laps and back. Run around, go up and down those steps." School is like military.

Yvonne discusses interracial issues and her response to one of the staff members.

▼

Yvonne has had friends of differing ethnic/regional backgrounds most of her life. Even so, both she and her family are concerned that she have more exposure to other groups:

I've had many white friends since I was a little kid. I still have those friends, from my younger days, and I'm still meeting new ones—Indians, Filipinos, things like that, lots of white people. I get along. I try to ignore color, and that works a lot, but then again, there's things that come out that go with our race. 'Cause you know, in history there are some things you can't change, and some things in my race, they're discriminating and racist against their own selves. I've noticed that too.

My high school is predominantly black. It's been like that for several years. My father was really disappointed at that, too, because he's an alumni, and when he went there, there were all kinds of people there. That's what I need, I need that environment. And, this environment [camp]—I'm really glad 'cause, he was glad too, 'cause he was worried I'd be around all my kind. I need to be around, more, you know, different races to understand how to work with them, because the field I want to get into, I'll most definitely have to be around them.

Staff members lead the workshops and other camp activities and therefore are an integral part of the camp experience. Yvonne feels there was one staff member with whom she developed a strong bond:

It's Mark, the oldest. He's so funny. He's good in science. I admire him, 'cause that's how I want to be. I don't want to be a person who is interested in the good things like science and arts and be *boring*. Then again, he's good with people and he knows a lot too. He's good in music and everything. He reminds me of my father, which was why it made me not miss him so much. He always tells us to be happy, because happiness is the key. That gave me such a positive attitude, even when I felt down.

In Yvonne's mind, coming to camp is a positive experience. Sensing that she lacked what she termed "people skills," she felt she "did open up more." Additionally, she feels that the camp experience encouraged her to become more involved in extracurricular activities in school:

> They keep stressing to be involved in a lot of things, 'cause they [colleges and universities] want a well-rounded person, and that's what I've got to work on. I'm not in any clubs, I don't know why, I never thought about it. [But] since I've been here, I want to meet more people, so I want to get involved in more clubs. In clubs you get to interact with everyone and learn at the same time, that's what I like.

Yvonne has other concluding thoughts about her camp experience:

> A lot more people should go to camp. I think they should probably go as a young person. But this is the first time I've ever gone to camp. I think it doesn't really matter what age you are. I mean, I think even the counselors have a good time, because this is a camp for them not just totally counseling us. But, I think camp should be stressed more. Not just for a place to go have fun or to get away from home—but it's more than that, I think. It's part of growing up.
>
> When they choose people for these camps and stuff, they shouldn't try to choose the "best" out of school. They should choose the ones that are good in ways but don't associate with people that much. If you're a well-rounded person and you open up to people, you can do that really good at school—you don't necessarily need camp that much.
>
> We can build a better generation if we have those people that aren't lacking in people skills. People skills are the most important.

Not all adolescents who come to the High/Scope camp are as talented or as perceptive as Yvonne.

GEORGE
George is a talented young man who is barely making it in school or society. There are many negative influences in George's life, not the least of which are teachers who

As a result of the High/Scope experience, she feels she will be more open to new activities and more understanding of others.

▾

George is a young person with high potential, but he has many difficulties at school and home.

▾

suggest that he "drop out of school." Although the Institute experience, from his point of view, does not appear to have greatly affected his life, from another point of view, the mere fact that he stayed, he listened, and he enjoyed it is a considerable accomplishment.

George is a 15-year-old freshman from a small town in northern Lower Michigan. He is tall, thin—almost gangly—and has long shaggy hair, which he keeps clean. He often carries himself with an air of defiance, and with his rather shaggy look, gives the impression of anger and toughness. His hair, which is both a source of pride to him and a source of conflict for him in his conservative rural town, is a constant reference point in the interview. George's family consists of a younger sister and a younger brother and his parents, who have been separated for approximately a year but are attempting a reconciliation. George will not be spending the summer at home:

> When I get home, I'm probably gonna be living with a neighbor, just for the summer.

George will be living with this neighbor because he "wants to" and because his parents think he is "old enough this year." He says he will be working for the neighbor:

> I'm gonna be like clean-up. He works for construction and I'm just going to go back at the end of the day and clean everything up.

George feels his parents do not put too many rules on him:

> They put rules, but not as much as some parents. Some parents are really strict; my parents aren't really that strict. My curfew on weekdays is 9:00 and on weekends is 2:00. That's 'cause I go out and party and stuff. I can't come back drunk, 'cause they don't like that too much. I'll go out partying, and then, like me and my friends just go for a ride for a couple of hours, sober up, like go back in the woods and just sit there and talk for a while until we're sober. And, if I'm like drunk at like 1:30 or 1:00 or midnight or something, I just have to call my mom and say I'm staying at a friend's house tonight or whoever's party I'm at.

In addition to "partying," sexual activity seems to be another favorite activity among George's friends. While readily admitting that it is common, George has concerns about this:

> There was this girl that I liked a lot, I was at her sister's house with her, and her sister was sleeping. We were up till about 4:30 in the morning, or 3:30, something like that. We were kissing a little bit and then she goes, "I want to have a kid." I said, "So do I, after I'm about 25." She said, "No, I mean tonight. I want to get pregnant tonight." That scared me.

Having been caught drinking by the police, George and his brother now have to attend a weekly group session with a probation officer:

> There's like a group of us that go. My little brother goes. It's like—well, we got caught drinking last October, and they didn't put it on our records. We talk about a lot of things. _____ [his probation officer] is pretty cool. We like, put in a couple of bucks, or a dollar or whatever, we go get stuff at the store, like munchies and pop and everything. We just sit there and talk and have candy and pop and chips, and a couple of times we had pizza. She [his probation officer] just sits there and talks to us like one of our friends—she wasn't really like a probation officer. It was more of a friend.

He discusses various problem-behavior incidents and difficult situations in and out of school.

George reports having a difficult time in school. He attends regularly, because if he misses more than 15 days, he loses his credits. He has already lost credit for other reasons, such as insulting a teacher who called him a burnout. Looking like a burnout appears to be a very sensitive subject for George.

Although he is interested in sports and drama, George does not participate in these activities in school. He says that the plays produced at his home school "are stupid," while those performed at the camp are "more interesting." He feels if the plays selected at his school were more interesting, he would participate. His lack of involvement in sports is directly linked to his hair style:

> Up until this year [I played basketball]. My coach won't let me on the team this year because I got long hair. I can play basketball at home. I do all the time. My coach must be prejudiced against people with long hair or some-

thing, because he won't let me on the team 'cause I got long hair.

All the same, the future for George, he believes, includes college:

> [I want to] go to college. Most people don't believe me, but I want to go to college. I want to go into construction, like housepainting and stuff. Them are the—I already got into them kind of 'cause I worked for Steve, and now I'm working for my neighbor. I want to go to U of M. Either that, or South Carolina. I was wanting to go to U of M for a while. Now I'm thinking I might want to go to South Carolina where my camp counselor went, Gerard. Might want to go there.

George feels he was chosen to participate in the High/Scope program because of his artistic abilities. He participated in several artistic experiences at camp, including making stained glass. Never having worked with stained glass before, George was disappointed.

> I picked stained glass because I had never stained glass before. I thought we were going to be staining glass—we didn't.

But George persisted and made a lamp. With pride, he proclaims that this was the "first 3-D stained glass thing ever made at High/Scope ever." Some of the other activities he participated in included creating a trout pond, council, and the trip to the University of Michigan. George likes council:

> I like council 'cause you can sit back and share. It's like me and Will and Karla and Debbie would all get by each other, and like, we weren't supposed to talk, but we'd whisper and stuff. We'd talk about what everybody else was talking about but just to the four of us. It was, like, special.

The region in Michigan where George lives has a Native American population. Because of this, he feels his attitudes towards people of other ethnic backgrounds have always been quite accepting. In particular, he feels that he already has accepting feelings towards African Americans and that these attitudes were not changed by the camp experience.

George explains his college aims and his beliefs about his talents. He describes how he has been developing some of his talents at the High/Scope Institute.

▾

I used to live in _____, and my best friend was black. I just think they're people. My girlfriend here is black. I like her; I'm gonna miss her a lot.

Getting along with others at camp was a challenge for George. He had problems with some of the campers and with some of the staff. He had particular problems with one other camper:

> We were gonna fight. He called me a burnout. 'Cause [another camper] said I do drugs, he was like telling everybody else in camp. So I went up to him and said, "Like, come on, buddy, you say I'm doing drugs, we're gonna have to butt."

Staff intervened and worked with both campers to handle their differences nonviolently:

> He apologized to me. He said, "I'm sorry, I know that I was wrong because I don't know you. I don't know if you do drugs or anything. But, I'm gonna talk to [the other camper] about it." [The other camper] just about got us to fight. I said, "I'm sorry about that too. I just didn't want you calling me a burnout, a druggie, before you even knew."

George's goal for himself in 5 years is to "mellow out a little." When questioned what this meant for him, he says:

> I don't want to go partying as much, because I'll be able to—I'll be driving and stuff a lot more than I am now, 'cause I don't have a driver's license. It's like if I'm partying a lot, I'm probably gonna be like driving home and like kill somebody or kill myself; that'd be stupid.

While Yvonne and George seem to illustrate the two ends of a spectrum of students who attend the camp program, Tom is probably more average.

TOM

Although plagued by family and personal problems, Tom is an appealing, personable young man. As is typical with adolescents, he can be superficial in his remarks yet periodically shares insights that are both meaningful and thoughtful. He is an adolescent for whom the Institute's goals appear to be especially rel-

George also reflects on problems and solutions he has encountered in the camp setting, and he talks about his goals for the future.

evant. Plagued with feelings of low self-esteem and unaccustomed to working with others, Tom has found the Institute experience to be both enlightening and confidence-boosting.

Like George, Tom is a 15-year-old high school freshman from a small town in northern Lower Michigan. Possessing dark hair and dark eyes, he is tall and heavyset. With his hand or foot, Tom keeps up a steady, nervous beating on the wooden deck where he is being interviewed. Tom describes how he gets along with his family:

> I didn't get along with my stepdad. We just always fight about everything. [We didn't get along] probably because we're so much alike. We both—well, we don't like to do a lot of things together, but we're so much alike and I hardly ever get along with anyone that's like me. I like to control situations and stuff the same way he does. So its like both of us fighting each other to control the same thing.

The "stepdad" Tom speaks of is his second stepfather. His real father and mother never married, and Tom just recently met his "real father":

> I just met him a couple of months ago, before I came here. It was interesting to finally find out who he was. This summer I'm supposed to go there [the town where his father lives] for a while. I always thought my stepdad was my dad—I found out [the truth] when I was, like, 6. At that age, I just never really thought about it.

Tom has six siblings from his parents and stepfather. They are not a close family and rarely engage in activities together:

> I'm usually gone. I, like, go with my friends places and stuff when I get home. You know, like fishing, swimming, or something.

For Tom, having a heavy build affects his life in numerous ways. For example, observations of him playing sports during the camp session reveal his particular talent in baseball. At the Institute, baseball is played with a "blooper ball," which is larger than a softball, fairly heavy, and easy to hit, but does not travel a great

Tom is a young man with some problems at home and some lack of confidence; he is eager to learn and wants to go to college.

▾

distance. Nevertheless, Tom has a talent for achieving great distances when batting; unfortunately, having hit the ball, because of his build, he has difficulty running the bases. This is not the first place he has encountered such a discrepancy:

> I don't play [at school], like, on a team 'cause they say, "Oh you can't play," and then I go out and play softball at lunch. I could probably make them [let me] play, but I don't want to be on their team if they want to be that way.

Tom has just recently moved and therefore changed schools:

> You know when a half year goes by? Whatever that's called, it was then [that I moved], right then—in January. I wouldn't have got to come here if I hadn't changed. My school doesn't offer it [the camp program], or it's not offered to them. One or the other.
> It didn't really bother me [to move]—well, I was kinda scared at first about making new friends and stuff. But it wasn't that hard.

The change in schools, at least on the surface, appears to have been a positive experience for Tom. He has been recruited to play football and he has made friends:

He talks about his participation in academics and his adjustment at school.

> At the other school I wanted to play football, but I didn't like the coach 'cause he was kind of a dork. Next year I'm gonna play football. I've never played it in high school or nothin . . .
> The first day I come there [to his new school] I went into my gym class and asked what I needed and stuff, and he goes, "Do you play football?" I said, "Nope." He said, "You're kidding!" He was the football coach.
> The friends I hang around with would be considered the "in" crowd at my old school 'cause they're all football players and stuff like that. But they never really pick on people.

Tom is also doing well academically, particularly in math courses.

> [My favorite subject is] algebra. I get an A in it. I never really liked it, but, well, you know, I'm so good at it. It just grew on me. [I'm taking] geometry. That's the only thing I can take. In our school, before you can take geometry you gotta take algebra and get a C or better. Before you

can take whatever's above geometry, you gotta take geometry and get a C or better. See, now, like in the other school I went to, you could double up; this school you can't.

Science is another of his favorite subjects, and he particularly likes his teacher.

He just wasn't like every other teacher, you know, stuffy with a tie or suit on everyday, "Do this, do that, no you don't do that." He teaches, you know; he's a really good teacher, but he doesn't really push you. He doesn't, like, sit there—like, if you're goofing around in class, he doesn't come up to you, "You do that work right now or get out." He'll just like, "Hey you should do that work or you're just gonna have to take it home," you know. Like, "You don't want to have to take it home, so you better do it." He's one of the teachers who recommended me to come here.

Tom wants to go to college and become a "computer repairman, like a computer technician or something like that." He wants to attend the University of Michigan, but he is uncertain because, he says, "They tell me it's really expensive."

College is very important to him because, he says,

If you don't go to college, you ain't gonna get a job worth anything. I mean, you could get a job, but like if you want to have a family and get a good size house and stuff, forget it.

Except for his cousin, Tom will be one of the first in his family to attend college:

My cousin will beat me there. He's the same age as me, but since I got held back in kindergarten, he went on. He's a year ahead of me. He's really smart. He's got a 4.0 and stuff.

Being in the High/Scope program gave Tom the opportunity to develop his interest in photography. He learned "how to, like, develop pictures, negatives, take photos, and stuff," and "how to get around in the darkroom." His favorite workshop was photography:

Yesterday we developed our negatives. We made some pictures. We're making seven of each one we want to

Tom describes his favorite academic subjects and his goals for college.

▼

make. We're gonna make a book for each one of us in the class. There's five of us and two counselors. We wanted to make a book of poetry and pictures—take a picture and write a poem about it, or a little short story, which I'll probably end up doing, 'cause I don't like poems—I can't write 'em. I can write stories real good.

Tom spent a great deal of his free time and independently scheduled time pursuing this hobby. During this time, he says, "I would go down in the shop or in the darkroom, I'll get the camera and take pictures." He describes what he did:

> I did photograms. You take a leaf or something and put it on the exposer thing, and it makes a print of it . . . everything else will be dark except for the thing you put on it. It was pretty cool.

Presently, Tom does not own a camera or have access to a darkroom at home to continue this interest.

Tom had a mixed reaction to other camp activities. He enjoyed the trip to the University of Michigan, but he felt uneasy at activities such as council or the musicales, where he might have to speak before the group. Nevertheless, he was observed during the first musicale explaining to the entire group what photograms were:

> Yeah [I talked], but I wasn't supposed to. I didn't know that I wasn't supposed to. They didn't have nothin' to do, so they wanted us to show our pictures. It was kind of like a big surprise to me.

While Tom readily admits that he did "okay," he nevertheless replies,

> Yeah . . . but I didn't know we were gonna. Otherwise I would have been all nervous and stuff. I was shocked. I didn't think she'd [the leader of the musicale] say that.

Tom feels that the trip to the University of Michigan was "helpful" and that it "explained things that you didn't know about college and stuff."

> We talked about grades, and like how to sign up, and how much of a pain it was. . . . Like, fraternities, the number of people, the expenses—whether it was cheaper to live on or off campus. I think it was cheaper to live off. I'm not sure. Tuition fees . . .

Experiences in the camp setting and on the field trips were both supportive and challenging, according to Tom.

I went to the nuclear fusion place, the museum of art, the football field—we saw the kicker, he was practicing—the buildings and stuff, some of the dorms and stuff (whatever they're called), the Union or something like that—what else? There were so many things.

I liked the nuclear place [the best]—looking down there and looking at that little nuclear reactor in the pool.

Tom reflects on comparisons between the High/Scope Institute and school and describes what he has gained from the Institute experience.

The purposes of many of the Institute's activities were not lost on Tom. While folk dancing was not one of his favorite activities (he "didn't mind it"), he did understand some of the rationale behind it:

To show everybody that trying new things probably isn't that bad. [Another camper] told us in our meeting with [the camp director], he told us that they all thought they were dumb at first when they were doing that, but then at the end, you like it. I think they do that every year to show people that trying new things is more fun than what you think it is. It can be interesting, you can like it. It shows people that trying new things isn't gonna hurt you.

He also feels he understands why the campers were asked to do work projects:

To show us that not everything in life is easy. That you will have to work in your life sometimes. Things just need to get done. Better to have us do it, and then give us an experience of how to do it, than to pay someone to come do it. It will help us be ready for life.

Differences between the High/Scope program and school are also apparent to Tom. He feels that

school's like that same old thing—go there, come home, go there, come home. Here you don't really do the same thing all the time. Things change, you know? There, you just go every day.

Lastly, Tom feels that the program has helped him to develop an important ability to work with others:

I like to do things on my own, and I learned that you can do things with other people. Like in school, you get in groups and stuff, [but] I don't like doing that, 'cause they just, like, cheat off of me. So I never got in groups, 'cause most of the kids in my class are stupid. Well they're not stupid; they just don't like doing it. Here, they're all at the same level as me. It's like everybody can put the same amount into it. So I learned to work with groups.

IN SUMMARY   These three unique individuals—Yvonne, George, and Tom—illustrate the different ways that the camp program's activities and experiences provided assistance and inspiration to participants. From the profiles, we see adolescents in the High/Scope program

- Striving towards an independent view of themselves
- Coping with personal desires, goals, struggles, frustrations, and growth
- Growing in awareness, understanding, and tolerance of others
- Growing in self-esteem
- Reaching out to adults and peers, sharing and resolving conflicts
- Exploring new experiences
- Setting goals in new directions
- Beginning to realize the connections between present activities and their futures

The High/Scope Institute Staff

Following a recruiting and interviewing process early in the year, the Institute director hired an assistant director and the other staff members. For the spring 1990 session, 14 staff members (8 females and 6 males) were hired to serve as counselors. Four counselors were college graduates, 9 were undergraduates, and 1 was a graduate student. Of the 14 counselors, 6 were from minority backgrounds: 4 females and 1 male were African American, and 1 male was Hispanic.

At the end of the session, the same researcher who observed and interviewed campers and some staff asked staff to respond to a brief questionnaire. Both the interviews and the questionnaire included open-ended questions about staff perceptions of the Institute experience

Staff members valued being able to effectively communicate with campers and provide them with guidance.

▼

and of the campers. Three illustrative staff responses, mainly from the questionnaires, are quoted next, with all names and identifying information changed or deleted. The staff members gave various reasons for choosing their roles in the High/scope program:

> To be a counselor. To obtain work experience with teens, to release myself from the outside world.

> It's a great opportunity to teach physics and learn from the experience. [I hope to] learn better methods to interest and excite younger people in the sciences, [to] find out how well I can teach.

> To be able to experience working with teenagers in a positive atmosphere. Also, to extend knowledge from myself to campers and receive positive reinforcement from all. [I hope to gain] a good feeling of accomplishment and positive attitudes. The remarks from the campers of truthful statements (to better myself) and the sense of a job well-done.

Regarding their Institute experiences, staff members' perceptions of the program and understanding of the campers revolved around various issues and experiences. For example, when asked to describe the most positive, effective experience that they had with a camper, Mark (a counselor) told of a compelling discussion he had with one of the campers:

> Unquestionably, that experience involved Joe. Joe is an extremely bright young man who initially focused all of his energy on demonstrating his desire for power, money, and fame.
> One evening, Joe asked to speak with me privately, and though this was around lights-out time, I sensed that something was troubling him deeply. I took Joe into a small room in the annex, and we sat with the lights off. He told me that he was having difficulties with two problems, the first revolved around his first love interest [another camper], and the second was a problem at home. We first discussed his relationship with [the other camper]. . . . After a bit of coaxing, he started to explain his home life. Apparently his father had left the family, and naturally, Joe felt tremendous resentment towards his father. Joe's mother placed considerable pressure on him to achieve academically. She was always saying that he "should have done better," that he "should have

worked harder." At some time during the explanation, Joe became quite upset, though it was almost undetectable at first. I comforted him verbally and by patting his shoulder. . . . [Another counselor entered the discussion] and both [the other counselor] and I related anecdotes of a similar nature and talked of the importance of setting one's goals and of the difficulties inherent in such an adult concept. We talked about the idea of being yourself irrespective of others' ideas and about how the true Joe is superior to any facade manufactured to impress or to meet anyone else's needs.

On the last day, Joe thanked the staff collectively for helping the "true Joe" to emerge, but I'm sure he was referring to the chat he had with [the other counselor] and me, in particular. I found it very easy to identify with Joe's problems, with the pressure of achieving at a young age and parental pressures, so I was very gratified to have helped him on such a personal level.

Other staff members related various kinds of personal discussions and conversations. As shown in the next three staff quotes, the campers themselves were the highlight of staff members' experience.

> The most positive experience I had with a camper was when a camper entrusted me with a very personal secret. It was during room time at night. All of the other campers had gone to sleep, and we stayed up talking. The camper told me he felt as if I were his older brother (one he never had). Then he told me about his problem. I was surprised at first but didn't let him know it. We discussed the situation, and by the end of that conversation, he felt very relieved about telling me. What I found so positive about this situation is that the boy finally opened up and trusted another individual besides his family.

> During workshop, I was showing [a camper] how to do something, and she told me that she realized that someone does care about her. It touched my heart to know that I had an effect on someone that way.

> [On visitor day] Sally's parents could not visit. [Another counselor] and I adopted her, and we worked in the kitchen and took a walk together. Sally talked about how she felt and what she feared. She was worried about her appearance, her lack of money for college, her [lack of] peer support. It was peaceful, and I felt it was a really productive experience.

When asked to evaluate council, the staff had vari-

Staff members reflected on council sessions and workshops.

▾

ous kinds of responses, as typified by these two staff quotes:

> After each council, our room group spoke about how they felt about the topic of council. The girls in my group, each of them said they did not enjoy the "decision-making" council (decision making was one of the topics for discussion). They felt that although the subject was a good one, it was not an appropriate topic for council. They felt that council should be a time to talk about emotional topics.

> The council about "opportunities" didn't go too well at the time but fostered a lot of good connections later. I had many talks with [my room group] and others about how they felt they needed to conquer obstacles.

A staff member described a camper's response to one of the workshops.

Regarding one particular camper and one particular workshop experience, one staff member had this to say:

> John . . . emerged with the greatest learning from our laser project. Out of all the science-related projects, the laser fabrication project really focused on the practical, engineering aspects as well as the conceptual, theoretical aspects of problem solving. John provided the most apt suggestions for the actual construction and the best grasp of the theory of photon production and wave alignment, in addition to other technical data. He impressed me greatly.

The researcher sensed a range in the maturity levels of staff members, due in part to their age differences. Also, because of their various roles across program activities, staff members varied in their levels of understanding of the program's processes and goals. Despite these variations, each staff member recounted positive and memorable incidents with campers. Staff also appeared to have had their own horizons expanded, especially regarding interpersonal relationships.

The Questionnaire Data

Each of the 46 campers responded to questionnaires, as described in the Evaluation Methods section. Some questionnaire data is missing because, as indicated previously, 2 rural camp participants, 1 male and 1 female (both white), left camp half-way through the camp session. These 2 participants filled out only the pre-camp questionnaire and are included only in that data analysis. Other participants, even though they filled out both questionnaires, failed to respond to some items, and thus were not included in analyses of those items. Unlike the interview method that was used to complete the questionnaires for the 5-year longitudinal study, the method of subjects filling out their own questionnaires is more prone to items being left blank, because subjects either do not understand or do not want to answer certain items.

Responding Participants—Their Region and Gender

Table 14.1 shows that there were nearly equal numbers of respondents from the rural and urban regions, and this included black as well as white participants. From the rural group, all were white. From the urban group, 19 respondents were black, 1 was white, and 1 had parents from India. As shown in Table 14.1, over 60% of each group—rural and urban—were females.

The *ages* of participants from the rural and urban regions of Michigan were not significantly different. Of

Although Institute participants included more females than males, there were comparable numbers of rural white and urban black participants.

Table 14.1

Distribution of Campers by Region

No./%	Rural			Urban		
	Males	Females	Total	Males	Females	Total
Number	9	16	25	8	13	21
Percent	36%	64%	100%	38%	62%	100%

The majority of Institute participants were just completing the ninth grade.

▼

all the camp participants, 84% were in the 14- to 15-year age-range. Overall, the age-range was 13 to 17 years, since participants included one 13-year-old and two 17-year-olds. The *grade levels* of participants ranged from 9th grade to 11th grade. The majority (82%) of the participants were just completing the 9th grade, with no significant differences in grade level for region or gender.

For all subsequent statistical analyses, results are presented first for the overall group and then for comparisons between the following subgroups: overall males versus overall females (gender), overall rural versus overall urban (region), and males versus females within each region.

Family Background of Campers

In the 1990 evaluation, study subgroups (gender and region) showed no significant differences in household size or type.

▼

Household size and type. Household sizes for campers ($n = 43$) ranged from 2 to 10, with the average being 4.63. Overall, 61% of the participants (10 males and 17 females) lived in two-parent households, and 36% (4 males and 12 females) lived in single-parent households. One male lived with relatives. There was no significant household difference for gender or region.

Education of parents. Table 14.2 contains data about the educational levels reached by campers' parents. It should be noted that there is missing data here, especially for fathers' education. This can be expected, since nearly 40% of campers were living in one-parent households, and many of these may not have known the absent parent's educational level. From Table 14.2 we can calculate that of mothers and fathers of campers, approximately 20% had neither completed high school nor received the GED (high school equivalency), 36% reached just the high school diploma or GED, and over 40% had some postsecondary education.

Table 14.2 allows us to next examine separately the educational levels of mothers and fathers. Overall, while 57% of mothers had a high-school-only level of education or less, 43% had some postsecondary education.

Table 14.2

Educational Background of Parents

Highest Educational Level Attained	No. (%) of Mothers	No. (%) of Fathers
Less than high school	7 (19%)	7 (24%)
High school/equivalent	14 (38%)	10 (34%)
Postsecondary technical/ vocational or some college	5 (13%)	6 (21%)
College (2 yr or more)	11 (30%)	6 (21%)
Total	37 (100%)	29 (100%)

Note. High school/equivalent indicates a high school diploma or completion of the equivalency (GED); *Postsecondary technical/ vocational or some college* includes up to 1 year of college.

(*Mother's educational level* was not provided by 5 urban campers and 2 rural campers.)

There was a significant difference between regions, with 11 out of 16 urban mothers (68%) having some postsecondary education, compared with 5 out of 21 rural mothers (24%) having some postsecondary education [$\chi^2(1) = 7.47$, $p < .01$]. There was also a significant difference for region within gender: Only 2 rural males reported having mothers with postsecondary education, whereas all the urban males reported having mothers with postsecondary education, which was a significant difference ($p = .01$, Fisher's exact test). In contrast, *mother's educational level* showed no significant difference for region within the female gender.

The number of participants who responded concerning *father's educational level* was just 63% of the sample, for reasons explained earlier. However, the

Significantly more urban than rural mothers— primarily mothers of urban male participants—had some postsecondary education.

There were no significant region or gender differences in fathers' educational level. ▾

Between urban versus rural, and males versus females, there were no significant differences for
• Parental employment
• Attitudes towards education
• Parent expectations
▾

overall educational levels were highly similar to those of mothers: 58% had a high-school-only level of education or less; 42% had postsecondary education. There were no significant differences for region or gender.

Employment of parents. The majority of campers' mothers (27 out of 45, or 60%) were employed. There was a nonsignificant trend of more female campers than male campers having employed mothers (70% versus 44%) [$\chi^2(1) = 3.02, p < .10$]. Of campers' fathers, 71% were employed, and there were no significant differences or trends for gender or region.

Parent attitudes towards education. One questionnaire item asked campers to rate their parents' attitudes about their children's *current education*. On a 4-point scale, 98% of parents were described as considering their children's education as *important* (18%) to *very important* (80%). On another 4-point scale item about homework, 76% of participants reported that their parents *frequently* emphasized the importance of doing homework, and 18% reported that their parents *sometimes* emphasized the importance of homework. There were no significant differences for region or gender.

Parent expectations. Campers were asked to indicate what their parents expected them to do after high school. Among a list of choices were enrolling in *college* (or other postsecondary education), enlisting in the *military*, and getting a *job*. Overall, 67% of campers (12 males and 18 females) replied that their parents expected them to go to *college*. There were no significant differences for gender or region. Only 1 camper (a male) indicated that his parents expected him to go into the *military*. Most parents appeared to hold expectations for education beyond high school for their talented children, but it is interesting that about one third did not.

Campers' Attitudes, Achievement, Behavior

Satisfaction with high school. Overall, approximately 40% of participants rated themselves as being *fairly* *satisfied* with high school, and 49% rated themselves *very satisfied*. The remaining 11% were *not satisfied with high school at all*. There were no significant differences for subgroups on high school satisfaction.

Recognition in high school and employment. Having received recognition for academic achievement in high school was found to be a major positive predictor of later higher education in the longitudinal study described in earlier chapters. Among the 1990 campers, Table 14.3 shows that only 2 rural campers (8%) reported being recognized for academic achievement. In contrast, 14 (67%) of urban campers had been recognized for academic achievement, which is a statistically significant difference [$\chi^2(1) = 17.32, p < .001$]. There was a significant difference for gender within urban campers, with more females than males being recognized achievers ($p = .00$, Fisher's exact test).

An indicator of a student's more general achievement is receiving some special recognition in high school activities that may or may not have some academic aspects (the school newspaper, theater productions, band, sports, social events). The pattern is the

Although most students were satisfied with high school, significantly more urban than rural students were high achievers in high school. This was especially true of urban females.

Table 14.3

Number of Recognized Achievers

Group	No. (%) of Rural Campers			No. (%) of Urban Campers		
	Males	Females	All	Males	Females	All
Recognized achievers	0 (0%)	2 (12%)	2 (8%)	4 (50%)	10 (77%)	14 (67%)
Others	9 (100%)	14 (88%)	23 (92%)	4 (50%)	3 (23%)	7 (33%)
Total	9 (100%)	16 (100%)	25 (100%)	8 (100%)	13 (100%)	21 (100%)

same here as it was for recognition for academic a-chievement. Significantly more urban campers (19 out of 20, or 95%) than rural campers (14 out of 25, or 56%) reported having received some kind of special recognition in high school (including academic recognition) [$\chi^2(1) = 8.64$, $p < .01$]. There were no significant differences for gender or region.

Since developing leadership skills is one of the goals of the High/Scope program, the 1990 campers were also asked about their **leadership experiences** in high school—about holding student government office, serving as athletic team captain, being editor of the school newspaper, and so forth. Overall, the majority (73%) of campers had not held leadership roles in high school. Only 2 out of 16 males (13%) had been elected to offices, compared with 10 out of 29 females (34%), a nonsignificant trend ($p = .10$, Fisher's exact test). There were no significant regional differences or trends.

Overall, the program participants were positive about high school. Participants included a mix of high achievers, leaders, and students with no special recognition for achievement or leadership. Because of their already-high levels of achievement, we would expect most urban campers to go on to higher education. From the longitudinal study, we know that the High/Scope program affected even those who had *not* achieved academic recognition in high school, since that study found the majority of nonrecognized campers going on to college. While this would lead us to expect that the majority of the 1990 camp participants—both rural and urban—will go on to higher education, the number may be greatest among the urban campers—that is, if ethnic/regional factors do not create unforeseen obstacles for them.

When asked about **employment**, the majority (76%) of campers (most of whom were aged 14 or 15) indicated that they did *not* hold a job. The employed participants were 9 females and 2 males.

Problem behavior. As pointed out in the discussion of the longitudinal study, problem behavior was found

> The majority of subjects in both groups—urban and rural—had not held offices or positions of leadership in school.

to be negatively related to subjects' postsecondary education levels. Among the 1990 campers, 27% indicated various kinds of problem-behavior incidents—getting into fights, shoplifting, using illegal substances. There were no significant differences for region or gender. Among males, 6 out of 16 (37%) reported being suspended from school at some point; this compared with 5 out of 29 females (17%), not a significant difference. Only 4 campers reported ever being arrested, but 7 reported delinquent acts (stealing money, destroying property). No females reported ever having been pregnant.

Only 7 campers reported ever using marijuana, and only 3 reported ever using other illegal substances. (According to national statistics, this usage is less than might be expected for this age group.) Just 3 campers indicated tobacco use, and 12 indicated some use of alcohol.

Influences—religion, role models, and experiences. The influence of religion was rated as *very important* by 15 campers (33%), as *important* by 4 campers (9%), as *somewhat important* by 19 campers (42%); 7 campers (16%) said it was *not important*. Significantly more urban campers than rural campers (60% versus 28%) said that religion was *important* or *very important* $[\chi^2(1) = 4.66, p < .05]$. This difference appeared to be primarily due to 5 out of 7 urban males rating religion as *important* or *very important*, compared with 2 out of 9 rural males doing so, which is a nonsignificant trend ($p = .07$, Fisher's exact test).

Influences from role models or experiences was positively related to postsecondary education level for High/Scope participants in the longitudinal research. For the 1990 evaluation, campers were asked to indicate any role model or experience that was a major source of influence in their lives. (They could cite as many persons or experiences as they wished.)

Overall, 32 out of 45 campers (80%) named 2 to 4 major influences from role models or experiences. Only 2 campers (4%), both urban, said they had no role

> **Some study subjects had behavior problems. In particular, there were several males whose school-related problems had resulted in school suspension.**
>
> ▾

> **Religion was especially important to urban participants, especially to urban males.**
>
> ▾

The majority of participants could cite 2–4 role models who had influenced their lives.

▾

models or influential experiences prior to coming to camp; 8 (17%) indicated just 1 source of influence; 16 (36%) indicated 2 sources of influence; and 16 (36%) had 3 to 4 sources of influences. There were no significant differences for region or gender.

In the longitudinal study, which explored role models and influential experiences more thoroughly, having influential experiences (such as the High/Scope Institute) was positively related to subjects' going on to postsecondary education. Thus we would expect that even those 1990 program participants who came to camp having had few major sources of influence in their past nevertheless stand a chance of being influenced towards higher education by the program's experiences and staff. While most 1990 campers did have 2 to 5 sources of past influence, the 10 campers who had fewer than this would appear to especially need the positive influences the camp program supplies.

Response to the High/Scope Program

Activities. Table 14.4 shows campers' responses to the different types of camp activities, including the instructional activities in various subjects. The data show that significantly more females than males liked folk dancing $[\chi^2(2) = 8.48, p < .01]$. There were no other significant differences for gender or region.

Of the *academic* activities, the computer activity was most well received. Of the *arts* activities, drama and art were the most well liked.

The majority of subjects understood the purpose of the work projects—to learn to take responsibility within a group effort.

▾

Work projects. Participants were asked to indicate what they found to be the most beneficial aspects of the work projects (no table). The majority (64%) indicated that the projects got them to take responsibility as part of a group effort, 50% indicated the projects taught them how to plan and complete a task, and 43% felt the projects enabled them to make a permanent and meaningful contribution to the camp. Only 3 participants indicated that the benefit was learning to do what they were told to do. In response to a question about what

Table 14.4

Participants' Ratings of Activities

Activity	No. (%) Who Did Not Like It Very Much	No. (%) Who Were Neutral	No. (%) Who Liked It a Lot	Total
Academic				
Computer	0 (0%)	16 (36%)	28 (64%)	44 (100%)
Writing	4 (9%)	26 (59%)	14 (32%)	44 (100%)
Physical science	3 (7%)	27 (64%)	12 (29%)	42 (100%)
Natural science	4 (10%)	29 (69%)	9 (21%)	42 (100%)
Arts				
Drama	2 (5%)	12 (27%)	30 (68%)	44 (100%)
Art	2 (5%)	15 (34%)	27 (61%)	44 (100%)
Dance	3 (7%)	17 (40%)	22 (52%)	42 (100%)
Music	2 (5%)	19 (43%)	23 (52%)	44 (100%)
Others				
Musicale	0 (0%)	5 (12%)	38 (88%)	43 (100%)
Photography	2 (5%)	20 (48%)	20 (48%)	42 (100%)
Folk dance	10 (23%)	20 (45%)	14 (32%)	44 (100%)

new things they learned, more females (16 out of 24, compared with 4 out of 12 males) indicated that they learned to work with specific new tools [$\chi^2(1) = 3.60$, $p < .10$]. The majority of campers (22 out of 36, or 61%) indicated that they learned new skills, and 9 out of 36 (25%) indicated that they learned to work with others.

Discussion sessions. Table 14.5 shows the campers' responses to discussion sessions on planning for the future, held by one of the camp directors. Campers were

Table 14.5

Frequency Distribution of Camper Ratings of Discussion Sessions

	No. (%) Rating Topic:			
Topic	Most Liked	Least Liked	Needs Further Discussion	Total
1. Career goals	40 (91%)	4 (9%)	0 (0%)	44 (100%)
2. Plans to reach goals	38 (90%)	1 (2%)	3 (7%)	42 (100%)
3. Educational goals	35 (81%)	5 (12%)	3 (7%)	43 (100%)
4. Personal goals	31 (73%)	7 (17%)	4 (10%)	42 (100%)
5. Improving personal problem-solving skills	20 (51%)	7 (18%)	12 (31%)	39 (100%)
6. Relating to parents	19 (46%)	6 (15%)	16 (39%)	41 (100%)
7. Practicing clear communication	16 (39%)	7 (17%)	18 (44%)	41 (100%)
8. Job interviewing	8 (20%)	9 (23%)	23 (57%)	40 (100%)

asked which topics they liked the most and the least and which ones needed to be discussed further.

Topics are ordered in Table 14.5 from most to least helpful, according to campers' ratings of them. Clearly, topics 1 through 4 indicate the campers' strong interest in their futures. Topics 5 and 6 indicate a strong interest in interpersonal growth and family relationships. Only topic 8 seemed to be of little concern to campers. We may assume that this is because they planned to go on to higher education, rather than employment, after high school. There were no significant differences for region or gender.

General response to major themes. The degree to which the camp program realizes its ideals was rated by participants, as shown in Table 14.6.

Items in Table 14.6 have been ordered from the most to the least positively rated by participants. Council and counselors were very positively rated by nearly all participants. The majority of participants agreed or strongly agreed that the Institute's ideals were realized. There were no significant differences for region. More females than males perceived council as positive [$\chi^2(1) = 5.38$, $p < .05$, Yates' correction].

Intergroup Attitudes and Relations

Since 1987 an important aspect of the camp program has been its diversity of participants— its mix of urban and rural teenagers and of blacks and whites. Therefore a series of analyses were conducted to examine the impact of the camp experience on the participants' intergroup attitudes and relationships.

Changes in attitude. In the precamp questionnaire, when participants were asked if they had friends of other ethnic/racial groups prior to the High/Scope Institute, 34 out of 44 (77%) reported having had friends of a different ethnic group (black participants had white friends and white participants had black friends). There was no significant difference between males and females regarding having friends of different ethnicity.

Participants' favorite discussion topics were those that focused on goals and planning to reach goals—career, educational, and personal.

▾

Participants' perceptions of the Institute experience revealed their highly positive reaction to council sessions, counselors, and group projects.

▾

Campers cited several specific ways that the Institute experience had positively influenced their attitudes towards people of other races.

▾

Table 14.6

Perceptions of the Overall Institute Experience

Ideal	Strongly Agree	Agree	Not Sure	Disagree	Strongly Disagree	Total
Council is positive.	31 (70%)	9 (21%)	3 (7%)	0 (0%)	1 (2%)	44 (100%)
Counselors value campers.	30 (68%)	7 (16%)	4 (9%)	0 (0%)	3 (7%)	44 (100%)
All participate in projects.	25 (57%)	11 (25%)	5 (11%)	3 (7%)	0 (0%)	44 (100%)
Groups mix regularly.	25 (57%)	14 (32%)	3 (7%)	0 (0%)	2 (5%)	44 (100%)
Cooperation is encouraged.	25 (57%)	13 (30%)	5 (11%)	1 (2%)	0 (0%)	44 (100%)
Activities include challenge, success.	20 (45%)	14 (32%)	8 (18%)	1 (2%)	1 (2%)	44 (100%)
Common bonds develop.	12 (27%)	19 (43%)	6 (14%)	4 (9%)	3 (7%)	44 (100%)

In the postcamp questionnaire, participants were asked if the Institute experience had affected their views towards other races, and 14 (32%) indicated that it *had* affected their views; this included 10 white participants (7 females, 3 males) and 4 black participants (3 females, 1 male).

Those participants who felt they had changed their views of persons from other ethnic/racial backgrounds explained that they learned (1) to understand that all people are essentially similar, (2) to be less afraid of meeting members of another race, (3) to like one another and become friends, (4) to see stereotypes as "dumb," and (5) to respect one another and realize people are equal.

Future roommate preference. Another question

pertinent to intergroup relationships asked respondents to name 4 campers of the same gender whom they would like to have as roommates if they were to return to camp at a future time. A subsequent question asked which additional persons they would choose if they could choose more than 4 roommates of the same gender. Male and female participants from the rural and urban regions were compared for their frequency of selecting *same-ethnic-group* versus *other-ethnic-group* roommates. (In this comparison, the urban camper of Indian ancestry was not included.)

Table 14.7 shows the number of "same-ethnic" versus "other-ethnic" roommate selections for the first set of 4 roommates campers selected. Frequencies are based on the total of same-ethnic or other-ethnic selections made by the subgroups shown in the table, counting up to 4 roommate selections per subject. One question to consider was the extent to which subjects' future-room-

On the postcamp question-naire, subjects were asked to choose a set of "future roommates," as if they were going to return to the Institute.

Table 14.7

Frequencies of Same- Versus Other-Ethnic-Group Roommate Selections

Roommate Choice	No. (%) of Rural Campers			No. (%) of Urban Campers		
	Males	Females	All	Males	Females	All
No. (%) of same-ethnic choices	12 (41%)	24 (42%)	36 (42%)	13 (42%)	32 (67%)	45 (57%)
No. (%) of other-ethnic choices	17 (59%)	33 (58%)	50 (58%)	18 (58%)	16 (33%)	34 (43%)
Total	29 (100%)	57 (100%)	86 (100%)	31 (100%)	48 (100%)	79 (100%)

Note. The frequencies refer to the numbers of same- versus other-ethnic roommates named by 8 rural males, 15 rural females, 7 urban males, and 13 urban females.

mate choices simply reflected whom they currently were rooming with. For the first 4 selections, approximately half of the participants did *not* choose a current roommate. Others either chose 1 or 2 current roommates; only 1 participant chose 3 current roommates, and only 1 chose 4 current roommates. The current-roommate factor (tendency to stay with the familiar) appears to have had only a limited effect on subjects' first 4 selections.

Overall, campers appeared to select same- and other-ethnic roommates with comparable frequencies, although males appeared to make somewhat more other-ethnic selections than females did. Comparing just urban males and females, we found the urban females clearly favored same-ethnic selections. Since there were fewer males, males had a smaller pool from which they could select friends, and thus members of the two ethnic groups may have gotten to know one another better.

When similar analyses were conducted on the second set of 4 roommates selected by participants, the same pattern of proportions of same- versus other-ethnic roommate selections was found, although, in this second selection, there was a greater tendency for subjects to select current roommates.

Reciprocity and friendship. Although campers tended to favor none or only one of their current roommates in their first set of roommate selections, this was not indicative that they failed to make friends at camp. Since the program included so many activities, and various combinations of participants were regularly resorted for subsequent activities, participants had many opportunities to get to know everyone.

A good index of friendship is the extent to which campers' selections for future roommates were reciprocated, that is, how frequently we found 2 campers selecting each other. Reciprocity was therefore assessed by scoring 1 point for each camper in cases where a pair of campers reciprocated (selected each other) for 1 of their 8 possible roommate choices (this included both

In general, subjects chose comparable proportions of same- and other-ethnic-group campers for roommates, although black females chose more same-ethnic-group roommates.

the first and second set of choices).

Overall, out of 8 roommate selections, campers had an average score of 3.43 (*SD* = 2.36) for reciprocations. There were only 4 participants (9%) who had no reciprocation; 13 (29%) had 1 to 2 reciprocations; 12 (27%) had 3 to 4 reciprocations; 10 (22%) had 5 to 6; and 5 (9%) had 7 to 8. It is clear from this that many mutual friendships were made.

An analysis of variance on the reciprocity data yielded a nonsignificant trend suggesting that black campers had more roommate selections reciprocated than did white campers [$F(1,41)$ = 2.90, $p < .10$]. A nonsignificant trend was also found for more reciprocity among urban than among rural campers [$F(1,42)$ = 2.84, $p < .10$]. This tendency suggests that black camp participants, especially females, appeared to make more friendships.

IN SUMMARY   There appeared to be a tendency, primarily among urban female campers, to prefer same-ethnic-group friends. However, even for the urban female participants (among whom there was a tendency for close relationships) there was also a fairly high rate of other-ethnic-group roommate selection. Overall, camp provided a positive intergroup experience in which many friendships were made between participants of like as well as different ethnic backgrounds.

General Attitudes Towards the High/Scope Institute Program

Would participants encourage other students to attend the Institute? A strong indicator of the positive response to the program is the fact that all female campers (100%) and 12 out of 14 male campers (86%) would encourage their friends to enroll in the High/Scope Institute if they had the opportunity. Campers gave a number of reasons as to why they thought their friends should come to the program. The most frequent responses included (1) "It is a great experience" (indi-

From an analysis of subjects' mutual roommate selections, it was apparent that most campers had made several friends in the program.

The campers highly recommended that others have this High/Scope experience, and the majority of them expressed an interest in returning to the Institute.

▼

cated by 42%); (2) "You learn a lot, including new things" (indicated by 29%); (3) "It is fun" (indicated by 24%); (4) "You meet new friends" (indicated by 22%); and (5) "It challenges you" (indicated by 10%). Only 2 subjects indicated that "getting away from school" was a reason to enroll in the program.

Would participants return next year if given the opportunity? All females campers (100%) and 12 out of 15 male campers (80%) responded that they would return to camp, which is another strong indication of their positive response to the program.

Impact of the Institute Experience on the Participants

Did the program affect participants' attitudes about achievement and locus of control? In the pre- and post-camp questionnaires, campers rated themselves on two types of attitudinal measures previously employed in the longitudinal study. The first is an *achievement motivation* measure based on 4-point scale responses to 23 statements relevant to the program's general achievement, social, and self-confidence goals. The second is a 16-item *locus-of-control* measure that employs 5-point scales to assess the extent to which a person views himself or herself as having control over life outcomes. Campers who did not respond to *all* the rating scales at *both* times of assessment were not included in the analyses.

A series of repeated-measures analyses of variance were conducted with these two attitudinal measures obtained from ratings precamp and postcamp. A significant difference for the total group was found, indicating an overall increase in *achievement motivation* across the 4-point scales: $M = 3.16$ ($SD = .43$) *precamp*, and $M = 3.36$ ($SD = .31$) *postcamp* [$F(1,35) = 16.57$, $p < .001$]. See Table 14.8.

The small cell-sizes for both region and gender made an examination of the potential interactions not appropriate. Taken separately, males and females also

Table 14.8

Change in Campers' Achievement Motivation

Group	n	Precamp		Postcamp	
		M	SD	M	SD
Males	15	3.12	.42	3.34	.32
Females	21	3.18	.39	3.38	.30
Total	36	3.16	.43	3.36	.31

showed significant increases. For *males*, $M = 3.12$ ($SD = .42$) *precamp*, compared with $M = 3.34$ ($SD = .32$) *postcamp* [$F(1,14) = 10.75$, $p < .01$]. For *females*, $M = 3.18$ ($SD = .39$) *precamp*, and $M = 3.38$ ($SD = .30$) *postcamp* [$F(1,20 = 7.05, p < .05$]. These findings that the Institute program does have a positive effect on participants' achievement motivation and self-confidence give strong validity to the program.

On the 5-point *locus-of-control* scales, participants maintained their already high sense of personal locus of control over the course of the Institute experience: $M = 4.02$ ($SD = .47$) *precamp*, and $M = 4.01$ ($SD = .41$) *postcamp*, not a significant difference.

The findings regarding participants' attitudes show that as the Institute provided broadening and challenging new experiences for participants, it also appeared to boost their achievement motivation and their self-confidence. The Institute experiences did not make participants feel any greater sense of personal locus of control than they had indicated at the beginning of the program. But more important, the experiences did *not* cause a more externally controlled orientation, as might be the case if campers' changes in achievement motivation and self-confidence were strictly situation-based.

From the precamp to the postcamp questionnaire, campers' achievement motivation increased significantly.

Did the program affect the participants' own expectations of pursuing higher education? In the precamp and postcamp questionnaires, campers were asked what they expected to be doing 5 years from now. Respondents simply wrote down their answers; no choices were given.

In the **precamp questionnaire**, 29 campers (67%) indicated that they expected to be in college. There was a nonsignificant trend for more urban campers (16 out of 20, or 80%) expecting to be in college, compared with 14 out of 25 rural campers (56%) [$\chi^2(1) = 2.88$. $p < .10$]. This pattern was especially the case for urban males, with 7 (100%) expecting to be in college, compared with 6 (67%) of the rural males ($p = .15$, Fisher's exact test). There were no significant differences or trends for gender or region.

In the **postcamp questionnaire**, 35 out of 43 (81%) expected to be in college in 5 years, including 20 out of 21 urban campers (95%), compared with 16 out of 23 rural campers (70%). Thus, again, more urban than rural campers expected to be in college, as indicated by a nonsignificant trend [$\chi^2(1) = 3.29$, $p < .10$, Yates' correction]. There were no other trends or significant differences for subgroups.

On the precamp questionnaire, 67% predicted that they would be in college in 5 years.

On the postcamp questionnaire, 81% expected to be in college in 5 years.

Table 14.9

Program Impact on Participants' 5-Year Expectations for College

| | Postcamp Expectation | | | | | |
| | Males | | Females | | Total | |
Precamp Expectation	College	No College	College	No College	College	No College
No college	0	3	7	4	7	7
College	11	1	17	0	28	1

It is important, in comparing the pre- versus post-camp expectations for college, to assess the direction of change in 5-year expectations for individuals. Table 14.9 shows the number of participants who from pre- to post-camp either *changed* or *did not change* their expectations. The direction of change in expectations includes three possibilities: (1) participants who, precamp, were *not* expecting college changed to expecting college; (2) participants who *were* expecting college changed to *not* expecting college; and (3) participants who maintained the same expectations from pre- to postcamp.

Overall, the college-bound category gained 7 females (3 rural and 4 urban) and lost 1 rural male. This net gain of 6 college-bound participants postcamp was a nonsignificant trend (binomial test, $p = .07$). The change was clearly among females, which was a significant gain (binomial test, $p = .02$.). There was no significant gain for males (binomial test, $p = 1.0$).

Postcamp, 73% of males and 86% of females expected to be in college. Females significantly increased their college expectations from pre- to postcamp.

▾

Campers were also asked how they planned to meet their economic needs 5 years from now. They could list as many sources as they expected. It is interesting that 34 said they expected to support themselves, at least in part, with a job. Only 6 expected to have a scholarship, and only 2 expected to get a loan. Only 9 campers expected that their parents would help. Although the majority planned on going to college, they appeared to still need further help in realistic economic planning, including help in how to find out about and qualify for the financial resources that exist for students like themselves.

Although the majority of campers wanted to attend college, it appeared that most needed to begin some specific economic planning.

▾

Major Findings

The following pages summarize the major findings of the 1990 evaluation of the High/Scope IDEAS program for talented disadvantaged and minority adolescents.

Family Background

Urban and rural program participants had highly similar socioeconomic backgrounds.

▾

- The socioeconomic backgrounds of rural and urban participants were highly similar. We found no significant differences between campers from different ethnic/regional backgrounds for single- and two-parent households, number in household, educational level of fathers, employment of parents, or parent expectations.

- Compared with the mothers of rural campers, significantly more urban mothers had some postsecondary education. This was primarily due to a large percentage of mothers of the urban males having postsecondary education.

Participants' Attitudes About High School and Recognition in High School

While most participants were satisfied with high school, their levels of high school achievement and leadership indicated a need for intervention.

▾

- On the precamp questionnaire, approximately one half of the campers (49%) rated high school as very satisfying, and the other half were either fairly satisfied (40%) or not satisfied (11%) with high school. Since the longitudinal study found that even the majority of those students who were dissatisfied with high school still went on to college, dissatisfaction with high school among some of the 1990 camp participants should not preclude their going on to college.

- Compared with rural campers, significantly more of the urban campers had been recognized for academic or general achievement in high school. Since the longitudinal study found that even campers who had not been recognized achievers in high school went on to college, we would expect the majority of 1990 campers—with or without high school recognition—to go on to college.

- There were no significant urban/rural differences in the numbers of campers who were high school student leaders. The majority, 73%, had held no office or position of leadership in high school thus far.

Problem Behavior

- Six out of 16 males (38%), compared with 5 out of 29 females (17%), reported that they had been suspended from school at some point, not a significant difference or trend.

- Only 7 campers reported ever committing delinquent types of activity, and only 4 reported having been arrested. These delinquency findings and the incidence of campers having been suspended from school indicates that while most participants did not have problem behavior, there were several participants with some behavior difficulty.

Religious Beliefs

- Significantly more urban campers (60%) than rural campers (28%) indicated that religion was important or very important to them. The difference was primarily due to a high valuing of religion among urban males.

Role Models and Influential Experiences

- Overall, 35 campers (77%) reported having experienced 2 to 5 major sources of influence from persons or experiences. The longitudinal study showed that having role models and influential experiences was related to campers going on to college after high school. Particularly for the 1990 campers who lacked role models and influential experiences, the camp experience should have been a useful source of alternative role models and experiences leading towards higher education.

Response to the Institute Experience

- The High/Scope program was very positively

Over one third of males and a number of females reported having problem behavior that led to school suspension—again indicating a need for intervention.

Influences from religion were especially strong for urban participants. Also, the majority of participants cited 2 or more influential role models or experiences.

Participants' ratings of the program and its components were very positive overall.

▼

perceived by male and female campers, both urban and rural, as indicated by interviews with individual campers and by the ratings campers gave program components on the postcamp questionnaire.

• Participants' responses to the questions about whether they would like to return to the camp and whether they would recommend it to friends were resoundingly positive. The reasons campers gave for valuing the Institute experience included that they learned a lot, gained new experiences, had fun, made new friends, and were challenged.

Achievement Motivation and Self-Confidence

There was a significant gain in participants' achievement motivation across the program period.

▼

• The impact of the Institute program was evident in the area of enhancing participants' achievement motivation and self-confidence. There was a significant pre- to postcamp gain in participants' ratings of their self-confidence and achievement motivation.

Peer Relationships

Positive relationships and friendships between same- and other-ethnic-group participants were indicated on several measures.

▼

• Overall, the urban-rural and black-white interactions provided by the camp program were a broadening experience in the young people's lives. This was especially the case for rural campers, who indicated relatively few past experiences with persons from African American ethnic backgrounds.

• Participants chose nearly equal proportions of same- and other-ethnic-group roommates for a future time. Although urban females chose same-ethnic-group roommates at a high rate, they named a considerable number of other-ethnic-group roommates, as well.

• Friendships (indicated by reciprocity in future roommate choices) were frequently made among both current roommates and nonroommates and across both same- and other-ethnic groups. There was a tendency for more friendships among females than among males, and among black females, in particular. The finding of approximately 3 friendships per camper is a strong indicator that the Institute's activities facilitated peer relationships, in general, and inter-ethnic peer relationships, in particular.

Expectations for College

• Males generally held steady from precamp to postcamp in their college expectations, with 11 out of 15 (73%) planning to be in college 5 years in the future. All urban males planned to go to college.

• Females made an impressive shift from pre- to postcamp, with a significant gain in the number planning to be in college in 5 years. Precamp, 17 out of 28 (61%) planned to be in college in 5 years, compared with 24 out of 28 (86%) postcamp. Although precamp there were significantly more urban than rural females planning on college, by the end of the camp experience, there was a shift towards nearly equal numbers of females from both regions planning on college.

SUMMARIZING THIS CHAPTER   Except for their multiethnic origins, the 1990 campers had backgrounds highly similar to the 1982 and 1983 campers who participated in the longitudinal study. With only one exception, campers from the longitudinal study completed high school; furthermore, the majority who completed high school also went on to college. We would thus expect that a solid majority of the 1990 cohort of talented disadvantaged and minority students will likewise pursue a college education.

By the end of the program, females had significantly increased their expectations regarding college.

▼

The 1990 program evaluation indicated a particularly positive impact on participants'
• Relationships with same- and other-ethnic-group peers
• Active learning and achievement attitudes
• Expectations to pursue higher education

——— • ———

Part **THREE**

An Overview: Future Directions for Policy and Development

SHERRI ODEN
DAVID P. WEIKART

Chapter FIFTEEN

Study Findings and Their Implications

A MAJOR PREMISE BEHIND THIS BOOK is that the nation's future depends on our ability to maintain and expand a highly educated and skilled work force. To do this, we must challenge previously untapped potential. The potential exists—in towns, rural areas, and inner cities—among the talented young people who are failing to finish high school or failing to achieve beyond high school because they are economically disadvantaged or from minority backgrounds.

Program models designed to challenge this untapped potential also exist, but they need refinement, expansion, and widespread replication if, by the twenty-first century, America's young adults are to "be able to participate, regardless of race, sex, or their economic status in childhood, in the social and political processes and sophisticated workplaces of the future" (Weill, 1988). To spur on the refinement, expansion, and replication of existing programs, in Parts 1 and 2 of this book, we have looked at 13 of these programs across the nation and, by observation, interviews, or data analysis, extracted information about why and how the various programs work. Part 3 contains urgent recommendations based on that information—recommendations aimed at policymakers as well as program evaluators, developers, and funders.

15

We must discover and develop the potential of all our young people. We cannot ignore the talents of those from economically disadvantaged and minority backgrounds.

▾

Two Evaluation Models

A Model Based on Knowledge About Students

Part 1 presented investigations of 12 nationally known programs (summarized on pp. 72–92). They are all extracurricular, precollege programs designed to challenge the potential of talented teenagers from economically disadvantaged and minority backgrounds. Each of these programs was found to be exemplary in some ways when it was compared with a model of "ideal-program" features (see insert). Because these features were derived from existing knowledge about the char-

Our charge is to spur on the refinement, expansion, and replication of existing programs, in part by identifying *ideal-program features.*

▾

The High/Scope longitudinal data provide an empirical model of factors that promote or detract from talented disadvantaged students' pursuit of higher education.

▾

IDEAL PROGRAM—Features

An ideal intervention program for adolescents should include these changes for *schools*:

- Advanced courses
- Improved laboratories and resources
- Hands-on problem-solving exercises
- Lessons and practice in using different learning styles
- Multidimensional screening procedures to identify high potential
- Teacher/staff training and retraining
- A professional support-group to work with teachers and students
- Curriculum modification to reflect minority contributions
- Remediation/enrichment in communication skills
- Restructuring of schools
- Residential summer classes
- A partnership between parents and schools/teachers

And these changes for *students*:

- Coaching in test-taking skills
- Coaching in study and time-management skills
- Tutoring for and by students
- Exposure to professionals in work settings
- Interaction with role models
- Personal counseling and discussions about racism
- Establishment of a peer support-group
- Assistance with college admission/financial aid

acteristics and needs of adolescents in the target populations, they should be considered when evaluating, improving, or designing educational programs for disadvantaged and minority students. We incorporate these features in our concluding recommendations.

Our concluding recommendations are also based on the research described in Part 2—a 5-year longitudinal study and a 1990 evaluation of High/Scope's month-long residential program for talented disadvantaged teenagers (summarized on pp. 142–145). Given the present lack of evaluation research of this type, the model based on High/Scope research is the driving force behind our recommendations.

A Model Based on the High/Scope Research

The longitudinal study. The High/Scope longitudinal research that was conducted to assess educational outcomes 5 years after students had participated in the 1982 and 1983 sessions of the High/Scope Institute for IDEAS found that significantly more students from the High/Scope program went on to postsecondary education— 73% from the program group versus 55% from the comparison group (Figure 15.1a). (Adult-education courses of a hobby or general-interest type were not counted as postsecondary education.) Perhaps even more important than these overall figures is the evidence of the program's impact among students with low to moderate achievement in high school, the "nonrecognized" achievers: In both program and comparison group, approximately half of the subjects had been recognized achievers and half had not been. In each group—program and comparison—over 80% of *recognized achievers* went on to postsecondary education. However, of the program group's *non*recognized achievers (Figure 15.1b), 65% went on to postsecondary education, whereas only 29% of their comparison-group counterparts did so, a statistically significant difference ($p < .01$). A more detailed summary of the longitudinal study follows.

Figure 15.1

Postsecondary Education Outcomes

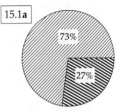

High/Scope Program Group

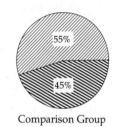

Comparison Group

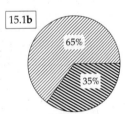

High/Scope Program Group
Nonrecognized Achievers

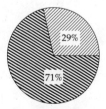

Comparison Group
Nonrecognized Achievers

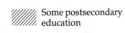 Some postsecondary education

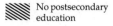 No postsecondary education

SUMMARIZING THE LONGITUDINAL STUDY

In the longitudinal research with the 1982 and 1983 High/Scope program cohorts, approximately 70% of both study sample groups— program and comparison—were interviewed for approximately an hour by telephone by interviewers who were not informed of the specific aims of the research. Because of several data collection strategies that were employed, subjects were not aware that the purpose of the interviews was to evaluate the High/ Scope program.

Statistical analyses indicated high initial comparability between program and comparison groups. The groups were not significantly different in socioeconomic background factors, achievement test scores, or age at time of interview (median age of subjects was approximately 21 years of age). However, there was some suggestion of an economic advantage in family background for the comparison group.

All major statistical analyses were conducted to examine the effectiveness of the main goals of the High/ Scope program, which are, in general, to increase the postsecondary educational attainment of the talented disadvantaged students for whom the program was designed. The following summary of specific findings is organized according to the major variables examined in the longitudinal investigation. In this summary, *significant difference* refers to $p < .05$, *nonsignificant trend* refers to $p < .10$, two-tailed tests.

EDUCATIONAL OUTCOMES

Educational Status

The educational variables employed in the research—educational level completed, *current postsecondary enrollment, and future educational plans—were found to have substantial statistical validity.* For both groups—program and comparison—there were significant and substantial positive correlations between subjects' levels of completed education, current enrollment in higher education, and plans for future education.

Nearly every study subject graduated from high school or received the GED certificate. Among program subjects, the rate of high school or GED completion was 98%, slightly higher than the 95% among comparison subjects. These rates somewhat exceed but are still comparable to typical rates of rural areas in the North Central States.

More program subjects than comparison subjects went on to postsecondary education, mostly at a college or university. Significantly more subjects from the High/Scope program obtained some postsecondary education—73% versus 55% of subjects from the comparison group. (On-the-job training courses not leading to professional certificates or college credit were not counted as postsecondary education.) Significantly more program subjects obtained specifically some *college* education— 68% compared with 50% of comparison students.

Gender was not a significant factor in the levels of postsecondary education attained by study subjects. Males and females in both study sample groups attained similar levels of postsecondary education. There was no statistically significant difference between the postsecondary education rates for males and females overall or within the program and comparison groups.

Areas of Study in College

College students in both sample groups in the study pursued a wide range of major areas of study, including humanities, sciences, engineering, education, business, and vocational/technical training. Although there were more program than comparison subjects who attended college, there were no significant differences between the two groups in areas of study, and only 22% of study subjects overall were pursuing vocational/technical courses of study in college.

More than half of the college students in both study sample groups began their postsecondary education at a 4-year college or university. In each group, of those with postsecondary education, approximately 41% had first attended a community or technical college and 59% had first attended a university or 4-year college.

Very few study subjects went to vocational or technical postsecondary schools. In each study sample group, 3 students attended short-term skill-training programs leading to certificates in such technical areas as dental hygiene, word processing, and computer operations.

Current Enrollment, Completed Education, and Future Educational Plans

Overall, over two thirds of subjects who had begun postsecondary education either were still enrolled or had already completed a degree or certificate. Of all subjects with some postsecondary experience, 55% were currently enrolled, 13% had already completed 2- or 4-year college degrees or postsecondary certificates, and 31% had left college without completing a degree. Though there were significantly more High/

Scope program subjects than comparison subjects with some postsecondary experience, there was no significant difference in the two groups' postsecondary "drop-out" rates. At the time of interview, of program subjects, 2 had completed vocational/technical certificates; 2 had completed 2-year college degrees, and 2 had completed 4-year college degrees; of comparison subjects, 2 had completed vocational/technical certificates, 3 had completed 2-year college degrees, and none had completed a 4-year college degree.

Of those study subjects who had dropped out of college, the majority (69%) planned to return to complete their education. Also, among female program subjects—in school, with degrees, or dropped out—80% had plans for further higher education, which was significantly more than among their program male or comparison female counterparts.

Military Service and Education

Significantly more of the High/Scope program subjects (18%) than of the comparison subjects (3%) served in the military at some point. Most subjects with some military service had also obtained some college-level education—before, during, or after military service.

FACTORS INFLUENCING EDUCATIONAL OUTCOMES

Recognized Achievement and Attitudes in High School

Slightly fewer than one half (47%) of study subjects were recognized achievers in high school, and they accounted for 61% of all subjects who went on to postsecondary education. Both groups—program and comparison—had similar proportions of recognized achievers. There were no significant differences in the proportions of recognized achievers from each study group who went on to postsecondary education; over 80% of recognized achievers from each group went on to postsecondary education.

The impact of the High/Scope program was most evident among those males and females who had not *been highly recognized for achievement in high school.* Overall, slightly over one half (53%) of study subjects were not recognized achievers, with approximately equal proportions of nonrecognized achievers in the program and comparison groups. However, the majority (65%) of the program's *non*recognized achievers went on to postsecondary education, whereas only 29% of their comparison group counterparts did so, which is a significant difference.

Especially among nonrecognized achievers, educational persistence was apparently fostered by the High/Scope program. For comparison subjects, *recognized achievement* correlated significantly with plans for further education. In contrast, for program subjects, because many nonrecognized as well as recognized achievers had plans for further education, there was no significant correlation between *recognized achievement* and *educational plans*.

Regardless of how High/Scope program subjects felt about high school, their receptivity towards postsecondary education was positively affected by the High/Scope program. For example, of the program subjects who were in any way dissatisfied with their last year of high school, 60% nevertheless went on to postsecondary education. This contrasts with their comparison group counterparts, only 38% of whom went on to postsecondary education, which was a significant difference.

Parent Expectations, Role Models, and Influential Experiences

The majority of study subjects with parents who held high educational expectations for them went on to postsecondary education. In both the program group and the comparison group, subjects who perceived high parent-expectations went on to postsecondary education (76% versus 68%, respectively) with no significant differences between groups.

The High/Scope program apparently had an especially positive effect on subjects whose parents had low educational expectations of them. Among program subjects with low parent-expectations, 69% nevertheless went on to postsecondary education, which was significantly more than the 37% of their comparison group counterparts who did so.

From their experiences in the High/Scope program, subjects apparently gained a higher estimation of their own potential and became less reliant on their parents' view of their potential. Whereas among comparison subjects, the variable *parent expectations* was significantly and positively correlated with all educational status variables (including *educational level, current (postsecondary) enrollment,* and *educational plans*), among program subjects, the *parent expectations* variable was not significantly correlated with any of the educational status variables.

High/Scope program subjects reported a broader range of role models/experiences that were influential and a somewhat greater number of influences overall than did comparison subjects. Program subjects reported a different pattern of influences than did comparison subjects: fewer influences from family and more influences from friends, from nonfamily adult role models, and from experiences, including the High Scope program. Teacher role models accounted for approximately 31% of all influences cited by both groups.

For program subjects, the High/Scope program may have increased receptivity to adopting positive role models beyond the family. Among program subjects, *role models/experiences* was significantly and positively correlated with *educational level* and *educational plans.* This was not the case among comparison subjects, but instead, *parent expectations* and *recognized achievement* were significantly and positively correlated with every educational status variable.

Problem Behavior

There were no significant differences between program and comparison groups in the overall amount of problem behavior. There were no significant differences between High/Scope and comparison groups for *some* versus *no* problem-behavior incidents (including suspension or expulsion from school, minor delinquency, serious delinquency, or marijuana use). Of all subjects, 27% reported no problem behaviors or incidents of the types surveyed. Another 24% of subjects reported only 1 or 2 problem behaviors or incidents.

There was a pattern of more problem behavior among male than among female study subjects. Overall, significantly more males than females had engaged in serious delinquency, been arrested by police, or been suspended or ex-

pelled from high school. More males (29% compared with 14% of females) had been suspended or expelled from high school.

In most cases, first arrests of study subjects occurred before subjects were 18 years of age. Since some students with problem behaviors had been encouraged to enroll in the High/Scope program, there was an expected nonsignificant trend of more first arrests before age 18 among program subjects than among comparison subjects, but no difference or trend in first arrests after subjects reached age 18. Overall, arrests occurred mainly among male subjects (12 male program subjects and 5 male comparison subjects). The problem behaviors that led to arrests were of the misdemeanor type; few subjects had spent even a small amount of time in jail.

Study subjects' rates of illegal substance use (and of alcohol and tobacco use) were comparable to or less than national rates. Overall, 48% of study subjects had at some point smoked marijuana, with no significant differences between program and comparison subjects. Significantly more program subjects (23%) than comparison subjects (6%) reported having ever tried other illegal substances. The program group's rate of ever having used illegal substances was comparable to 1988 national rates for 18- to 24-year-olds; the comparison group's rate was unusually low.

Study subjects with more behavior problems tended to obtain less or no post-secondary education. Frequency of problem behavior was significantly and negatively correlated with educational level for both the program and the comparison group.

Marital Status

The majority of study subjects were living on their own, apart from their parents. Of High/Scope program subjects, 71% were living in their own households, apart from their parents, which was not significantly different from comparison subjects, 60% of whom lived on their own. (Subjects at college were not counted as living on their own unless they resided in their own apartments or dormitories 12 months of the year.)

More comparison than program subjects had remained single. Significantly more comparison subjects than program subjects were single (never married, not cohabiting) at the time of interview—67% versus 50%, respectively.

More male subjects than female subjects had remained single. Significantly more males than females (71% versus 46%, respectively) had remained single (had never married and were not cohabiting with a spouse-equivalent at the time of interview). Significantly more male than female comparison subjects (82% versus 50%) had remained single. These latter two percents compared with 58% of male program subjects and 43% of female program subjects, not a significant difference.

Single marital status was less related to educational level for High/Scope subjects than it was for comparison subjects. Among program subjects with postsecondary education, only 54% had remained single, compared with 74% of comparison subjects with postsecondary education—a significant difference.

*Among program females, single marital status was somewhat less related to hav-*ing some college-level education than it was among comparison females. For High/Scope females, solid majorities of both single (93%) and married (70%) subjects had some college-level education. Among female comparison subjects, rates of having some college-level education were 67% for single females and 47% for married females.

Remaining single did make a difference in the likelihood of study subjects' staying in school (postsecondary) or completing a postsecondary degree. Of those study subjects currently in college or with a college degree, 71% were single and 29% were married or cohabiting. In contrast, of study subjects who had been enrolled but then had dropped out of college, 60% were married and 40% were single. This relationship between staying single and securing education was stronger among males than among females.

Remaining single was somewhat related to study subjects' making plans for beginning or completing postsecondary education, especially among comparison subjects. Although there was a pattern of negative correlations between *marital status* (ranging from staying single to being married or cohabiting) with the educational status variables for both program and comparison subjects, the only significant correlation was an inverse correlation between *marital status* (married or cohabiting) and *educational plans*, and this was found only for comparison subjects.

Childrearing

Nearly every study subject delayed having children until after high school. Only 1 subject in each group—program and comparison—had a child before the age of 18 years. This 3% rate is comparable to the 3% national rate of pre-age-18 childbirth for females. At ages 18 and 19, 3 females in each study group bore children. This 5% post-age-18 childbirth rate is somewhat less than the 8% national rate.

The majority of study subjects were not yet parents at the time of interview. Overall, approximately 18% of study subjects had children (only 1 from each group was a single parent), with no significant difference between program and comparison groups in the proportions having children.

More female subjects than male subjects were parents at the time of interview. Significantly more females (25%) than males (9%) had children. These rates are comparable to national rates for 18- to 24-year-olds.

Employment

The majority of subjects were employed full- or part-time. Overall, 75% of study subjects were employed at the time of interview, with no significant differences between males and females or between program and comparison subjects.

The majority of employed study subjects worked full-time. There were no significant differences between groups in the numbers of employed subjects who worked full-time—68% of program subjects and 77% of comparison subjects.

Compared with not-enrolled subjects, more subjects who were enrolled in postsecondary school were employed part-time. For both the program and the comparison group, 56% of subjects who were currently enrolled in postsecondary education worked part-

time; this compared with only 13% of not-enrolled subjects working part-time. Program females enrolled in school seemed to be the most determined (or perhaps the least financially supported) group, since almost all were employed.

The majority of study subjects currently enrolled in school (postsecondary) reported some financial support either from school or from parents. Nearly 83% of all currently enrolled postsecondary students received some financial support. Nearly 30% of all currently enrolled students received aid from both the school and their parents; 53% received some financial support from one or the other source; and 17% received no financial support at all. Dividing the program and comparison groups into currently enrolled students with one, two, or no sources of financial aid revealed a borderline trend ($p < .13$) suggesting that a greater proportion of the program subjects had no financial means, other than their own resources, to support their education.

Economic Difficulty

Study subjects' personal economic difficulty was related to parental family economic background. Subjects' own economic difficulty since high school—their receipt of public assistance such as AFDC, food stamps, unemployment insurance, Medicaid—was related to less parental employment and greater family use of public assistance when subjects were growing up.

Only a small group of study subjects received AFDC or food stamps, but as expected, more program than comparison subjects were in this group. A small group of study subjects (8%) received welfare, including significantly more program subjects (9 program versus 2 comparison subjects). This difference was expected, since the program subjects came from somewhat less-advantaged economic backgrounds. Of the 9 program subjects, 4 were employed at least part-time, and of the 2 comparison subjects, neither was employed.

Study subjects' personal economic difficulty was related to educational level. Those subjects who had obtained the least education represented the major-

ity of both the unemployed and the welfare recipients.

Subjects with the least economic resources also obtained the least education, but this was less the case among program subjects than among comparison subjects. For comparison subjects', *economic difficulty* (personal use of public assistance) was significantly and inversely correlated with *educational level.* Among program subjects, the correlation of these same two variables was also inverse, but it was not significant.

The 1990 evaluation. Another evaluation of High/Scope's program was conducted with students from the 1990 program, about 3 years after the program had expanded to include not only rural white disadvantaged teenagers but also inner-city teenagers. A special aim of this evaluation was to examine interactions between participants from diverse cultural backgrounds. The 1990 evaluation indicated that the program's students, though from different ethnic and regional backgrounds (rural white and, predominantly, urban black), were highly similar in socioeconomic background. Also, despite ethnic/regional background differences, both groups of students had highly positive and similar responses to the program. Furthermore, sociometric analyses of students' peer selections at the end of the program period revealed nearly the same proportion of friendships between students from different ethnic/regional backgrounds as between students from the same ethnic/regional background.

The path analyses. For subjects in High/Scope's longitudinal study, educational outcomes appeared to have been influenced by participation in the High/Scope program and also by such factors as parental level of education and economic difficulty. Therefore, we decided to conduct several statistical path analyses on the longitudinal research data to gain more understanding of how major variables may have worked together to affect these disadvantaged students' pursuit of higher education. The result was the empirically based model of paths to postsecondary education presented next. While the model is a summary of findings from a long-term study of participants from a specific program, we think it should prove generally useful to developers and evaluators of programs aimed at promoting higher-education outcomes for disadvantaged adolescents.

For the various path analyses of the longitudinal data, we selected potential influence variables—subjects' family backgrounds, school backgrounds, personal economic difficulty—from previous descriptive and correlational analyses (in Part 2) and from other

The longitudinal study's summary path-analysis model and the 1990 findings suggest that programs should develop experiences and strategies that

- **Motivate talented but low-achieving students**
- **Facilitate positive multi-ethnic relationships**
- **Broaden students' positive sources of influence**
- **Guide parents in supporting development of their children's potential**
- **Guide students in planning paths to higher education**
- **Help students to learn effective problem solving**

▾

research on disadvantaged youth (in Part 1). Overall, the variables selected for the path analyses accounted for the majority of the variance in subject *educational level* and *educational plans*.

Based on the results of the several path analyses, the summary model in Figure 15.2 shows the following **positive paths** to *educational level* (postsecondary):

- *Parent expectations* and encouragement
- Positive influences from *role models and experiences* (including intervention programs)
- *Recognized achievement* in high school
- *Educational plans* (postsecondary)

Figure 15.2

Summary Model of Paths to Postsecondary Education

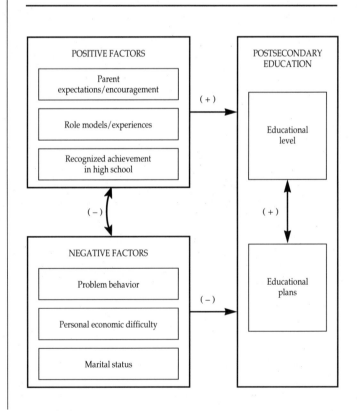

Negative paths to *educational level* (postsecondary) were as follows:

- *Problem behavior*
- Personal *economic difficulty*
- *Marital status* (being married/cohabiting)

Note also that the Figure 15.2 summary model shows *educational plans* and *educational level* completed by a subject as having a reciprocal effect. This means that study subjects who completed some level of postsecondary education also tended to have plans to complete higher levels (degrees) of postsecondary education, and vice versa.

One of our path analyses differentiated subjects according to membership in the program group or the comparison group. The results of this analysis showed that participation in the High/Scope program made a major contribution to subjects' pursuit of postsecondary education. Furthermore, the size of this contribution was sufficient to compensate for such negative background factors as low parent-expectations and lack of recognition for achievement in high school. In the absence of negative factors, program participation, combined with other positive background factors, had even greater influence on subjects' pursuit of postsecondary education.

In two other path analyses—one we conducted for the program group and one we conducted for the comparison group—some differences were found in which influence variables had major **positive effects** on postsecondary education:

For **comparison subjects**, the students with postsecondary education were those who had been recognized for achievement in high school, who had parents with high expectations for them, who were enrolled in postsecondary courses at the time of interview, and who were planning further education. Role models and influential experiences had negligible or no effect on the comparison subjects' pursuit of postsecondary education.

Overall, the path analyses indicated that the High/Scope Institute for IDEAS expanded students' paths to postsecondary education and compensated for limiting background influences.

▾

In contrast, for the High/Scope **program subjects**, role models and influential experiences (including the High/Scope program), had a major positive effect on their pursuit of postsecondary education, whereas recognized achievement in high school had negligible or no effect. We also found that program subjects who had completed some postsecondary education, even if they were not enrolled at the time of interview, had plans for further education. As with the comparison group, program subjects' being currently enrolled in postsecondary education and having plans for further education were major influences on *educational level*. The *parent expectations* variable was less of an influence on *educational plans* among program subjects than among comparison subjects.

Two variables had **negative effects** on pursuit of postsecondary education for both **program** and **comparison groups**: (1) having had *problem behaviors*, primarily in high school and (2) having had *economic difficulty* since high school. Also, for comparison subjects, *marital status* (getting married or cohabiting) negatively affected future *educational plans*, but for program subjects, *marital status* had little or no effect on future *educational plans*.

A final path analysis focusing on family background (specifically, parents' economic and educational status) suggested that in families where parents had low educational or economic levels, subjects' own educational and economic attainment were also low. From the earlier path analyses, we learned that for students who did not have the benefit of program intervention, parent expectations were the primary source of influence. Therefore, program intervention is particularly needed for students whose parents provide little support or do not encourage higher education goals. An especially critical function of programs thus should be to broaden students' sources of influence—through active, engaging learning activities and through exposure to and interaction with young adults who have college experience.

Considering the results of the various path analyses, we can conclude that the High/Scope program increased the number of disadvantaged students going on to postsecondary education and planning to complete degrees. Included in this expanded group are those students we would expect to go on to college—the highly recognized achievers—but also those students who had not been highly recognized achievers in high school, whose parents did not have expectations for them to pursue postsecondary education.

A Word About Gender in Paths to Postsecondary Education

Gender does appear to play a role in young peoples' life choices and outcomes. For example, nationally, more females than males enroll in college and complete degrees. At the same time, relatively few females enter math- and science-related fields, and few females reach the highest levels in business and the professions (Adelman, 1991; American Council on Education, 1991). Also, gender seems to play an important part in the problems disadvantaged and minority teenagers face today (for example, the high dropout rate among males and the high incidence of single-parenting among females). For all these reasons, we analyzed data for gender differences in the longitudinal study. In the High/Scope longitudinal research, the gender of subjects was found to have no significant, direct effect on study subjects' postsecondary education levels. This may indicate that factors that *were* found to affect subjects' educational levels (for example, parent expectations, role models, and experiences such as the High/Scope program) were strong for both males and females.

It is interesting to consider how the High/Scope program worked for both males and females. Though there were no significant differences in the proportions

There is increasing effort to encourage females to join math- and science-related fields and to become leaders in business and the professions.

of males versus females going on to postsecondary education in the High/Scope or comparison group, the data did indicate that the life circumstances of males and females differed, particularly in terms of marital status and having children, with more females than males being married (or cohabiting) and having children. One might have expected these different life circumstances to have lessened the positive effect of the High/Scope program for female subjects by adding stress or causing some to drop out of college, but the data indicate that this was not generally the case.

Females—Encouraging Results

In the longitudinal study, though females had to contend with limiting circumstances financially and otherwise, they made postsecondary gains and had plans to complete college degrees.

Given the growing number of single-parent, female-headed households, the economic projections for young female adults from low-income backgrounds who have low educational attainment are especially dismal (U.S. Bureau of the Census, 1990a). Since resources for these young women to pursue postsecondary education and improve their employability are very limited, it is particularly encouraging that in the High/Scope longitu-dinal study, females were found to benefit. Though a current national trend is for more females than males (from all minority backgrounds) to enroll in college, the longitudinal study on rural white disadvantaged subjects indicated that females in the study's comparison group were not part of this trend. However, females in the program group were consistent with the national trend.

Although economic barriers appeared to have been somewhat greater for the High/Scope program's females than for their comparison group counterparts, the majority of program females (by about age 21) had either completed or at least pursued some postsecondary education (their attainments included some 2-year and 4-year college degrees). Furthermore, of subjects with some college experience, more females than males had plans to persist towards completion of a degree.

Research on achievement motivation indicates that

teachers do not typically communicate as high expectations to their female students as they do to their male students. For example, several studies by Dweck and colleagues (cited in Henderson & Dweck, 1990) found that in mathematics and science, female students become decreasingly interested and skilled (relative to male students) as they go through school. This may be, at least in part, because of low teacher-expectations, lack of role models, and females' belief that they lack the necessary ability. The results of the High/Scope longitudinal study show that such mindsets can be altered. Females from the High/Scope program appear to have gained considerable motivation to persist in their education. Nearly every High/Scope program female who remained single went on to postsecondary education, and the majority of married (or cohabiting) females also went on to postsecondary education and stayed in school. Of those married or cohabiting females who had dropped out of college, the majority had plans to complete their degrees. It is also interesting that 5 females from the High/Scope group and no females from the comparison group had joined the military. Clearly, the program had a strong positive influence that served to offset the limitations of early marriage and economic difficulty for the female participants.

Males—An Altered Course

For males from minority and disadvantaged backgrounds, both problem behavior (including delinquency) and personal economic difficulty can be limiting factors in their efforts to develop their achievement potential. Even so, of the 1982–83 High/Scope programs' 11 young adults (predominantly males) with a history of the most problematic behaviors, over one third went on to postsecondary education. Furthermore, only 2 males from the High/Scope program were neither employed nor enrolled in postsecondary education, and far more High/Scope than comparison males had served in the military. Regarding marital status, even though more

Many High/Scope males started families early, and some experienced problem behaviors, but contrary to national trends, their educational levels were not significantly different from those of the program females.

program than comparison males had left home and were married or cohabiting, twice as many of the program married/cohabiting males had at least some postsecondary education—but being married or cohabiting did appear to present obstacles to their staying in school.

The Long-Range Promise of Program Intervention

The High/Scope program participants' greater amount of postsecondary education has both short-term and long-range economic impact.

▾

Overall, the empirical model derived from the High/Scope longitudinal data illustrates the potential power of programs designed to promote higher education for talented disadvantaged teenagers. Even when such students' academic achievement has been marginal—when they have not been recognized for achievement in their high schools or have not had the benefit of strong expectations and economic support from parents, they can be motivated to go to college. The role models and experiences provided by programs like the High/Scope program can provide them with the skills, resources, and encouragement to pursue higher education.

U.S. Bureau of the Census data show that for each additional year of higher education, the average monthly income is greater for both men and women.

▾

The increased pursuit of higher education by the students who participated in High/Scope's adolescent program produces benefits beyond additional learning for individuals. Among the benefits of program participants' higher education is greater expected income for themselves and thus higher aims and achievements for their families in the years to come. A U.S. Bureau of the Census (1987) report indicated that a college degree brings a significantly higher income than a high school diploma does. In 1987, men with 4-year college degrees earned an average monthly income of $2,777, and women with 4-year college degrees earned an average monthly income of $1,388. In contrast, for men and women with only high school diplomas, average monthly earnings would have been $1,578 and $785, respectively. Every additional year of postsecondary education or training leads to greater average earnings. Furthermore, with the increase in jobs requiring high levels of skill and education, earning gaps between college and high school graduates have been steadily increasing over the past 20 years. When program intervention helps individuals to ultimately earn higher wages, society profits from their greater productivity and economic contributions. Such profits can far exceed intervention "costs."

Implications for Program Development and Policy Direction

The model programs described in this book, in challenging their talented students, support adolescent development and at the same time address the specific obstacles to achievement that minority and disadvantaged students face. Recognizing that adolescents are developing identities separate from their parents and growing towards emotional and economic independence, the programs build in opportunities for students to form relationships with peers and adults who serve as positive role models outside the family. The programs also provide students with engaging instructional activities designed to support and advance the adolescents' growing cognitive abilities—their capacities for abstract thinking, forming and testing hypotheses, and critical thinking.

Throughout this book, we have talked about the national need for a more highly skilled and educated work force. As this need grows more urgent, extracurricular precollege programs such as this book describes will become more numerous. Many of the new programs will replicate or improve on existing programs. Located in various settings—within high schools, on college campuses, and at residential camps—both old and new programs will fulfill two functions: The programs will be *interventions*, in that they can serve minority and disadvantaged students in ways they are not

> **The intervention programs described in this book show that programs can serve as laboratories for developing or refining educational approaches.**
>
> ▼

> **Many approaches demonstrated in intervention programs can be employed in schools, both to support the development students gain from program participation and to increase school effectiveness for all students.**
>
> ▼

served in traditional schools. The programs will also be *"laboratories" for the development of instructional and motivational strategies* not used in traditional schools.

When talented adolescents are changed in positive ways by intervention programs, the benefits to them can be further enhanced if *schools* also change their curricula and methods to support the students' newly gained knowledge and motivation. (For example, a curriculum change that intervention programs might influence schools to bring about would be an increase in advanced courses and laboratories; a possible change in schools' instructional methods would be the incorporation of active-learning and cooperative learning projects.) The following recommendations thus address those interested in developing and improving extracurricular precollege programs as well as those interested in making related changes in schools. Based on both the *model of ideal-program features* developed in Part 1 and the empirically based *model of paths to postsecondary education* developed in Parts 2 and 3, the recommendations are these:

The following pages present our recommendations.

———— • ————

▼

Expand the number and types of programs available for high-potential disadvantaged students.

Programs should include more disadvantaged adolescents whose talents may be overlooked. Programs and schools should develop and use a variety of methods of assessment to identify such students. As shown in this book, a variety of assessment approaches can be used to identify less-than-obvious potential in students. The longitudinal study of the High/Scope program demonstrated that even high school students who are not highly recognized for academic achievement but who show some promise of achievement can be successfully encouraged to pursue higher education.

Programs should continue to include disadvantaged students with obvious talent. We know that disadvantaged and minority students who score high on national achievement tests, get As and Bs in high school academic courses, and have no behavioral problems are the most likely to go on to postsecondary education. However, they should not be excluded from intervention programs. In precollege programs, these already-achieving students can serve as peer role models, and because they often do not have sufficient knowledge of future opportunities, their exposure to program experiences can secure and further advance their potential.

A greater number of intervention programs should direct students to a wide range of areas of study. We should continue to encourage disadvantaged young people to go into technical and scientific fields, where they are currently underrepresented. However, so far, the increase in disadvantaged and minority graduates in some of these fields has produced a decline in graduates in some nontechnical fields. This is because the overall number of minority and disadvantaged teenagers going on to postsecondary education is not increasing sufficiently. For some groups, such as African American males, the number is actually decreasing (American Council on Education, 1991).

The changing nature of the workplace and the complexity of our society require a populace that is liberally educated as well as technically literate. Many have argued that programs need most of all to foster critical and flexible thinking in students, so they will be prepared for a *variety* of work roles in their futures (e.g., National Center on Education and the Economy, 1990; National Commission on Children, 1991).

Intervention programs should be located in a variety of settings—middle schools, high schools, colleges, and residential settings. Variation in program location and duration (a weekend, one to several weeks, a summer) can further expand the availability of programs for students. In particular, more *residential* programs or program components should be developed. The High/

Scope longitudinal data show that residential programs can increase the number of high-potential students who follow high school graduation with college enrollment, military service, or independent living.

Programs with a residential aspect, like the High/Scope program and other programs reviewed in Part 1, may be especially effective because they take students out of familiar surroundings that include various obstacles to achievement—peer pressure for nonachievement, lack of alternatives for constructive use of nonschool time, low expectations from parents or teachers. Furthermore, experiencing life in a residential setting—a college campus, a camp, or some similar facility—may convince an adolescent that living away from familiar surroundings can be a positive experience, and this may make going away to college or military service seem possible. Also, because of its informality, a residential setting can foster students' active participation in learning, cooperation with peers, and formation of positive relationships with role models and with peers from other ethnic/racial backgrounds.

▼

Enhance teachers' training to facilitate their interactions with minority and disadvantaged students and their parents.

Teachers in programs and schools need training—both preservice and inservice—that provides them with awareness of differences in students' cultural backgrounds. Teachers especially need to be aware of obstacles disadvantaged teenagers face in developing their identities and realizing their achievement potential. Teacher training, whether held on site or at colleges or universities, should increase teachers' knowledge of (1) a range of methods to assess achievement potential, (2) variations in students' cognitive and learning styles related to their cultural backgrounds, (3) communication processes related to different languages and language usage, (4) historical roots and current customs of ethnic groups, (5) obstacles to students' achievement and identity formation that are related to growing up with poverty and discrimination, and (6) methods of engaging students in active-learning to enhance student motivation and responsibility.

Teachers should receive training in ways to involve parents of high-potential disadvantaged adolescents in their children's education. Teachers need training and experience with techniques such as providing alternative time-schedules for parent-teacher discussions and meetings, developing activities and events that parents feel comfortable participating in, informing parents about their children's potential for higher education and about ways this potential can be realized.

Curricula should include cultural and historical content about students' ethnic backgrounds. Identity development in adolescents from ethnic minority backgrounds can be further supported by textbooks, educational materials, and instruction that give greater attention to the contributions to various fields that have been made by persons from minority groups.

▼

Restructure instruction to include active participation of students in learning and to include challenging advanced content.

Instruction in programs and schools should build in active-learning opportunities to promote students' cognitive development, specific academic skills, problem-solving strategies, and achievement motivation. Research presented in this book points to the abstract, formal content and methods of high school instruction as a major source of difficulty for minority and disadvantaged students. Because of the close connection between adolescents' cognitive growth and their social development, the learning and achievement motivation of high school students may be better fostered by a variety of instructional methods—by active-learning situations that involve more hands-on participation by students, more informal interactions between adults/teachers and students, and greater peer interaction. As discussed in Part 1, many programs are experimenting with such innovative ways to tap into the achievement potential of adolescents.

Instruction should emphasize group learning activities that allow for peer interaction, support, and role modeling. Learning activities in which peers work cooperatively in small groups can foster learning, motivation, and peer support for achievement (Slavin & Madden, 1989). In such contexts, teachers can encourage peers to help one another in mastering academic content, developing problem-solving strategies, and learning time-management and planning skills. And since every student can make some kind of contribution to a group project or experiment, group activities give teachers good opportunities to provide positive feedback and guidance for individual students. In peer-group projects, students can also find opportunities to make unique contributions that may reflect their particular learning styles or ethnic backgrounds.

Peer-group learning activities, which are found in some of the model programs in Part 1 and in the High/ Scope program in Part 2, are similar to many workplace experiences in that they encourage individual contributions and require teamwork at the same time. Evaluators of the future needs of the work force have pointed to the need for schools to include more activities that simulate the workplace, more cooperative projects that foster students' critical and flexible thinking and their creative problem solving.

Programs and schools should provide out-of-school active-learning experiences that expose teenagers to a variety of opportunities for future work and education. Such out-of-school learning experiences as visiting colleges and work settings, making field trips to historical sites and cultural events, or participating in volunteer programs in the community can expand horizons for disadvantaged and minority students. These wider experiences can build students' confidence and help them to break away from limited mindsets and goals (Simons, Finlay, & Yang, 1991).

Schools need to provide the necessary advanced courses, materials, and facilities to prepare high-potential students for postsecondary education. Remedial classes and "coaching" may also be needed to ensure that students have the necessary skills and knowledge for advanced studies. Research in this book points out that too often, high-potential disadvantaged students go on to postsecondary education but find that they lack advanced preparation in their area of interest, have below-college-level basic skills, or lack study and test-taking skills. Inadequate materials and facilities and a lack of advanced courses are among the typical realities of schools these students have come from. Also, some high-potential students, whether due to specific learning disabilities, prior educational limitations, or earlier lack of motivation, need remedial help in academic skills and "survival techniques." For these students, coaching in study, time-management, and test-taking skills—as well as tutoring in basic academic skills—must accompany or precede any advanced studies. Both schools and intervention programs should address this need.

▼

Include staff and other adults who can serve as positive role models, and design learning situations to facilitate interactions of students with role models.

Programs and schools should provide positive adult role models as major motivators for high-potential teenagers from families with limited economic and educational resources and experiences. Whenever possible, role models should come from backgrounds similar to those of the students, to provide examples that achievement is possible even if one is from an economically disadvantaged or minority background. Public school teachers often have limited value as role models because they are not from economically disadvantaged or minority backgrounds, and many low-income parents are limited as role models because they themselves have had poor educational experiences and preparation. It is also unfortunate that in low-income neighborhoods today, children have less exposure than in the past to extrafamilial role models of high-achieving adults (Wilson, 1987; Brooks-Gunn, Duncan, Kato, & Sealand, 1991). Although the impact of role models needs further study, some evidence in Parts 1 and 2 of this book suggests that role models play an important role in motivating disadvantaged teenagers.

The design of program and school learning activities should facilitate students' relating to role models. The informal, active-learning situations we have recommended for schools and programs readily lend themselves to role-modeling purposes. Role models, whether they are business professionals, camp counselors, teachers, or peers, are likely to be most effective with students when they are engaged with them in a common effort— one in which each person's learning or communication style and unique contributions are valued. Informal group learning situations allow role models to provide students with specific practical help and guidance, such as academic tutoring, advice about dealing with discrimination, or counseling about selecting colleges and obtaining financial aid.

▼

Expand postsecondary financial aid and guidance for obtaining aid.

Government, private foundations, and institutions of higher education should increase scholarships and other kinds of financial aid to disadvantaged, high-potential students. The High/Scope research found that many of the students from the High/Scope Institute for IDEAS who entered postsecondary education had little or no resources from scholarships or from parents to finance their education. Thus the majority of them needed to hold jobs to pay for both their education and their living expenses. (The lack of scholarships is not surprising, because—except for sports scholarships—financial aid is typically more limited for students who have not been the most highly recognized achievers in high school.) While for some disadvantaged students, financial difficulty is probably a reason for dropping out of college permanently or temporarily, for others it is the reason they simply never enroll.

Everyone stands to gain from providing disadvantaged students with more financial aid or more access to available aid for postsecondary education. Since over the course of a person's lifetime, income increases for every additional year of postsecondary education, disadvantaged young people who gain even some postsecondary education can hold better-paying, higher-skill jobs. This can add to the nation's productivity and at the same time decrease the costs of providing public assistance.

High schools, colleges, and intervention programs should use a variety of methods to increase disadvantaged and minority students' knowledge about ways to finance postsecondary education. Too often, as discussed in Part 1 of this book, parents and students lack knowledge of how to gain access to financial aid. Seeing college as unaffordable, parents may discourage their teenaged children from aspiring to college. Many disadvantaged students and their parents assume that no aid, other than sports scholarships, is available.

Counselors and other educators can work to better inform students and parents through several mechanisms: providing individual financial planning sessions with parents and students, at school or at home; providing special programs and workshops featuring speakers from colleges and universities; sponsoring field trips to college and university financial aid offices; seeking out specific kinds of scholarships, such as art, forensics, or mathematics scholarships; identifying colleges that have national reputations in the areas students are especially interested in; enlisting college students from minority and disadvantaged backgrounds to be mentors to high school students on how to obtain financial aid information; and conducting community fund raising events and involving local businesses in donating scholarship money for more students to go to college.

▼

Conduct research about intervention program effectiveness, methods, and long-term impact.

Programs should conduct research to assess their effectiveness in fostering the achievement of talented minority and disadvantaged youth. Qualitative and quantitative approaches that employ preprogram, postprogram, ongoing, and longitudinal research designs can be used to assess programs, as demonstrated in this book. When feasible, studies should include the use of a comparison group—a no-treatment group, a placebo group, or an alternative-program group.

Research on programs should include evaluation methods to determine programs' areas of strength and areas needing further development. For example, in the 1990 evaluation of the High/Scope program (Chapter 14), data from the student and staff interviews and from naturalistic observations of program activities make possible a comparison between the program's stated goals and objectives and students' responses to the program. Naturalistic observations can also answer the questions of how program processes work. Quantitative methods, which were used both in the High/Scope 1990 evaluation and the High/Scope longitudinal study, provide another approach. Quantitative methods can include gathering data about achievement test scores, grades, class standing, college participation, military service, employment, and economic status of program participants.

Research should also include analysis of program impact on individuals. As research on programs increases, it should include data analysis strategies that evaluate how effective programs are for individuals as well as groups. Analyses should allow evaluators to determine whether a program helps all its participants, not just whether a program group in general made greater gains than a comparison group. Furthermore, individual analyses allow evaluators and program developers to see how helpful a program is for persons with specific kinds of difficulties—learning disabilities, physical handicaps, or major psychological problems. Using this research approach is more fruitful if assessment goes beyond test scores to include other indicators of progress, such as increased motivation to persist in spite of obstacles or initial setbacks, improved ability to work with others, and so forth.

Research should also assess the long-term impact of programs in order to increase the knowledge about educating disadvantaged adolescents and provide a basis for policy planning. We need more longitudinal research like that presented in Part 2—research that includes follow-up interviews with former program participants in their young-adult years. Longitudinal studies will provide the ultimate and necessary assessment of programs' contributions to advancing the higher education of talented disadvantaged students. Such studies will also contribute to the research base on the impact of intervention programs. National longitudinal evaluations of precollege programs (both in-school and extracurricular) can provide accountability and establish generalizability for various program models, enabling policymakers to set national priorities for investments in program development.

A Final Recommendation

Basic to all that we have presented is a major societal directive for educators, parents, and policymakers. *We must change our view of talented disadvantaged and minor-*

ity students' potential for achievement, with the firm belief that our higher expectations will enhance their achievement. The world of students who grow up in poverty or as members of a minority group has many limits, and among these limits is the students' own sense that no one expects them to achieve, that they don't have "what it takes." As stated by the Commission on the Skills of the American Workforce, "More than any other country in the world, the United States believes that natural ability, rather than effort, explains achievement" (National Center on Education and the Economy, 1990). Indeed, recent research reviewed by Henderson and Dweck (1990) suggested that while minority students may lack access to needed educational experiences (as was explored in Part 1), they may also have come to believe that intelligence is fixed and that achievement, rather than depending on their effort, is primarily the result of specific ability that they either have or do not have. Coupled with their perception that they have low academic ability, this belief can lead to low or modest educational aspirations, even for talented students.

With problems in how we assess their achievement potential and in how we express our expectations for their achievement, we cause many students to believe their early failures are due to lack of ability. Consequently they fail to put in the effort necessary for further cognitive development and eventual mastery of a field of knowledge. However, research presented in this book demonstrates that intervention programs can motivate high-potential adolescents who have not been high achievers to expect more of themselves and hence to strive towards better futures.

Technical Notes for the High/Scope Longitudinal and 1990 Studies

In this appendix, we describe each basic type of variable and coding procedure that was applied to the data from the High/Scope longitudinal study and the High/Scope 1990 evaluation. We also define and explain some specific complex variables used in the data analyses in one or both studies, especially those variables that were derived from the original coding of the variables. (The interview questions, the interviewer manual, the 1990 questionnaires, and the coding manuals are available from the authors.) At the end of this appendix are correlational tables and Figures A.1 and A.2 that were discussed in Chapters 13 and 15.

Throughout the part of the appendix that pertains to coding and variables, how variables were treated in the data analyses is noted. Most of the variables used in the data analyses in the longitudinal and 1990 studies were described in Part 2. In the following discussion, we will refer to questions used to generate data specifically from the longitudinal data as *interview* questions (described in Chapters 8–13); for the 1990 evaluation, we will refer to *questionnaire* questions or items (described in Chapter 14).

In the longitudinal study, except for students' achievement test scores, 1107 variables were directly coded from subjects' responses to a predetermined, fixed set of 263 interview questions. In the 1990 study, 501 variables were directly coded from subjects' responses to a total of 171 questions from the pre- and postprogram questionnaires, which contained a large number of questions that were identical or highly similar to those used in the longitudinal study. Next, we describe the coding procedures.

Procedures for Coding and Recoding Variables

In this section, we discuss the major kinds of variable coding used in both the longitudinal and the 1990 studies. The majority of the data were in the form of subjects' responses to *rating-scale*, *assorted-choice*, *yes-no*, or *open-ended* interview questions. For most subject responses to the rating-scale, assorted-choice, and yes-no types of questions, the categories used for coding were the same category choices that had been provided for subjects. For the open-ended interview questions, since there were no set, preconceived response choices, the researchers constructed categories to code subjects' responses. The following pages describe the specific coding procedures that were used.

Main Types of Data Coding

Subjects' nonresponses and "don't know" responses were coded as *missing* responses. If a subject had been tracked out of a question or sequence of questions, researchers used a code indicating those responses as *nonapplicable*. Frequency counts were made on the number of missing and nonapplicable responses.

For the *rating-scale questions*, interviewers read scale choices to a subject after asking a question. Typical "anchor" labels—"all of the time," "sometimes," "never," and so on—were read to subjects, and the assignment of numerical scale values or scores corresponding to the anchor labels took place during the coding of the data.

In *assorted-choice questions*, subjects were typically asked if any item from a list read to them was applicable to them. An example is the question "When you were 4 or 5 years old, what type of household did you live in?" Item choices for this question were "house," "duplex," "apartment," and so on. In coding the subjects' selections for assorted-choice questions, arbitrary numbers were typically assigned to the subjects' selections, so these data could be analyzed for frequency counts of each choice.

Yes-no questions were often actually a listing of items pertaining to a major question, such as "Do you now receive money or the equivalent from the following government sources?"

Each response to an item was coded with a number indicating "yes" and another number indicating "no."

For coding the subjects' responses to *open-ended questions*, mutually exclusive categories were developed, based on some responses that were anticipated and some responses generated from a random sampling of subjects' actual responses to the questions. For example, in answer to the open-ended question "What are your future goals?" a subject's responses might match with the following categories: "get a job," "get a degree," "go to the military," "get married," "have children," or "other." In coding a subject's responses to open-ended questions, if any of the subject's responses matched a given category, that category was given a score of 1 (to indicate "yes"). If none of the subject's responses matched the category, that category was given a score of 0 (indicating "no mention"). A category of "other" was also included to count subject responses that did not fit into any given category.

In cases where subjects' responses generated a large number of diverse categories (or in cases where some categories were considered less important than other categories), categories were assigned arbitrary numbers, and a limited number of a subject's first-mentioned responses (generally up to 4 category responses) were coded using the arbitrarily assigned category numbers.

In general, in the analyses of the categorical data, researchers conducted frequency counts of the categories. They treated the codes assigned to subjects' responses either as actual scores or as markers for frequency counting. When the analyses of the frequency distributions revealed a low frequency or no frequency of occurrence, the variable was modified (by computer) by combining across two or more coding levels, as appropriate. Sometimes additional variables were developed from the coded data by using the computer to combine variables or by using the scoring techniques explained next.

Specific Variables

As already indicated, to address some research questions, or to meet the requirement for specific kinds of data analyses, researchers recoded some variables by computer, thereby creating a newly derived variable. Most variables are simply the result of combining previously coded levels that turned out to be low in frequency of occurrence, and the final coding levels for these variables were described in Part 2. Other variables that were recoded by combining two or more variables or by transforming the original codes into a scale are next defined and explained. Some other variables that are included next were not recoded, but since they are complicated, we explain them here in more detail than found in Part 2.

For each of the following major variables, we provide the general variable name, description, and codes (including how the code was indicated or quantified), as well as major derived variables. In some cases, we also indicate relevant data analyses issues.

Household composition included size of household and household structure (for example, whether it was single-parent, two-parent). The coded data consisted of the number and types of people living in the household. Subjects were asked to indicate the total number of each type of household member (for example, 3 brothers, 2 sisters, 1 mother, 1 father) at age 5, at elementary school age, and at teen age, as well as the current household

composition. Specific derived variables were summary counts of the total number of household members and the total numbers of different types of household members (such as total number of parents, of children, of other adults). The overall score of household members was developed by adding the totals for various types of household members and then adding 1 for the subject. The household variables corresponding to the three different time periods in the subjects' life were analyzed and described separately. Another major derived variable was the number of single-parent versus two-parent households.

Birth order was a variable indicating the subject's order of birth in the family. Subjects were asked to indicate the number of older and the number of younger siblings in the family. From these coded values, researchers derived a score to indicate the subject's birth order among the siblings (1 = first, 2 = second, and so on). This score was derived from the coded data by counting the number of older siblings that a subject indicated and adding 1 for the subject.

Sources of stress variables concerned the amount and types of stress due to problems in the family or to situations that subjects themselves reported experiencing. The *family stress* variables consisted of the total amount of stress and the types of stress derived from subjects' coded responses to two questions. One question used in the longitudinal study interview and in the 1990 study questionnaire pertained to reasons why changes had occurred in the household, and the other question inquired whether subjects had experienced any difficult problems or events (in or out of the household) in growing up. The rationale for combining coded responses to these two questions was that difficult problems and household changes were both likely to be related to significant stress. Only those difficult problems or situations most likely to be stressful were included in the derived stress variables. Family stress included a parent's death, parental separation or divorce, parental alcoholism or illness, or the existence of physical or sexual (subject) abuse. The *self-stress* variables—concerning subjects' own problems, such as alcoholism, illegal substance use, illness, or psychological problems—were separated out from the family stress variables. The family stress total score and self-stress total score variables were examined in data analyses both separately and as a single stress variable.

Parent expectations for subjects referred to specific kinds of post-high-school expectations that subjects perceived their parents to hold for them. The coding of the assorted parent-expectation choices was rescored by using a 0–4 scale indicating the lowest to the highest levels of education or training that parents expected. This variable was used in various data analyses that required a scale of some type. The new scoring was: 0 = no expectations, 1 = a job, 2 = military, 3 = vocational/technical education, and 4 = 2-year or 4-year college or university. For one analysis, another variable derived from this scoring was *low expectations* (combining levels 0 and 1) versus *high expectations* (combining levels 2–4).

Educational level was the highest completed educational level reported by a subject for mother, father, and self. Responses were coded according to a scale ranging from 1 (for elementary school) to 16 (for doctoral degree or other graduate degrees beyond the master's level). Educational level variables were used as continuous variables in several analyses. For some

descriptive purposes, as described in Part 2, several levels of the 16-point scale were collapsed to form the following 5 categories:

1. Less than high school
2. High school diploma or GED
3. Some postsecondary education (postsecondary technical courses, completed certificate, or 1 year of college)
4. Two years or more of postsecondary education at a college or university
5. Four-year college or university degree or higher

In the few cases of missing responses, mother's and father's educational level was counted as high school in analyses using continuous data. Although the educational level variable was not used for the subjects in the 1990 study of the program (since the subjects were still in high school), it was used for parents.

Educational plans was the educational level that a subject, at the time of interview, planned to complete, and it was coded using the same 16-point scale used to code the educational level completed. For data analyses using continuous data, if a subject indicated no further educational plans, the subject's current level of education was entered as the subject's educational plans score—since the difference between completed education and level of educational aspiration indicated no further education.

Current enrollment and *past enrollment* pertained to variables from the longitudinal interview data that indicated the times and types of subjects' postsecondary enrollment (in a school, college, or other training) at the time of the interview and at any previous time. An assorted-choice list of possible types of postsecondary schools or other educational programs was used for the coding of the subjects' responses. For certain data analyses, the coded responses for current and past postsecondary school enrollments were recoded into the following scale: 1 = military training not at a college, 2 = 2-year college, 3 = 4-year college or university. These current and past enrollment variables were not used in the 1990 study of the program, since the subjects were still in high school.

Job types or *occupations* referred to the types of occupations that were coded for mother's, father's, and subject's jobs across the subject's life. Data analyses included frequency distributions primarily for the types of jobs of mothers, fathers, and subjects at various points in time. Each job was coded using the U.S. Bureau of the Census codes first established in 1970 (U.S. Bureau of the Census, 1971). In the 1970 census codes, over 400 three-digit codes identify occupational titles. These titles are typically placed into 12 major types of occupations (indicated by the first digit in each occupation's code). The ordering of the major classifications ranges roughly from highest to lowest in salary and, to some extent, in prestige. In the present research, researchers collapsed classifications when low frequencies were found. They also added some codes for jobs not found in the 1970 census codes. Also, prior to data analyses, they moved some occupations to higher or lower classification levels to reflect current educational-training requirements or income status.

More-recent occupational coding schemes have changes that reflect the researchers' concerns about the 1970 classifications. Though the U.S. Bureau of the Census 1980 Standard Occupational Classification (SOC) System appears to have addressed some of the problems of classifying occupations, determining the status of jobs remains controversial (Campbell & Parker, 1983; Stevens & Featherman, 1981; and Osborn, 1987).

Role models/experiences in the longitudinal study referred to the numbers and types of major influences that subjects perceived in their lives regarding 4 major achievement behaviors—working cooperatively with others, reflectivity (thinking before reacting), persisting at a task, and striving for excellence. For each of these achievement behaviors, a "yes" or "no" was coded, depending on whether or not subjects indicated they had experienced any sources of influence regarding the behavior—mother, father, teacher, a program, and so on.

The *number of subjects with some source of influence* was determined by scores that ranged from 0 (for "no influences") to 1 (for "some influences") for each of the 4 behaviors. Other derived variables were the *number of influences per behavior* (influences as unit of analysis)—from 0 to 3 types of influence per behavior, and the total number of *types of influences* (influences as unit of analysis) across behaviors—from 0 to 3 types of influence per behavior, up to a total of 12 influences.

The different types of influences also were coded to allow for frequency counting of each specific type of role model or experience (up to 3 different influences per behavior, but only 1 individual type of influence per behavior). Thus, the mathematics teachers, for example, would be counted just once per behavior. Subjects were asked to include both positive and negative sources of influence and to explain their effects. Positive and negative influences were coded and analyzed separately.

For certain data analyses that required continuous data, researchers summed influences across behaviors. The effect of this was that frequently reported types of influence—often a parent or grandparent—were allowed to be counted across behaviors (one count for each type of role model or experience per behavior for which it was cited by the subject). Thus, for example, if a subject cited his father for 3 out of the 4 behaviors, and his mother for 2 behaviors, and an experience for 1 behavior, the subject's total score for role models/experiences across behaviors was 6. The rationale for this scoring was that it is reasonable to assume that a role model or experience mentioned frequently by a subject should be given appropriate weight.

In the 1990 study, subjects were asked to name persons who had an influence on them and to tell how each person had an influence. Up to 10 different types of persons who had a positive influence were coded per subject.

Recognized achievement referred to awards or recognition subjects received for various kinds of academic achievements and activities in high school. The variable was derived from a large set of coded categories of recognition subjects might mention in response to an open-ended question. Although subjects could report more than one type of recognition and more than one type of academic recognition, this variable only included whether or not a subject had received any academic recognition.

Family economic difficulty referred to the frequency of subjects' families receiving some form of welfare or public assistance. Researchers coded a rating corresponding to each of two time-periods in subjects' lives—the elementary school years and the teen years, each referring to a 7-point rating scale. The ratings ranged from 0 (never) to 6 (all of the time). Sometimes the variables were analyzed separately; other times they were combined to gain an assessment of the

overall family use of public assistance.

Personal economic difficulty referred to subjects' own use of public assistance since high school. The main variables for subjects' economic difficulty since high school included *use of public assistance* (1 = no use, 2 = yes, some use); the *total amount of time in months* that they received some form of public assistance; the *specific types* of public assistance received (AFDC, food stamps, Medicaid); and the *amount of money (or money equivalent) per month* received in each type of assistance. Since only a small number of subjects were currently receiving any public assistance, the variable indicating public assistance use since high school was the major indicator of subjects' personal economic difficulty. This variable was not used in the 1990 study, since subjects were still in high school and therefore not receiving public assistance on their own.

Problem behavior referred to subjects' reported problem-behavior incidents, such as physical fighting, shoplifting, stealing, vandalism, using illegal substances, or being arrested. The codes were derived from subjects' responses to 18 five-point frequency scales, from a categorizing of the incidents by type, and from a categorizing of the incidents by levels of seriousness. The scale used with subjects was 1 = not at all, 2 = once, 3 = twice, 4 = 3 or 4 times, and 5 = 5 or more times. This was rescored as follows: 0 = not at all, 1 = once, 2 = twice, 3 = 3 or 4 times, and 4 = 5 or more times.

For many analyses, researchers summed the subjects' frequency ratings across all 18 scales and calculated average and median scores per subject. For each interview question about problem-behavior incidents, subjects were asked to describe either the only incident reported or the most serious one, if there was more than one. In the coding, subjects' descriptions were categorized for each type of incident. For some analyses, these items were grouped according to the type or seriousness of the incident, which resulted in the following 4 categories: (1) suspension or expulsion from high school for behavior problems; (2) minor delinquency (such as getting into fights, shoplifting, vandalizing school property); (3) serious delinquency (such as car theft, robbery); (4) arrest by police; and (5) use of illegal substances (marijuana, other illegal substances).

In the longitudinal study, subjects were also asked how old they were at their first arrest (if applicable) and subsequent arrests. Most subjects did not recall or report their ages at subsequent times of arrests. From the data on first arrests, a variable was derived to count the number of subjects' first, arrests before reaching age 18 versus after reaching age 18. The rationale for this variable was that at age 18 or later, a subject was definitely beyond the age of participation in the High/Scope program; age 18 also marks the time when illegal activity moves from juvenile into criminal jurisdiction. On subsequent questions, subjects who had been arrested were asked how much time they had spent in jail or on probation. For jail or probation time, if any, researchers derived summary scores of total hours and days.

Locus of control referred to the extent to which subjects perceived having personal control over what happens in their lives. Overall variables were derived from codes corresponding to 16 five-point ratings that subjects made in response to items read to them. Subjects responded in degrees of agreement ranging from 1–5 (1 = disagree, 2 = mostly disagree, 3 = neither (neutral), 4 = mostly agree, 5 = agree). Ratings were selected from questions from the University of

Michigan's Institute for Social Research Monitoring the Future survey of high school students (Bachman, Johnston, & O'Malley, 1986).

In some cases a strong sense of personal control and confidence (considered a positive response) was indicated by *agreement* with the statement, but in other cases a strong sense of personal control and confidence was indicated by *disagreement* with the statement. Prior to data analyses, these latter scale responses were reversed to make all high scores indicate positive responses. In most analyses, researchers calculated average and median scores across the 16 items to achieve one overall score per subject.

Achievement motivation ratings were subjects' responses to a series of attitudinal statements about their own self-esteem, risk taking, and striving for achievement. Each statement was read to a subject, and the subject rated the extent to which the statement was descriptive of himself or herself. The overall variables were derived from the codes corresponding to 23 four-point scales (1 = not true of you, 2 = somewhat true of you, 3 = true of you, 4 = very true of you). In some cases the most positive response was "very true of you," and in other cases the most positive response was "not true of you." Prior to data analyses, these latter scale responses were reversed to make high scores indicate positive responses. For most analyses, researchers calculated average and median scores across the 23 items to get one overall score per subject.

Other Specific Variables From the 1990 Study

In addition to the specific variables just described, on the 1990 study pre- and postprogram questionnaires, subjects were asked to rate many aspects of the program experience, as described in Chapter 14. From these ratings, coded according to their quantitative values, researchers derived overall and subcategory average and median scores to be used in the analyses. The additional key variables used in the 1990 study were as follows:

Future expectations were subjects' expectations of where they would be in 5 years (when they would be about 20 years old). Subjects made two predictions, one on the preprogram and one on the postprogram questionnaire. Each of the 2 subject-responses was coded as follows: 1 = college, 2 = military, 3 = a job, 4 = marriage. In one of the data analyses, researchers collapsed these levels to compare how many subjects gave at-college versus not-at-college predictions.

Prior other-race friends pertained to whether subjects had friends of other racial/ethnic backgrounds prior to the program and how many of these friends they had. The codes of subjects' responses included yes/no categorization and coding of the total number of other-race friends. Subjects were also asked how the program had affected their attitudes towards persons of other racial/ethnic groups. Subjects' responses to this question were coded into categories. The main analyses were the following frequency counts: how many subjects said they previously had other-race friends, how many subjects reported attitudinal effects resulting from the program, and how many types of effects they had experienced.

Sociometric roommate selections referred to the same-gender roommates that subjects said they would select if they had the opportunity to return to the program again. Each roommate who was nominated (selection is here referred to as nomination) was coded

using the nominee's identification code, which was then specifically entered into the roommate data set of the nominator. The resulting data set thus included the identification codes given by each subject and the identification codes received by each subject. From these data, researchers derived variables by comparing the ethnic/racial and regional backgrounds of nominators with those of nominees.

More specifically, a major variable that was derived from these data included *same- versus other-race selections* of subjects. To derive these data from the roommate nominations of subjects (4 "first-choice" roommates and an additional 4 "reserve" roommates were asked for), the coding procedures included codes for whether or not the race of each roommate nominated by the subject was the same or different from that of the subject. From the data, researchers also derived a variable referring to how many of a subjects' selections were from their *current roommates*. A third derived variable, *reciprocity* (mutual selection), referred to how many of a subject's roommate nominations were reciprocated by the nominees.

The two sets (of 4 first-choice and 4 reserve roommate selections) were analyzed separately for same- versus other-race and for current- versus not-current roommates. All 8 selections were combined for scoring and analyzing the reciprocity of subjects' selections.

Intercorrelations Among Influence Variables

Table A.1 shows the correlation coefficients (Pearson product-moment) between the major influence variables

Table A.1

Intercorrelations of Influence Variables

Influence Variable	2	3	4	5	6
Campers (*n* = 66)					
1. Recognized achievement	.15	-.06	-.07	-.18	-.06
2. Parent expectations	—	.02	-.10	.06	.24
3. Role models/ experiences	—	—	.02	-.07	.11
4. Problem behavior	—	—	—	-.09	-.07
5. Marital status	—	—	—	—	.03
6. Economic difficulty	—	—	—	—	—
Noncampers (*n* = 64)					
1. Recognized achievement	.13	.11	-.36**	-.04	-.16
2. Parent expectations	—	-.01	.00	-.06	.04
3. Role models/ experiences	—	—	-.10	-.13	-.05
4. Problem behavior	—	—	—	-.28*	.12
5. Marital status	—	—	—	—	.16
6. Economic difficulty	—	—	—	—	—

*Note. Marital status ranged from single to married/cohabiting. Economic difficulty refers to subjects' personal (not family) economic difficulty. *p < .05, **p < .01, two-tailed tests.*

(these are shown separately for campers and noncampers). Recall that in Chapter 13 (Table 13.1) we presented the correlations between these influence variables and the educational status variables. In Chapter 13 these influences were further examined in causal path analyses.

Path Analyses Technical Notes and Figures

Chapter 13 presented a series of path analyses causal models to explain how key influence variables were related to educational status variables—*educational level*, *educational plans*, and *current enrollment*. In our path analyses (which are unlike multiple regression analyses, where prediction is the main purpose and tests of significance are important), we were interested in examining variables to explain their effects on educational outcomes. Variables that are strong predictors of a dependent variable can sometimes fail to provide any understanding of *why* the variables are predictors (see Li, 1975, for further discussion.)

Figure A.1, presented here and discussed in Chapter 13, illustrates how subjects' participation in the High/Scope program affected their educational levels 5 years later. Examining all the major variables together, along with the High/Scope program variable, allowed for this analysis of the High/Scope contribution. For this causal model, LISREL computer software (Jöreskog & Sörbom, 1989) was used to create several new factors: *parent education* (educational levels of the subject's mother and father), *negative factor* (subject's personal economic difficulties and frequency of problem behavior); and *positive factor* (recognized academic achievement and role models/experiences). The negative and positive factors were induced latent variables, as shown in the model. (The variables involved for generating the negative and positive factors were not correlated). Because of the nature of an induced variable, the direct cause from each positive and negative factor affecting educational level is obtained by multiplying the coefficients within the linkage of any two variables. The High/Scope program can thus be compared with each variable directly. From this model, both direct and indirect causes can be calculated.

Figure A.2 shows another path analysis model referred to in Chapter 13. This path analysis model was developed to explain some of the effects of subjects' family background variables, subjects' attitudes towards achievement and locus of control, and subjects' personal economic situations.

Figure A.1

Path Analysis With Latent Variables Leading to Educational Level

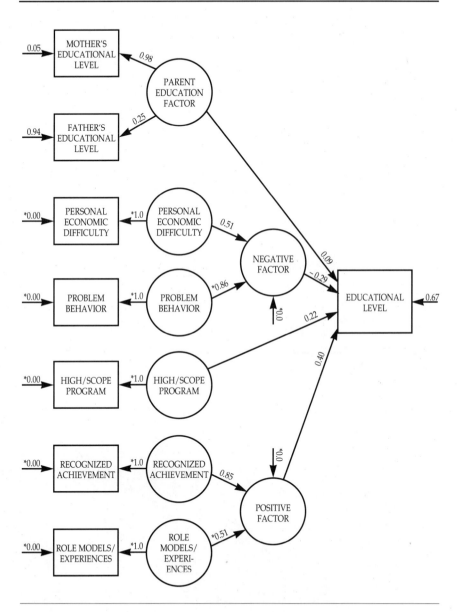

Note. Data are pooled for groups, standardized solution. $N = 130$; $\chi^2 = 5.31$, $df = 10$; Ratio = $\chi^2/df = 0.53$; CN (critical number) = 422; GFI (goodness-of-fit index) = 0.99; AGFI (adjusted goodness-of-fit index) = 0.99; RMR (root mean square residual) = 0.02; *parameter is fixed.

Figure A.2

Confirmatory Factor Analysis for Subjects' Background Variables, Attitudes, and Personal Economic Difficulty

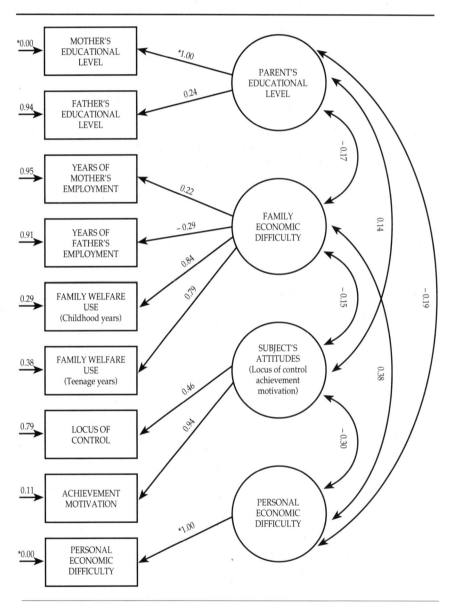

Note. Data are pooled for groups, standardized solution. $N = 130$; $\chi^2 = 13.95$, $df = 25$; χ^2/df = 0.56; CN (critical number) = 349; GFI (goodness-of-fit index) = 0.98; AGFI (adjusted goodness-of-fit index) = 0.95; RMR (root mean square residual) = 0.04; *parameter is fixed.

References

Adams, R. L., & Phillips, B. N. (1972). Motivation and achievement differences among children of various ordinal birth positions. *Child Development, 43,* 155–164.

Adelman, C. (1991). *Women at thirtysomething: Paradoxes of attainment* (U.S. Department of Education and Office of Educational Research and Improvement). Washington, DC: U.S. Government Printing Office.

Alter, J., McDonald, D. H., Murr, A., & Padgett, T. (1989, January 23). Out of sight, out of mind: Forgetting the civil rights movement. *Newsweek,* pp. 52–53.

American Council on Education. (1988). *Sixth annual status report 1987—Minorities in higher education.* Washington, DC: American Council on Education.

American Council on Education. (1991). *Minorities in higher education* (Ninth Annual Status Report 1990). Washington, DC: Author.

Bachman, J. G., Johnston, L. D., & O'Malley, P. M. (1986). *Monitoring the Future: Questionnaire responses from the nation's high school seniors, 1984.* Ann Arbor, MI: University of Michigan, Institute for Social Research.

Bachman, J. G., Johnston, L. D., & O'Malley, P. M. (1991). *Monitoring the Future: Questionnaire responses from the nation's high school seniors, 1988.* Ann Arbor, MI: University of Michigan, Institute for Social Research.

Baldwin, A. (1987). Undiscovered diamonds: The minority gifted child. *Journal of Education of the Gifted, 10*(4), 271–285.

Ball, S., & Bogatz, J. (1972). Summative research on Sesame Street: Implications for the study of preschool children. In A. D. Pick (Ed.), *Minnesota symposia on child psychology, Vol. 6* (pp. 3–17). Minneapolis: University of Minnesota Press.

Bandura, A. (1986). *Social foundations of thought and action.* Englewood Cliffs, NJ: Prentice-Hall.

Bangert-Drowns, R., Kulik, J., & Kulik, C. (1983). Effects of coaching programs on achievement test performance. *Review of Educational Research, 53*(4), 499–518.

Banks, J. A. (1981). Stages of ethnicity: Implications for curriculum reform. In J. A. Banks (Ed.), *Multi-ethnic education: Theory and practice* (pp. 129–139). Boston: Allyn & Bacon.

Belsky, J., & Isabella, R. A. (1985). Marital and parent-child relationships in family of origin and marital change following the birth of a baby: A retrospective analysis. *Child Development, 56,* 342–349.

Berger, K. S. (1986). *The developing person through childhood and adolescence* (2nd ed.). New York: Worth.

Bernstein, B. (1972). A sociolinguistic approach to education with some reference to educability. In J. J. Gumperz and D. Hymes (Eds.), *Directions in sociolinguistics.* New York: Holt, Rinehart & Winston.

Berrueta-Clement, J. R., Schweinhart, L. J., Barnett, W. S., Epstein, A. S., & Weikart, D. P. (1984). *Changed lives: The effects of the Perry Preschool program on youths through age 19* (Monographs of the High/Scope Educational Research Foundation No. 8). Ypsilanti, MI: High/Scope Press.

Bloom, B. S. (1974). Time and learning. *The American Psychologist, 29*(9), 682–688.

Bloom, B. S. (1980). Early learning in the home. In B. Bloom (Ed.), *All our children learning* (pp. 67–88). New York: McGraw-Hill.

Bloom, B. S. (1982). *Human characteristics and school learning.* New York: McGraw-Hill.

Bloom, B. S., Englehart, M. D., Furst, E. J., Hill, W. H., & Krathwohl, D. R. (1956). *Taxonomy of educational objectives. Handbook 1: Cognitive domain.* New York: McKay.

Bowman, P., & Howard, C. (1985). Race-related socialization, motivation, and academic achievement: A study of black youth in three-generation families. *Journal of the American Academy of Child Psychiatry, 24*(2), 134–141.

Bredderman, T. (1983). Effects of activity-based elementary science on student outcomes: A qualitative synthesis. *Review of Educational Research. 53*(4), 499–518.

Broman, S. H., Nichols, P. L., & Kennedy, W. A. (1975). *Preschool IQ: Prenatal and early developmental correlates.* Hillside, NJ: Lawrence Erlbaum.

Bronfenbrenner, U. (1979). *The ecology of human development.* Cambridge, MA: Harvard University Press.

Brooks-Gunn, J., Duncan, G. J., Kato, P., & Sealand, N. (1991, April). *Do neighborhoods influence child and adolescent behavior?* Paper presented at the biennial meeting of the Society for Research in Child Development, Seattle, WA.

Brophy, J. E., & Good, T. L. (1974). *Teacher-student relationships: Causes and consequences.* New York: Holt, Rinehart & Winston.

Cadmus, H. (1974). *The behavioral and structural dynamics of social stratification as manifested in a racially integrated first-grade classroom.* Unpublished doctoral dissertation, University of Florida, Gainesville.

Campbell, D. R. (1986). Developing mathematical literacy in a bilingual classroom. In J. Cook-Gumperz (Ed.), *The social construction of literacy* (pp. 156–184). New York: Cambridge University Press.

Campbell, R. T., & Parker, R. N. (1983). Substantive and statistical considerations in the interpretation of multiple measures of SES. *Social Forces, 62*, 450–466.

Carnegie Corporation of New York. (1990, Winter/Spring). Adolescence: Path to a productive life or a diminished future? *Carnegie Quarterly, 35*(1, 2).

Carnegie Council on Adolescent Development. (1989). *Turning points. Preparing American youth for the 21st century* (The report of the Task Force on Education of Young Adolescents). Washington, DC: Author.

Children's Defense Fund. (1990, January/March). *Latino youths at a crossroads.* Washington, DC: Author, Adolescent Pregnancy Prevention Clearinghouse.

Chronicle of Higher Education. (1991, August). *Chronicle of Higher Education Almanac, 38*(1), 39–104.

Clark, R. (1983). *Family life and school achievement: Why poor black children succeed or fail.* Chicago: University of Chicago Press.

Clift, E. (1989, January 23). The Bush clan: Inaugurating a new family dynasty? *Newsweek*, pp. 24–25.

Cohen, R. (1969). Conceptual styles, culture conflict, and nonverbal tests of intelligence. *American Anthropologist*, 71(5), 828–856.

Collins, J. (1986). Differential instruction in reading groups. In J. Cook-Gumperz (Ed.), *The social construction of literacy* (pp. 117–137). New York: Cambridge University Press.

Comer, J. P. (1980). *School power: Implications of an intervention project*. New York: The Free Press.

Cook-Gumperz, J. (1986). Introduction: The social construction of literacy. In J. Cook-Gumperz (Ed.), *The social construction of literacy* (pp. 1–15). New York: Cambridge University Press.

Cross, W. E. (1978). The Thomas and Cross models of psychological nigrescence: A review. *The Journal of Black Psychology*, 5, 13–31.

Duncan, G. J. (1984). *Years of poverty. Years of plenty. The changing economic fortunes of American workers and families*. Ann Arbor, MI: University of Michigan, Survey Research Center.

Dweck, C. S. (1986). Motivational processes affecting learning. *American Psychologist*, 41(10), 1040–1048.

Eder, D. (1986). Organizational constraints on reading group mobility. In J. Cook-Gumperz (Ed.), *The social construction of literacy* (pp. 138–155). New York: Cambridge University Press.

Elkind, D. (1974). *Children and adolescents: Interpretive essays on Jean Piaget*. New York: Oxford University Press.

Ellis, J. E. (1988, March 14). The black middle class. *Business Week*, pp. 62–70.

Entwisle, D. R. (1990). Schools and the adolescent. In S. S. Feldman & G. R. Elliott (Eds.), *At the threshold. The developing adolescent* (pp. 197–224). Cambridge, MA: Harvard University Press.

Erikson, E. H. (1963). *Childhood and society* (2nd ed.). New York: Norton.

Freire, P. (1970). *Pedagogy of the oppressed*. New York: The Seabury Press.

Gallagher, J. J. (1985). *Teaching the gifted child* (3rd ed.). Boston, MA: Allyn & Bacon.

Gardner, H. (1983). *Frames of mind*. New York: Basic Books.

Gay, G. (1985). Implications of selected models of ethnic identity development for educators. *Journal of Negro Education*, 54(1), 43–55.

Gay, G. (1987, January). *Multicultural education*. Presentation at the 1st Annual Faculty Workshop on Multicultural Education, University of Nebraska–Lincoln, Teachers College.

Gay, G. (1988, January). *The substance of ethnic/racial diversity: How do you have a subtle impact in the classroom?* Presentation at the 2nd Annual Faculty Workshop on Multicultural Education, University of Nebraska–Lincoln, Teachers College.

Ginsburg, H. (1972). *The myth of the deprived child*. Englewood Cliffs, NJ: Prentice-Hall.

Ginsburg, H. (1986). The myth of the deprived child: New thoughts on poor children. In U. Neisser (Ed.), *The school achievement of minority children: New perspectives* (pp. 169–189). Hillsdale, NJ: Lawrence Erlbaum.

Golden, M., & Birns, B. (1976). Social class and infant intelligence. In M. Lewis (Ed.), *Origins of intelligence* (pp. 299–351). New York: Plenum.

Good, T., & Brophy, J. (1987). *Looking in classrooms* (3rd ed.). New York: Harper & Row.

Gordon, E. W., Gordon, S. G., Lloyd, S. K., Margolis, E. M., Nembhard, J. G., & Armour-Thomas, E. (1987). *A report to the field: A descriptive analysis of programs and trends in engineering education for ethnic minority students*. New York: National Action Council for Minorities in Engineering, Inc.

Gottlieb, D. (1966). Teaching and students: The views of Negro and white teachers. *Sociology of Education, 37*(4), 345–353.

Gronlund, N. E. (1985). *Measurement and evaluation in teaching* (5th ed.). New York: Macmillan.

Hale-Benson, J. (1986). *Black children: Their roots, culture, and learning styles.* Baltimore: The Johns Hopkins University Press.

Hall, V. C., & Kaye, D. B. (1980). Early patterns of cognitive development. *Monographs of the Society for Research in Child Development, 45*(2, Serial No. 184).

Hare, B., & Castenell, L. (1985). No place to run, no place to hide: Comparative status and future prospects of black boys. In M. Spencer, G. Brookins, & W. Allen (Eds.), *Beginnings: The social and affective development of black children* (pp. 201–214). Hillsdale, NJ: Lawrence Erlbaum.

Harter, S. (1982). The perceived competence scale for children. *Child Development, 53*, 87–97.

Harvard Committee on Race Relations. (1980). *A study of race relations at Harvard College* (A report prepared for the Office of the Dean of Students, Harvard College). Cambridge, MA: Harvard College.

Heath, S. B. (1982). Questioning at home and at school: A comparative study. In G. Spindler (Ed.), *Doing the ethnography of schooling: Educational anthropology in action* (pp. 96–101). New York: Holt, Rinehart & Winston.

Henderson, V. L., & Dweck, C. C. (1990). Motivation and achievement. In S. S. Feldman & G. R. Elliott (Eds.), *At the threshold. The developing adolescent* (pp. 308–329). Cambridge, MA: Harvard University Press.

Hetherington, M. E., Camara, K. A., & Featherman, D. L. (1983). Achievement and intellectual functioning of children from one-parent households. In J. Spence (Ed.), *Achievement and achievement motives* (pp. 205–284). San Francisco: Freeman.

Hetherington, M. E., Cox, M., & Cox, R. (1982). Effects of divorce on parents and children. In M. Lamb (Ed.), *Nontraditional families* (pp. 233–288). Hillsdale, NJ: Lawrence Erlbaum.

Hetherington, M. E., & Parke, R. D. (1986). *Child psychology: A contemporary viewpoint* (3rd ed.). New York: McGraw-Hill.

Hilliard, A. G., Jr. (1976). *Alternatives to IQ testing: An approach to the identification of gifted "minority" children* (Final Report). Sacramento, CA: California State Department of Education, Sacramento Division of Special Education. (ERIC Document Reproduction Service No. ED 147 009).

Hirsch, E. D., Jr. (1988). *Cultural literacy: What every American needs to know.* New York: Vintage Books.

Holt, G. S. (1972). "Inversion" in black communication. In T. Kochman (Ed.), *Rappin' and stylin' out: Communication in urban black America* (pp. 152–159). Chicago: University of Illinois Press.

Honzik, M. P., MacFarlane, J. W., & Allen, L. (1948). The stability of mental test performance between two and eighteen years. *Journal of Experimental Education, 18*(2), 309–324.

Hudson Institute. (1987). *Workforce 2000. Work and workers for the 21st century.* Indianapolis, IN: Author.

Hundleby, J. D., & Mercer G. W. (1987). Family and friends as social environments and their relationship to young adolescents' use of alcohol, tobacco, and marijuana. *Journal of Marriage and the Family, 49*, 151–164.

Jacob, E. (1987). Qualitative research traditions: A review. *Review of Educational Research, 57*(1), 1–50.

Jensen, A. R. (1969). How much can we boost IQ and scholastic achievement? *Harvard Educational Review, 39*(1), 1–123.

Johnson, S. O. (1987). Panel presentation on recruitment/marketing strategies for minorities in teacher education. In E. J. Middleton & E. J. Mason (Eds.), *Proceedings of the National Invitational Conference on Recruitment and Retention of Minority Students in Teacher Education, March 29–April 1* (pp. 81–83). Lexington, KY: University of Kentucky.

Jöreskog, K. G., & Sörbom, D. (1989). *LISREL 7. A guide to the program and applications* (2nd ed.). Chicago: SPSS, Inc.

Keith, T. Z., Reimers, T. M., Fehrmann, P. G., Pottsbaum, S. M., & Aubey, L. W. (1986). Parental involvement, homework, and TV time: Direct and indirect effects on high school achievement. *Journal of Educational Psychology, 78*(5), 373–380.

Kelly, M. A. (1983). *Race relations at the University of Rochester* (Report to the Division of Student Affairs). Rochester, NY: University of Rochester.

Kennedy, W. A. (1969). A follow-up normative study of Negro intelligence and achievement. *Monographs of the Society for Research in Child Development, 34*(2, Serial No. 126).

Kinsler, K. (1990). Structured peer collaboration: Teaching essay revision to college students needing writing remediation. *Cognition and Instruction, 7*(4), 303–321.

Kinsler, K., Romero, M., Kelly, M., Graves, S., & Mercado, C. (1991). *The QUEST Program faculty handbook on cultural diversity*. Unpublished manuscript, Hunter College of the City University of New York, Division of Programs in Education, New York.

Kunjufu, J. (1985). *Countering the conspiracy to destroy black boys* (Vols. 1 & 2). Chicago: African-American Images.

Labov, W. (1970). The logic of nonstandard English. In F. Williams (Ed.), *Language and poverty: Perspectives on a theme* (pp. 153–189). Chicago: Markman.

Labov, W. (1972). *Language in the inner city: Studies in the black English vernacular*. Philadelphia: University of Pennsylvania Press.

Leigh, G. K., & Loewen, I. R. (1987). Utilizing developmental perspectives in the study of adolescence. *Journal of Adolescent Research, 2*(3), 303–320.

Leslie, C., & Springen, K. (1989, October 16). Can parents save schools? *Newsweek*, p. 74.

Li, C. C. (1975). *Path analysis—A primer*. Pacific Grove, CA: Boxwood Press

Marsella, A. J. (1990). Ethnocultural identity: The "new" independent variable in cross-cultural research. *Focus, 4*(2), 14–15.

McKey, R. H., Condelli, L., Ganson, H., Barrett, B. J., McConkey, C., & Plantz, M. C. (1985). *The impact of Head Start on children, families, and communities: Final report of the Head Start Evaluation, Synthesis, and Utilization Project*. Washington, DC: U.S. Government Printing Office.

McLoyd V. C., & Wilson, L. (1990). Maternal behavior, social support, and economic conditions as predictors of distress in children. In V. C. McLoyd & C. A. Flanagen (Eds.), *Economic stress: Effects on family life and child development. New directions for child development. No. 46* (pp. 49–69). San Francisco: Jossey-Bass.

National Center for Education Statistics. (1988). *National Education Longitudinal Study of 1988. A profile of the American eighth grader. NELS:88. Student descriptive summary* (U.S. Department of Education, Office of Education Research and Improvement). Washington, DC: U.S. Government Printing Office.

National Center for Education Statistics. (1989). *Changes in educational attainment: A comparison among 1972, 1980, and 1982 high school seniors* (U.S. Department of Education, Office of Education Research and Improvement). Washington, DC: U.S. Government Printing Office.

National Center for Education Statistics. (1991). *Youth indicators 1991. Trends in the well-being of American youth* (U.S. Department of Education, Office of Educational Research and Improvement). Washington, DC: U.S. Government Printing Office.

National Center on Education and the Economy. (1990). *America's choice: High skills or low wages!* (The report of the Commission on the Skills of the American Workforce). Rochester, NY: Author.

National Commission on Children. (1991). *Beyond rhetoric. A new American agenda for children and families* (Final Report of the National Commission on Children). Washington, DC: U.S. Government Printing Office.

National Commission on Excellence in Education. (1983). *A nation at risk: The imperative for educational reform.* Washington, DC: U.S. Government Printing Office.

National Opinion Research Center. (1986a). *Four years after high school: A capsule description of 1980 seniors* (A report prepared for the Center for Statistics, U.S. Department of Education). Washington, DC: U.S. Government Printing Office.

National Opinion Research Center. (1986b). *Two years after high school: A capsule description of 1980 sophomores* (A report prepared for the Center for Statistics, U.S. Department of Education). Washington, DC: U.S. Government Printing Office.

National Research Council. (1989). *Everybody counts. A report to the nation on the future of mathematics education.* Washington DC: National Academy Press.

Ogbu, J. U. (1978). *Minority education and caste: The American system in cross-cultural perspective.* New York: Academic Press.

Ogbu, J. U. (1985). A cultural ecology of competence among inner-city blacks. In M. Spencer, G. Brookins, & W. Allen (Eds.), *Beginnings: The social and affective development of black children* (pp. 45–66). Hillsdale, NJ: Lawrence Erlbaum.

Ogbu, J. U. (1986). The consequences of the American caste system. In U. Neisser (Ed.), *The school achievement of minority children: New perspectives* (pp. 19–56). Hillsdale, NJ: Lawrence Erlbaum.

Orr, E. W. (1987). *Twice as less: Black English and the performance of black students in mathematics and science.* New York: Norton.

Osborn, A. F. (1987). Assessing the socioeconomic status of families. *Sociology, 21*(3), 429–448.

Paige, R. (1987). Keynote address: The recruitment and retention of minorities in teacher education. *Proceedings of the National Invitational Conference on the Recruitment and Retention of Minority Students in Teacher Education, March 29–April 1.* Lexington, KY: University of Kentucky.

Piaget, H. (1983). Piaget's theory. In Paul H. Mussen (Ed.), *Handbook of child psychology: Vol. 1. History, theory, and methods* (pp. 103–128). New York: Wiley. (Original work published in 1970.)

Quality Education for Minorities Project. (1990). *Education that works: An action plan for the education of minorities.* Cambridge, MA: Massachusetts Institute of Technology, QEM Project.

Raudenbusch, S. W. (1984). Magnitude of teacher expectancy effects on pupil IQ as a function of credibility of expectancy induction: A synthesis from 18 experiments. *Journal of Educational Psychology, 76*(1), 85–97.

Richardson, R. C., Jr., & Bender, L. W. (1985). *Students in urban settings: Achieving the baccalaureate degree* (ASHE-ERIC Higher Education Report No. 6). Washington, DC: Association for the Study of Higher Education.

Rosenthal, R., & Jacobsen, L. (1968). *Pygmalion in the classroom.* New York: Holt.

Santmire, T. E. (1987). *Child development and education.* Unpublished manuscript, University of Nebraska—Lincoln, Department of Educational Psychology.

Shipman, S., & Shipman, V. (1985). Cognitive styles: Some conceptual, methodological, and applied issues. In E. W. Gordon (Ed.), *Review of educational research* (Vol. 12). Washington, DC: American Educational Research Association.

Shulman, L. S. (1988). Disciplines of inquiry in education: An overview. In. R. M. Jaeger (Ed.), *Complementary methods for research in education* (pp. 3–21). Washington, DC: American Educational Research Association.

Siegel. S. (1956). *Nonparametric statistics for the behavioral sciences.* New York: McGraw-Hill.

Simons, J. M., Finlay, B., & Yang, A. (1991). *The adolescent and young adult fact book.* Washington, DC: Children's Defense Fund.

Slack, W. V., & Porter, D. (1980). The Scholastic Aptitude Test: A critical appraisal. *Harvard Educational Review, 50*(2), 154–175.

Slaughter, D. T., & Epps, E. G. (1987). The home environment and academic achievement of black American children and youth: An overview. *Journal of Negro Education, 56*(1), 3–20.

Slavin, R. E., & Madden, N. A. (1989). Effective classroom programs for students at risk. In R. E. Slavin, N. L. Karweit, & N. A. Madden (Eds.), *Effective programs for students at risk* (pp. 23–51). Boston: Allyn & Bacon.

Soar, R. S., & Soar, R. M. (1979). Emotional climate and management. In P. L. Peterson & H. J. Walberg (Eds.), *Research on teaching: Concepts, findings, and implications.* Berkeley, CA: McCutchan.

Spanard, J. A. (1990). Beyond intent: Reentering college to complete the degree. *Review of Educational Research, 60,* 309–344.

Stevens, G., & Featherman, D. L. (1981). A revised socioeconomic index of occupational status. *Social Science Research, 10,* 364–395.

Subotnik, R. F. (1989). Teaching gifted students. In J. A. Banks & C. A. McGee Banks (Eds.), *Multicultural education: Issues and perspectives* (pp. 269–285). Newton, MA: Allyn & Bacon.

Task Force on Women, Minorities, and the Handicapped in Science and Technology. (1989). *Changing America: The new face of science and engineering* (Final Report). Washington, DC: Author (ERIC Document Reproduction Service No. ED 317 386).

Thomas, C. W. (Ed.). (1971). *Boys no more: A Black psychologist's view of community.* Beverly Hills, CA: Glencoe Press.

Torrance, E. P. (1965). *Creativity in the classroom.* Englewood Cliffs, NJ: Prentice-Hall.

Trujillo, C. M. (1986). A comparative examination of classroom interactions between professors and minority and nonminority college students. *American Educational Research Journal, 23*(4), 629–642.

U.S. Bureau of the Census. (1971). *1970 census of population alphabetical index of industries and occupations.* Washington, DC: U.S. Government Printing Office.

U.S. Bureau of the Census. (1986). *Characteristics of the population below the poverty level: 1984* (Current Population Reports, Series P-60, No. 152). Washington, DC: U.S. Government Printing Office.

U.S. Bureau of the Census. (1987). *What's it worth? Educational background and economic status* (Current Population Reports, Series P-70, No. 21). Washington, DC: U.S. Government Printing Office.

U.S. Bureau of the Census. (1989). *Studies in marriage and the family. Singleness in America. Single parents and their children. Married-couple families with children* (Current Population Reports, Special Studies, Series P-23, No. 162). Washington, DC: U.S. Government Printing Office.

U.S. Bureau of the Census. (1990a). *Money income and poverty status in the United States: 1989. Advance data from the March 1990 Current Population Survey* (Current Population Reports, Series P-60, No. 168). Washington, DC: U.S. Government Printing Office.

U.S. Bureau of the Census. (1990b). *Statistical abstract of the United States: 1990* (110th ed.). Washington, DC: U.S. Government Printing Office.

U.S. Congressional Budget Office. (1987). *Educational achievement: Explanations and implications of recent trends.* Washington, DC: U.S. Government Printing Office.

U.S. Congressional Research Service & U.S. Congressional Budget Office. (1985). *Children in poverty.* Washington, DC: U.S. Government Printing Office.

U.S. Department of Education. (1991). *America 2000: An education strategy. Sourcebook.* Washington, DC: Author.

U.S. Department of Education, Office of Educational Research and Improvement. (1988). *Youth indicators 1988: Trends in the well-being of American youth.* Washington, DC: U.S. Government Printing Office.

U.S. Department of Justice. (1983). *Report to the nation on crime and justice. The data* (No: NCJ-87068). Rockville, MD: National Criminal Justice Reference Service.

Vasta, R. (1979). *Studying children.* San Francisco: W. H. Freeman & Co.

Verway, D. I. (Ed.). (1987). *Michigan statistical abstract* (20th ed., 1986–87). Detroit, MI: Wayne State University, School of Business Administration, Bureau of Business Research.

Vygotsky, L. S. (1962). *Thought and language.* Cambridge, MA: MIT Press.

Weill, J. D. (1988). *New trends in poverty* (A speech to the Civil Caucus of the National Legal Aid and Defender Association at the annual conference of the National Legal Aid and Defender Association, Miami). Washington, DC: Children's Defense Fund.

Wells, G. (1986). The language experience of five-year-old children at home and at school. In J. Cook-Gumperz (Ed.), *The social construction of literacy* (pp. 69–93). New York: Cambridge University Press.

White, J. L. (1984). *The psychology of blacks.* Englewood Cliffs, NJ: Prentice-Hall.

White, K. (1982). The relations between socioeconomic status and academic achievement. *Psychological Bulletin, 91*(3), 461–481.

William T. Grant Foundation Commission on Work, Family, and Citizenship. (1988). *The forgotten half: Pathways to success for America's youth and young families. Final report.* Washington, DC: Youth and America's Future—The William T. Grant Commission on Work, Family, and Citizenship.

Wilson, W. J. (1987). *The truly disadvantaged. The inner city, the underclass, and public policy.* Chicago: University of Chicago Press.

About the Authors

SHERRI ODEN is a senior research associate at the High/Scope Educational Research Foundation and director of High/Scope's research on adolescent programs and on the long-term effects of Head Start. Her research has been published in *Child Development, Developmental Psychology*, and other journals and books in the fields of human development and education. Prior to coming to High/Scope, she was a professor of education and psychology at the University of Rochester and at the Graduate School of Wheelock College in Boston.

MARIO A. KELLY is an assistant professor in the Department of Educational Foundations and Counseling Programs at Hunter College of the City University of New York, where he teaches courses in child development, educational psychology, and educational evaluation. In addition to his teaching responsibilities, Kelly is involved in several school-college collaborative projects and regularly works with teachers, parents, and high school students. Kelly's research interests include the study of minority youth development and achievement,

moral development, and the impact of cultural diversity on the teaching-learning process.

ZHENKUI MA has been a research associate and director of data analysis, computer programming, and statistics at the High/Scope Foundation. He has published research articles on statistics and survey sampling, and he has taught courses at the University of Michigan. He has recently become a research associate in the Biology Division of the University of Montana.

DAVID P. WEIKART is founder and president of the High/Scope Educational Research Foundation. He has authored numerous research and policy publications in the fields of education and psychology and is especially known for initiating the High/Scope Perry Preschool Study—a longitudinal study of the effects of preschool education on the lives of disadvantaged children. His work with talented teenagers goes back to 1963, when, together with Phyllis Weikart, he founded the High/Scope camp program, today known as the High/Scope Institute for IDEAS.